SM

SUPPLEMENT TO
A BIBLIOGRAPHY OF
UNITED STATES–LATIN AMERICAN
RELATIONS SINCE 1810

SUPPLEMENT TO
A BIBLIOGRAPHY OF
UNITED STATES–
LATIN AMERICAN
RELATIONS SINCE 1810

Compiled and Edited by

MICHAEL C. MEYER

University of Nebraska Press • Lincoln and London

Copyright © 1979 by the University of Nebraska Press

All Rights Reserved

Library of Congress Cataloging in Publication Data

Meyer, Michael C
    Supplement to A bibliography of United States-Latin American relations since 1810.

    Includes index.
    1. Latin America—Foreign relations—United States—Bibliography.   2.   United States—Foreign
relations—Latin America—Bibliography.   I.   Trask, David F. A bibliography of United States-Latin
American relations since 1810.   II.   Title.   III.   Title: A bibliography of United States-Latin
American relations since 1810.
Z6465.L29T7 suppl [F1418]   016.32773'08   79-1243
ISBN 0-8032-3051-6

Preface to Supplement

Ten years ago, together with David F. Trask and Roger R. Trask, I compiled and edited a volume which appeared under the title *A Bibliography of United States–Latin American Relations Since 1810: A Selected List of Eleven Thousand Published References*. The citations included in that volume were collected during the period 1965 to 1967 and the first printing of the study was published by the University of Nebraska Press in 1968. Because the volume was considered useful by Latin American historians and United States diplomatic historians, and because a substantial amount of published material has appeared in the intervening years, a number of colleagues urged us to prepare a supplement. My two original collaborators, however, have left the academic world for historical positions in government and, as a result, the preparation of the supplement fell to me.

The organization of the present study is essentially the same as that of its predecessor and it should be considered a companion volume. A few supplementary chapter subsections have been added to accommodate newly important hemispheric trends and diplomatic events. In 1967, for example, the bibliography of multinational corporations and dependency theory, or of Inter-American law of the sea, did not warrant separate categories. Today they do. The chronological sections have been updated to include the Nixon and Ford administrations as well as the Inter-American conferences that have occurred in the last decade. The cross references direct the reader to appropriate sections of the original volume as well as the supplement.

The preparation of this supplement afforded me the opportunity not only to collect and organize titles published since the original effort but also to include older publications that were not uncovered in time to appear in the 1968 volume. Well over three-quarters of the citations included here, however, do carry publication dates since 1965.

M. C. M.

Preface to Original Volume

The history of United States–Latin American relations is of vital concern to all who inhabit the Western Hemisphere, and it is of increasing importance elsewhere in the world. Given the significance of this field, it is surprising that no comprehensive bibliographical guide to its literature has heretofore been available in one volume. To be sure, interested investigators have been able to turn to a number of exceedingly useful bibliographical works dealing in part with the history of United States–Latin American relations. Among these are the classic work of Bemis and Griffin, *Guide to the Diplomatic History of the United States, 1775–1921* (item 335); the *Index to Latin American Periodical Literature, 1929–1960* (item 277); the four-volume set entitled *Foreign Affairs Bibliography* (item 56) made available by the Council on Foreign Relations; Humphreys' *Latin American History: A Guide to the Literature in English* (item 218); and the indispensable *Handbook of Latin American Studies* (item 208). (All item numbers refer to the original volume.) Nevertheless, these works and comparable materials pose difficulties because they deal with other fields as well as hemispheric relations and are limited in their coverage by chronology, topic, organization, scope, and type of listing. Accordingly, any adequate bibliographical search has required the historical investigator to consult a large number of volumes not necessarily developed to meet his particular needs. For example, Bemis and Griffin do not survey the years after 1921, nor do they list materials published after 1935. The periodical *Index* lists only items from serial publications for the period 1929–1960, although supplements for more recent years are becoming available. *Foreign Affairs Bibliography* lists only books published during the period 1919–1962. Humphreys does not list material available in languages other than English. The *Handbook of Latin American Studies*, perhaps the most comprehensive in its coverage, now extends to some twenty-eight volumes covering publications since 1934.

Our objective as compilers has been to provide in one volume an extensive listing of published sources and authorities which both collates and expands the corpus of previous general lists of references for the history of United States–Latin American relations. This bibliography includes published materials of all kinds—books, articles, pamphlets, documents, and the like—in a wide variety of languages, particularly English, Spanish, Portuguese, French, German, Italian, Russian, and Japanese. We have not attempted to list unpublished materials, although we have cited a large number of guides to manuscript collections in Chapter I. The only exceptions to this rule are a large sampling of unpublished doctoral dissertations and a very small number of mimeographed items of particular significance. We make no claim to have incorporated all materials relevant to our subject, but we believe that no other work of comparable scope and convenience is now available.

Organization. The bibliography is organized in two main sections, which are supplemented by several specialized chapters. Chapters III–X provide a chronological survey of United States–Latin American relations from the beginning of the national independence movements in Latin America in 1810 until the present. The periodization adopted for this chronological survey is based on the conventional perspective of historians in the United States. Chapters XIII–XXIV offer a country-by-country survey. Each country's chapter is periodized according to the perspective of historians from that nation. In addition, Chapter I includes an extensive list of guides and aids; Chapter II covers general studies of the field and other useful works; Chapter XI surveys the course of the Pan American movement since 1889; and Chapter XII lists works relating to certain Latin American movements of a political, ideological, and cultural nature which have exerted considerable influence on the course of hemispheric relations—in particular, Pan Hispanism, Yankeephobia, and Aprismo. We have made no attempt to survey hemispheric relations with Spain prior to the independence movements or to cover relations with areas of the Western Hemisphere which have remained dependent on European nations or the United States, such as the British West Indies, the Guianas, and Puerto Rico. We have attempted to make the work helpful to users with various perspectives and intentions, including those peculiar not only to students in the United States but to those of other countries. We believe that the country chapters are of particular utility to Latin American users.

Citation. Each item is cited in full only once, but cross references from the original citation are provided for other relevant sections of the bibliography. All citations are alphabetized by author (or by title if no author is given) within sections or subsections. The conventional English alphabet is used for this purpose. Names and words beginning with Spanish letters like *ll* and *ch* are not listed separately but are incorporated into the alphabetization as in English. The same practice is used for other languages. A typical citation for a book-length publication or pamphlet includes author, title, edition (if relevant), volumes (if relevant), place of publication, and year of publication. For example:

> 8702. Orellana, J. G. *Resumen Histórico del Ecuador*. 2d ed., 2 vols., Quito, 1948.

The citations for dissertations include author, title, university, and year accepted. For example:

> 2564. Van Aken, M. J. "Origins of the Pan-Hispanic Movement to 1866," U. of California Diss., 1956.

The citations for items from periodicals or other serial publications include author, title, symbol for publication, volume number, year of publication, and page numbers. For example:

> 7357. Olney, R. "Fortification of the Panama Canal," *AJIL* 5 (1911) 298–301.

A list of symbols for periodicals and serial publications appears at the beginning of the bibliography. There is also a separate list of other abbreviations used in citations. If additional information is needed to locate a given item, it is added to the basic form, e.g., the month of publication or the number of the publication.

Annotation. Annotations are included occasionally to provide additional publication data, to clarify content, or to identify the author or subject in instances where this information may be helpful to the user. No critical comments are made; annotations are entirely descriptive in nature. If a listing has been translated or is available in more than one place, this information is provided in the annotation. A clarification is given if the title is susceptible of diverse interpretation. For example:

> 3758. Lieuwen, E. *Arms and Politics in Latin America*. N.Y., 1960.
> Rev. ed. in pb., N.Y., 1963. Part I discusses the role of the military; Part II considers military aspects of United States–Latin American policy. The revised edition contains a new chapter on Cuba.

Cross References. Lists of cross references appear at the conclusion of sections and subsections. These inserts refer the searcher either to entire sections elsewhere in the bibliography where other relevant items appear, or to the numbers of individual citations which may prove useful. The cross references provide a necessary link between the chronological chapters (III–X) and the country chapters (XIII–XXIV). The full citation for cross-referenced items is listed in the place where the work makes its primary contribution.

Users of this bibliography will note that certain areas of interest have received much more attention in the past than others, e.g., United States–Mexican relations or the New Pan Americanism, whereas others, like United States–Costa Rican relations or United States–Paraguayan relations, have been studied far less extensively. In the latter case, we have included general items which may be useful in the absence of specialized information. Our bibliography reflects the amount of labor expended on any given topic rather than the quality or depth of those labors. We leave to those who consult this work the task of rendering critical judgments and selecting from the available materials those items they wish to consult.

Despite rigorous efforts, we realize that our bibliography undoubtedly contains a certain number of errors and omissions. We ask that users inform us of any they note so that they might be corrected in the future. We will be satisfied with our compilation if it proves as helpful to its users as those imposing bibliographical works we have relied upon so heavily in the course of our own endeavor, especially those mentioned at the outset of this Preface, have been to us.

D. F. T.
M. C. M.
R. R. T.

Contents

Abbreviations

Ala.	Alabama	Me.	Maine
Arg.	Argentina	Mich.	Michigan
Ariz.	Arizona	Minn.	Minnesota
Aug.	August	MIT	Massachusetts Institute of Technology
B.A.	Buenos Aires	Mo.	Missouri
Calif.	California	N.C.	North Carolina
Cd.	Ciudad	N.d.	No date
Colo	Colorado	Nebr.	Nebraska
Comm.	Committee	New ed.	New Edition
Comp.	Compiler	N.J	New Jersey
Cong.	Congress	N.M.	New Mexico
Conn.	Connecticut	No.	Number
C.R.	Costa Rica	Nov.	November
Dec.	December	N.p.	No place
Del.	Delaware	N.s.	New series
D.F.	Distrito Federal	N.Y.	New York
Diss.	Dissertation	NYU	New York University
Doc.	Document	O.	Ohio
D.R.	Dominican Republic	OAS	Organization of American States
Ed.	Editor; edition	Oct.	October
Eng.	England; English	Okla.	Oklahoma
Exec.	Executive	Ore.	Oregon
Feb.	February	O.s.	Old series
Fla.	Florida	Pa.	Pennsylvania
Fr.	French	PAU	Pan American Union
Ga.	Georgia	Pb.	Paperback
Ger.	Germany; German	Phil.	Philadelphia
Ia.	Iowa	P.I.	Philippine Islands
IAS	Inter-American System	Port.	Portugal; Portuguese
Ill.	Illinois	P.R.	Puerto Rico
Ind.	Indiana	Pseud.	Pseudonym
Jan.	January	Pt.	Part
Kan.	Kansas	Rept.	Report
Ky.	Kentucky	Rev. ed.	Revised edition
L.A.	Los Angeles	R.I.	Rhode Island
La.	Louisiana	Rio	Rio de Janeiro
LN	League of Nations	Russ.	Russian
Mar.	March	S.C.	South Carolina
Mass.	Massachusetts	Sept.	September
Md.	Maryland	Ser.	Series

Sess.	Session	USDC	United States Department of Commerce
So.	South	USDD	United States Department of Defense
Sp.	Spanish	USDN	United States Department of the Navy
Suppl.	Supplement	USDS	United States Department of State
Tenn.	Tennessee	USDW	United States Department of War
Tex.	Texas	USIA	United States Information Agency
Trans.	Translator	USLC	United States Library of Congress
Tri.	Trimester	USNA	National Archives of the United States
U.	University	Va.	Virginia
UCLA	University of California at Los Angeles	Ven.	Venezuela
UNAM	Universidad Nacional Autónoma de México	Vol.	Volume
		Vt.	Vermont
USC	United States Congress	Wash.	Washington
U.S.C.	University of Southern California	Wis.	Wisconsin
USCH	United States Congress, House of Representatives	WPA	Works Progress Administration
		W.Va.	West Virginia
USCS	United States Congress, Senate	Wyo.	Wyoming
USDAG	United States Department of Agriculture		

Key to Journals and Other Serials

AAAPSS   *Annals of the American Academy of Political and Social Science*. Philadelphia, Pa.

AAW   *Arizona and the West*. Tucson, Ariz.

ABAJ   *American Bar Association Journal*. Chicago, Ill.

ACIISC   *Anuario Colombiano de Historia Social y de la Cultura*. Bogotá, Colombia.

AEA   *Anuario de Estudios Americanos*. Seville, Spain.

AER   *American Economic Review*. Ithaca, N.Y.

AHR   *American Historical Review*. Washington, D.C.

AJES   *American Journal of Economics and Sociology*. New York, N.Y.

AJIL   *American Journal of International Law*. New York, N.Y.

AJS   *American Journal of Sociology*. Chicago, Ill.

AL   *América Latina*. Moscow, Soviet Union.

AME   *American Mercury*. New York, N.Y.

AOAS   *Annals of the Organization of American States*. Washington, D.C.

APAU   *Americas*. Washington, D.C.

APSR   *American Political Science Review*. Baltimore, Md.

AQ   *American Quarterly*. Philadelphia, Pa.

ASILP   *American Society of International Law Proceedings*. Washington, D.C.

AUC   *Anales de la Universidad de Cuenca*. Cuenca, Ecuador.

BACH   *Boletín de la Academia Chilena de la Historia*. Santiago, Chile.

BACPS   *Boletín de la Academia de Ciencias Políticas y Sociales*. Caracas, Venezuela.

BAGNDR   *Boletín del Archivo General de la Nación*. Cd. Trujillo, D.R.

BAGNM   *Boletín del Archivo Nacional de la Nación*. Mexico, D.F.

BAHL   *Boletín de la Academia Hondureña de la Lengua*. Tegucigalpa, Honduras.

BANH   *Boletín de la Academia Nacional de Historia*. Quito, Ecuador.

BANHA   *Boletín de la Academia Nacional de la Historia*. B.A., Argentina.

BANHC   *Boletín de la Academia Nacional de la Historia*. Caracas, Venezuela.

BAPH   *Boletín de Academia Panameña de la Historia*. Panama City, Panama.

BEP   *Boletín de Estudios Políticos*. Mendoza, Argentina.

BHA   *Boletín de Historia y Antigüedades*. Bogotá, Colombia.

BHR   *Business History Review*. Boston, Mass.

BIHA   *Boletín del Instituto de Historia Argentina Doctor Emilio Ravignani*. B. A. Argentina.

BINM   *Boletín del Instituto Nacional Mejía*. Quito, Ecuador.

BJ   *Boletín Jurídico*. Quito, Ecuador.

BJD   *Boletín Jurídico Venezolano*. Caracas, Venezuela.

BMRE   *Boletín del Ministerio de Relaciones Exteriores*. Montevideo, Uruguay.

BMREC   *Boletín del Ministerio de Relaciones Exteriores y Culto*. B.A., Argentina.

BPAU   *Bulletin of the Pan American Union*. Washington, D.C.

BSBDI   *Boletim de Sociedade Brasileira do Direito Internacional*. Rio de Janeiro, Brazil.

CA   *Cuadernos Americanos*. Mexico, D.F.

CAL   *Cahiers des Amériques Latines*. Paris, France.

CAR   *Caravelle: Cashiers du Monde Hispanique et Luso-Brésilliene*. Toulouse, France.

CB   *Cadernos Brasileiros*. Rio de Janeiro, Brazil.

CDI   *Cuadernos del Instituto*. Mendoza, Argentina.

CDLA *Casa de las Americas*. Havana, Cuba.

CE   *Century*. New York, N.Y.

CH   *Current History*. New York, N.Y.

CHA   *Cuadernos de Historia y Arqueología*. Quito, Ecuador.

CHSQ *California Historical Society Quarterly*. San Francisco, Calif.

CJ   *Cavalry Journal*. Washington, D.C.

CL   *Clio: Revista Bimestre de la Academia Dominicana de la Historia*. Cd. Trujillo, D.R.

COMEX *Comercio Exterior*. Mexico, D.F.

COM   *Commonweal*. New York, N.Y.

COMB *Combate*. San José, C.R.

CPS   *Ciencias Políticas y Sociales*. Mexico, D.F.

CQ   *Caribbean Quarterly*. Mona, Jamaica.

CR   *Contemporary Review*. London, England.

CS   *Caribbean Studies*. San Juan, P.R.

DE   *Desarrollo Económico*. B.A., Argentina.

DEC   *The Developing Economics*. Tokyo, Japan.

DFA   *Derecho y Reforma Agraria*. Mérida, Venezuela.

DH   *Diplomatic History*. Wilmington, Delaware.

EBLA *Economic Bulletin for Latin America*. New York, N.Y. (UN)

EDCC *Economic Development and Cultural Change*. Chicago, Ill.

EHI   *Estudos Históricos*. Marília, Brazil.

EHIPS *Estudios de la Historia de las Instituciones Políticas y Sociales*. Santiago, Chile.

ENV   *Enviado, Revista de Política y Ciencias Sociales*. B.A., Argentina.

ESC   *Estudios sobre el Comunismo*. Santiago, Chile.

ESTA *Estudios: Revista Argentina de Cultura Información y Documentación*. B.A., Argentina.

ESTLA *Estudios Latinoamericanos*. Warsaw, Poland.

ESTR *Estrategia*. B.A., Argentina.

EX   *Extra*. Tegucigalpa, Honduras.

EYO   *Este y Oeste*. Caracas, Venezuela.

FA   *Foreign Affairs*. New York, N.Y.

FHQ   *Florida Historical Quarterly*. Jacksonville, Fla.

FI   *Foro International*. Mexico, D.F.

FPAR *Foreign Policy Association Reports*. New York, N.Y.

FRON *Fronteras 1976*. San Diego, Calif.

GAZ   *Gazdasag*. Budapest, Hungary.

GLJ   *Georgetown Law Journal*. Washington, D.C.

GR   *Geographical Review*. New York, N.Y.

GU   *Guardacostas: Revista Oficial de la Prefectura Naval*. B.A., Argentina.

HAHR *Hispanic American Historical Review*. Durham, N.C.

HBA   *Historiografía y Bibliografía Americanista*. Seville, Spain.

HIH   *Historia del Instituto de Historia*. Universidad Católica de Chile. Santiago, Chile.

HIS   *Historian*. Albuquerque, N.M.

HISPR *Historia*. San Juan, P.R.

HM   *Historia Mexicana*. Mexico, D.F.

HRTH *Historia, Revista Trimestral de Historia Argentina, Americana, y Española*. B.A., Argentina.

HU   *Humanitas*. Monterrey, Nuevo León, Mexico.

IAA   *Ibero-Amerikanisches Archiv*. Berlin, Germany.

IAF   *International Affairs*. London, England.

IAP   *Ibero-Americana Pragensia*. Prague, Czechoslovakia.

IBR   *Inter-American Bibliographical Review*. Washington, D.C.

IC   *International Conciliation*. New York, N.Y.

IEA   *Inter-American Economic Affairs*. Washington, D.C.

IJ   *International Journal*. Toronto, Canada.

ILR   *International Labour Review*. Geneva, Switzerland.

INA   *Inter-American*. Washington, D.C.

IO   *International Organization*. Boston, Mass.

IRB   *Inter-American Review of Bibliography (Revista Interamericana de Bibliografía)*. Washington, D.C.

IV   *Ideas y Valores*. Bogotá, Colombia.

IYE   *Investigaciones y Ensayos*. B.A., Argentina.

JAGS *Journal of the American Geographical Society*. New York, N.Y.

JAHI *Journal of American History*. New Haven, Conn.

JCS   *A Journal of Church and State*. Waco, Tex.

JEH	*Journal of Economic History*. New York, N.Y.		PAN	*Panorama: Testigo de Nuestro Tiempo*. B.A., Argentina.
JFE	*Journal of Farm Economics*. Lancaster, Pa.		PAPS	*Proceedings of the Academy of Political Science*. New York, N.Y.
JIA	*Journal of International Affairs*. New York, N.Y.		PB	*Problemas Brasileiros*. São Paulo, Brazil.
JIAS	*Journal of Inter-American Studies*. Gainesville, Fla.		PEI	*Política Externa Independente*. Rio de Janeiro, Brazil.
JLAS	*Journal of Latin American Studies*. London, England.		PH	*Patrimonio Histórico*. Panama City, Panama.
JMH	*Journal of Modern History*. Chicago, Ill.		PHR	*Pacific Historical Review*. Berkeley, Calif.
JP	*Journal of Politics*. Gainesville, Fla.		PHY	*Phylon: Review of Race and Culture*. Atlanta, Ga.
JPR	*Journal of Peace Research*. Oslo, Norway.			
JQ	*Journalism Quarterly*. Urbana, Ill.		PIA	*Public and International Affairs*. Princeton, N.J.
JUS	*La Justicia*. Mexico, D.F.			
JW	*Journal of the West*. Manhattan, Kan.		PMH	*Pennsylvania Magazine of History and Biography*. Philadelphia, Pa.
			POI	*Política Internacional*. Havana, Cuba.
KKN	*Keizai Keiei Kenkyu Nenpo*. Kobe, Japan.		POL	*Politeia*. Caracas, Venezuela.
			POLEM	*Polémica: Primera Historia Argentina Integral*. B.A., Argentina.
L	*Lotería*. Panama City, Panama.			
LARR	*Latin American Research Review*. Austin, Tex.		PROBIN	*Probleme Internationale*. Bucharest, Rumania.
LHI	*Louisiana History*. Baton Rouge, La.		PSQ	*Political Science Quarterly*. New York, N.Y.
MA	*Mid-America*. Chicago, Ill.			
MAF	*Military Affairs*. Washington, D.C.		RACHS	*Records of the American Catholic Historical Society*. Philadelphia, Pa.
MAMH	*Memorias de la Academia Mexicana de la Historia*. Mexico, D.F.		RAGHN	*Revista de la Academia de Geografía e Historia de Nicaragua*. Managua, Nicaragua.
MANHG	*Memoria de la Academia Nacional de Historia y Geografía*. Mexico, D.F.		RAHGH	*Revista de la Academia Hondureña de Geografía e Historia*. Tegucigalpa, Honduras.
MCG	*Marine Corps Gazette*. New York, N.Y.			
MJPS	*Midwest Journal of Political Science*. Detroit, Mich.		RAK	*Raten Amerika Kenkyu*. Tokyo, Japan.
MR	*Monthly Review*. New York, N.Y.		RBCU	*Revista Bimestre Cubana*. Havana, Cuba.
MVHR	*Mississippi Valley Historical Review*. Bloomington, Ind.		RBEP	*Revista Brasileira de Estudos Políticos*. Belo Horizonte, Brazil.
			RCEDR	*Revista de Ciencias Económicas*. Santo Domingo, D.R.
N	*Nation*. New York, N.Y.		RCEHMP	*Revista del Centro de Estudios Histórico-Militares del Perú*. Lima, Peru.
NAR	*North American Review*. New York, N.Y.			
NCHR	*North Carolina Historical Review*. Raleigh, N.C.		RCHG	*Revista Chilena de Historia y Geografía*. Santiago, Chile.
NDQ	*North Dakota Quarterly*. Grand Forks, N.D.		RCS	*Revista de Ciencias Sociales*. Rio Piedras, P.R.
NH	*Nebraska History*. Lincoln, Nebr.			
NHIS	*Nuestra Historia*. Panama City, Panama.		RCU	*Revista Cubana*. New York, N.Y.
NMHR	*New Mexico Historical Review*. Albuquerque, N.M.		RDCPB	*Revista de Direito e Ciência Política*. Rio de Janeiro, Brazil.
NR	*New Republic*. New York, N.Y.		RDCSP	*Revista de Derecho y Ciencias Sociales*. Asunción, Paraguay.
NS	*Nueva Sociedad*. San José, C.R.		RDI	*Revista de Derecho Internacional*. Havana, Cuba.
OR	*Orbis*. Philadelphia, Pa.			
OSAHQ	*Ohio State Archaeological and Historical Quarterly*. Columbus, O.		RDICD	*Revista de Derecho Internacional y Ciencias Diplomáticas*. Rosario, Argentina.

RDN   *Revista de la Defensa Nacional*. B.A., Argentina.

RE   *Revista de Las Españas*. Madrid, Spain.

REP   *Revista de Estudios Políticos*. Madrid, Spain.

REPORT *Reporter*. New York, N.Y.

RFDCS   *Revista de la Facultad de Derecho y Ciencias Sociales*. B.A., Argentina.

RFDSCU *Revista de la Facultad de Ciencias Sociales*. Montevideo, Uruguay.

RFDM   *Revista de la Facultad de Derecho de México*. Mexico, D.F.

RFOR   *Revista Forense*. Rio de Janeiro, Brazil.

RGDIP   *Revue Générale de Droit International Public*. Paris, France.

RHA   *Revista de Historia de América*. Mexico, D.F.

RHIS   *Revista de História*. São Paulo, Brazil.

RHMC   *Revue D'Histoire Moderne et Contemporaine*. Paris, France.

RHU   *Revista Histórica*. Montevideo, Uruguay.

RIHGB   *Revista do Instituto Histórico e Geográfico Brasileiro*. Rio de Janeiro, Brazil.

RIN   *Revista de Indias*. Madrid, Spain.

RJEHM   *Revista de la Junta de Estudios Históricos de Mendoza*. Mendoza, Argentina.

RJV   *Revista Jurídica Veracruzana*. Japala, Veracruz, Mexico.

RMCPS   *Revista Mexicana de Ciencias Políticas y Sociales*. Mexico, D.F.

RMS   *Revista Mexicana de Sociología*. Mexico, D.F.

RNC   *Revista Nacional de Cultura*. Caracas, Venezuela.

RP   *Review of Politics*. Notre Dame, Ind.

RPC   *Revista del Pensamiento Centroamericano*. Managua, Nicaragua.

RPDI   *Revista Peruana de Derecho Internacional*. Lima, Peru.

RPI   *Revista de Política Internacional*. Madrid, Spain.

RRVHR   *Red River Valley Historical Review*. Durant, Okla.

RS   *Rural Sociology*. Ithaca, N.Y.

RSPI   *Revista di Studi Politici Internazionale*. Florence, Italy.

RUH   *Revista de la Universidad de la Habana*. Havana, Cuba.

SAISR   *SAIS Review*. Washington, D.C.

SAQ   *South Atlantic Quarterly*. Durham, N.C.

SCID   *Studies in Comparative International Development*. New Brunswick, N.J.

SECOLAS *Southeastern Conference on Latin American Studies Annals*. Carrollton, Ga.

SHQ   *Southwestern Historical Quarterly*. Austin, Tex.

SIN   *Sinsegye*. Seoul, Korea.

SLR   *Stanford Law Review*. Palo Alto, Calif.

SM   *Sprawy Miedzynarodowe*. Warsaw, Poland.

SO   *Society*. New Brunswick, N.J.

SPSSQ   *Southwestern Political and Social Science Quarterly*. Austin, Tex.

SSC   *Social Science*. Winfield, Kan.

SSSQ   *Southwestern Social Science Quarterly*. Austin, Tex.

STU   *Studia, Revista Semestral*. Lisbon, Portugal.

TA   *The Americas*. Washington, D.C.

TAR   *Tarsadalmi Szemle*. Budapest, Hungary.

TARE   *Tareas*. Panama City, Panama.

TC   *Trabajo y Communicaciones*. La Plata, Argentina.

TE   *El Trimestre Económico*. Mexico, D.F.

TES   *Todo Es Historia*. B.A., Argentina.

TIFL   *Texas International Law Forum*. Austin, Tex.

TRHS   *Transactions of the Royal Historical Society*. London, England.

UA   *Universidad de Antioquía*. Medellín, Colombia.

UES   *La Universidad de el Salvador*. San Salvador, El Salvador.

UNI   *Universidad*. Santa Fe, Argentina.

USDSB   *United States Department of State Bulletin*. Washington, D.C.

USNIP   *United States Naval Institute Proceedings*. Annapolis, Md.

VS   *Vital Speeches of the Day*. Pelham, N.Y.

WA   *World Affairs*. Washington, D.C.

WAI   *World Affairs Interpreter*. Los Angeles, Calif.

WP   *World Politics*. Princeton, N.J.

WPQ   *Western Political Quarterly*. Salt Lake City, Utah.

WS   *Waseda Shogaku*. Tokyo, Japan.

WT   *World Today*. London, England.

WW   *World's Work*. New York, N.Y.

YR   *Yale Review*. New Haven, Conn.

Chapter I Guides and Aids

A. BIBLIOGRAPHY

1. BIBLIOGRAPHY OF BIBLIOGRAPHIES

1. Boehm, E. H. (ed.). *Bibliographies on International Relations and World Affairs: An Annotated Directory*. Santa Barbara, Calif., 1965.

2. Cardozo, A. *Bibliografía de Bibliografías Agrícolas Bolivianas*. 2d ed., Bogotá, 1974.

3. Cardozo, L. "Bibliografía de las Bibliografías Humanísticas sobre Latinoamérica," *BANHC* 60 (Jan.–Mar., 1977) 101–110.

4. Collison, R. L. *Bibliographies: Subject and National*. Rev. ed., N.Y., 1968.

5. Culebra de Soberanes, C. "Bibliografías sobre América Latina: Ciencias Sociales," *FI* 12 (Oct.–Dec., 1971) 229–269.

6. Downs, R. B., and F. B. Jenkins (eds.). *Bibliography: Current State and Future Trends*. Urbana, Ill., 1967.

7. Foster, D. W., and V. R. Foster (comps.). *Manual of Hispanic Bibliography*. Seattle, Wash., 1970.
   A guide to almost 800 reference works.

8. Geoghegan, A. R. *Bibliografía de Bibliografías Argentinas, 1807–1970*. B.A., 1970.

9. Gropp, A. E. (comp.). *A Bibliography of Latin American Bibliographies*. Metuchen, N.J., 1968.

10. ———. *A Bibliography of Latin American Bibliographies Published in Periodicals*. 2 vols., Metuchen, N.J., 1976.
    Compilation from more than 1,000 periodicals. Contains name and subject index.

11. ———. *A Bibliography of Latin American Bibliographies: Supplement*. Metuchen, N.J., 1971.

12. Laval, R. A. *Bibliografía de Bibliografías Chilenas*. Santiago, 1915.

13. Musso Ambrosi, L. A. *Bibliografía de Bibliografías Uruguayas*. Montevideo, 1964.

14. Sheehy, E. P. *Guide to Reference Works*. 9th ed., Chicago, 1976.

15. Siles Guevara, J. *Bibliografía de Bibliografías Bolivianas*. La Paz, 1969.

16. Susto, J. A. "Panorama de la Bibliografía en Panamá," *IRB* 41 (Jan.–Mar., 1968) 3–27.
    Lists bibliographies by year of publication.

17. Zimmerman, I. *Current National Bibliographies of Latin America: A State of the Art Study*. Gainesville, Fla., 1971.

I-A-1 cross references: In the Trask, Meyer, and Trask Bibliography see items 1-23.

2. GENERAL BIBLIOGRAPHY

18. Brock, C. *The Literature of Political Science: A Guide for Students, Librarians and Teachers*. N.Y., 1969.

19. Delupis, I. *Bibliography of International Law*. London, 1975.

20. Dexter, B. (ed.). *The Foreign Affairs 50-Year Bibliography: New Evolution of Significant Books on International Relations, 1920–1970*. N.Y., 1970.

21. Flynn, A. H. *World Understanding: A Selected Bibliography*. Dobbs Ferry, N.Y., 1965.

22. Gould, W. L., and M. Barkum. *Social Science Literature: A Bibliography for International Law*. Princeton, N.J., 1972.

23. Gray, R. A. (ed.). *Serial Bibliographies in*

1

the *Humanities and Social Sciences*. Ann Arbor, Mich., 1969.

24. Grupo de Trabajo para la Integración de la Información. *Catálogo Colectivo de Publicaciones Periódicas en Desarrollo Social y Económico*. Lima, 1972.

25. Harmon, R. B. *Political Science: A Bibliographical Guide to the Literature*. N.Y., 1965.

26. Harvard University. Law School. Library. *Catalog of International Law and Relations*. 20 vols., Cambridge, Mass., 1965–1967.

27. Moussa, F. *Diplomatie Contemporaine: Guide Bibliographique*. Geneva, 1964.

28. Regional Economic Development Institution. *Bibliography of Resource Material in the Field of Regional Economic Development*. Wash., 1966.

29. Roach, J. *A Bibliography of Modern History*. Cambridge, Eng., 1968.

30. Rogers, A. *The Humanities: A Selective Guide to Information Sources*. Littleton, Colo., 1974.

31. Wasserman, P., and E. Herman. *Library Bibliographies and Indexes*. Detroit, Mich., 1975.

I-A-2   cross references: In the Trask, Meyer, and Trask Bibliography *see items 24–142.*

3. LATIN AMERICA IN GENERAL

32. Ajia Keizai Kenkyujo. *Raten Amerika no Klizai Togo ni Kansuro Bunken to Zasshi Kijo*. 2 vols., Tokyo, 1964–1967.
     Translated title: "Bibliography on Economic Integration in Latin America."

33. Bayitch, S. A. *Latin America and the Caribbean: A Guide to Works in English*. Coral Gables, Fla., 1967.

34. Benito, M. *Latinamerika I Svensk Bibliografi: América Latina en la Bibliografía Sueca, 1959–1969*. Stockholm, 1971.

35. *Bibliografía Jurídica de América Latina, 1910–1965*. 5 vols., Santiago, 1965–1970.
     Contains 17,000 entries.

36. Bingaman, J. W. *Latin America: A Survey of Holdings at the Hoover Institution on War, Revolution and Peace*. Stanford, Calif., 1972.
     A valuable bibliographical tool for

contemporary Latin America, especially political movements of the left.

37. Brunnschweiler, T. *Current Periodicals: A Select Bibliography in the Area of Latin American Studies at Michigan State University*. East Lansing, Mich., 1968.
     Vol. 3 in the monograph series of the Latin American Studies Center. Lists 740 periodicals with publisher and call number.

38. Chaffee, W. A., and H. M. Griffin. *Dissertations on Latin America by U.S. Historians, 1960–1970*. Austin, Tex., 1973.

39. Charno, S. M. (comp.). *Latin American Newspapers in the United States Libraries*. Austin, Tex., 1968.
     Project sponsored by the Conference on Latin American History. Contains data on about 5,500 Latin American newspapers.

40. Chilcote, R. H. *Revolution and Structural Change in Latin America: A Bibliography on Ideology, Development and the Radical Left (1930–1965)*. 2 vols., Stanford, Calif., 1970.

41. Cortés Conde, R., and S. J. Stein (eds.). *Latin America: A Guide to Economic History, 1830–1930*. Berkeley, Calif., 1977.
     The most comprehensive volume of its kind. Contains over 4,500 titles, all annotated, and a series of perceptive historiographical essays.

41a. Deal, C. (ed.) *Latin America and the Caribbean: A Dissertation Bibliography*. Ann Arbor, Mich., 1978.
     Contains over 7,000 titles from United States and Canadian universities.

41b. Domínguez, J. I. "Consensus and Divergence: The State of the Literature on Inter-American Relations in the 1970's," *LARR* 13 (Spring, 1978) 87–126.

42. Dorn, G. M. (ed.). *Latin America, Spain and Portugal: An Annotated Bibliography of Paperback Books*. Wash., 1976.
     Lists 2,202 paperback titles. Major revision of volume published in 1971.

43. Einaudi, L., and H. Goldhamer. *An Annotated Bibliography of Latin American Military Journals*. Santa Monica, Calif., 1965.

44. Esquenazi-Mayo, R., and M. C. Meyer (eds.). *Latin American Scholarship Since*

World War II: Trends in History, Political Science, Literature, Geography, and Economics. Lincoln, Nebr., 1971.

A series of essays analyzing the trends in the scholarly literature of each field.

45. Gardner, M. A. The Press of Latin America: A Tentative and Selected Bibliography in Spanish and Portuguese. Austin, Tex., 1973.

46. Griffin, C. C., and J. B. Warren (eds.). Latin America: A Guide to the Historical Literature. Austin, Tex., 1971.

Sponsored by the Conference on Latin American History, this volume is the most valuable of its kind. Contains over 7,000 annotated citations compiled by leading scholars in the field.

47. Hanson, C. A. Dissertations on Iberian and Latin American History. Troy, N.Y., 1975.

A useful listing of over 3,500 dissertations from U. S., Canadian, British and Irish universities.

48. International Conferences of American States. Bibliografía de las Conferencias Americanas. Wash., 1954.

49. Kantor, H. Latin American Political Parties: A Bibliography. Gainesville, Fla., 1968.

50. Keesing, B. Economic Problems of Latin America: A Selected Bibliography. N.Y., 1966.

51. Klein, M. T. Bibliographie zur Soziologie und Demographie Lateinamerikas. Hamburg, 1968.

52. Lambert, M. Bibliographie Latino-Américaniste: France, 1959–1972. Mexico, 1973.

52a. León, P. R. "Los Estudios sobre Iberoamérica en el Canadá," HBA 16 (Mar., 1972) 71–98.

53. Lindenberg, K. Fuerzas Armadas y Política en América Latina: Bibliografía Selecta. Santiago, 1972.

54. Mings, R. C. The Tourist Industry in Latin America: A Bibliography for Planning and Research. Monticello, Ill., 1974.

54a. Molineu, H. (comp.). Multinational Corporations and International Investment in Latin America: A Selected and Annotated Bibliography with an Annotated Film Bibliography. Athens, O., 1978.

55. Morris, J. E., and E. Córdova. Bibliog-

raphy of Industrial Relations in Latin America. Ithaca, N.Y., 1967.

56. National Foreign Trade Council. Sources of Marketing and Economic Information on Latin America. N.Y., 1975.

57. Naylor, A. Accounts of Nineteenth-Century South America: An Annotated Checklist of Works by British and American Observers. London, 1969.

Lists 320 travel accounts.

58. Ross, S. R., et al. Historiografía Contemporánea de América Latina. Tunja, Colombia, 1975.

59. Ross, S. R. "Recent United States Bibliographical Contributions to Latin American Historiography," RHA 77–78 (1974) 207–218.

60. Russell, C., J. A. Miller, and R. E. Hildner. "The Urban Guerrilla in Latin America: A Select Bibliography," LARR 9 (Spring, 1974) 37–79.

Contains 261 annotated items.

61. Sable, M. H. Communism in Latin America: An International Bibliography. Los Angeles, 1968.

62. ———. Latin American Agriculture: A Bibliography. Milwaukee, Wis., 1970.

Over 1,000 titles. Not annotated.

63. ———. Latin American Studies in the Non-Western World and Eastern Europe. Metuchen, N.J., 1970.

In spite of the title, this is an extensive bibliography rather than a guide to Latin American studies.

64. ———. The Guerrilla Movement in Latin America Since 1950: A Bibliography. Milwaukee, Wis., 1977.

A 57-page pamphlet listing 487 sources.

65. Schaefer, J. Bibliographie zur Politik und Zeitgeschichte der Iberoamerikanischen Länder. Hamburg, 1965.

66. Seara Vásquez, M. "Guía de Lecturas para el Estudiante de Ciencias Diplomáticas," CPS 9 (July–Sept., 1963) 495–520.

67. Stein, S. J., and S. J. Hunt. "Principal Currents in the Economic Historiography of Latin America," JEH 31 (Mar., 1971) 222–253.

67a. Thompson, L. S. "Latin America and Related Material in Microfilm," IRB 24 (Apr.–June, 1974) 162–166.

68. Toto, J. del (comp.). A Bibliography of the

Collective Biography of Spanish America. Detroit, Mich., 1971.

A guide to 488 published sources useful for prosopographic research.

69. Tulane University. Latin American Library. *Catalogue of the Latin American Library of the Tulane University*. 9 vols., Boston, 1970.

70. USDA. *Latin America and the Caribbean: Analytical Survey of Literature*. Wash., 1969.

71. Vaughan, D. R. (comp.). *Urbanization in Twentieth-Century Latin America: A Working Bibliography*. Austin, Tex., 1970.

72. Villalón, A. *Bibliografía Jurídica de América Latina (1810–1965)*. Santiago, 1969.

73. Weaver, J. L. *Latin American Development: A Selected Bibliography, 1950–1967*. Santa Barbara, Calif., 1969.

Items arranged by country without annotation.

74. Wilgus, A. C. *Latin America in the Nineteenth Century: A Selected Bibliography of Books of Travel and Description Published in English*. Metuchen, N. J., 1973.

Contains almost 1,200 titles, some with annotations.

75. Woodbridge, H. C., and D. Newberry (eds.). *Basic List of Latin American Materials in Spanish, Portuguese and French*. Amherst, Mass., 1975.

I-A-3 cross references: In the Trask, Meyer, and Trask Bibliography *see items* 143–330, 614, 1077–1148, 4365.

4. UNITED STATES

76. Brown, J. C. *Administration of United States Foreign Affairs: A Bibliography*. University Park, Pa., 1968.

77. Doenecke, J. D. *The Literature of Isolationism: A Guide to Non-Interventionist Scholarship*. Colorado Springs, Colo., 1972.

78. Fowler, W. B. *American Diplomatic History Since 1890*. Northbrook, Ill., 1975.

A topically arranged bibliography listing over 2,800 titles.

79. Jones, W. C. "American Studies Research in Progress: 1974–1975," *AQ* 27 (1975) 296–305.

80. Millett, A. R., and B. F. Franklin (comps.). "Doctoral Dissertations in Military Affairs," *MA* 38 (Feb., 1974) 12–16.

80a. Simmons, M. E. *U.S. Political Ideas in Spanish America before 1830: A Bibliographical Study*. Bloomington, Ind., 1977.

81. Stewart, W. J. (comp.). *The Era of Franklin D. Roosevelt: A Selected Bibliography of Essays, Dissertations, and Periodical Literature, 1945–1971*. Hyde Park, N.Y., 1973.

81a. USDS. Office of the Historian. *Major Publications of the Department of State: An Annotated Bibliography*. Wash., 1977.

USDS Publication No. 7843. A 27-page pamphlet.

82. U.S. National Archives and Record Service. General Services Administration. *List of National Archives Microfilm Publications*. Wash., 1968.

Contains the price of each set of microfilm.

83. Wynar, B. D. (ed.). *American Reference Books Annual: 1970*. 2 vols., Littleton, Colo., 1970.

I-A-4 cross references: In the Trask, Meyer, and Trask Bibliography *see items* 331–425, 780, 781, 786, 799, 1149–1187.

5. ARGENTINA

84. Caffese, M. E., and C. F. Lafuente. *Mayo en la Bibliografía*. B.A., 1961.

85. Córdoba, A. O. *Bibliografía de Juan Bautista Alberdi*. B.A., 1969.

86. Cordone, H. "Bibliografías: Peronismo," *ENV* 2 (1970) 93–95.

87. Ferrari, G. "Bibliografía de Base sobre Política Exterior Argentina," *BIHA* 14–15 (1970–1971) 74–97.

88. Geoghegan, A. R. *Obras de Referencia de Argentina, 1964–1969*. B.A., 1970.

Describes 93 reference works.

89. Halperín Donghi, T. *El Revisionismo Histório Argentino*. B.A., 1970.

90. Hualde de Pérez Guihou, M. "Aporte para una Bibliografía Crítica de la Revolución de Mayo," *BEP* 9 (1958) 116–150.

91. Instituto Bibliográfico "Antonio Zinny." *Indice Historgráfico Argentino, 1970*. B.A., 1973.

Contains more than 2,000 items on Argentine history published in 1970.

92. Pla, A. J. *Ideología y Método en la Historiografía*. B.A., 1972.

93. Rey Balmaceda, R. *Bibliografía Geográfica Argentina*. B.A., 1975.

94. Universidad de Buenos Aires. *Tesis Presentadas a la Universidad de Buenos Aires, 1961–1962*. B.A., 1966.

I-A-5 cross references:
a) See item 8.
b) In the Trask, Meyer, and Trask *Bibliography* see items 426–475, 1188–1218.

6. BOLIVIA

95. Abecia Baldevieso, V. *Historiografía Boliviana*. La Paz, 1965.

96. Christman, C. L. "The Chaco War: A Tentative Bibliography of Its Diplomacy," *TA* 26 (July, 1969) 54–65.

97. Costa de la Torre, A. *Catálogo de la Bibliografía Boliviana: Libros y Folletos 1900–1963*. La Paz, 1968.

98. Guttentag Tichauer, W. *Bibliografía Boliviana del Año 1974*. Cochabamba, Bolivia, 1975.

99. Muñoz Reyes, J. *Bibliografía Geográfica de Bolivia*. La Paz, 1967.

100. Quintero Mesa, R. *Latin American Serial Documents: A Holdings List*. Vol. 6: *Bolivia*. N.Y., 1972.
    Based on holdings located in 407 libraries.

I-A-6 cross references:
a) See items 2, 15.
b) In the Trask, Meyer, and Trask *Bibliography* see items 476–490, 1219–1228.

7. BRAZIL

101. Bartley, R. H. "A Decade of Soviet Scholarship in Brazilian History," *HAHR* 50 (Aug., 1970) 445–446.

102. Brasil. Ministério das Relações Exteriores. *Lista dos Periódicos Existentes na Biblioteca do Itamaraty*. Rio, 1966.

103. Hanson, C. A. "Dissertations on Luso-Brazilian Topics: A Bibliography of Dissertations Completed in the United States, Great Britain and Canada, 1892–1970," *TA* 30 (Oct., 1973) 251–267 and 30 (Jan., 1974) 373–403.

104. Lacombe, A. J. "Fontes para o Estudo da História do Brasil," *RHA* 43 (June, 1957) 31–49.

105. Matos, O. Nogueira de. "José Honório Rodrigues e a Historiografia Brasileira," *RHIS* 43 (Oct.–Dec., 1971) 527–534.

105a. Ramos, D. H. A. "Levantamento das Pesquisas sobre Asuntos Brasileiros Feitas en Universidades Americanas: 1960–1970," *RHIS* 49 (July–Sept., 1974) 281–308.

I-A-7 cross references: In the Trask, Meyer, and Trask Bibliography *see items 439, 491–556c, 1229–1254.*

8. CENTRAL AMERICA AND THE CARIBBEAN IN GENERAL

106. Comitas, L. *Caribbeana 1900–1965: A Topical Bibliography*. Seattle, Wash., 1968.

107. Dossick, J. J. "Doctoral Research on the Caribbean and Circum-Caribbean Accepted by American, British and Canadian Universities," *CS* 8 (July, 1978) 89–96.

108. Peraza Sarausa, F. *Bibliografía Cubana, Complementos: 1936–1961*. Gainesville, Fla., 1966.
    Contains 3,955 entries for the Caribbean area.

109. Snarr, D. N. "Ph.D. Dissertations Dealing with Social Change and Development in Central America and Panama," *RS* 40 (Fall, 1975) 284–318.

110. ———, and E. L. Brown. "An Analysis of Dissertations on Central America: 1960–1974," *LARR* 12 (1977) 187–202.

I-A-8 cross references:
a) See item 284.
b) In the Trask, Meyer, and Trask *Bibliography* see items 557–571a, 784, 1254a–1260.

9. CHILE

111. Avila Martel, A. *Panorama de la Historiografía Jurídica Chilena*. B.A., 1949.

112. Banco Central de Chile. *Bibliografía Económica de Chile, 1960–1968*. Santiago, 1969.
113. Chile. Dirección de Bibliotecas, Archivos y Museos. Biblioteca Nacional. *Bibliografía General de la Revista Estudios: 1932–1957*. Santiago, 1969.
114. Jobet, J. C. *Literatura Histórica Chilena: Historiografía Chilena*. Santiago, 1949.
115. ———. "Notas sobre los Estudios Históricos en Chile," *TC* 20 (1970) 207–233.
116. Millares Carlo, A. "Andrés Bello, Ensayo Bibliográfico," *RHA* 67–68 (Jan.–Dec., 1969) 211–231.
117. Paunes Gálvez, H. *Bibliografía Histórica de Chile, 1917–1950: Tesis para Optar al Título de Profesora de Estado en Historia, Geografía, Educación Cívica y Economía Política*. Santiago, 1957.
      Contains 2,843 works.
118. Stharsky, H., and M. Riesch (eds.). *Bibliographical Notes for Understanding the Military Coup in Chile*. Wash., 1974.
119. Vial Correa, G. "Historiografía de la Independencia de Chile," *HIH* 4 (1965) 165–190.
120. Williams, L. H. (comp.). *The Allende Years: A Union List of Chilean Imprints, 1970–1973*. Boston, 1977.
121. Woll, A. "The Catholic Historian in Nineteenth Century Chile," *TA* 33 (June, 1977) 470–489.

I-A-9 *cross references:*
a) See item 12.
b) In the Trask, Meyer, and Trask *Bibliography* see items 439, 572–608, 1261–1282.

10. COLOMBIA

122. Grases, P., and M. Pérez Vila. "Gran Colombia: Referencias Relativas a la Bibliografía sobre el Período Emancipador en los Países Grancolombinos," *AEA* 21 (1964) 733–777.
123. Ocampo López, J. *Historiografía y Bibliografía de la Emancipación del Nuevo Reino de Granada*. Tunja, Colombia, 1969.
123a. Ramsey, R. W. "Critical Bibliography on La Violencia in Colombia," *LARR* 8 (Spring, 1973) 3–44.
124. Vegalara, H., and E. Wiesner Durán.

Bibliografía Comentada sobre el Desarrollo Económico y la Economía Colombiana. 2 vols., Bogotá, 1959–1961.
125. Watson, G. H. *Colombia, Ecuador and Venezuela: An Annotated Guide to Reference Materials in the Humanities and Social Sciences*. Metuchen, N.J., 1971.

I-A-10 *cross references: In the Trask, Meyer, and Trask* Bibliography *see items* 609–635, 889, 890, 893, 1283–1295a.

11. COSTA RICA

126. Costa Rica. Instituto Geográfico Nacional. *Publicaciones del Instituto Geográfico Nacional: 1954–1972*. San José, C.R., 1973.
127. Kantor, H. *Bibliography of José Figueres*. Tempe, Ariz., 1972.
      Contains titles by Figueres and about him.

I-A-11 *cross references: In the Trask, Meyer, and Trask* Bibliography *see items* 636–644, 1296–1299, 2480a.

12. CUBA

128. Blanch y Blanco, C. *Bibliografía Martiana, 1954–1965*. Havana, 1965.
129. Cozeah, J. D., *et al*. *Cuban Guerrilla Training Centers and Radio Havana: A Select Bibliography*. Wash., 1968.
130. González, M. P. "A Selective Bibliography of the Cuban Revolution against Machado (1928–1933)," *RBCU* 50 (Sept.–Oct., 1942) 209–231.
131. Peraza Sarausa, F. (ed.). *Revolutionary Cuba: A Bibliographical Guide, 1967*. Coral Gables, Fla., 1969.
      Contains 911 entries.
132. ———. "Bibliografía Cubana de la Segunda Guerra Mundial," *RUH* 2 (Mar., 1943) 87–91 and 6 (July, 1945) 486–488.
133. Pérez, L. A. *The Cuban Revolutionary War, 1953–1958: A Bibliography*. Metuchen, N.J., 1976.
134. Schulman, I. A., and E. Miles. "A Guide to the Location of Nineteenth-Century Cuban Magazines," *LARR* 12 (1977) 69–102.

135. Snow, P. G. "The Cuban Revolution: A Partial List of Books and Pamphlets," *CS* 2 (Jan., 1963) 62–65.
136. Trelles y Govin, C. M. *Bibliografía Social Cubana*. Havana, 1969.
    Lists about 700 references covering the period 1717 to 1924.

I-A-12 cross references: In the Trask, Meyer, and Trask Bibliography see items 645–682, 1300–1311, 7448.

13. DOMINICAN REPUBLIC

137. Ferguson, Y. H. "The Dominican Intervention of 1965: Recent Interpretations," *IO* 17 (Autumn, 1973) 517–548.
138. Florén Lozano, L. *Bibliografía de la Bibliografía Dominicana, 1930–Mayo 1952*. Cd. Trujillo, D.R., 1952.
139. Grabendorf, W. *Bibliographie zu Politik und Gesellschaft der Dominikanischen Republik: Neuere Studien, 1961–1971*. Munich, 1973.
140. Hitt, D. S., and L. C. Wilson. *A Selected Bibliography of the Dominican Republic: Century after the Restoration of Independence*. Wash., 1968.
141. Mella Chavier, P. "Bibliografía Histórica Dominicana: Publicaciones Aparecidas en 1958 y 1959," *CL* 27 (Jan.–Jur 1959) 109–112.
142. Wiarda, H. J. *Materials for the Study of Politics and Government in the Dominican Republic, 1930–1966*. Santiago, D. R., 1968.

I-A-13 cross references: In the Trask, Meyer, and Trask Bibliography see items 648, 683–696, 751, 752, 1312–1317.

14. ECUADOR

142a. Larrea Holguín, J. *Bibliografía Jurídica del Ecuador*. Quito, 1974.
    Extensive guide to the legal literature.
143. Norris, R. E. "Estudios Norteamericanos sobre la Historia del Ecuador," *AUC* 28 (July–Dec., 1971) 179–189.

I-A-14 cross references:
a) See items 122, 125.
b) In the Trask, Meyer, and Trask *Bibliography* see items 697–711, 1318–1328.

15. EL SALVADOR

I-A-15 cross references: In the Trask, Meyer, and Trask Bibliography see items 712–721, 1328a–1331.

16. GUATEMALA

144. Burgess, P. *José Rufino Barrios: Una Bibliografía*. Guatemala, 1972.
145. Ray, J. A. "Revolution and Liberation: A Review of Recent Literature on the Guatemalan Situation," *HAHR* 38 (1958) 239–255.

I-A-16 cross references: In the Trask, Meyer, and Trask Bibliography see items 722–737a, 1332–1335.

17. HAITI

I-A-17 cross references: In the Trask, Meyer, and Trask Bibliography see items 638–652a, 1336–1337.

18. HONDURAS

145a. Durón, J. F. "Las Publicaciones Hondureñas de 1971," *BAHL* 15 (Nov., 1972) 7–38.
146. García, M. A. *Anuario Bibliográfico Hondureño, 1961–1971*. Tegucigalpa, 1973.
147. ———. *Bibliografía Hondureña*. 2 vols., Tegucigalpa, 1971–1972.

I-A-18 cross references: In the Trask, Meyer, and Trask Bibliography see items 753–759c, 1338–1339.

19. MEXICO

148. Avilés, R. *Bibliografía de Benito Juárez*. Mexico, 1972.
149. Barrios, E. (ed.). *Bibliografía de Aztlán: An Annotated Chicano Bibliography*. San Diego, Calif., 1971.
149a. Cole, G. *American Travellers to Mexico, 1821–1972: A Descriptive Bibliography*. Troy, N.Y., 1978.
150. Comité Mexicano de Ciencias Históricas. *Catálogo de Tesis sobre Historia de México*. Mexico, 1976.
    Mimeographed listing of over 1,000 theses.

151. Dabbs, J. A. *Mariano Riva Palacio Archives: A Guide*. 3 vols., Mexico, 1967–1972.

The first two volumes list more than 10,000 items. The third volume is the index.

152. Fernández Esquivel, R. M. *Las Publicaciones Oficiales de México: Guía de Publicaciones Periódicas y Seriadas, 1937–1967*. Mexico, 1968.

Updates Annita Ker's guide to Mexican government publications.

153. Grajales, G. *Guía de Documentos para la Historia de México Existentes en la Public Record Office de Londres, 1827–1830*. Mexico, 1967.

154. Johnson, C. W. *México en el Siglo XX: Una Bibliografía Social y Política de Publicaciones Extranjeras, 1900–1969*. Mexico, 1969.

155. Mendoza López, M. *Catálogo General del Archivo del Ayuntamiento de la Ciudad de México*. Mexico, 1972.

The catalog of 7,400 volumes covers the sixteenth through the twentieth centuries.

156. Meyer, E. *Conciencia Norteamericana sobre La Revolución de 1910*. Mexico, 1970.

Studies U.S. historiography of the Mexican Revolution.

157. Meyer, M. C. "A Venture in Documentary Publication: Isidro Fabela's *Documentos Históricos de la Revolución Mexicana*," *HAHR* 52 (Feb., 1972) 123–129.

Suggests ways in which the documentary set may be used.

158. Nogales, G. (ed.). *The Mexican Americans: A Selected and Annotated Bibliography*. Stanford, Calif., 1971.

Lists and annotates the major works. Both monographs and articles.

159. Perales Ojeda, A. *Las Obras de Consulta: Reseña Histórico Crítica*. Mexico, 1962.

160. Pino, F. *Mexican Americans: A Research Bibliography*. 2 vols., East Lansing, Mich., 1974.

Contains over 15,000 entries.

161. Quintero Mesa, R. (comp.). *Latin American Serial Documents: A Holdings List*. Vol. 4: *Mexico*. Ann Arbor, Mich., 1970.

162. Richmond, D. W. "The Venustiano Carranza Archive," *HAHR* 56 (May, 1976) 290–294.

Describes the documents in Mexico City's CONDUMEX historical collection.

163. Sáenz Cirlos, V. J. *Guía de Obras de Consulta sobre México en el Campo de las Ciencias Sociales*. Austin, Tex., 1968.

Based upon works in the U. of Tex. Latin American collection.

164. Steele, C., and M. P. Costeloe, *Independent Mexico: A Collection of Mexican Pamphlets in the Bodleian Library*. London, 1973.

Contains references to 1,446 Mexican pamphlets, most from the early nineteenth century.

165. Velásquez Gallardo, P. *Catálogo Colectivo de Publicaciones Periódicas Existentes en Bibliotecas de la República Mexicana*. Mexico, 1968.

166. Ymhoff Cabrera, J. *Catálogo de Obras Manuscritas de la Biblioteca Nacional de México*. Mexico, 1975.

I-A-19   cross references: In the Trask, Meyer, and Trask Bibliography *see items 185a, 296, 760–869, 1340–1364, 5778a, 6228, 6239.*

20. NICARAGUA

I-A-20   cross references: In the Trask, Meyer, and Trask Bibliography *see items 870–883, 1365, 2480a, 7051.*

21. PANAMA

167. Castillero R., E. J. "Bibliografía de la Independencia de Panamá," *L* 24 (Nov., 1957) 28–37.

168. Herrera, C. D. de. *Bibliografía de los Trabajos de Graduación y Tesis Presentados en la Universidad de Panamá*. Panama, 1960.

169. ———. *Bibliografía Existente en la Biblioteca Universitaria sobre el Canal de Panamá y Nuestras Relaciones con los Estados Unidos de Norteamérica*. Panama, 1964.

170. Herrera, F. A. "Bibliografía de Panamá de 1960 a 1963," *L* 118 (Sept., 1965) 67–97.

170a. Moscote, R. E. "Las Corrientes Historiográficas Contemporáneas y la Historia Nacional," *PH* 1 (Mar., 1972) 35–47.

171. Panamá. Biblioteca Nacional. *Bibliografía Panameña*. Panama, 1953.
172. Soler, R. "Contribución a la Bibliografía Histórica en Lengua Francesa sobre el Canal de Panamá," *L* 22 (Sept., 1957) 87–93.
173. Susto Lara, J. A. *Panorama de la Bibliografía en Panamá (1619–1967).* Panama, 1971.

I-A-21   cross references:
a)   See item 16.
b)   In the Trask, Meyer, and Trask *Bibliography* see items 884–900, 1366–1369.

22. PARAGUAY

174. Amarilla de Ferreira, R. I. *Bibliografía de Tesis Entregadas a la Facultad de Derecho y Ciencias Sociales de la Universidad Nacional de Asunción*. Asunción, 1975.
175. Fernández Caballero, C. F. S. *The Paraguayan Bibliography: A Retrospective and Enumerative Bibliography of Printed Works of Paraguayan Authors*. Wash., 1970.
176. Hahner, J. E. "The Archivo Nacional in Asunción," *LARR* 6 (Fall, 1971) 131–132.
177. Irala Burgos, A. "Nuevas Corrientes de la Historiografía Paraguaya," *IRB* 42 (Apr.–June, 1968) 125–141.
178. Mareski, S. and O. Ferraro. *Bibliografía para el Estudio de los Mensajes Presidenciales del Paraguay*. Asunción, 1973.
179. Williams, J. H. "The Archivo Nacional in Asunción, Paraguay," *LARR* 6 (Spring, 1971) 101–118.
180. ———. "Paraguayan Historical Resources: Part I, the Paraguayan National Archives," *TA* 34 (July, 1977) 113–123.

I-A-22   cross references: In the Trask, Meyer, and Trask Bibliography *see items 710, 901–910, 1370–1376.*

23. PERU

181. Basadre, J. *Bibliografía General de la Etapa Republicana*. Lima, 1968.
182. Herbold, C., and S. Stein. *Guía Bibliográfica para la Historia Social y Política del Perú en el Siglo Veinte (1895-1960)*. Lima, 1971.

183. Martínez, H., M. Cameo C., and J. Ramírez S. *Bibliografía Indígena Andina Peruana: 1900–1968*. Lima, 1969.
184. Matos Mar, J., and R. Ravines. *Bibliografía Peruana de Ciencias Sociales: 1957–1969*. Lima, 1971.
        Contains approximately 2,000 items.
185. Moreyra y Paz Soldán, C. *Bibliografía Regional Peruana*. Lima, 1976.
186. Samame Boggio, M. *Minería Peruana: Bibliografía*. Breña, Peru, 1974.
187. Universidad Nacional Mayor de San Marcos. *Catálogo de Tesis de la Facultad de Derecho*. Lima, 1944.

I-A-23   cross references: In the Trask, Meyer, and Trask Bibliography *see items 707, 911–937, 1377–1387.*

24. URUGUAY

188. *Anuario Bibliográfico Uruguayo. 1972.* Montevideo, 1975.
189. *Anuario Bibliográfico. 1973.* Montevideo, 1975.
        Contains 11,000 items published in Uruguay.
190. *Anuario Bibliográfico Uruguayo. 1974.* Montevideo, 1976.

I-A-24   cross references:
a)   See item 13.
b)   In the Trask, Meyer, and Trask *Bibliography* see items 938–951, 1388–1395.

25. VENEZUELA

191. Blonval López, A. *Bibliografía Jurídica y Fiscal Venezolana*. 2 vols., Caracas, 1966.
        Contains almost 5,000 items, many of which are on international law. Arranged topically.
192. Bonafanti, C., A. T. Cova, and A. de Costa. *Catálogo de la U.C.V.* Caracas, 1969.
        Library catalog of the Universidad Central de Venezuela.
193. Carrera Damas, G. "La Historiografía Venezolana Actual," *IV* 32–34 (Jan.–Mar., 1969) 77–82.
194. Grases, P. *Temas de Bibliografía y Cultura Venezolana*. 2d ed., Caracas, 1973.
195. Lombardi, J. V., G. Carrera Damas, and

R. E. Adams. *Venezuelan History: A Comprehensive Working Bibliography*. Boston, 1977.

Lists 4,647 works without annotations.

196. Rodríguez Gallad, I. *El Petróleo en la Historiografía Venezolana*. Caracas, 1974.

197. Sullivan, W. M. *Bibliografía Comentada de la Era de Cipriano Castro, 1899–1908*. Caracas, 1977.

198. Villasana, A. R. *Ensayo de un Repertorio Bibliográfico Venezolano: Años 1808–1950*. 4 vols., Caracas, 1969–1970.

I-A-25   cross references:
a) See items 122, 125.
b) In the Trask, Meyer, and Trask *Bibliography* see items 952–983, 1396–1401.

B. OTHER GUIDES AND AIDS

1. GENERAL GUIDES AND AIDS

198a. Amstutz, M. R. (ed.). *Economics and Foreign Policy: A Guide to Information Sources*. Detroit, Mich., 1977.

199. *The Annual Register of World Events*. N.Y., 1972.

200. Banks, A. S. (ed.). *Political Handbook of the World: 1976*. N.Y., 1976.

Contains up-to-date information about all countries.

201. Broek, J. O. M. *A Geography of Mankind*. N.Y., 1968.

202. Calvo, C. *Dictionnaire Manuel de Diplomatie et de Droit International Public et Privé*. Berlin, 1885.

Defines terms used in international relations and international law.

203. *Dictionnaire de la Terminologie du Droit Internationale, Public sous le Patronage de l'Union Académique Internationale*. Paris, 1960.

204. Gilbert, M. *Recent History Atlas: 1870 to the Present Day.*. N.Y., 1969.

205. Hammond, C. S. *Diplomat World Atlas*. Maplewood, N.J., 1961.

206. Hanesch, G. *Internationale Terminologie: Diplomatie, Vertrage, International Organisationen, Konferenzen*. Stuttgart, 1954.

207. Harmon, R. B. *The Art and Practice of Diplomacy: A Selected and Annotated Guide*. Metuchen, N.J., 1971.

208. *International Encyclopedia of the Social Sciences*. 17 vols., N.Y., 1968.

208a. *The International Who's Who, 1977–1978*. Detroit, Mich., 1977.

Contains over 17,000 listings.

209. Keeton, G. W., and G. Schwarzenberger (eds.). *The Yearbook of World Affairs, 1976*. Boulder, Colo., 1976.

210. Kernig, C. D. (ed.). *Marxism, Communism and Western Society: A Comparative Encyclopedia*. 8 vols., N.Y., 1972–1974.

211. Palomar, J. I. *Diccionario Diplomático Consular*. 2 vols., B.A., 1937.

212. Plano, J. C., and R. Olton. *The International Relations Dictionary*. N.Y., 1969.

213. Shaim, A. (ed.). *International Organizations: Yearbook, 1975*. Boulder, Colo., 1976.

214. Vasco, M. A. *Diccionario de Derecho Internacional*. Quito, 1963.

215. Zawodny, J. K. *Guide to the Study of International Relations*. San Francisco, 1966.

I-B-1   cross references:
a) See items 18–31.
b) In the Trask, Meyer, and Trask *Bibliography* see items 24–142, 984–1076.

2. LATIN AMERICA IN GENERAL

216. Arce, F. de. *Compendio de Geografía, Historia y Constituciones de América*. Madrid, 1929.

217. Asociación Latinoamericana de Instituciones Financieras de Desarrollo. *Directorio Latinoamericano de Instituciones Financieras de Desarrollo*. Lima, 1971.

218. Bartley, R. H., and S. L. Wagner. *Latin America in Basic Historical Collections: A Working Guide*. Stanford, Calif., 1972.

219. Bernard, J. *Guide to the Political Parties of South America*. Baltimore, Md., 1973.

A country-by-country breakdown.

220. Bourne, R. *Political Leaders of Latin America*. Baltimore, Md., 1969.

Biographical sketches of heads of state.

221. Butland, G. J. *Latin America: A Regional Geography*. 3d ed., N.Y., 1972.

222. Comisión Económica para América Latina. *Anuario Estadístico de América Latina*. 4 vols., N.Y., 1974.

Statistical yearbook for 1973.

223. Condarco Morales, R. *Atlas Histórico de América*. La Paz, 1968.

224. Darino, E. *Guía de Referencia de Hispanoamérica*. Montevideo, 1975.

225. ———. *Revistero: Directorio Crítico de Publicaciones Periódicas y Seriadas de Hispanoamérica*. Montevideo, 1975.

226. Delpar, H. (ed.). *Encyclopedia of Latin America*. N.Y. 1974.

227. Haro, R. P. *Latin American Research in the United States and Canada, a Guide and Directory*. Chicago, 1971.

228. Hilton, R. (ed.). *Who's Who in Latin America: A Biographical Dictionary of Notable Living Men and Women of Latin America*. 7 vols. in 2, 3d ed., Detroit, Mich., 1971.

   A reprinting of the work long considered standard. Readers must keep in mind that the study was published originally in 1945.

229. Kielman, C. V. "The University of Texas Archives. An Analytical Guide to the Historical Manuscripts Collections in the University of Texas Library," U. of Tex. Diss., 1966.

230. Mantilla, G. *Who's Who among Latin Americans in Washington*. Wash., 1976.

   Biographical sketches.

231. Martin, M. R. *Encyclopedia of Latin American History*. Indianapolis, Ind., 1966.

232. Mauro, F. "Comment Développer les Recherches Francaises sur l'Histoire de l'Amérique Latine," *RHMC* (Oct.–Dec., 1967) 424–435.

   Discusses sources and documents in France for the study of Latin America.

233. Merino, A. *Geografía de América*. Bogotá, 1975.

234. Morais, C. *Diccionario de Reforma Agraria Latinoamericana*. San José, C.R., 1973.

235. Morales Padrón, F. (ed.). *El Americanismo en Europa*. Seville, Spain, 1970.

   Provides a list of European institutions which specialize in Latin American affairs.

236. ———. *Guía de Americanistas Españoles*. Seville, Spain, 1971.

237. OAS. General Secretariat. *Pan American Associations in the United States, with a Supplementary List of Other Inter-American and General Associations*. Wash., 1971.

238. Odell, P. R., and D. A. Preston. *Economies and Societies in Latin America: A Geographical Interpretation*. N.Y., 1973.

239. PAU. Departamento de Asuntos Culturales. *Guía de Instituciones y Sociedades en el Campo de las Ciencias Sociales*. Wash., 1950.

240. Raten Amerika Kenkyujo. *Raten Amerika Jilen*. Tokyo, 1964.

   Translated title: "Dictionary of Latin America."

241. Sable, M. H. *Latin America: A Guide to the Literature, Organizations and Personnel*. Metuchen, N.J., 1971.

241a. ———. *Latin American Jewry: A Research Guide*. Cincinnati, O., 1978.

242. Seckinger, R. L. "A Guide to Selected Diplomatic Archives of South America," *LARR* 10 (Spring, 1975) 127–153.

243. Siefer, E. *Neuere Deutsche Lateinamerika-Forschung: Institute und Bibliotheken in der Bundesrepublik Deutschland und in Berlin*. Hamburg, 1971.

   A guide to research institutes and libraries specializing in Latin America in the German Federal Republic and West Berlin.

244. Tatlow, F. J. (ed.). *Directory of Scholars in Latin American Teaching and Research in Canada: 1969–1970*. Ottawa, 1970.

245. Ulibarri, G. S., and J. P. Harrison. *Guide to Materials on Latin America in the National Archives of the United States*. Wash., 1974.

   Supplements the volume published in 1961 under the same title.

246. Vivó, P. (comp.). *Sources of Current Information on Latin America*. Wash., 1971.

   Describes 150 periodicals which treat Latin America.

247. Walne, P. (ed.). *A Guide to Manuscript Sources for the History of Latin America and the Caribbean in the British Isles*. London, 1973.

   An extremely comprehensive guide to public and private papers in British and Irish archives.

248. Webb, K. E. *Geography of Latin America: A Regional Analysis*. Englewood Cliffs, N.J., 1972.

249. Wilgus, A. C. *Historical Atlas of Latin America*. N.Y., 1969.

New edition of the basic historical atlas published first in 1943.

250. Zubatsky, D. S. (comp.). *Doctoral Dissertations in History and the Social Sciences on Latin America and the Caribbean Accepted by the Universities in the United Kingdom, 1920–1972*. London, 1972.

I-B-2   cross references:
a) See items 38–75.
b) In the Trask, Meyer, and Trask *Bibliography* see items 143–330, 1077–1148, 1172, 1344, 4530.

3. United States

251. Fox, W. T. R., and A. B. Fox "The Teaching of International Relations in the United States," *WP* 3 (1961) 339–359.
252. Freidel, F. (ed.). *Harvard Guide to American History*. Rev. ed., 2 vols., Cambridge, Mass., 1974.
253. Gustafson, M. O. *The National Archives and Foreign Relations Research*. Athens, O., 1974.
254. Hopkins, J. G. E. (ed.). *Concise Dictionary of American Biography*. 2d ed., N.Y., 1977.
255. Leidy, W. P. (comp.). *A Popular Guide to Government Publications*. N.Y., 1976.
255a. McCoy, D. R. *The National Archives, America's Ministry of Documents, 1934–1968*. Chapel Hill, N.C., 1978.
256. Powers, P. W. *A Guide to National Defense: The Organization and Operation of the U.S. Military Establishment*. N.Y., 1964.
257. Schmeckebier, L. F., and R. B. Eastin. *Government Publications and Their Use*. Rev. ed., Wash., 1969.
257a. *Who Was Who among North American Authors, 1921–1939*. 2 vols., Detroit, Mich., 1976.
Contains 11,200 biographical sketches.

I-B-3   cross references:
a) See items 76–83.
b) In the Trask, Meyer, and Trask *Bibliography* see items 331–425, 1149–1187.

4. Argentina

257b. Buonocore, D. *Libreros, Editores e Impre-sores de Buenos Aires: Esbozo para una Historia del Libro Argentino*. B.A., 1974.

258. Escardó, F. *Nueva Geografía de Buenos Aires*. B.A., 1971.
259. Fitzgibbon, R. H. *Argentina: A Chronology and Fact Book, 1516–1973*. Dobbs Ferry, N.Y., 1974.
260. Guiffra, C. A. *Guía de Bibliotecas Argentinas*. B.A., 1967.
261. Matijevic, N. *Guía de las Bibliotecas Universitarias Argentinas*. Bahía Blanca, Arg., 1971.
262. *Quién Es Quién*. B.A., 1974.
Contains 15,000 biographical sketches of notable Argentines.
263. Sosa de Newton, L. *Diccionario Biográfico de Mujeres Argentinas*. B.A., 1974.

I-B-4   cross references:
a) See items 84–94.
b) In the Trask, Meyer, and Trask *Bibliography* see items 426–475, 1188–1218, 1278, 4527.

5. Bolivia

264. Ahlfeld, F. E. *Geografía Física de Bolivia*. La Paz, 1969.
265. Heath, D. *Historical Dictionary of Bolivia*. Metuchen, N.J., 1972.
266. Urquidi, C. *A Statement of the Laws of Bolivia in Matters Affecting Business*. 3d ed., Wash., 1962.

I-B-5   cross references:
a) See items 95–100.
b) In the Trask, Meyer, and Trask *Bibliography* see items 476–490, 1219–1228, 1278.

6. Brazil

267. Brasil. Conselho Nacional de Geografia. *Atlas Geográfico Escolar*. Rio, 1970.
268. Brazil. Ministério das Relações Exteriores. *Indice da Coleção dos Atos Internacionais*. Rio, 1968.
List of treaties and conventions to which Brazil is a party.
269. ———. Presidência da República. Conselho Nacional de Pesquisas. *Quem na Biblioteconomia e Documentação no Brasil*. Rio, 1971.
270. Brinches, V. *Dicionário Biobibliográfico*

Luso-Brasileiro. 2 vols., São Paulo, 1965.

271. Correa, V. "Desenvolvimento dos Estudos Históricos no Brasil," *RHA* 27 (June, 1949) 45–58.

272. Fitzgibbon, R. H. (ed.). *Brazil: A Chronology and Fact Book, 1488–1973*. Dobbs Ferry, N.Y., 1974.

273. Florenzano, Z. (comp.). *Diccionario do Comercio Exterior*. São Paulo, 1973.

274. Lacerda, C. (ed.). *Enciclopêdia Século XX*. 13 vols., Rio, 1973.

275. Lacombe, A. J. *Introdução ao Estudo da História do Brasil*. São Paulo, 1974.
   A guide to the history of Brazil, rather than an introductory history.

276. Lombardi, M. *Brazilian Serial Documents: A Selective and Annotated Guide*. Bloomington, Ind., 1974.
   Contains 1,370 titles.

277. Reipert, H. J. *História da Biblioteca Pública Municipal Mário de Andrade*. São Paulo, 1972.
   The municipal library of São Paulo has over 850,000 volumes.

278. Ribeiro Filho, J. S. *Diccionario Biobibliográfico de Escritores Cariocas (1565–1965)*. Rio, 1965.

279. Rodrigues, J. H. "Os Estudos Brasileiros e os Brazilianists," *RHIS* 54 (July–Sept., 1976) 189–219.
   Expresses concern of foreign Brazilianists dominating the historical profession.

280. ————. *A Pesquisa Histórica no Brasil*. 2d ed., São Paulo, 1970.

281. Silva, G. do Couto. *Geopolítica do Brasil*. Rio, 1967.

282. Suassuna, A., *et al*. *Atlas Cultural do Brasil*. Rio, 1972.

I-B-6   cross references:
a) See items 101–105.
b) In The Trask, Meyer, and Trask *Bibliography* see items 491–556c, 1229–1254.

7. CENTRAL AMERICA AND THE CARIBBEAN IN GENERAL

283. Kapp, K. S. *Central America: Early Maps up to 1860*. North Bend, O., 1974.

284. Rodríguez, M., and V. C. Peloso. *A Guide for the Study of Culture in Central America: Humanities and Social Sciences*. Wash., 1968.

285. Veliz, C. (ed.). *Latin America and the Caribbean: A Handbook*. N.Y., 1968.
   Contains a historical sketch and contemporary political and economic analysis.

I-B-7   cross references:
a) See items 106–110.
b) In the Trask, Meyer, and Trask *Bibliography* see items 557–571a, 1254a–1260.

8. CHILE

286. Bizzarro, S. *Historical Dictionary of Chile*. Metuchen, N.J., 1972.

287. Cortes, L., and J. Fuentes. *Diccionario Político de Chile*. Santiago, 1967.

288. *Diccionario Biográfico de Chile*. 16th ed., Santiago, 1976.
   Contains biographical sketches of over 16,000 Chileans.

289. Echeverría y Reyes, A. *Geografía Política de Chile*. 2 vols., Santiago, 1888–1889.
   Contains descriptions of the political and administrative subdivisions of the country.

290. Figueroa, P. P. *Diccionario Biográfico de Chile*. Santiago, 1924.

291. Freudenthal, J. R. "Development and Current Status of Bibliographic Organization in Chile," U. of Mich. Diss., 1972.

292. Fuentes, J., and L. Cortés. *Diccionario Histórico de Chile*. Santiago, 1963.

293. Sociedad Chilena de Historia y Geografía. *Geografía de Chile: Física, Humana y Económica*, Santiago, 1968.

I-B-8   cross references:
a) See items 111–121.
b) In the Trask, Meyer, and Trask *Bibliography* see items 572–608, 1261–1282.

9. COLOMBIA

294. *Diccionario Geográfico de Colombia*. 2 vols., Antioquía, Colombia, 1972.

295. Martinson, T. L. *Research Guide to Colombia*. Mexico, 1975.

296. Mendoza Neira, P. *Colombia en Cifras*. Bogotá, 1963.

297. Perry, O. *Quién Es Quién en Colombia*. Bogotá, 1970.
297a. Soler Delgado, F. A. *Geografía Económica de Colombia*. Bogotá, 1977.
298. Solís Moncada, J. *Almanaque Histórico de Antioquia*. Medellín, 1968.
299. Urrutia Montoya, M., and M. Arubla (eds.). *Compendio de Estadísticas Históricas de Colombia*. Bogotá, 1970.
300. Vergara y Velasco, F. J. *Nueva Geografía de Colombia Escrita por Regiones Naturales*. Bogotá, 1975.
301. Vilar, P. *Nueva Geografía de Colombia*. Bogotá, 1945.
302. Weil, T. E., *et al*. *Area Handbook for Colombia*. Wash., 1970.

I-B-9   cross references:
a) See items 122–125.
b) In the Trask, Meyer, and Trask *Bibliography* see items 609–635, 1283–1295a.

10. COSTA RICA

303. Blutstein, H. I., *et al*. *Area Handbook for Costa Rica*. Wash., 1970.
304. Creedman, T. S. *Historical Dictionary of Costa Rica*. Metuchen, N.J., 1977.
305. González Víquez, C. *Personal del Poder Ejecutivo de Costa Rica, 1821–1936*. San José, C.R., 1958.
    Title is misleading, as this edition has been brought up to 1958 by Ricardo Fernando Peralta.
306. Montero Barrantes, F. *Geografía de Costa Rica*. Barcelona, 1892.
307. Noreiga, F. F. *Diccionario Geográfico de Costa Rica*. San José, C.R., 1923.
308. Stephenson, P. (ed.). *Costa Rican Factbook*. Wash., 1966.
309. Trejos Quiros, J. *Geografía Ilustrada de Costa Rica*. 22d ed., San José, C.R., 1968.
310. Welles, H. *Costa Rican Factbook 1970*. Wash., 1970.

I-B-10   cross references:
a) See items 126–127.
b) In the Trask, Meyer, and Trask *Bibliography* see items 636–644, 1296–1299.

11. CUBA

311. Black, J. K., *et al*. *Area Handbook for Cuba*. 2d ed., Wash., 1976.
312. Canet Alvarez, G. *Atlas de Cuba*. Cambridge, Mass., 1949.
313. *La Encyclopedia de Cuba*. 3 vols., Madrid, 1973–1974.
314. Núñez Jiménez, A. *Geografía de Cuba*. 3 vols., Havana, 1972.
315. Peraza Sarausa, F. *Diccionario Biográfico Cubano*. Coral Gables, Fla., 1968.
316. Valdés, N. P., and E. Lieuwen. *The Cuban Revolution: A Research Study Guide, 1959–1969*. Albuquerque, N.M., 1971.
    Contains 3,839 items and discusses holdings of libraries and book stores specializing in Cuban publications.

I-B-11   cross references:
a) See items 128–136.
b) In the Trask, Meyer, and Trask *Bibliography* see items 645–682, 1300–1311.

12. DOMINICAN REPUBLIC

317. Deschamps, E. *La República Dominicana: Directorio y Guía General*. Santiago de los Caballeros, D.R., 1974.
    Facsimile reproduction of 1906 volume.
318. Fleury, V. G. Ricart, and P. R. Bisono. *Cien Dominicanos Célebres*. Santo Domingo, 1973.
319. Franco, F. J., *et al*. *Enciclopedia Dominicana*. 4 vols., Santo Domingo, 1975.
320. Fuente, S. de la. *Geografía Dominicana*. Santo Domingo, 1976.
321. García, J. G. *Rascos Biográficos de Dominicanos Célebres*. Santo Domingo, 1971.
    Short sketches of famous nineteenth-century Dominicans.
322. Martínez, R. *Diccionario Biografico-Histórico Dominicano, 1821–1930*. Santo Domingo, 1971.
323. Robert, T. D., *et al*. *Area Handbook for the Dominican Republic*. Wash., 1966

I-B-12 cross references:
a) See items 137–142.

b) In the Trask, Meyer, and Trask *Bibliography* see items 683–696, 1312–1317.

13. ECUADOR

324. Bork, A. W., and G. Maier. *Historical Dictionary of Ecuador*. Metuchen, N.J., 1973.
325. Paz y Mino, L. T. *Atlas Escolar del Ecuador*. Quito, 1936.

I-B-13   cross references:
a) See item 143.
b) In the Trask, Meyer, and Trask *Bibliography* see items 697–711, 1223, 1318–1328.

14. EL SALVADOR

326. Blutstein, H. I., *et al. Area Handbook for El Salvador*. Wash., 1971
327. Cardona Lazo, A. *Diccionario Geográfico de la República de El Salvador*. San Salvador, 1945.
328. Flemion, P. F. *Historical Dictionary of El Salvador*. Metuchen, N.J., 1972.
329. Fonseca, P. S. *Geografía Ilustrada de El Salvador*. Barcelona, 1926.
330. Gallardo, R. *Las Constituciones de El Salvador*. Madrid, 1961.
331. Godfrey, H. F. *Your El Salvador Guide*. N.Y., 1968.

I-B-14   cross references: In the Trask, Meyer, and Trask Bibliography *see items 1328a–1331.*

15. GUATEMALA

332. Obiols, G. A. (ed.). *Diccionario Geográfico de Guatemala*. 2 vols., Guatemala, 1961–1962.
333. PAU. Department of Legal Affairs. *A Statement of the Laws of Guatemala in Matters Affecting Business*. Wash., 1965.

I-B-15   cross references:
a) See items 144–145.
b) In the Trask, Meyer, and Trask *Bibliography* see items 722–737a, 1332–1335.

16. HAITI

I-B-16   cross references: In the Trask, Meyer, and Trask Bibliography *see items 1336–1337.*

17. HONDURAS

334. Aguilar B., C. A. *Texto de Enseñanza de la Geografía de Honduras*. 2 vols., Tegucigalpa, 1960–1970.
335. Aguilar Pinel, C. *Geografía de Honduras*. Comayagua, 1945.

I-B-17   cross references:
a) See items 146–147.
b) In the Trask, Meyer, and Trask *Bibliography* see items 753–759c, 1223, 1338–1339.

18. MEXICO

336. Alisky, M. *Who's Who in Mexican Government*. Tempe, Ariz., 1969.
     An alphabetical listing and brief biographical sketches of leading government officials.
337. *Anglo-American Directory of Mexico: 1968–1969*. Mexico, 1969.
338. Barberena, E. B. (comp.). *Directorio de la Ciudad de México*. Mexico, 1967.
     Bilingual edition.
339. Bataillon, C. *Les Regiones Geógraphiques au Mexique*. Paris, 1968.
340. Clagett, H., and D. M. Valderrama. *A Revised Guide to the Law and Legal Literature of Mexico*. Wash., 1973.
     Updates the volume published originally in 1945.
341. Covo, M. *Las Instituciones de Investigación Social en la Ciudad de México*. Mexico, 1969.
342. *Diccionario Porrúa de Historia, Biografía y Geografía de México*. 3d ed., 2 vols., Mexico, 1971.
     One of the most comprehensive guides of its kind.
343. *Directorio Jurídico Biográfico Mexicano*. Mexico, 1972.
344. García de Miranda, E. *Atlas: Nuevo Atlas Porrúa de la República Mexicana*. Mexico, 1974.

345. Martínez, J. L. "Bibliotecas en México: Análisis y Programa," *CA* 34 (May–June, 1975) 35–54.

346. Morales Díaz, C. *Quién Es Quién en la Nomenclatura de la Ciudad de México*. Mexico, 1962.

347. Ocampo de Gómez, A. M., and E. Prado Velásquez. *Diccionario de Escritores Mexicanos*. Mexico, 1967.

348. Salas Artega, G. *Directorio de Asociaciones e Institutos Científicos y Culturales de la República Mexicana*. Mexico, 1959.

349. Wilkie, J. W. "New Hypotheses for Statistical Research in Recent Mexican History," *LARR* 6 (Summer, 1971) 3–17.

I-B-18   cross references:
a) See items 148–166.
b) In the Trask, Meyer, and Trask *Bibliography* see items 760–869, 1340–1364.

19. NICARAGUA

350. Incer Barquero, J. *Geografía Ilustrada de Nicaragua*. Managua, 1976.

351. Meyer, H. K. *Historical Dictionary of Nicaragua*. Metuchen, N.J., 1972.

352. Ryan, J. J., *et al. Handbook for Nicaragua*. Wash., 1970.

I-B-19   cross references: In the Trask, Meyer, and Trask Bibliography *see items 870–883, 1365.*

20. PANAMA

353. Hedrick, B. C., and A. K. Hedrick. *Historical Dictionary of Panama*. Metuchen, N.J., 1970.

354. Letgers, L. H. (ed.). *Area Handbook for Panama*. Wash., 1962.

355. Ortega C., J. C. *Gobernantes de la República de Panamá, 1903–1968*. Panama, 1965.

356. *Panamá: 50 Años de la República*. Panama, 1953.
     A series of bio-bibliographies.

I-B-20   cross references:
a) See items 167–173.
b) In the Trask, Meyer, and Trask *Bibliography* see items 884–900, 1366–1369, 7294.

21. PARAGUAY

357. Ferreira Gubetich, H. *Geografía del Paraguay*. 12th ed., Asunción, 1975.

358. González, J. N. *Geografía del Paraguay*. Mexico, 1964.

359. Kolinsky, C. J. *Historical Dictionary of Paraguay*. Metuchen, N.J., 1973.

360. Sosa de Maciel, R. *Directorio de Bibliotecas Paraguayas*. Asunción, 1976.

I-B-21   cross references:
a) See items 174–180.
b) In the Trask, Meyer, and Trask *Bibliography* see items 901–910, 1370–1376.

22. PERU

361. Arévalo Alvarado, A. *Manual Legal de la Industria Pesquera del Perú*. 2 vols., Lima, 1968.

362. Beltroy, M. *Peruanos Notables de Hoy: Biografías de Peruanos Representativos Contemporáneos*. Lima, 1957.

363. *Directorio de Bibliotecas Especializadas del Perú*. Lima, 1972.

364. García Rosell, C. *Geografía del Perú*. 3 vols., Lima, 1966–1967.

365. Tauro, A. *Diccionario Enciclopédico del Perú*. 3 vols., Lima, 1966–1967.

366. Velarde, J. M. *Peruanos Ilustres*. Lima, 1975.

I-B-22   cross references:
a) See items 181–187.
b) In the Trask, Meyer, and Trask *Bibliography* see items 911–937, 1377–1387.

23. URUGUAY

367. Araujo, O. *Gobernantes del Uruguay*. Montevideo, 1903.

368. De María, I. *Hombres Notables del Uruguay*. Montevideo, 1939.

369. Weil, T. E., *et al. Area Handbook for Uruguay*. Wash., 1971.

I-B-23   cross references:
a) See items 188–190.
b) In the Trask, Meyer, and Trask *Bibliography* see items 938–951, 1388–1395.

24. VENEZUELA

370. Anderson, A. *Tax and Trade Guide: Venezuela*. Chicago, 1966.

371. Carrera Damas, G. *Historiografía Marxista Venezolana y Otras Temas*. Caracas, 1967.

372. Marín, O. (comp.). *Directorio de Bibliotecas Venezolanas*. Caracas, 1973.

373. Mariñas Otero, L. *La Constituciones de Venezuela (1811–1961)*. Madrid, 1965.

374. Milares Carlo, A. *Estudio Bibliográfico de los Archivos Venezolanos y Estranjeros de In-* *terés para la Historia de Venezuela*. Caracas, 1971.

375. Rudolph, D. K., and G. A. Rudolph. *Historical Dictionary of Venezuela*. Metuchen, N.J., 1971.

376. Venegas Filardo, P., and L. M. Arce (eds.). *Enciclopedia de Venezuela*. 12 vols., Caracas, 1973–1975.

I-B-24   *cross references:*

 a) See items 191–198.

 b) In the Trask, Meyer, and Trask *Bibliography* see items 952–983, 1396–1401.

Chapter II   Basic Works for the Study of United States–Latin American Relations

A. SURVEYS AND INTERPRETATIONS OF LATIN AMERICAN HISTORY

377. Alba, V. *The Latin Americans*. N.Y., 1969.

378. Al'Perovich, M. S., and L. Yu Slezkin. *Novaia Istorüa stran Latinskoi Ameriki*. Moscow, 1970.

   The first serious Latin American survey text for university students in the Soviet Union.

379. Bartos, L. *Úvod do Dějin, Společénskho Zrízení a Kultury Spanelské Ameriky*. Prague, Czechoslovakia, 1964.

   Translated title: "An Introduction to History, Social Conditions, and Culture of Spanish America."

380. Belmonte, J. *Historia Contemporánea de Iberoamérica*. 3 vols., Madrid, 1971.

   Covers both the nineteenth and twentieth centuries with heavy emphasis on the period since 1930.

381. Blakemore, H. *Latin America*. N.Y., 1973.

   A brief historical sketch.

382. Burns, E. *Latin America: A Concise Interpretive History*. Englewood Cliffs, N.J., 1972.

   A greater emphasis on Brazil than most survey histories.

382a. Camacho, G. *Latin America: A Short History*. London, 1973.

383. Chaunu, P. *Historia de América Latina*. B.A., 1970.

   A short survey history covering both colonial and national periods.

383a. Chevalier, F. *L'Amérique Latine: De l'independence a nos jours*. Paris, 1977.

384. Collier, S. *From Cortés to Castro: An Introduction to the History of Latin America, 1492–1973*. N.Y., 1973.

385. Cúneo, D. *Breve Historia de América Latina*. B.A., 1968.

386. Davis, H. E. *Latin American Thought: A Historical Introduction*. Baton Rouge, La., 1972.

387. Ellis, J. A. *Latin America: Its Peoples and Institutions*. Beverly Hills, Calif., 1975.

388. Gomes, L. S. *América Latina: Seus Aspectos, sua História, seus Problemas*. Rio, 1966.

389. Halperin Donghi, T. *Historia Contemporánea de América Latina*. 2d ed., Madrid, 1970.

   Covers the nineteenth and twentieth centuries with heavy emphasis on economic history.

390. Hilton, R. *The Latin Americans: Their Heritage and Their Destiny*. N.Y., 1973.

391. Liss, S. B., and P. K. Liss (eds.). *Man, State and Society in Latin American History*. N.Y., 1972.

   Selected readings.

392. Lucena, S. M. *Historia de América Latina: Epocas Indígenas, Hispánica y Republicana*. Bogotá, 1975.

393. Mauro, F. *L'Amerique Espagnole et Portugaise de 1920 á nos Jours*. Paris, 1975.

394. Morales Padrón, F. *Historia de Hispanoamérica*. Seville, Spain, 1972.

   Twentieth-century treatment is weak.

395. Nakaya, K. *Raten Amerika Shi*. Tokyo, 1964.

   Translated title: "History of Latin America."

396. Pike, F. B. *Spanish America, 1900–1970:*

18

Tradition and Social Innovation. N.Y., 1973.

Treats the relationships between the status quo and the forces of change.

397.   ———. *Latin American History: Select Problems, Identity, Integration, and Nationhood*. N.Y., 1969.

398.   Ramos, J. A. *Historia de la Nación Latinamericana*. B.A., 1968.

399.   Raten Amerika Kyokai. *Raten Amerika no Rekishi*. Tokyo, 1964.

Translated title: "History of Latin America."

400.   Rothchild, J. (ed.). *Latin America: Yesterday and Today*. N.Y., 1973.

401.   Ruiz, R. E. (ed.). *Interpreting Latin American History from Independence to Today*. N.Y., 1970.

401a.   Shafer, R. J. *A History of Latin America*. Lexington, Mass., 1978.

402.   Silvert, K. H. *Essays in Understanding Latin America*. Philadelphia, Pa., 1977.

403.   Tulchin, J. (ed.). *Problems in Latin American History: The Modern Period*. N.Y., 1973.

II-A cross references: In the Trask, Meyer, and Trask Bibliography *see items 1402–1481.*

B. HISTORIES OF GREATER AMERICA

404.   Balseiro, J. A. *The Americas Look at Each Other: Essays on the Culture and Life of the Americas*. Coral Gables, Fla., 1969.

405.   Cárdenas Nannetti, J. *Historia de América*. Bogotá, 1977.

An introductory survey.

406.   Cohen, D. W., and J. P. Green (eds.). *Neither Slave nor Free: The Freedman of African Descent in the Slave Societies of the New World*. Baltimore, Md., 1972.

Ten essays originally delivered at a Johns Hopkins U. symposium.

407.   Foner, L., and E. D. Genovese (eds.). *Slavery in the New World: A Reader in Comparative History*. Englewood Cliffs, N.J., 1969.

408.   Hoetink, H. *Slavery and Race Relations in the Americas: Comparative Notes on Their Nature and Nexus*. N.Y., 1973.

409.   Lane, A. J. (ed.). *The Debate over Slavery: Stanley Elkins and His Critics*. Urbana, Ill., 1971.

Latin American sections by Eugene Genovese, Marvin Harris, and Herbert Klein.

409a.   Morales Padrón, F. *Historia General de América*. 2d ed., 2 vols., Madrid, 1975.

410.   Muñoz, J. B. *Historia del Nuevo Mundo*. Mexico, 1975.

411.   Price, R. *Maroon Societies: Rebel Slave Communities in the Americas*. Garden City, N.Y., 1973.

Treats runaway slave communities in Spanish America, Brazil, and the French and English Caribbean.

411a.   Rubin, V., and A. Tuden (eds.). *Comparative Perspectives on Slavery in New World Plantation Societies*. N.Y., 1977.

412.   Urbanski, E. S. *Angloamérica: Análisis de dos Civilizaciones*. Madrid, 1965.

II-B cross references: In the Trask, Meyer, and Trask Bibliography *see items 423, 1482–1526, 1717, 4431.*

C. SURVEYS OF LATIN AMERICAN GOVERNMENT

413.   Adie, R. F., and G. E. Poitras. *Latin America: The Politics of Immobility*. Englewood Cliffs, N.J., 1974.

Designed as an introductory text to Latin American politics.

414.   Burnett, B. G., and K. F. Johnson. *Political Forces in Latin America: Dimensions of the Quest for Stability*. Belmont, Calif., 1968.

A country-by-country analysis by specialists with emphasis on the post–World War II period.

415.   Edelmann, A. T. *Latin American Government and Politics: The Dynamics of a Revolutionary Society*. Homewood, Ill., 1969.

A traditional textbook.

416.   Fitzgibbon, R. H. *Latin America: A Panorama of Contemporary Politics*. N.Y., 1971.

416a.   Jaguaribe, H. *Political Development: A General Theory and a Latin American Case Study*. N.Y., 1973.

417.   Jorrín, M., and J. Martz. *Latin American Political Thought and Ideology*. Chapel Hill, N.C., 1970.

The work was finished by Professor Martz after Miguel Jorrín's death.

418. Lazar, A. von. *Latin American Politics: A Primer*. Boston, 1971.
419. McDonald, R. H. *Party Systems and Elections in Latin America*. Chicago, 1971.
420. Williams, E. J. *Latin American Political Thought: A Developmental Perspective*. Tucson, Ariz., 1974.
421. ————, and F. J. Wright. *Latin American Politics: A Developmental Approach*. Palo Alto, Calif., 1975.

II-C   cross references: In the Trask, Meyer, and Trask Bibliography *see items 1527–1544.*

D. WORKS ON UNITED STATES FOREIGN RELATIONS

1. GENERAL HISTORIES

422. Bosch García, C. *La Base de la Política Exterior Estadounidense*. Mexico, 1975.
423. Cole, W. S. *An Interpretive History of American Foreign Relations*. Homewood, Ill., 1968.
424. Ferrell, R. H. (ed.). *America as a World Power, 1872–1945*. N.Y., 1971.
425. ————. *Foundations of American Diplomacy, 1775–1872*. Columbia, S.C., 1968.
426. Gardner, L. C. (ed.). *American Foreign Policy, Present to Past*. N.Y., 1974.
427. ————, W. La Faber, and T. J. McCormick. *Creation of the American Empire: U.S. Diplomatic History*. Chicago, 1973.
428. Gelfand, L. E. (ed.). *Essays on the History of American Foreign Relations*. Reading, Mass., 1971.
429. Kaplan, L. S. *Recent American Foreign Policy: Conflicting Interpretations*. Homewood, Ill., 1968.
430. Merli, F. J., and T. A. Wilson (eds.). *Makers of American Diplomacy: From Benjamin Franklin to Henry Kissinger*. N.Y., 1974.
430a. Paterson, T. G. *Major Problems in American Foreign Policy: Documents and Essays*. 2 vols., Lexington, Mass., 1978.
430b. ————, J. G. Clifford, and K. J. Hagan. *American Foreign Policy: A History*. Lexington, Mass., 1977.
431. Ransom, H. H. (ed.). *An American Foreign Policy Reader*. N.Y., 1965.
432. Sanford, C. L. (ed.). *Manifest Destiny and*

the Imperialism Question. N.Y., 1971.
Concentrates on nineteenth and early twentieth centuries with brief coverage of the period since 1945.

433. Smith, D. *The American Diplomatic Experience*. Boston, 1972.
434. Williams, W. A. (ed.). *From Colony to Empire: Essays in the History of American Foreign Relations*. N.Y., 1972.

II-D-1   cross references: In the Trask, Meyer, and Trask Bibliography *see items 1545–1567.*

2. SPECIAL STUDIES AND INTERPRETATIONS

435. Ambrose, S. E. *Rise to Globalism: American Foreign Policy, 1938–1970*. Baltimore, Md., 1971.
436. Appleton, S. *United States Foreign Policy: An Introduction with Cases*. Boston, 1968.
437. Aron, R. *Peace and War: A Theory of International Relations*. N.Y., 1967.
438. Barnett, V. M., Jr. (ed.). *The Representation of the United States Abroad*. N.Y., 1965.
Indicates how the role of the foreign service and State Department has changed in recent years.
439. Bartlett, C. J. *The Rise and Fall of the Pax Americana: United States Foreign Policy in the Twentieth Century*. N.Y., 1975.
440. Braeman, J. (ed.). *Twentieth Century American Foreign Policy*. Columbus, O., 1971.
James Wilkie and Allan Millett treat relations with Latin America.
441. Brandon, D. *American Foreign Policy: Beyond Utopianism and Realism*. N.Y., 1966.
Treats the twentieth century.
442. Brown, J. A. C. *Techniques of Persuasion: From Propaganda to Brainwashing*. Middlesex, Eng., 1963.
443. Burton, J. W. *International Relations: A General Theory*. Cambridge, Eng., 1965.
444. ————. *Systems, States, Diplomacy and Rules*. Cambridge, Eng., 1968.
445. Cardozo, M. H. "Diplomatic Immunities, Protocol and the Public," *JIA* 17 (1963) 61–69.
446. Clark, E. *Diplomat: The World of International Diplomacy*. N.Y., 1973.

447. Cobbledick, J. R. *Choice in American Foreign Policy: Options for the Future*. N.Y., 1973.
Devotes one chapter to policy options in Latin America.

448. Combs, J. A. (ed.). *Nationalist, Realist, and Radical: Three Views of American Diplomacy*. N.Y., 1972.

449. Coplin, W. D. *Introduction to International Politics: A Theoretical Overview*. Chicago, 1971.

450. Denza, E. *Diplomatic Law: Commentary on the Vienna Convention on Diplomatic Relations*. Dobbs Ferry, N.Y., 1976.

451. Deutsch, K. W. *The Analysis of International Relations*. Englewood Cliffs, N.J., 1968.

452. Ekirch, A. A., Jr. *Ideas, Ideals and American Diplomacy: A History of Their Growth and Interaction*. N.Y., 1966.

453. Fann, K. T., and D. C. Hodges (eds.). *Readings in U.S. Imperialism*. Boston, 1971.

454. Fisher, G. H. *Public Diplomacy and the Behavioral Sciences*. Bloomington, Ind., 1972.

455. Flemming, T. J. *West Point: The Men of Times of the United States Military Academy*. N.Y., 1969.

456. Friedman, J. R., C. Bladen, and S. Rosen (eds.). *Alliance in International Politics*. Boston, 1970.

457. Grenville, J. A. S., and G. B. Young. *Politics, Strategy and American Diplomacy: Studies in Foreign Policy, 1873–1917*. New Haven, Conn., 1966.

458. Harrison, H. V. *The Role of Theory in International Relations*. N.Y., 1964.

459. Higham, R. (ed.). *Intervention or Abstention: The Dilemma of American Foreign Policy*. Lexington, Ky., 1975.
Examples and analyses are taken from the twentieth century.

460. Holsti, K. J. *International Politics: A Framework for Analysis*. Englewood Cliffs, N.J., 1972.

461. Hudson, M. *Super Imperialism: The Economic Strategy of American Empire*. N.Y., 1972.
Covers the period since 1920.

462. Jervis, R. *The Logic of Images in International Relations*. Princeton, N.J., 1970.

463. Kolko, G. *The Roots of American Foreign Policy*. Boston, 1969.

464. Lefever, E. *Ethics and United States Foreign Policy*. N.Y., 1957.

465. Lens, S. *The Forging of the American Empire*. N.Y., 1971.

466. May, E. R. *"Lessons" of the Past: The Use and Misuse of History in American Foreign Policy*. N.Y., 1973.

467. McCarthy, E. J. *The Limits of Power: America's Role in the World*. N.Y. 1967.

468. Merritt, R. (ed.). *Foreign Policy Analysis*. Lexington, Mass., 1975.

469. Middleton, D. *Retreat from Victory: A Critical Appraisal of American Foreign Policy and Military Policy from 1920 to 1970*. N.Y., 1973.

470. Morgenthau, H. J. "Common Sense and Theories of International Relations," *JIA* 21 (1967) 207–214.

471. Northedge, F. S., and M. J. Grieve. *A Hundred Years of International Relations*. N.Y., 1971.

472. O'Connor, R. G. *Force and Diplomacy: Essays Military and Diplomatic*. Coral Gables, Fla., 1972.
Covers 1920 to the 1960s.

473. Osgood, R. E. *Alliances and American Foreign Policy*. Baltimore, Md., 1968.

474. Pearson, L. B. *Diplomacy in the Nuclear Age*. Toronto, 1959.

475. Plischke, E. *United States Diplomats and Their Missions: A Profile of American Diplomatic Emissaries Since 1778*. Wash., 1975.

476. Rosenau, J. N. *International Politics and Foreign Policy: A Reader in Research and Theory*. N.Y., 1969.

477. Scribner, E. *A Casebook of American Foreign Policy Problems*. Portland, Me., 1977.

478. Seabury, P. *Power, Freedom and Diplomacy: The Foreign Policy of the United States of America*. N.Y., 1963.

479. Spanier, J. *Games Nations Play: Analyzing International Politics*. N.Y., 1975.

480. Trask, D. F. *Victory without Peace*. N.Y., 1968.
Interpretive account of U.S. foreign policy in the twentieth century.

481. Ward, B. *Nationalism and Ideology*. N.Y., 1966.

482. Woodruff, W. *America's Impact on the World: A Study of the Role of the United States in the World Economy, 1750–1970.* N.Y., 1975.

II-D-2   *cross references: In the Trask, Meyer, and Trask* Bibliography *see items 1568–1649.*

3. THE CONDUCT OF FOREIGN RELATIONS

483. Bailey, T. A. *The Art of Diplomacy: The American Experience.* N.Y., 1968.

484. Blancké, W. W. *The Foreign Service of the United States.* N.Y., 1969.

485. Bletz, D. F. *The Role of the Military Professional in U.S. Foreign Policy.* N.Y., 1972.

486. Briggs, E. *Anatomy of Diplomacy: The Origin and Execution of American Foreign Policy.* N.Y., 1968.

487. Burke, L. H. *Ambassador at Large: Diplomat Extraordinary.* The Hague, 1972.

488. Burton, J. W. *Systems, States: Diplomacy and Rules.* N.Y., 1968.

489. Carlton, J. *Presidential Vetoes, 1892–1945.* Athens, Ga., 1967.

490. Challener, R. D. *Admirals, Generals and American Foreign Policy, 1898–1914.* Princeton, N.J., 1973.
    Treats the influence of the military on foreign policy.

491. Cohen, B. C. *The Press and Foreign Policy.* Princeton, N.J., 1963.

492. Destler, I. M. *Presidents, Bureaucrats, and Foreign Policy.* Princeton, N.J., 1972.

493. Estes, T.S., and E. A. Lightner, Jr. *The Department of State.* N.Y., 1976.

494. Etzold, T. H. *The Conduct of American Foreign Relations: The Other Side of Diplomacy.* N.Y., 1977.

495. Frankel, J. *The Making of Foreign Policy.* N.Y., 1963.

496. Grassmuch, G. L. *Sectional Biases in Congress on Foreign Policy.* Baltimore, Md., 1951.

497. Harmon, R. B. *The Art and Practice of Diplomacy: A Selected and Annotated Guide.* Metuchen, N.J., 1971.

498. Harr, J. E. *The Anatomy of the Foreign Service: A Statistical Profile.* N.Y., 1965.

499. ———. *The Professional Diplomat.* Princeton, N.J., 1969.

500. Haviland, H. F., Jr. *The Formulation and Administration of United States Foreign Policy.* Wash., 1960.

501. Henkin, L. *Foreign Affairs and the Constitution.* Mineola, N.Y., 1972.

502. Hill, T. M. "The Senate Leadership and International Policy," Washington U. Diss., 1970.

503. Hinckley, B. *The Seniority System in Congress.* Bloomington, Ind., 1971.

504. Johnson, R. A. *The Administration of United States Foreign Policy.* Austin, Tex., 1971.

505. Landecker, M. *The President and Public Opinion: Leadership in Foreign Affairs.* Wash., 1968.

506. Leigh, M. *Mobilizing Consent: Public Opinion and American Foreign Policy, 1937–1947.* Westport, Conn., 1976.

507. Linehan, P. E. *The Foreign Service Personnel System: An Organizational Analysis.* Boulder, Colo., 1976.

508. Plischke, E. *Conduct of American Diplomacy.* 3d ed., Princeton, N.J., 1967.

509. Radosh, R. *American Labor and United States Foreign Policy.* N.Y., 1969.

510. Ransom, H. H. *Central Intelligence and National Security.* Cambridge, Mass., 1958.

511. ———. *The Intelligence Establishment.* Cambridge, Mass., 1970.

512. Rosenau, J. N. (ed.). *Domestic Sources of Foreign Policy.* N.Y., 1967.

513. Schlesinger, A. M. *The Imperial Presidency.* Boston, 1973.
    Treats the growing power of the presidency.

514. Schulzinger, R. D. *The Making of the Diplomatic Mind: The Training, Outlook and Style of United States Foreign Service Officers, 1908–1931.* Middletown, Conn., 1975.

515. Seidman, H. *Politics, Position and Power: The Dynamics of Federal Organization.* N.Y., 1971.

516. Simpson, S. *Anatomy of the State Department.* Boston, 1967.

517. Steiner, Z. S. *Present Problems of the Foreign Service.* Princeton, N.J., 1961.

518. ———. *The State Department and the Foreign Service: The Wriston Report—Four Years Later.* Princeton, N.J., 1958.

519. USCH. *Hearings on the Improvement of the*

Foreign Service. (62d Cong., 1st Sess.) Wash., 1912.

520. USCS. Committee on International Operations. *Negotiation and Statecraft*. (91st Cong., 2d Sess.) Wash., 1970.

521. USDS. *Diplomacy for the Seventies: A Program of Management Reform for the Department of State*. Wash., 1970.

522. ————. *Toward a Stronger Foreign Service*. Wash., 1954.

Recommends an enlargement of the foreign service.

523. ————. *Vienna Convention on Diplomatic Relations and Optional Protocol on Disputes*. Wash., 1961.

524. Warwick, D. P. *A Theory of Public Bureaucracy: Politics, Personality and Organization in the State Department*. Cambridge, Mass., 1975.

525. Wilcox, F. O. *Congress, the Executive and Foreign Policy*. N.Y., 1971.

526. Wilson, C. E. *Diplomatic Privileges and Immunities*. Tucson, Ariz., 1967.

527. Wood, J. R., and J. Serres. *Diplomatic Ceremonial and Protocol*. N.Y., 1970.

528. Young, R. "Diplomatic Immunities," *ABAJ* 39 (Sept., 1953) 839–840.

II-D-3 cross references:
a) See items 842, 930, 1024, 1099.
b) In the Trask, Meyer, and Trask *Bibliography* see items 1650–1707, 2113a.

4. DOCUMENTARY COLLECTIONS

529. Grenville, J. A. S. *The Major International Treaties, 1914–1973: A History and Guide with Texts*. N.Y., 1974.

Chapter XII treats Inter-American treaties.

530. Isreal, F. L. (ed.). *Major Peace Treaties of Modern History, 1648–1967*. 4 vols., N.Y., 1967.

531. Link, A. S., and W. M. Leary, Jr. (eds.). *The Diplomacy of World Power: The United States, 1889–1920*. N.Y., 1970.

532. Miller, H. (ed.). *Treaties and Other International Acts of the United States, 1783–1855*. 6 vols., Wash., 1931–1942.

533. Rockway, T. P. (ed.). *Basic Documents in United States Foreign Policy*. Rev. ed., Princeton, N.J., 1968.

Contains the Monroe Doctrine, Rio Pact, Alliance for Progress, and many other documents treating United States–Latin American relations.

534. Schlesinger, A. M. (ed.). *The Dynamics of World Power: A Documentary History of U.S. Foreign Policy, 1945–1973*. 5 vols., N.Y., 1973.

535. *Treaties and Alliances of the World: An International Survey Covering Treaties in Force and Communities of States*. N.Y., 1968.

536. Whiteman, M. M. *Digest of International Law*. 11 vols., Wash., 1963–1968.

II-D-4 cross references:
a) See items 919, 925.
b) In the Trask, Meyer, and Trask *Bibliography* see items 1708–1731, 1733, 1860, 2102.

E. UNITED STATES–LATIN AMERICAN RELATIONS: COMPREHENSIVE WORKS

537. Burr, R. N. *Our Troubled Hemisphere: Perspectives on United States–Latin American Relations*. Wash., 1967.

Emphasis on the period since World War II.

538. Callcott, W. F. *The Western Hemisphere: Its Influence on United States Policies to the End of World War II*. Austin, Tex., 1968.

539. Connell-Smith, G. *The United States and Latin America: An Historical Analysis of Inter-American Relations*. N.Y., 1974.

An interpretation by an English historian.

540. Davis, H. E., J. J. Finan, and F. T. Peck. *Latin American Diplomatic History*. Baton Rouge, La., 1977.

Arranged chronologically. Davis treats the period to 1860, Peck the period between 1860 and 1930, and Finan the period since 1930.

541. Fournial, G., and R. Labarre. *De Monroe à Johnson: La Politique des États-Unis en Amerique Latine*. Paris, 1966.

542. Gil, F. G. *Latin American–United States Relations*. N.Y., 1971.

Survey from the period of independence to the Nixon administration.

543. Glauert, E. T., and L. T. Langley (eds.).

The United States and Latin America. Reading, Mass., 1971.

Readings which approach the topic from the U.S. point of view.

544. Hopkins, J. W. *Latin America in World Affairs: The Politics of Inequality*. Woodbury, N.Y., 1977.

A survey with emphasis on the post–World War II period.

545. Karnes, T. L. *Readings in the Latin American Policy of the United States*. Tucson, Ariz., 1972.

Useful as a teaching aid for courses in United States–Latin American relations.

546. Korolev, N. V. *Strany Latinskoi Ameriki v Mezhdunarodnkh Otnosheniiakh, 1898–1962*. Kishinev, USSR, 1972.

Translated title: "The Countries of Latin America in International Relations, 1898–1962."

547. Pla, J. J. (ed.). *América Latina y Estados Unidos de Monroe (1823) a Johnson (1965)*. B.A., 1971.

548. Rama, C. M. *La Imagen de los Estados Unidos en la América Latina: De Simón Bolívar a Allende*. Mexico, 1975.

549. Stuart, G. H., and J. L. Tigner. *Latin America and the United States*. 6th ed., Englewood Cliffs, N.J., 1975.

A major revision of the comprehensive survey originally written by Stuart alone.

550. Walton, R. J. *The United States and Latin America*. N.Y., 1972.

A broad survey based on well-known and rather dated secondary materials.

II-E cross references: In the Trask, Meyer, and Trask Bibliography *see items 1732–1750.*

F. UNITED STATES–LATIN AMERICAN RELATIONS: SPECIAL STUDIES

551. Atkins, G. P. *Latin America in the International Political System*. N.Y., 1977.

Topically arranged and comprehensive in coverage. Emphasis on the period since World War II.

552. Bailey, N. A. *Latin America in World Politics*. N.Y., 1967.

553. Barclay, G. S. J. *Struggle for a Continent: The Diplomatic History of South America, 1917–1945*. London, 1971.

Heavy emphasis on United States–Argentine relations.

554. Blasier, C. *The Hovering Giant: U.S. Responses to Revolutionary Changes in Latin America*. Pittsburgh, Pa., 1976.

Treats the U.S. and the Mexican, Bolivian, Guatemalan, and Cuban revolutions.

555. Bosch, J. *De Cristóbal Colón a Fidel Castro: El Caribe, Frontera Imperial*. Madrid, 1970.

A historical denunciation of imperialism in the Caribbean by the former president of the Dominican Republic.

556. Bright, R. D. "The Influence of North American Organized Labor in Latin America," Howard U. Diss., 1969.

557. Browning, D. S. "Inter-American Fisheries Resources: A Need for Cooperation," *TIFL* 2 (Winter, 1966) 1–39.

558. Calvert, P. *Latin America: Internal Conflict and International Peace*. N.Y., 1969.

Treats twentieth-century diplomatic history.

559. Canyes, M., *et al. Copyright Protection in the Americas*. Wash., 1962.

560. Catholic Inter-American Cooperation Program. *Cultural Factors in Inter-American Relations*. Notre Dame, Ind., 1968.

Proceedings of the Fifth Conference.

561. Clementi, H. *Formación de la Conciencia Americana: Tres Momentos Claves*. B.A., 1972.

The author views the Walker filibustering expedition, the U.S. Civil War, and the role of the United States in the independence of Panama as key factors conditioning Inter-American relations.

562. Davis, H. E., *et al. Latin American Foreign Policies: An Analysis*. Baltimore, Md., 1975.

563. Durán Abarca, W. *La Autodeterminación de las Colonias en América*. Lima, 1966.

564. Ferguson, Y. H. *Contemporary Inter-American Relations: A Reader in Theory and Issues*. Englewood Cliffs, N.J., 1972.

565. Gardner, M. A. *The Inter-American Press Association: Its Fight for Freedom of the Press, 1926–1960*. Austin, Tex., 1967.

566. Kane, W. E. *Civil Strife in Latin America: A Legal History of U.S. Involvement*. Baltimore, Md., 1972.

Stresses U.S. interventions, direct and indirect, in Latin American internal affairs.

567. Liu, K. H. *Mei-Kuo Ch'in Lüeh La-Ting-Mei-Chou-Chien Shih*. Peking, 1957.

Translated title: "A Brief History of U.S. Invasions of Latin America."

567a. Newton, W. P. *The Perilous Sky: U.S. Aviation Diplomacy and Latin America, 1919–1931*. Coral Gables, Fla., 1978.

568. Shapiro, S. (ed.). *Cultural Factors in Inter-American Relations*. Notre Dame, Ind., 1969.

569. Tambs, L. A. (ed.). *United States Policy toward Latin America: Antecedents and Alternatives*. Tempe, Ariz., 1976.

Thirteen essays delivered at a December, 1975, conference. Emphasis on the post–World War II period.

570. Trueblood, E. G. *The U.S. Cultural Relations Program with Latin America: The Formative Years*. Tucson, Ariz., 1977.

Covers the period 1938 to 1942 and recounts the author's personal experiences.

571. Vigil, A. S. *The Ugly Anglo: An Analysis of White Extremism in Latin American Relations*. N.Y., 1967.

572. West, R. *The Gringo in Latin America*. London, 1967.

Coverage of the twentieth century with greatest emphasis on the post–World War II period.

573. Wolff, T. "Inter-American Maritime Disputes over Fishing in the 20th Century," U. of Calif. Santa Barbara Diss., 1968.

II-F cross references: In the Trask, Meyer, and Trask Bibliography *see items 1751–1765, 2894, 4535.*

G. GENERAL WORKS ON THE MONROE DOCTRINE

574. Alfaro, R. J. "Un Siglo de la Doctrina Monroe," *L* 16 (Mar., 1971) 19–29.

575. Bingham, H. *The Monroe Doctrine: An Obsolete Shibboleth*. N.Y., 1976

New edition of the work published in 1913.

576. Dozer, D. M. (ed.). *The Monroe Doctrine: Its Modern Significance*. Tempe, Ariz., 1976.

Contains new articles not included in the 1965 edition.

577. Oswald, J. M. (ed.). *The Monroe Doctrine: Does It Survive?* N.Y., 1968.

578. Poetker, J. S. *The Monroe Doctrine*. Columbus, O., 1967.

579. Queuille, P. *L'Amerique Latine, la Doctrine Monroe et le Panamericanisme*. Paris, 1969.

580. Williamson, M. R. "An Historical Study of the Application of the Monroe Doctrine by the United States in International Conferences," NYU Diss., 1928.

581. Wilson, C. M. *The Monroe Doctrine: An American Frame of Mind*. Princeton, N.J., 1971.

II-G cross references:

a) For origins of the Monroe Doctrine, see items 631–636.

b) For European violations of the Monroe Doctrine during the nineteenth century, see items 667–710.

c) For the status of the Monroe Doctrine during the imperialist era, see item 820.

d) For the status of the Monroe Doctrine from 1921 to 1938, see items 896–897.

e) In the Trask, Meyer, and Trask *Bibliography* see items 1766–1804, 1989–2053, 2060a, 2063, 2066, 2068, 2069, 2073, 2077, 2081, 2086, 2090, 2093, 2100, 2103, 2108, 2116–2118, 2121, 2129, 2130, 2132, 2137, 2139, 2140, 2150–2348, 2947a–2983, 3113–3127, 3243–3260, 3547–3555, 3872, 4507–4519.

Chapter III The United States and the Period of Latin American Independence

A. GENERAL WORKS

582. Acevedo, E. O. "América y los Sucesos Europeos de 1810," *ESTA* 513 (May, 1960) 154–176.

583. Bagu, S. "El Orden Nacional Hasta 1815," *POLEM* 4 (1970) 85–95.

584. Baker, M. D. "The United States and Piracy during the Spanish American Wars of Independence," Duke U. Diss., 1946.

585. Barros Borgoño, L. *La Primera Relaciones Diplomáticas de las Naciones Americanas.* B.A., 1938.

586. Bartley, R. H. "Russia and Latin American Independence, 1808–1826," Stanford U. Diss., 1971.

587. Bowman, C. H. "Manuel Torres, a Spanish American Patriot in Philadelphia, 1796–1822," *PMH* 108 (1972) 153–172.

588. Duarte French, J. *América de Norte a Sur: ¿Corsarios o Libertadores?* Bogotá, 1975.

589. Dunblar Temple, E. *La Posición de las Grandes Potencias ante la Emancipación Hispano-Americana y la Política Internacional del Perú en sus Primeras Relaciones Diplomáticas.* Lima, 1965.

590. Enciso Recio, L. M. *La Opinión Pública Española y la Independencia Hispanoamericana, 1819–1820.* Valladolid, Spain, 1967.

591. Friede, J. *La Otra Verdad: La Independencia Americana Vista por los Españoles.* Bogotá, 1972.

592. Fulton, N. *Relaciones Diplomáticas entre España y Los Estados Unidos a Fines del Siglo XVIII.* Madrid, 1970.

593. Godechot, J. *Europa y América en la Epoca Napoleónica (1800–1815).* Barcelona, 1969.

594. Graham, R. *Independence in Latin America: A Comparative Approach.* N.Y., 1972.

595. Gribbin, W. "A Matter of Faith: North America's Religion and South America's Independence," *TA* (Apr., 1975) 470–487.

596. Gronet, R. W. "Early Latin American–United States Contacts: An Analysis of Jeremy Robinson's Communications to the Monroe Administration, 1817–1823," Catholic U. of America Diss., 1970.

597. Heredia, E. A. *Planes Españoles para Reconquistar Hispanoamérica, 1810–1818.* B.A., 1975.

598. Humphreys, R. A. "Anglo-American Rivalries and Spanish American Independence," *TRHS* 16 (1966) 131–156.

599. Jova, J. J. "Hispanic America and U.S. Independence," *APAU* 28 (1976) 5–12.

600. Kaplan, L. S. *Colonies into Nation: American Diplomacy, 1763–1801.* N.Y., 1972.

601. Ketcham, R. *James Madison.* N.Y., 1971.

   Treats the relationship between domestic and foreign policy.

602. Kinsbruner, J. *The Spanish American Independence Movement.* Hinsdale, Ill., 1973.

603. Lima, L. F. B. *A Independência na América Latina.* Rio, 1969.

604. Lynch, J. *The Spanish American Revolutions, 1808–1826.* N.Y., 1973.

   A comprehensive one-volume treatment.

605. Malone, D. *Jefferson, the President.* Boston, 1971.

606. Nicholson, I. *The Liberators: A Study of Independence Movements in Spanish America*. N.Y., 1967.

607. Peterson, D. *Thomas Jefferson and the New Nation*. N.Y., 1970.

608. Reyes Flores, A. "La Actitud de Estados Unidos ante la Independencia Latinoamericana," *RCEHMP* 19 (1971) 191–197.

609. Rodríguez, J. E. *The Emergence of Spanish America: Vicente Rocafuerte and Spanish Americanism, 1808–1832*. Berkeley, Calif., 1975.

609a. Rodríguez, M. *La Revolución Americana de 1776 y el Mundo Hispánico: Ensayos y Documentos*. Madrid, 1976.

610. Savelle, M. *Empires to Nations: Expansion in America, 1713–1824*. Minneapolis, Minn., 1974.

611. Seckinger, R. L. "South American Power Politics during the 1820's," *HAHR* 56 (May, 1976) 241–267.

611a. Simmons, M. E. *Santiago F. Puglia, an Early Philadelphia Propagandist for Spanish American Independence*. Chapel Hill, N.C., 1977.

612. Smelser, M. *The Democratic Republic, 1801–1815*. N.Y., 1968.

613. Varg, P. A. *Foreign Policies of the Founding Fathers*. East Lansing, Mich., 1963.
Covers the years 1776 to 1812.

614. Wood, G. S. *The Creation of the American Republic, 1776–1787*. Williamsburg, Va., 1969.

III-A cross references:

a) For works treating the influence of the United States in independence movements of particular countries, see the country chapters (XIII–XXIV).

b) See also items 2404, 2880.

c) In the Trask, Meyer, and Trask *Bibliography* see items 1622, 1805–1896, 1993, 2009, 2539, 7439, 7456, 8831, 9349.

B. ACQUISITION OF EAST AND WEST FLORIDA

615. Baker, M. "The Spanish War Scare of 1816," *MA* 45 (1963) 67–78.

616. Bradley, J. W. "W. C. C. Claiborne and Spain: Foreign Affairs under Jefferson and Madison," *LHI* 12 (Fall, 1971) 297–314 and 13 (Winter, 1972) 5–26.
Treats Claiborne's relations with the Spanish in West Florida.

617. Din, Gilbert C. "The Irish Mission to West Florida," *LHI* 12 (Fall, 1971) 315–334.

618. Ellsworth, L. F. (ed.). *The Americanization of the Gulf Coast, 1803–1850*. Pensacola, Fla., 1972.

619. Gold, R. L. *Borderland Empires in Transition: The Triple-Nation Transfer of Florida*. Carbondale, Ill., 1969.
Treats the period 1763 to 1765.

620. Howard, C. N. "Alleged Spanish Grants in British West Florida," *FHQ* 22 (Oct., 1943) 74–85.

621. ———. *The British Development of West Florida, 1763–1764*. Berkeley, Calif., 1947.

622. Johnson, C. *British West Florida, 1763–1783*. New Haven, Conn., 1943.

623. ———. "Expansion in West Florida, 1770–1779," *MVHR* 20 (Mar., 1934) 481–496.

624. Miller, J. B. "Juan Nepomuceno de Quesada, Spanish Governor of East Florida, 1790–1795," Fla. State U. Diss., 1974.

625. McDermott, J. F. (ed.). *The Spanish in the Mississippi Valley, 1762–1804*. Urbana, Ill., 1974.

626. Mowat, C. L. *East Florida as a British Province, 1763–1784*. Berkeley, Calif., 1943.

627. Siebert, W. H. "How the Spaniards Evacuated Pensacola in 1763," *FHQ* 11 (Oct., 1932) 48–57.

628. Starr, J. B. *Tories, Dons and Rebels: The American Revolution in British West Florida*. Gainesville, Fla., 1976.

629. White, D. H. "The Forbes Conspiracy in Spanish Florida, 1801–1806," *FHQ* 52 (Jan., 1974) 274–285.

III-B cross references: In the Trask, Meyer, and Trask Bibliography see items 1823, 1853, 1897–1941, 2062.

C. ADAMS-ONÍS (TRANSCONTINENTAL) TREATY

III-C cross references: In the Trask, Meyer, and Trask Bibliography see items 1815, 1846, 1908, 1911, 1934, 1942–1971.

D. RECOGNITION OF LATIN AMERICAN INDEPENDENCE

630. Campbell, R. B. "Henry Clay and the Emerging Nations of Spanish America, 1815–1829," U. of Va. Diss., 1966.

III-D   cross references:
  a) For works pertaining to U.S. recognition of particular countries, see the appropriate country chapters (XIII-XXIV).
  b) For works on the general question of recognition in international law, see items 1597–1603.
  c) See also item 3459.
  d) In the Trask, Meyer, and Trask *Bibliography* see items 1972–1988, 2006, 4557–4566.

E. ORIGINS OF THE MONROE DOCTRINE, 1815–1823

631. Ammon, H. *James Monroe: The Quest for National Identity*. N.Y., 1971.

632. Körner, K. W. (ed.). *La Independencia de la América Española y la Diplomacia Alemana*. B.A., 1968.

633. Kossok, M. *Historia de la Santa Alianza y la Emancipación de América Latina*. B.A., 1968.

634. May, E. R. *The Making of the Monroe Doctrine*. Cambridge, Mass., 1975.
   Treats U.S. domestic considerations which influenced the formulation of the doctrine.

635. Mir, P. *Las Raíces Dominicanas de la Doctrina de Monroe*. Santo Domingo, 1974.

636. Perkins, B. *Castlereagh and Adams: England and the United States, 1812–1823*. Berkeley, Calif., 1964.

III-E   cross references: In the Trask, Meyer, and Trask Bibliography *see items 1807, 1808a, 1815, 1823, 1829, 1831, 1837, 1840a, 1847a, 1849, 1854–1856, 1867a, 1871, 1873, 1876a, 1886, 1888, 1974, 1989–2053, 2121, 2140, 2578, 9588.*

Chapter IV United States–
Latin American Relations, 1823–1895

A. GENERAL WORKS, BIOGRAPHIES, AND SPECIAL STUDIES

637. Campbell, S. *The Transformation of American Foreign Relations, 1865–1900*, N.Y., 1976.

638. Daniel, E. R. "Spanish American Travelers in the United States before 1900: A Study in Inter-American Literary Relations," U. of N.C. Diss., 1959.

639. Davis, K. E. *The Presidency of Rutherford B. Hayes*. Westport, Conn., 1972.

640. Eblen, J. E. *The First and Second U.S. Empires: Governors and Territorial Government, 1784–1912*. Pittsburgh, Pa., 1968.

641. García Mérou, M. *Historia de la Diplomacia Americana: Política Internacional de los Estados Unidos*. 2 vols., B.A., 1904.
Covers the nineteenth century.

642. Hagan, K. J. *American Gunboat Diplomacy and the Old Navy, 1877–1889*. Westport, Conn., 1973.

643. Healy, D. *U.S. Expansionism: The Imperialist Urge in the 1890's*. Madison, Wis., 1970.

644. Hollingsworth, J. R. (ed.). *American Expansion in the Late Nineteenth Century: Colonialist or Anti-Colonialist*. N.Y., 1968.

644a. Iriye, A. *From Nationalism to Internationalism: U.S. Foreign Policy to 1914*. London, 1977.

645. Johannesen, R. L. "John Quincy Adams Speaking on Territorial Expansion, 1836–1848," Kan. U. Diss., 1964.

646. Lobo, H. *De Monroe a Rio-Branco*. Rio, 1912.

647. May, E. R. *American Imperialism: A Speculative Essay*. N.Y., 1968.
Covers the period 1890 to 1903.

648. Medina Castro, M. *Estados Unidos y América Latina: Siglo XIX*. Havana, 1968.
A critical and comprehensive survey of relations in the nineteenth century.

649. Morgan, H. W. *From Hayes to McKinley*. Syracuse, N.Y., 1969.

650. Morrison, J. H. *History of American Steam Navigation*. N.Y., 1903.

651. Nichols, J. P. "The United States Congress and Imperialism, 1861–1897," *JEH* 21 (1961) 526–538.

652. North, C. *The Economic Growth of the United States, 1790–1860*. N.Y., 1960.

653. Paolino, E. N. *The Foundation of the American Empire: William Henry Seward and U.S. Foreign Policy*. Ithaca, N.Y., 1973.
Secretary of State, 1861–1869.

654. Pardo, E. *La Ilusión Yanqui*. Madrid, 1919.
Treats U.S. intervention in Latin America in the nineteenth century.

655. Platt, D. C. M. *Latin America and British Trade, 1806–1914*. N.Y., 1973.
Considerable emphasis on British rivalry with the United States.

656. Plesur, M. *America's Outward Thrust: Approaches to Foreign Affairs, 1865–1890*. DeKalb, Ill., 1971.

657. Pletcher, D. M. "Inter-American Trade in the Early 1870's—A State Department Survey," *TA* 23 (1977) 593–612.
Survey undertaken in the Grant administration to increase U.S. trade in the

face of European competition.

658. Rothman, D. J. *Politics and Power: The United States Senate, 1869–1901*. Cambridge, Mass., 1966.

659. Scribner, R. L. "The Diplomacy of William L. Marcy, Secretary of State, 1853–1857," U. of Va. Diss., 1949.

660. Sievers, H. J. *Benjamin Harrison: Hoosier President*. Indianapolis, Ind., 1968.

661. Silbey, J. H. *The Transformation of American Politics, 1840–1860*. Englewood Cliffs, N.J., 1967.

662. Soler, R. *Clase y Nación en Hispanoamérica: Siglo XIX*. Panama, 1975.

663. Spetter, A. B. "Harrison and Blaine: Foreign Policy 1889–1893," Rutgers U. Diss., 1967.

664. USDS. *The United States Consular System: A Manual for Consuls and also for Merchants, Shipowners and Masters in Their Consular Transactions Comprising the Instructions of the Department of State in Regard to Consular Emoluments, Duties Privileges and Liabilities*. Wash., 1856.

665. Van Deusen, G. G. *William Henry Seward*. N.Y., 1967.
Secretary of State, 1861–1869.

666. Winchester, R. C. "James G. Blaine and the Ideology of American Expansionism," U. of Rochester Diss., 1966.
Secretary of State, 1881 and 1889–1892.

IV-A   cross references:
a) For works pertaining to the Washington Conference of 1889, see item 1810.
b) In the Trask, Meyer, and Trask *Bibliography* see items 2054–2149, 2500, 2503, 2513, 2948, 2951, 4902a–4916a, 6670, 6677, 6683, 7891, 7894, 9985.

B. EUROPEAN VIOLATIONS OF THE MONROE DOCTRINE

1. FRANCE AND GREAT BRITAIN IN THE LA PLATA, 1838–1850

667. Barba, E. M. "Rosas y los Intereses Británicos en la Argentina," *POLEM* 16 (1970) 149–159.

668. Botta, V. P. *El Bloqueo Francés en Zárate*. B.A., 1969.

669. Costa, E. *English Invasion of the River Plate*. B.A., 1937.

670. Destefani, L.H. *Los Marinos en las Invasiones Inglesas*. B.A., 1975.

671. Iñigo Carrera, H. J. "Caudillos en las Invasiones Inglesas," *TES* 34 (1970) 56–63.

672. Rebollo Paz, L. "La Intervención Anglo-Francesa (1845–1850). ¿Por qué Venció Rosas?" *PAN* 149 (1971) 62–63.

673. Rodríguez, A. G. "Las Invasiones Inglesas y su Apresto Militar," *BANHA* 43 (1970) 397–407.

674. Salidas, A. *Por que se Produjo el Bloqueo Anglo-Francés*. B.A., 1974.

IV-B-1   cross references: In the Trask, Meyer, and Trask Bibliography *see items 2150–2177, 2182b, 9583, 9586, 9594, 9597, 9600.*

2. THE PASTRY WAR (MEXICO), 1838

675. Hernández Guerrero, D. "La Intervención Francesa en México—1838," UNAM Diss., 1965.

IV-B-2   cross references: In the Trask, Meyer, and Trask Bibliography *see items 2177a–2182b.*

3. BRITISH INCURSIONS ON THE MOSQUITO COAST

676. *Como Reincorporó Nicaragua su Costa Oriental: La Mosquitia, Desde la Colonia Hasta su Reincorporación Definitiva*. Managua, 1944.

677. Levett, E. P. "Negotiations for Release from the Inter-Oceanic Obligations of the Clayton-Bulwer Treaty," U. of Chicago Diss., 1941.

IV-B-3   cross references: In the Trask, Meyer, and Trask Bibliography *see items 2183–2189.*

4. SPANISH RECONQUEST OF SANTO DOMINGO, 1861–1865

678. Balcacer, J. D. *Pedro Santana: Historia Política de un Déspota*. Santo Domingo, 1974.

679. Bándara, J. de la. *Anexión y Guerra de Santo Domingo*. 2 vols., Santo Domingo, 1975.

680. González Tablas, R. *Historia de la*

Dominación y Última Guerra de España en Santo Domingo. Santo Domingo, 1974.

681. Puente García, E. de la. "1861–1885: Anexión y Abandono de Santo Domingo, Problemas Críticos," *RIN* 22 (July–Dec., 1962) 411–472.

682. Tolentino, H. *La Traición de Pedro Santana*. Santo Domingo, 1968.

IV-B-4   cross references: In the Trask, Meyer, and Trask Bibliography *see items 2190–2202.*

5. ATTEMPTED RECONQUEST OF CHILE AND PERU, 1863–1866

682a. Bermúdez Miral, O. "Repercusiones en Cobija de la Guerra con España," *RCHG* 143 (1975) 46–72.

683. Chirinos Soto, E. *La Guerra del Perú y España*. Lima, 1966.

684. Delgado, L. H. *Guerra entre el Perú y España*. Lima, 1966.

685. Perú. *Memoria que Presenta el Ministro de Estado en el Despacho de Relaciones Exteriores, al Congreso de 1870*. Lima, 1870.

   Contains documentation on the war with Spain.

686. Ward, J. G. S. "The Activities of Spain on the Pacific Coast of South America, and Her War with the Confederation of the Andes, 1860–1886," U. of London Diss., 1940.

IV-B-5   cross references:
a) See also item 771.
b) In the Trask, Meyer, and Trask *Bibliography* see items 1780, 2203–2232.

6. FRENCH INTERVENTION IN MEXICO, 1862–1867

687. Aguirre, M. J. *La Intervención Francesa y el Imperio en México*. 2d ed., Mexico, 1969.

688. Almada, F. R. "La División de Operaciones," *HU* 9 (1968) 431–455.

   Treats military operations during the French intervention.

689. Arnaiz y Freg, A., and C. Bataillon (eds.). *La Intervención Francesa y el Imperio de Maximiliano*. Mexico, 1965.

690. Arriaga, A. *La Patria Recobrada: Estampas de México y los Mexicanos durante la Intervención Francesa*. Mexico, 1967.

691. Barrows, F. M. "Mexican Empire of Napoleon III and the Military Preparation of the United States," Georgetown U. Diss., 1934.

692. Belenki, A. B. *La Intervención Extranjera en México, 1861–1867*. Mexico, 1966.

   Sp. trans. of the work published originally in Russ. (1960).

692a. Black, S. J. "Napoleon III and the French Intervention in Mexico: A Quest for Silver," U. of Okla. Diss., 1974.

693. Blackburn, C. B. "Military Opposition to Official State Department Policy Concerning the Mexican Intervention, 1862–1867," Ball State U. Diss., 1969.

694. Blumberg, A. *The Diplomacy of the Mexican Empire, 1863–1867*. Philadelphia, Pa., 1971.

695. Bock, C. H. *Prelude to Tragedy: The Negotiation and Breakdown of the Tripartite Convention of London, October 31, 1861*. Philadelphia, Pa., 1966.

696. Brunon, J. *Camerone. Carte et Plans par Raoul Brunon*. Paris, 1963.

697. Desternes, S., and H. Chandet. *Maximiliano y Carlota*. Mexico, 1967.

   Trans. by Adolfo A. de Alba.

698. Hanna, A. J., and K. A. Hanna. *Napoleon III and Mexico: American Triumph over Monarchy*. Chapel Hill, N.C., 1971.

   Examines the intervention from the perspective of the U.S. government.

699. Leich, J. F. "Maximiliano de México: Recuerdos y Reflexiones sobre la Intervención Intercontinental," *CA* 34 (Mar.–Apr., 1975) 146–160.

700. Niklewic, K. *Meksyk za Panowania Maksymiljana I*. 2d ed., Warsaw, Poland, 1961.

   Translated title: "Mexico under Maximilian I."

701. Poulton, G. M. "Great Britain and the Intervention in Mexico, 1861–1865," Miami U. Diss., 1976.

702. Schefer, C. *Los Orígenes de la Intervención Francesa en México*. Mexico, 1963.

703. Schroeder, S. *The Fall of Maximilian's Empire as Seen from a United States Gun Boat*. N.Y., 1887.

   Log book of a U.S. naval officer in Veracruz.

704. Tamayo, J. L. "Las Relaciones de México

con los Estados Unidos durante la Intervención Francesa y el Imperio," *CA* 160 (Sept.–Oct., 1967) 170–186.

705. Torre Villar, E. de la. *La Intervención Francesa y el Triunfo de la República*. Mexico, 1968.

IV-B-6   cross references:
a) For general accounts of the period, see items 2099–2124.
b) See also item 665.
c) In the Trask, Meyer, and Trask *Bibliography* see items 1780, 2059, 2098, 2115, 2125, 2180, 2233–2337, 5845–5930.

7. OTHER VIOLATIONS

706. Aguilar, O. *Centroamérica baja el Impacto del Imperialismo Británico en el Siglo XIX*. Guatemala, 1963.

707. Sánchez Lamego, M. A. *La Invasión Española de 1829*. Mexico, 1971.

708. Urquijo, M. *Los Proyectos Españoles para Reconquistar el Río de la Plata, 1820–1833*. B.A., 1958.

709. Villacrés Moscoso, J. W. "El General Flores y su Proyectado Protectorado Francés para Ecuador," *CHA* 8 (1958) 35–71.

710. Wagner de Reyna, A. *La Intervención de las Potencias Europeas en Latinoamérica, 1864 a 1868*. Lima, 1974.

IV-B-7   cross references: In the Trask, Meyer, and Trask Bibliography *see items 2020, 2052, 2064, 2093, 2116, 2337a–2348, 7460.*

C. TRANS-ISTHMIAN DIPLOMACY, 1823–1895

1. GENERAL WORKS

711. Allen, C. *France in Central America: Felix Belly and the Nicaraguan Canal*. N.Y., 1966.
Treats United States–French rivalry.

712. Folkman, D. I. *The Nicaragua Route*. Salt Lake City, Utah, 1972.

713. Pensa, H. *La République et le Canal de Panama*. Paris, 1906.
A history of French efforts in the nineteenth century and French rivalry with the United States.

714. Rodríguez Serrano, F. *El Canal por Nicaragua*. Managua, 1968.

Treats Nicaraguan interest in a canal from the middle of the nineteenth century to the opening of the Panama Canal.

715. Williams, M. H. "San Juan River–Lake Nicaragua Waterway, 1502–1921," La. State U. and Agricultural and Mechanical College Diss., 1971.

IV-C-1   cross references: In the Trask, Meyer, and Trask Bibliography *see items 2103, 2186, 2349–2368, 5871.*

2. TRANS-ISTHMIAN DIPLOMACY, 1823–1850

716. Campbell, A. F. *Remarks on a British Railway and Its Construction by the British Government, from the Atlantic to the Pacific Ocean, Commencing at the Gulf of Honduras*. London, 1849.

717. Garay, J. de. *Survey of the Isthmus of Tehuantepec*. London, 1844.

718. Pérez Venero, A. "Reseñas Históricas sobre Varios Proyectos para la Construcción de una Vía Transístmica," *L* 192 (Nov., 1971) 60–75.
Treats railway construction plans in the first half of the nineteenth century.

IV-C-2   cross references:
a) See also items 2050, 2401, 2486, 2488, 2489, 2558.
b) In the Trask, Meyer, and Trask *Bibliography* see items 2072a, 2189, 2369–2397, 6693, 7040a, 8275.

3. TRANS-ISTHMIAN DIPLOMACY, 1851–1870

719. Gisborne, L. *The Isthmus of Darien in 1852: A Journal of the Expedition of Inquiry for Juncture of the Atlantic and Pacific*. London, 1853.

720. Rodríguez, M. "The 'Prometheus' and the Clayton-Bulwer Treaty," *JMH* 36 (1964) 260–278.
Treats a violation of the treaty in 1851.

721. Schott, J. L. *Rails across Panama: The Story of the Building of the Panama Railroad, 1849–1855*. Indianapolis, Ind., 1967.

722. Tomes, R. *Panama in 1855: An Account of the Panama Railroad*. N.Y., 1855.

723. Woodbridge, P. *Los Contratos Webster-Mora y las Implicaciones sobre Costa Rica y Nicaragua*. San José, C.R., 1967.

Treats Webster's efforts to gain transit rights on the San Juan River and Lake Nicaragua in 1857–1858.

IV-C-3 cross references:

a) See also items 2117, 2121, 2122.

b) In the Trask, Meyer, and Trask *Bibliography* see items 2380a, 2397a–2429, 5856, 5873, 5896.

4. TRANS-ISTHMIAN DIPLOMACY, 1871–1895

724. Ammen, D. *American Isthmian Canal Routes*. Philadelphia, Pa., 1889.

725. Crowell, J. "The United States and a Central American Canal, 1869–1877," *HAHR* 49 (Feb., 1969) 27–52.

726. Mock, J. R. "Panama and Nicaragua Canal Rivalry, 1870–1903," U. of Wis. Diss., 1930.

727. Peacock, G. *Notes on the Isthmus of Panama and Darien with References to a Railroad and Canal for Joining the Atlantic and Pacific Oceans*. London, 1879.

728. USCH. *Reports of Explorations and Surveys to Ascertain the Practicability of a Ship Canal between the Atlantic and Pacific Oceans by Way of the Isthmus of Darien*. (42d Cong., 3d Sess., House Misc. Doc. 113.) Wash., 1874.

729. ———. *Report of Historical and Technical Information Relating to the Problem of Interoceanic Communications by Way of the American Isthmus*. (47th Cong., 2d Sess., House Exec. Doc. 107.) Wash., 1883.

730. USCS. *Message . . . Covering Report of Secretary of State . . . in Relation to the Proposed Interoceanic Canal between the Atlantic and Pacific Oceans*. (46th Cong., 2d Sess., Sen. Exec. Doc. 112.) Wash., 1880.

IV-C-4 cross references:

a) See also items 2126, 2436, 2485, 2490.

b) In the Trask, Meyer, and Trask *Bibliography* see items 2061, 2090, 2430–2458.

D. FILIBUSTERING EXPEDITIONS

731. Cordero Croceri, J. R. "Costa Rica y la Guerra contra los Filibusteros," *UA* 43 (Jan.–June, 1966) 77–92.

732. Fornell, E. W. "Texas and Filibusters in the 1850's," *SHQ* 59 (Apr., 1956) 411–428.

733. Guier, E. *William Walker*. San José, C.R., 1971.

734. Partido Revolucionario Dominicano. *Un Error de Washington: La Resurrección del Imperialismo Militar Norteamericano en el Caribe*. Havana, 1949.

735. Rosegarten, F. *Freebooters Must Die! The Life and Death of William Walker, the Most Notorious Filibuster of the Nineteenth Century*. Wayne, Pa., 1976.

Treats Walker's activities in Sonora, Baja California, and Central America.

736. Stout, J. A. *The Liberators: Filibustering Expeditions into Mexico 1848–1862; and the Last Thrust of Manifest Destiny*. Los Angeles, 1973.

Treats activities of six filibusters.

737. TePaske, J. J. "Appleton Oaksmith, Filibuster Agent," *NCHR* 35 (Oct., 1958) 427–447.

Oaksmith participated with Walker in Nicaragua.

IV-D cross references:

a) For filibustering in Cuba, see items 2634, 2635.

b) For filibustering in Mexico, see items 2041–2043, 2047, 2104, 2112a, 2113.

c) For filibustering in Nicaragua, see item 2491.

d) See also items 795, 2469, 2535.

e) In the Trask, Meyer, and Trask *Bibliography* see items 2006, 2103, 2459–2493, 2546, 2761, 2771, 5848, 5854, 5855, 5855a, 5860, 5867, 5902, 5926, 5928, 5989, 7037–7040, 7045, 7046, 7050, 7052, 7054, 7057–7059, 7062, 7064, 7065, 7441, 7446, 7449, 7452, 7457, 7462, 7464, 7471–7473, 7478, 7480.

E. OLNEY COROLLARY OF 1895

738. Carson, D. K. "Richard Olney: Secretary of State, 1895–1897," U. of Ky. Diss., 1969.

739. Eggert, G. G. *Richard Olney: Evolution of a Statesman*. University Park, Pa., 1974.

IV-E cross references:

a) For works on the Venezuelan–British

Guiana dispute, see items 2960–2970.

b) In the Trask, Meyer, and Trask *Bibliography* see items 2076a, 2076b, 2104a, 2112, 2112b, 2143, 2494–2515, 2630, 8562–8605a.

F. THE OLD PAN AMERICANISM

1. FORMULATION OF THE CONCEPT

740. Ayala, S. F. *Bolívar y el Sistema Interamericano*. Quito, 1962.

741. Bakula Budge, M. C. *Los Ideales de Bolívar en la Integración de los Pueblos Hispanomericanos*. Lima, 1975.

742. Bolívar, J. R. *Bolívar y la Integración Latinoamericana*. Caracas, 1973.

743. Callorda, P. E. *Idea de una Liga que Responda a los Conceptos Panamericanos del Congreso de Bolívar*. Havana, 1928.

744. Fitzgerald, G. E. *The Political Thought of Bolivar: Selected Writings*. The Hague, 1971.

Contains some famous documents and some obscure ones.

744a. Gandía, E. "El Pensamiento Político de Simón Bolívar y la Unidad de América," *BANHC* 58 (Apr.–Jun., 1975) 241–251.

745. Gurri, D. A. *Simón Bolívar: El Ideal Panamericano del Libertador*. Montevideo, 1966.

746. Hudson, R. M. "The Last Years of Simón Bolívar, 1828–1830: A Study in Futility," U. of N.C. Diss., 1965.

747. Lievano Aguirre, I. *Bolivarismo y Monroismo*. Caracas, 1971.

Discusses early Pan Americanism, the Congress of Panama of 1826, and the Monroe Doctrine.

748. Mayochi, E. M. *Espíritu Americanista de la Epopeya Sanmartiniana*. B.A., 1970.

749. Ortega, E. C. *Bolívar y la Revolución Sudamericana*. B.A., 1973.

Contains section on Bolívar's ideas for the early integration of Latin America.

750. Quevedo, N. *Bolívar, Legislador y Jurista*. Caracas, 1974.

751. Townsend Ezcurra, A. *Las Ideas de Bolívar en la Integración de los Pueblos Latinoamericanos*. Lima, 1975.

752. Van Loon, H. *Fighters for Freedom: Jefferson and Bolívar*. N.Y., 1964.

IV-F-1 cross references: In the Trask, Meyer, and Trask Bibliography *see items 1816, 1859, 2009, 2516–2564, 4456, 9556.*

2. CONGRESS OF PANAMA, 1826

753. Castillero Reyes, E. J. *Bolívar en Panamá*. Panama, 1976.

754. ———. *Historia Sintética del Congreso de Panamá de 1826*. Panama, 1956.

755. ———. *Intimidades del Congreso de Panamá de 1826*. Panama, 1956.

756. Clare, Jr., H. *Los Delegados al Congreso Anficiónico de Panamá*. Panama, 1967.

757. Comisión Nacional del Sesquicentenario del Congreso de Panamá. *Sánchez Carrión y el Congreso de Panamá*. Lima, 1976.

758. Cova, J. A. *El Libertador y el Congreso de Panamá*. Caracas, 1955.

758a. "Documentos Relativos al Congreso de Panamá (22 de Junio a 15 de Julio, 1826," *NHIS* 17 (June, 1976) 289–301.

759. Drago, M. J. *El Congreso de Panamá*. B.A., 1970.

Discusses general Inter-American relations at the time of the Congress of Panama.

760. Escarra J., H. E. *Bolívar, El Congreso de Panamá y el Nacionalismo Latinoamericano*. Caracas, 1977.

A prize-winning essay of 61 pages.

761. Fernández del Castillo, A. *El Congreso de Panamá y su Fracaso en Tacubaya*. Mexico, 1969.

762. Garay, N. *Idea de una Liga que Corresponda a los Conceptos Panamericanos del Congreso de Bolívar*. Panama, 1926.

763. González, E. *Influencia del Congreso de Bolívar sobre el Panamericanismo Actual*. Caracas, 1926.

764. Grimaldi, E. *En el Centenario del Congreso de Bolívar, 1826–1926*. Panama, 1926.

765. Guimaraes, A. *O Congreso de Bolívar*. Panama, 1927.

766. LeFevre, J. F. *Documentación Inédita del Congreso de Panamá de 1826*. Panama, 1937.

767. Pacheco Quintero, J. *El Congreso Anficiónico de Panamá y la Política Internacional de los Estados Unidos*. Bogotá, 1971.

Argues that the United States did not want the congress to succeed.

768. Pereira, C. *La Gran Bretaña y el Congreso de Panamá*. San José, C.R., 1926.

769. Porras Barrenechea, R. *El Congreso de Panamá*. Lima, 1975.

770. Vaughn, E. "Algunos Apuntes sobre Edward James Dawkins, Comisionado Británico en el Congreso de Panamá, 1826," *BACH* 53 (Jan.–Mar., 1966) 69–131.

IV-F-2   cross references:
a) See also item 747.
b) In the Trask, Meyer, and Trask *Bibliography* see items 1862, 2006a, 2020, 2516, 2565–2598, 4435, 5583, 8203, 8211, 8236.

3. ATTEMPTS AT ORGANIZATION, 1826–1889

771. Academia Diplomática del Perú. *El Congreso Americano de Lima de 1864*. Lima, 1964.

Deals with effort to treat the Spanish military venture on the west coast of South America.

772. *Bases de Unión Americana Discutidas y Aprobadas por la Sociedad de la Unión Americana de Santiago*. Santiago, 1897.

773. Vivian, J. F. "The South American Commission to the Three Americas Movement: The Politics of Pan Americanism, 1884–1890," American U. Diss., 1971.

IV-F-3   cross references:
a) For works on the general concept of Pan Americanism, many of which treat the period before 1889, see items 1548–1569.
b) For works treating Pan Hispanism, as opposed to Pan Americanism, see items 1911–1962.
c) In the Trask, Meyer, and Trask *Bibliography* see items 2063a, 2103, 2120a, 2203a, 2215, 2260, 2558, 2562, 2564, 2595, 2598–2622, 4385–4506, 5313–5384.

Chapter V   The Spanish-American War, 1895–1900

A. GENERAL WORKS, BIOGRAPHIES, AND SPECIAL STUDIES

774. Brown, C. H. *Correspondent's War: Journalists in the Spanish-American War*. N.Y., 1967.

775. Dallek, R. (ed.). *1898: McKinley's Decision, the United States Declares War on Spain*. N.Y., 1969.

    Selected readings and documents.

776. Duncan, G. W. "The Diplomatic Career of William Rufus Day, 1897–1898," Case Western Reserve U. Diss., 1976.

    Day was Assistant Secretary of State at the time of the Spanish-American War.

777. Dupotey Fideaux, H. *Gómez, Calixto y el Marqués en el Diario de Valdés-Domínguez*. Havana, 1972.

778. Eggert, G. G. "Our Man in Havana: Fitzhugh Lee," *HAHR* 47 (Nov., 1967) 463–485.

    Treats the activities of the U.S. consul general in bringing on the war.

779. Flint, G. *Marching with Gómez: A War Correspondent's Field Notebook Kept during Four Months with the Cuban Army*. Boston, 1898.

780. Foner, P. S. *The Spanish-Cuban-American War and the Birth of American Imperialism*. 2 vols., N.Y., 1972.

    Based on Cuban archives. Reflects the Cuban point of view.

781. Holbo, P. S. "The Convergence of Moods and the Cuban Bond 'Conspiracy' of 1898," *JAHI* 55 (1968) 54–72.

782. Keller, A. *The Spanish-American War: A Compact History*. N.Y., 1969.

783. Linderman, G. F. *The Mirror of War: American Society and the Spanish-American War*. Ann Arbor, Mich., 1974.

784. Miller, R. H. *American Imperialism in 1898: The Quest for National Fulfillment*. N.Y., 1970.

785. Natal, C. R. *Puerto Rico y la Crisis de la Guerra Hispanoamericana*. Hato Rey, P.R., 1975.

785a. Seager, R. *Alfred Thayer Mahan: The Man and His Letters*. Annapolis, Md., 1977.

    A biography of the naval strategist who influenced Theodore Roosevelt.

786. Vahle, C. W. "Congress, the President and Overseas Expansion, 1897–1901," Georgetown U. Diss., 1967.

787. Wexler, A. R. "Historians, Society, and the Spanish-Cuban War of 1898," Ind. U. Diss., 1972.

V-A   cross references:

a) See item 643.

b) In the Trask, Meyer, and Trask *Bibliography* see items 2623–2676, 2754, 2764, 2765, 2878, 7428, 7549, 7555, 7556.

B. BACKGROUND OF THE CONFLICT, 1868–1898

788. Beck, E. R. "The Martínez Campos Government of 1879: Spain's Last Chance in Cuba," *HAHR* 56 (May, 1976) 268–289.

789. Cabrera, R. *Cuba and Cubans*. Philadelphia, Pa., 1896.

790. Crouch, T. W. *A Yankee Guerrillero: Frederick Funston and the Cuban Insurrection, 1896–1897*. Memphis, Tenn., 1975.

    Funston was an artillery officer with Calixto García's rebels.

791. Figueredo Socarrás, F. *La Revolución de Yara, 1868–1878*. Havana, 1968.

792. Foner, P. S. *Antonio Maceo: The "Bronze Titan" of Cuba's Struggle for Independence*. N.Y., 1977.

793. García Verdugo, V. *Cuba contra España*. Madrid, 1869.
Treats the beginning of the war.

794. Guerra, R. *Guerra de los 10 Años*. 2 vols., Havana, 1972.

795. Halkiotis, S. H. "Neutrality and Enforcement: The U.S.A. and Cuban Filibustering, 1895–1898," U. of N.C. Diss., 1976.

796. Lizaso, F. "José Morales Lemus y su Gestión Diplomática en los Estados Unidos," *RCU* 1 (Jan.–June, 1968) 143–155.
Tried to have President Grant and Secretary of State Fish extend belligerency to rebels during Ten Years' War.

796a. McWilliams, T. S. "Procrastinations Diplomacy: Hannis Taylor and the Cuban Business Disputes, 1893–97," *DH* 2 (Winter, 1978) 63–80.

797. Morgan, H. W. "The De Lome Letter: A New Appraisal," *HIS* 26 (1963) 36–49.

798. Piñera, H. "El Fundamento Teórico de la Guerra de los Diez Años," *RCU* 1 (Jan. 1–June, 1968) 13–40.

798a. Preece, C. A. "Insurgent Guests: The Cuban Revolutionary Party and Its Activities in the United States, 1892–1898," Georgetown U. Diss., 1976.

799. Rickover, H. G. *How the Battleship Maine Was Destroyed*. Wash., 1976.
Holds that the explosion was internal.

800. Soulere, E. A. *Historia de la Insurrección de Cuba, 1869–1879*. 2 vols., Barcelona, 1879–1880.

801. Taylor, H. "A Review of the Cuban Question and Its Economic, Political, and Diplomatic Aspects," *NAR* 165 (Nov., 1897) 610–635.

801a. Texera, F. C. "An American Dilemma: The Cuban Question, 1897–1898," Fla. State U. Diss., 1975.

V-B   cross references:
a) For general works on the United States and Spanish Cuba, see items 2632–2636.

b) In the Trask, Meyer, and Trask *Bibliography* see items 2056, 2076a, 2099b, 2099c, 2113a, 2677–2789, 7438–7499.

C. CONDUCT OF THE WAR, 1898

802. Cosmas, G. A. "An Army for Empire: The United States Army in the Spanish-American War, 1898–1899," U. of Wis. Diss., 1969.

803. Dierks, J. C. *A Leap to Arms: The Cuban Campaign of 1898*. Philadelphia, Pa., 1970.

804. Gómez Núñez, S. *La Guerra Hispano-Americana: Puerto Rico y Filipinas*. Madrid, 1902.
Emphasizes the military history.

805. Jones, V. C. *Roosevelt's Rough Riders*. Garden City, N.Y., 1971.

V-C   cross references: In the Trask, Meyer, and Trask Bibliography *see items 2790–3807, 7618a, 9408.*

D. EUROPEAN INTERESTS

V-D   cross references:
a) See item 845.

b) In the Trask, Meyer, and Trask *Bibliography* see items 2808–2828, 3085–3092, 7544.

E. LEGAL ASPECTS

V-E   cross references: In the Trask, Meyer, and Trask Bibliography *see items 2829–2839b, 2843, 2845.*

F. PARIS PEACE SETTLEMENT

V-F   cross references: In the Trask, Meyer, and Trask Bibliography *see items 2840–2863.*

G. AFTER-EFFECT: THE IMPERIALIST DEBATE

806. Axeen, D. L. "Romantics and Civilizers: American Attitudes toward War, 1898–1902," Yale U. Diss., 1969.

807. Beisner, R. L. *Twelve against Empire: The Anti-Imperialists, 1898–1900*. N.Y., 1968.
Treats Republican opposition to imperialism.

808. Cobbledick, J. R. "Anti-Imperialism in the United States, 1893–1902," Tufts U. Diss., 1966.

809.   Coletta, P. "Bryan, Anti-Imperialism and Missionary Diplomacy," *NH* 44 (Sept., 1968) 167–187.

810.   Legaspi, E. C. "The Rhetoric of the Anti-Imperialist Movement, 1898–1900, with Special Emphasis on the Role of the Anti-Imperialist League," Cornell U. Diss., 1967.

811.   Marina, W. F. "Opponents of Empire: An Interpretation of Anti-Imperialism, 1898–1921," U. of Denver Diss., 1968.

811a. Matré, R. A. "The Chicago Press and Imperialism, 1889–1902," Northwestern U. Diss., 1961.

812.   Tompkins, E. B. *Anti-Imperialism in the United States, 1890–1920*. Philadelphia, Pa., 1970.

813.   ———. "The Old Guard: A Study of the Anti-Imperialist Leadership," *HIS* 30 (1968) 366–388.

814.   ———. "Scylla and Charybdis: The Anti-Imperialist Dilemma in the Election of 1900," *PHR* (1967) 143–161.

815.   Welch, R. E. "Senator George Frisbie Hoar and the Defeat of Anti-Imperialism, 1898–1900," *HIS* 26 (1964) 362–380.

815a. Zimmerman, J. A. "Who Were the Anti-Imperialists and the Expansionists of 1898 and 1899? A Chicago Perspective," *PHR* 46 (Nov., 1977) 589–601.

V-G   cross references: In the Trask, Meyer, and Trask Bibliography *see items* 2631c, 2676, 2747, 2854, 2864–2891, 2906, 2925, 2944, 3048, 6720, 7529, 7596, 7597, 7600.

Chapter VI   The Imperialist Era and Latin America, 1900–1921

A. GENERAL WORKS AND INTERPRETATIONS

816. Abrams, R. M. "United States Intervention Abroad: The First Quarter of the Century," *AHR* 79 (Feb., 1974) 72–102.
    Emphasizes Caribbean interventions.

817. Alejandro, A. *La Nueva Política Internacional Sudamericana*. Lima, 1903.
    A collection of articles originally published in *El Comercio*.

817a. Kist, G. J. "The Role of Thomas C. Dawson in United States–Latin American Diplomatic Relations, 1897–1912," Loyola U. Diss., 1971.

818. Nieto, R. *El Imperio de los Estados Unidos y Otros Ensayos*. Mexico, 1927.

819. Tulchin, J. S. "Dollar Diplomacy and Non-Intervention: The Latin American Policy of the United States," Harvard U. Diss., 1965.

VI-A   cross references:
a) Many of the general works on U.S. relations with the Central American–Caribbean area also treat the subject of imperialism. See items 2396–2400 and 2406–2412.
b) See also items 811, 1566.
c) In the Trask, Meyer, and Trask *Bibliography* see items 1587, 1591, 1608, 1611, 1736, 2631c, 2722, 2731, 2762, 2869, 2892–2947, 3193, 3297, 6706–6818.

B. THE MONROE DOCTRINE AND INTERVENTION

820. Jolibois, J. Fils. *La Doctrine de Monroe*. Port-au-Prince, 1932.

VI-B   cross references: In the Trask, Meyer, and Trask Bibliography *see items 1766–1804, 2117, 2947a–2983, 2984a, 3031, 3259, 4600.*

C. THE ROOSEVELT AND TAFT ADMINISTRATIONS, 1901–1913

821. Aquarone, A. *Le Origini dell'imperialismo Americano: Da McKinley a Taft (1897–1913)*. Bologna, Italy, 1973.

822. Burton, D. H. *Theodore Roosevelt*. N.Y., 1972.

823. ———. *Theodore Roosevelt: Confident Imperialist*. Philadelphia, Pa., 1968.

824. Cadenhead, I. E. *Theodore Roosevelt: The Paradox of Progressivism*. N.Y., 1974.

825. Chessman, G. W. *Theodore Roosevelt and the Politics of Power*. Boston, 1968.

826. Coletta, P. E. *The Presidency of William Howard Taft*. Lawrence, Kan., 1973.

827. Esthus, R. A. *Theodore Roosevelt and the International Rivalries*. Waltham, Mass., 1970.

828. González de Arrili, B. *Roosevelt: América para los Yanquis*. B.A., 1913.

829. Minger, R. E. *William Howard Taft and the United States Foreign Policy: The Apprenticeship Years, 1900–1908*. Urbana, Ill., 1975.

830. Mulhollen, P. E. "Philander C. Knox and Dollar Diplomacy, 1909–1913," U. of Tex. Diss., 1966.

831. Muth, E. W. "Elihu Root: His Role and Concepts Pertaining to United States Policies of Intervention," Georgetown U. Diss., 1966.

832. Scholes, W. V., and M. V. Scholes. *The Foreign Policies of the Taft Administration*. Columbia, Mo., 1970.

VI-C *cross references:*
 a) For works treating the role of President Theodore Roosevelt's administration in separating Panama from Colombia, see items 821–832.
 b) For works on the Mexico City Conference of 1901, see items 1811–1814; for the Rio de Janeiro Conference of 1906, see items 1815–1821; for the Buenos Aires Conference of 1910, see items 1822–1825.
 c) For works on the Central American Peace Conference of 1907, held in Washington, D.C., see item 1849.
 d) See also items 2407, 2651.
 e) In the Trask, Meyer, and Trask *Bibliography* see items 2624, 2628, 2656, 2873, 2877, 2882, 2891, 2909, 2984–3035, 4917–4944, 5128–5135, 6724, 6987, 7197, 7586, 8082, 8290–8382, 8612b, 8615.

D. WILSON'S ADMINISTRATION, 1913–1921

833. Bell, S. *Righteous Conquest: Woodrow Wilson and the Evolution of the New Diplomacy*. Port Washington, N.Y., 1972.
834. ———. "Woodrow Wilson and the Evolution of the New Diplomacy," U. of Wis. Diss., 1969.
834a. Block, R. H. "Southern Opinion of Woodrow Wilson's Foreign Policies, 1913–1917," Duke U. Diss., 1968.
835. Carter, P. M. "Congressional and Public Reaction to Wilson's Caribbean Policy, 1913–1917," U. of Colo. Diss., 1970.
836. Coletta, P. E. *William Jennings Bryan: Progressive Politician and Moral Statesman, 1909–1915*. Lincoln, Nebr., 1969.
837. Kaplan, E. A. "The Latin American Policy of William Jennings Bryan, 1913–1915," NYU Diss., 1970.
838. Kaufman, B. I. *Efficiency and Expansion: Foreign Trade Organization in the Wilson Administration, 1913–1921*. Westport, Conn., 1974.
839. ———. "United States Trade and Latin America: The Wilson Years," *JAHI* 58 (Sept., 1971) 342–363.

Trade with Latin America grew tremendously during the Wilson years.

840. Knott, A. W. "The Pan American Policy of Woodrow Wilson, 1913–1921," U. of Colo. Diss., 1968.
841. Levin, N. G., Jr. *Woodrow Wilson and World Politics*. N.Y., 1968.
842. Livermore, S. W. "Deserving Democrats: The Foreign Service under Woodrow Wilson," *SAQ* 69 (Winter, 1970) 144–160.
842a. Safford, J. J. *Wilsonian Maritime Diplomacy, 1913–1921*. New Brunswick, N.J., 1978.
843. Smith. D. M. *Aftermath of War: Bainbridge Colby and Wilsonian Diplomacy, 1920–1921*. Philadelphia, Pa., 1970.
     Colby was Secretary of State.
844. Tumulty, J. P. *Woodrow Wilson as I Know Him*. Garden City, N.Y., 1921

VI-D *cross references:*
 a) For material relating specifically to World War I, see Chapter VII.
 b) See also items 2850, 2853, 3030, 3070.
 c) In the Trask, Meyer, and Trask *Bibliography* see items 2898, 2899, 3006, 3036–3083, 6185, 6855, 6979, 7075a, 7078, 7079, 7091, 7224, 7241, 7311a, 7504, 7508, 7908, 7909.

E. EUROPEAN INTRUSIONS AND THE UNITED STATES RESPONSE

845. Bines, J. P. "The United States and the European Balance of Power: 1890–1908," U. of Va. Diss., 1976.
846. Manignat, L. F. *L'Amérique Latine au XXᵉ Siécle: 1889–1929*. Paris, 1973.

VI-E *cross references: In the Trask, Meyer, and Trask* Bibliography *see items 2810, 2811, 2815, 2827, 3084–3092, 3104, 3105, 3177, 6180a.*

F. ECONOMIC RELATIONS IN THE IMPERIALIST ERA

847. Abrahams, P. P. "The Foreign Expansion of American Finance and Its Relationship to the Foreign Economic Policies of the United States, 1907–1921," U. of Wis. Diss., 1967.

847a. Parrini, C. *Heir to Empire: United States Economic Diplomacy, 1916–1923*. Pittsburgh, Pa., 1969.

b) In the Trask, Meyer, and Trask *Bibliography* see items 1582, 2631c, 2929, 2934, 2973, 3092a–3102, 3203.

VI-F *cross references:*

a) See also items 1984, 2929, 2983, 3030.

Chapter VII   Latin America and World War I

A. GENERAL WORKS

848. Coffman, E. M. *The War to End All Wars*. N.Y., 1968.

849. Giddens, J. A. "American Foreign Propaganda in World War I," Fletcher School Diss., 1967.

850. Morato, O. *América del Sur y la Futura Paz Europea: Historiando de Porvenir*. Montevideo, 1918.

851. Rosenberg, E. S. "World War I and the Growth of U.S. Preponderance in Latin America," State U. of N.Y. Stony Brook Diss., 1973.

852. Small, M. "The United States and the German Threat to the Hemisphere, 1905–1914," *TA* 28 (Jan., 1972) 252–270.

    The German threat to Latin America was not very significant.

853. Tulchin, J. S. *The Aftermath of War: World War I and U.S. Policy toward Latin America*. N.Y., 1971.

    Covers the period 1914 to 1925.

854. Zeman, Z. A. B. *The Gentlemen Negotiators: A Diplomatic History of the First World War*. N.Y., 1971.

VII-A   *cross references: In the Trask, Meyer, and Trask* Bibliography *see items 2928, 3040, 3041, 3043, 3045, 3047, 3054, 3055, 3062, 3070, 3073, 3076, 3079, 3103–3112.*

B. THE MONROE DOCTRINE AND THE WAR

VII-B   *cross references:*
  a)   See item 878.
  b)   In the Trask, Meyer, and Trask *Bibliography* see items 1768, 3113–3127.

C. NEUTRALITY AND BELLIGERENCY, 1914–1918

855. Alington, A. F. *The Lamps Go Out: 1914 and the Outbreak of War*. London, 1969.

856. Badía, C. *El Factor Geográfico en la Política Sudamericana*. Madrid, 1919.

857. Baecker, T. *Die Deutsche Mexicopolitik*. Berlin, 1971.

858. Blakeley, G. T. *Historians on the Homefront: American Propagandists for the Great War*. Lexington, Ky., 1970.

859. Cooper, J. M., Jr. *The Vanity of Power: American Isolation and the First World War*. Westport, Conn., 1969.

860. González Blanco, E. *Iberismo y Germanismo: España ante el Conflicto Europeo*. Valencia, Spain, 1917.

861. Gregory, R. *The Origins of American Intervention in the First World War*. N.Y., 1971.

862. Trask, D. F. *Captains and Cabinets: Anglo-American Naval Relations, 1917–1918*. Columbia, Mo., 1972.

863. Turner, L. C. F. *The Coming of the First World War*. London, 1968.

864. Walworth, A. *America's Movement: 1918. American Diplomacy at the End of World War I*. N.Y., 1977.

865. Zárate, R. *España y América: Proyecciones y Problemas Derivadas de la Guerra*. Madrid, 1917.

    Author, a Peruvian officer, was stationed in Spain during the war.

VII-C   *cross references:*
  a)   See also item 3193.
  b)   In the Trask, Meyer, and Trask *Bibliography* see items 3036, 3047a, 3067, 3069, 3071, 3078, 3128–3142, 6180a, 7540.

D. LATIN AMERICAN RESPONSES TO WORLD WAR I

866. Basile, J. Van Der Karr. "World War I as a Turning Point in Argentine History: As Seen Especially through a Study of Fiscal and Budgetary Legislation during the War Years," NYU Diss., 1972.

867. Conil Paz, A. *La Neutralidad Argentina y la Primera Guerra Mundial*. B.A., 1976.

868. Gerhardt, R. C. "Inglaterra y el Petróleo Mexicano durante la Primera Guerra Mundial," *HM* 25 (July–Sept., 1975) 118–142.

869. Gravil, R. "Argentina and the First World War," *RHIS* 54 (Oct.–Dec., 1976) 385–418.

869a. "Informes Diplomáticas de los Representantes del Imperio Alemán en el Uruguay, 1912–1915," *RHU* 46 (1975) 117–202.

869b. Rosenberg, E. S. "Anglo-American Economic Rivalry in Brazil during World War I," *DH* 2 (Spring, 1978) 131–152.

870. Rowe, L. S. *El Perú y la Guerra de 1914*. Lima, 1975.

871. Ryan, R. *La Primera Guerra Mundial y la Presidencia de Yrigoyen*. B.A., 1921.

VII-D cross references: In the Trask, Meyer, and Trask Bibliography see items 3143–3177.

Chapter VIII   From Imperialism to the Good Neighbor Policy, 1921–1938

A. GENERAL WORKS AND INTERPRETATIONS

872. Berger, H. W. "Union Diplomacy: American Labor's Foreign Policy in Latin America, 1932–1955," U. of Wis. Diss., 1966.

873. Currie, G. R. "Latin America and the Era of Disarmament: The First Stage 1920–1925," U. of Minn. Diss., 1970.

873a. González Casanova, P. *América Latina en los Años Treïnta*. Mexico, 1977.

874. Green, D. *The Containment of Latin America: A History of the Myths and Realities of the Good Neighbor Policy*. N.Y., 1971.

   A revisionist interpretation.

875. Ramírez Necochea, H. *Los Estados Unidos y América Latina, 1930–1965*. B.A., 1966.

876. Shepard, W. R. "Uncle Sam, Imperialist," *NR* 49 (Jan. 29, 1936) 330–332.

877. Wilson, J. H. *American Business and Foreign Policy, 1920–1933*. Lexington, Ky., 1971.

VIII-A   cross references:
   a)   See also items 853, 567a.
   b)   In the Trask, Meyer, and Trask *Bibliography* see items 158, 1555, 1733, 1736, 1757, 1760, 2894, 2947, 3178–3209a, 5411.

B. LATIN AMERICA AND THE LEAGUE OF NATIONS

878. Carrasco, J. *Bolivia ante la Liga de las Naciones*. La Paz, 1919.

   The author was a Bolivian delegate to the League of Nations.

879. Cecil, R. *A Great Experiment*. N.Y., 1941.

880. Downing, M. L. "Hugh R. Wilson and American Relations with the League of Nations, 1927–1937," U. of Okla. Diss., 1970.

881. Escala, V. H. *El Congreso de Panamá y la Sociedad de las Naciones*. Rome, 1924.

882. LN. *Dispute between Bolivia and Paraguay: Appeal of the Bolivian Government under Article 15 of the Covenant*. Geneva, 1935.

883. ———. *Dispute between Bolivia and Paraguay: Records of the Special Session of the Assembly*. Geneva, 1934.

884. ———. *Dispute between Bolivia and Paraguay: Statement of the Paraguayan Case Submitted to the Assembly by the Paraguayan Government, September 6, 1934*. Geneva, 1934.

885. ———. Official Journal. *Dispute between Bolivia and Paraguay: Appeal of the Bolivian Government under Article 15 of the Covenant*. Geneva, 1934.

886. ———. *L'Oeuvre de la Société des Nations dans ses Rapports avec le Programme de la Septieme Conférence Internationale Americaine*. Geneva, 1933.

887. Martínez Legorreta, O. "La Actuación de México en la Liga de las Naciones: El Caso de España," UNAM Diss., 1965.

888. Morales, E. *El Canal de Panamá y la Liga de las Naciones*. Panama, 1918.

889. Ostrower, G. B. "The United States, the League of Nations, and Collective Security," U. of Rochester Diss., 1970.

890. Paraguay. Ministerio de Relaciones Exteriores y Culto. *Exposición de la Causa del Paraguay en su Conflicto con Bolivia*. Asunción, 1934.

The Paraguayan case as presented to the League of Nations.

891. Schiffer, W. *Repertoire of Questions of General International Law before the League of Nations, 1920–1940*. Geneva, 1942.

892. Soares, J. C. de Macedo. *Le Bresil et la Société des Nations*. Paris, 1927.

893. Stone, R. *The Irreconcilables: The Fight against the League of Nations*. Lexington, Ky., 1970.

894. Torriente, C. de la. *Actividades de la Liga de las Naciones*. Havana, 1923.

895. Wright, Q. *Mandates under the League of Nations*. Chicago, 1930.

VIII-B   cross references: In the Trask, Meyer, and Trask Bibliography see items 3210–3242.

C. THE MONROE DOCTRINE AND THE CHANGING IMAGE

896. Cresson, W. P. *Diplomatic Portraits: Europe and the Monroe Doctrine*. Boston, 1923.

Views of European diplomats on the Monroe Doctrine.

897. García Calderón, F. "A Latin American Criticism of the Monroe Doctrine," *CH* 29 (Jan., 1929) 548–553.

VIII-C   cross references: In the Trask, Meyer, and Trask Bibliography see items 2980, 3123, 3219b, 3221, 3223, 3226a, 3240, 3243–3260.

D. THE HARDING, COOLIDGE, AND HOOVER ADMINISTRATIONS: BACKGROUND TO THE GOOD NEIGHBOR POLICY, 1921–1933

898. Cleaver, C. G. "Frank B. Kellogg: Attitudes and Assumptions Influencing His Foreign Policy Decisions," U. of Minn. Diss., 1956.

899. Conwell, M. J. "Opinion-Makers and Foreign Policy: The Concept of America's Role in World Affairs, the 1920's," Mich. State U. Diss., 1977.

900. Ellis, L. E. *Republican Foreign Policy, 1921-1933*. New Brunswick, N.J., 1968.

Relations with Latin America treated in two chapters.

901. Grieb, K. J. *The Latin American Policy of Warren G. Harding*. Fort Worth, Tex., 1976.

Argues that Harding initiated a more positive Latin American policy.

902. Lowerre, N. K. J. "Warren G. Harding and American Foreign Affairs, 1915–1923," Stanford U. Diss., 1968.

903. McCoy, D. R. *Calvin Coolidge: The Quiet President*. N.Y., 1967.

904. Murray, R. K. *The Harding Era: Warren G. Harding and His Administration*. Minneapolis, Minn., 1969.

905. Robinson, E. E., and V. D. Bornet. *Herbert Hoover: President of the United States*. Stanford, Calif., 1975.

906. Schultejann, Sister M. A. "Henry L. Stimson's Latin American Policy, 1929–1933," Georgetown U. Diss., 1967.

907. Schwartz, J. A. *The Interregnum of Despair: Hoover, Congress, and the Depression*. Urbana, Ill., 1970.

908. Sessions, G. A. "The Clark Memorandum Myth," *TA* 34 (July, 1977) 40–58.

908a. Wilson, J. F. *Herbert Hoover: Forgotten Progressive*. Boston, 1975.

908b. Woodward, N. E. "Postwar Reconstruction and International Order: A Study of the Diplomacy of Charles Evans Hughes, 1921–1925," U. of Wis. Diss., 1970.

VIII-D   cross references:
a) For works on the Santiago Conference of 1923, see items 1826–1828; for the Havana Conference of 1928, see items 1829–1831.
b) See also items 2213, 2225, 2602, 2754, 3405.
c) In the Trask, Meyer, and Trask *Bibliography* see items 1760, 3246, 3258, 3261–3329b, 4945–4975b, 5136–5149.

E. FRANKLIN D. ROOSEVELT AND THE GOOD NEIGHBOR POLICY, 1933–1938

909. Beck, R. T. "Cordell Hull and Latin

America, 1933–1939," Temple U. Diss., 1977.

910.   Capestany Abreu, M. *Roosevelt Ciudadano Eminente de América*. Havana, 1941.

911.   Castillo Torre, J. *La Nueva Diplomacia de América*. Mexico, 1936.

912.   Cooper, W. C. "New Light on the Good Neighbor Policy," U. of Pa. Diss., 1972.

913.   Flynn, G. Q. *Roosevelt and Romanism: Catholics and American Diplomacy, 1937–1945*. Westport, Conn., 1976.

914.   Givens, L. D. "Official United States' Attitudes toward Latin American Military Regimes, 1933–1960," U. of Calif. Davis Diss., 1970.

915.   Graff, F. "The Strategy of Involvement: A Diplomatic Biography of Sumner Welles, 1933–1943," U. of Mich. Diss., 1971.

916.   Hull, C. *The Memoirs of Cordell Hull*. 2 vols., N.Y., 1948.

917.   Jablon, H. "Cordell Hull, the State Department, and Foreign Policy of the First Roosevelt Administration, 1933–1935," Rutgers U. Diss., 1967.

917a. Liggio, L. P. and J. J. Martin (eds.). *Watershed of Empire: Essays on New Deal Foreign Policy*. Colorado Springs, Colo., 1976.
       Critical of F.D.R.'s foreign policy.

918.   Millington, T. M. "The Latin American Diplomacy of Sumner Welles," Johns Hopkins U. Diss., 1966.

919.   Nixon, E. B. (ed.). *Franklin D. Roosevelt and Foreign Affairs*. 3 vols., Cambridge, Mass., 1969.
       Selected documents.

920.   Zamora y López, J. C. *The New Deal*. Havana, 1937.

VIII-E   cross references:
  a)   For accounts of the seventh Inter-American Conference at Montevideo (1933), see items 1832–1835.

  b)   For the eighth Inter-American Conference at Lima (1938), see items 1836–1838.

  c)   For the special Conference on the Maintenance of Peace at Buenos Aires (1936), see items 1850–1853.

  d)   See also items 2597, 2662, 2665, 2669, 2674, 2864, 2928, 2936, 3107, 3404.

  e)   In the Trask, Meyer, and Trask *Bibliography* see items 1757, 3073b, 3330–3402, 3450, 3454, 3483, 3814, 4976–5063, 7598, 7615, 9120, 10163.

F. INTER-AMERICAN TRADE AND COMMERCE, 1921–1938

921.   Adams, F. C. *Economic Diplomacy: The Export-Import Bank and American Foreign Policy, 1934–1939*. Columbia, Mo., 1976.

922.   Berglund, A. "The Reciprocal Trade Agreement Act of 1934," *AER* 25 (Sept., 1935) 411–425.

922a. Elston, J. M. "Multinational Corporations and American Foreign Policy in the Late 1930's," U. of Mich. Diss., 1976.

923.   Gardner, L. C. *Economic Aspects of New Deal Diplomacy*. Madison, Wis., 1964.

924.   Stewart, D. *Trade and Hemisphere: The Good Neighbor Policy and Reciprocal Trade*. Columbia, Mo., 1975.
       Revisionist view contending that economic policies of the Roosevelt administration were simply a guise for imperialism.

VIII-F   cross references:
  a)   See also items 2657, 2671, 2860, 2931, 2933, 2985a.

  b)   In the Trask, Meyer, and Trask *Bibliography* see items 3334a, 3403–3433.

Chapter IX   Latin America and World War II

A. GENERAL WORKS AND SPECIAL STUDIES

925. Buchanan, A. R. (ed.). *The United States and World War II: Military and Diplomatic Documents*. Columbia, S.C., 1972.

926. Fernández Larraín, S. *La Verdad en el Caso Español: Contestación al Ministro de RR. EE*. Santiago, 1947.
     Treats Latin American relations with Spain during World War II.

927. Fox, A. B. *The Power of Small States: Diplomacy in World War II*. Chicago, 1959.

928. Green, D. E. "Security and Development: The United States' Approach to Latin America, 1940–1948," Cornell U. Diss., 1967.

928a. Grishin, Y. "El Fracaso de los Planes Hitlerianos en América Latina," *AL* 2 (1975) 45–56.

929. Hines, C. W. "United States Diplomacy in the Caribbean during World War II," U. of Tex. Diss., 1968.

930. Leigh, M. *Mobilizing Consent: Public Opinion and American Foreign Policy, 1937–1947*. Westport, Conn., 1976.

931. McCann, F. D. "Aviation Diplomacy: The United States and Brazil, 1939–1941," *IEA* 21 (Spring, 1968) 33–50.

932. Nálevka, V. "El Consorcio de Bata en América Latina durante la Segunda Guerra Mundial," *IAP* 5 (1971) 183–191.
     Bata was a Czech citizen in Latin America who cooperated with the Germans during the war.

933. ———. "Restablecimientos de Relaciones Diplomáticas entre el Gobierno Checosloslovako en el Exilio y los Países de América Latina," *IAP* 2 (1968) 93–113.

934. Simonson, W. N. "Nazi Infiltration in South America, 1933–1945," Tufts U. Diss., 1964.

IX-A   *cross references:*
a) For general works on the response of the Inter-American system to World War II, see items 1750–1751.
b) See also items 875, 914, 915, 989.
c) In the Trask, Meyer, and Trask *Bibliography* see items 3145, 3186, 3356, 3362, 3373, 3377, 3380, 3387, 3389, 3434–3448, 3607, 5344.

B. BACKGROUND OF WORLD WAR II AND THE PERIOD OF UNITED STATES NEUTRALITY, 1937–1941

935. Baker, L. *Roosevelt and Pearl Harbor: A Great President in a Time of Crisis*. N.Y., 1970.

936. Fehrenbach, T. R. *F.D.R.'s Undeclared War, 1939–1941*. N.Y., 1967.

937. Frye, A. *Nazi Germany and the American Hemisphere, 1933–1941*. New Haven, Conn., 1967.
     Emphasizes Nazi propaganda activities in the hemisphere.

938. Hodge, R. W. "Lining Up Latin America: The United States Attempts to Bring About Hemisphere Solidarity, 1939–1941," Mich. State U. Diss., 1968.

939. Nálevka, V. "El Acuerdo de Munich y la América Latina," *IAP* 6 (1972) 111–126.
     Argues that the fall of Czechoslovakia

helped convince Latin America to support Allied war effort.

940. Russett, B. M. *No Clear and Present Danger: A Skeptical View of the United States Entry into World War II.* N.Y., 1972.

IX-B   cross references:
a) For information concerning the First and Second Consultative Conferences at Panama (1939) and Havana (1940), see items 1855–1859.
b) In the Trask, Meyer, and Trask *Bibliography* see items 1756, 2938, 3398, 3449–3520, 3682, 3697, 5189a–5229, 10098.

C. THE PERIOD OF BELLIGERENCY, 1941–1945

941. Greenfield, K. R. *American Strategy in World War II: A Reconsideration.* Baltimore, Md., 1970.
942. Kolko, G. *The Politics of War: The World and United States Foreign Policy, 1943–1945.* N.Y., 1968.
943. Weathers, B. E., Jr. "A Study of the Methods Employed in the Acquisition of Air Bases in Latin America for the Army Armed Forces in World War II," U. of Denver Diss., 1971.

IX-C   cross references:
a) For works dealing with the Third Consultative Conference at Rio de Janeiro (1942), see items 1860–1862.
b) For works dealing with the Conference on the Problems of War and Peace at Mexico City (1945), see items 1863–1867.
c) See also item 1089.
d) In the Trask, Meyer, and Trask *Bibliography* see items 3521–3546, 5216–5255a.

D. THE MONROE DOCTRINE AND WORLD WAR II

IX-D   cross references: In the Trask, Meyer, and Trask Bibliography *see items 3547–3555.*

E. ECONOMIC RELATIONS DURING THE WAR

944. Blumenthal, M. D. "The Economic Good Neighbor: Aspects of United States Economic Policy toward Latin America in the Early 1940's as Revealed by the Activities of the Office of Inter-American Affairs," U. of Wis. Diss., 1968.
945. Fernández Guedes, J. *O Cafe Brasileiro en 1942.* Rio, 1943.
946. Guerra y Sánchez, R. "Sugar: Index of Cuban-American Cooperation," *FA* 20 (July, 1942) 743–756.
947. Gustafson, M. O. "Congress and Foreign Aid: The First Phase, UNRRA, 1943–1947," U. of Nebr. Diss., 1966.
948. Muñiz, P. E., and C. M. Cox. *Petróleo en Sudamérica: Nacionalización e Imperialismo.* B.A., 1941.
949. O'Brien, A. F. "The Politics of Dependency: A Case Study of Dependency in Chile, 1938–1945," U. of Notre Dame Diss., 1977.
    Treats U.S. copper policy in Chile during World War II.
950. USDA. Bureau of Agricultural Economics. *Sugar During the World War and in the 1939 European War.* Wash., 1940.
951. Williams, B. H. "The Coming of Economic Sanctions into American Practice," *AJIL* 37 (July, 1943) 386–396.

IX-E   cross references: In the Trask, Meyer, and Trask Bibliography *see items 3408, 3409f, 3418, 3556–3606, 3615, 3639, 3699, 3706–3708, 3801, 3817, 3835.*

F. HEMISPHERE DEFENSE

IX-F   cross references:
a) For arrangements made at the Consultative Conferences held at Panama (1939), Havana (1940), and Rio de Janeiro (1942), see items 1855–1862.
b) For information concerning the Conference on War and Peace at Mexico City (1945), see items 1863–1867.
c) See also item 1189.

d) In the Trask, Meyer, and Trask *Bibliography* see items 3557, 3559, 3569, 3599, 3601, 3607–3627, 3667, 5189a–5255a.

G. MEXICO AND WORLD WAR II

952. Cárdenas de la Peña, E. *Gesta en el Golfo: La Segunda Guerra Mundial y México*. Mexico, 1966.

953. Clash, T. W. "United States–Mexican Relations, 1940–1946: A Study of U.S. Interests and Policies," State U. of N.Y. Buffalo, 1972.

954. Harrison, Donald F. "United States– Mexican Military Cooperation during World War II," Georgetown U. Diss., 1976.

955. Santoro, C. E. "United States–Mexican Relations during World War II," Syracuse U. Diss., 1967.

956. Smith, K. W. "The U.S. Cultural Crusade in Mexico, 1938–1945. A Case Study in Person-to-Person Peacemaking," U. of Calif. Berkeley Diss., 1972.

957. Stegmaier, H. I., Jr. "From Confrontation to Cooperation: The United States and Mexico, 1938–1945," U. of Mich. Diss., 1970.

957a. Volland, K. *Das Dritte Reich und Mexiko*. Bern, 1976.

IX-G   cross references:
a) See also item 2237.
b) In the Trask, Meyer, and Trask *Bibliography* see items 3627a–3646, 6293.

H. CENTRAL AMERICAN– CARIBBEAN REGION AND WORLD WAR II

958. Cooley, J. A. "The United States and the Panama Canal, 1938–1947: Policy Formulation and Implementation from Munich through the Early Years of the Cold War," O. State U. Diss., 1972.

958a. Grieb, K. J. "Guatemala and the Second World War," *IAA* 3 (1977) 377–394.

959. Martin, L., and S. Martin. "Nazi Intrigues in Central America," *AME* 53 (July, 1941) 66–73.

960. Phillips, R. H. "Cuba Goes to War," *INA* 2 (May, 1943) 22–26.

IX-H   cross references:
a) See also item 132.
b) In the Trask, Meyer, and Trask *Bibliography* see items 3647–3667.

I. SPANISH SOUTH AMERICA AND WORLD WAR II

961. Argentina. Cámara de Diputados Comisión Investigadora. *Informe Confidencial de las Actividades Nazis en la República Argentina*. B.A., 1941.

962. ————. Ministerio de Relaciones Exteriores y Culto. *Decretos sobre la Neutralidad de la República Argentina en el Estado de Guerra en Europa*. B.A., 1939.

963. Francis, M. J. *The Limits of Hegemony: United States Relations with Argentina and Chile during World War II*. Notre Dame, Ind., 1977.

963a. ————. "The United States and Chile during the Second World War: The Diplomacy of Misunderstanding," *JLAS* 9 (May, 1977) 91–113.

964. Matsushita, H. "A Historical View of Argentine Neutrality during World War II," *DEC* 11 (Sept., 1973) 272–296.

965. Perú. Ministerio de Relaciones Exteriores. *Medidas de Control sobre Actividades Comerciales y Financieras de Nacionales de Países de Eja Establecidas por el Gobierno del Perú durante el Actual Conflicto Mundial*. Lima, 1943.

966. Pyle, N. R. "A Study of the United States' Propaganda Efforts and Pro-Allied Sentiments in Argentina during World War II," Georgetown U. Diss., 1968.

967. Rudgers, D. G. "Challenge to the Hemisphere: Argentina Confronts the United States, 1938–1947," George Washington U. Diss., 1972.

967a. Stemplowski, R. "Las Potencias Anglosajonas y el Neutralismo Argentina (1939–1945)," *ESTLA* 3 (1976) 129– 160.

968. Sutin, S. E. "The Impact of Nazism on the Germans of Argentina," U. of Tex. Austin Diss., 1975.

969. Tulchin, J. S. "The Argentine Proposal for Non-Belligerency, April, 1940," *JIAS* 11 (Oct., 1969) 571–604.

970. Woods, R. B. "United States Policy toward Argentina from Pearl Harbor to San Francisco," U. of Tex. Diss., 1972.

IX-I *cross references:*
a) See also items 949, 2934, 3133.

b) In the Trask, Meyer, and Trask *Bibliography* see items 3595, 3668–3708, 4746, 4848, 4861, 5229, 5234, 5248, 9484, 9764, 9804.

J. BRAZIL AND WORLD WAR II

971. Duarte, P. de Q. *O Nordeste na II Guerra Mundial: Antecedentes e Ocupação*. Rio, 1971.
   Treats defense of the northeast during the war.

971a. Hilton, S.E. "Brazilian Diplomacy and the Washington–Rio de Janeiro 'Axis' during the World War II Era," *HAHR* 59 (May, 1979) 200–229.

971b. ———. *Suástica sobre o Brasil: A História da Espionagem Alemã no Brasil, 1934–1944*. Rio, 1977.

972. McCann, F. D., Jr. "Brazil and the United States and the Coming of World War II, 1937–1942," Ind. U. Diss., 1967.

973. ———. "Vargas and the Destruction of the Brazilian Integralista and Nazi Parties," *TA* 26 (July, 1969) 15–34.

974. Moraes, J. B. M. *The Brazilian Expeditionary Force by Its Commander*. Wash., 1966.
   Trans. from the Portuguese ed.

975. Silva, H. *1942: Guerra no Continente*. Rio, 1972.
   Details Brazilian participation in the war.

976. ———. *1939: Véspera de Guerra*. Rio, 1972.
   Treats Vargas's foreign policy at the beginning of the war.

977. ———. *O Ciclo de Vargas*. Vol. XI: *1939: Véspera de Guerra*. Rio, 1972.

978. ———. *O Ciclo de Vargas*. Vol. XII: *1942:Guerra no Continente*. Rio, 1972.

979. Simões, R. Mattos Almeida. *A Presença do Brasil na 2ª Guerra Mundial: Uma Antologia*. Rio, 1966.

980. Tavares, A. de Lyra. *História da Arma de Engenharia: Capítulo da FEB*. João Pessoa, Brazil, 1966.

IX-J *cross references:*
a) See also items 931, 945, 3534.

b) In the Trask, Meyer, and Trask *Bibliography* see items 3595, 3709–3724, 4734, 10098.

Chapter X   The United States and Latin America Since World War II

A. GENERAL WORKS AND SPECIAL STUDIES

981. Agee, P. *Inside the Company: CIA Diary*. Harmondworth, Eng., 1975.

982. ———. *Latin America: More Cloak Than Dagger*. London, 1974.

   Revelations about CIA operations in Latin America by a former agent.

983. Alba, V. *Nationalists without Nations: The Oligarchy versus the People in Latin America*. N.Y., 1969.

984. Aron, R. *The Imperial Republic, the United States and the World, 1945–1973*. Englewood Cliffs, N.J., 1974.

985. Astiz, C. *As Eleições Norteamericanas e seus Reflexos sobre a Política Exterior para a América Latina*. Brasília, 1972.

   A 37-page pamphlet on the presidential elections.

986. Bacon, R. C. "United States Policy toward Latin American Dictators," U.S.C. Diss., 1959.

987. Baker, R. K. "Military Intervention and Status Deprivation in Post-War Latin America," U. of Pa. Diss., 1966.

   Argues that intervention is likely to occur when traditional privileges are curtailed.

988. Betancourt, R. *The Democratic Revolution in Latin America*. Storrs, Conn., 1965.

   A Brien McManon lecture delivered by the president of Venezuela at the U. of Conn.

989. Bierck, H. A. *The United States and Latin America, 1933–1968*. London, 1969.

990. Bode, K. A. "An Aspect of United States Policy in Latin America: The Latin American Diplomats' View," *PSQ* 85 (1970) 471–491.

991. ———. "Latin American Diplomats in Washington, D.C.: Backgrounds and Attitudes," U. of N.C. Diss., 1967.

992. Bohlen, C. E. *The Transformation of American Foreign Policy*. N.Y., 1969.

993. Bosch, J. *Pentagonism: A Substitute for Imperialism*. N.Y., 1968.

   By the former president of the Dominican Republic.

994. Braden, S. *Diplomats and Demagogues: The Memoirs of Spruille Braden*. New Rochelle, N.Y., 1971.

   The author's varied Latin American career found him as chairman of the U.S. delegation to the Chaco Peace Conference, ambassador to Colombia, Cuba, and Argentina, and Assistant Secretary of State for Latin American Affairs.

995. Bradford, C. A. *Forces for Change in Latin America: U.S. Policy Implications*. Wash., 1971.

   Treats both political and economic policy.

996. Brandon, H. *The Retreat of American Power*. N.Y., 1973.

997. Bronheim, D. "Latin America Diversity and United States Foreign Policy," *PAPS* 30 (1972) 167–176.

998. Brown, S. *The Faces of Power: Constancy and Change in the U.S. Foreign Policy from Truman to Johnson*. N.Y., 1968.

999. Chalmers, D. A. (ed.). *Changing Latin America: New Interpretations of Its Politics and Society*. N.Y., 1972.

   Proceedings of a Columbia U. symposium held in 1972.

1000. Ciria, A. *América Latina: Contribuciones al Estudio de su Crisis.* Caracas, 1968.
Broadly ranging essays.

1001. Commission on United States–Latin American Relations. *The Americas in a Changing World: A Report of the Commission on United States–Latin American Relations.* N.Y., 1975.

1002. Cotler, J., and R. R. Fagen (eds.). *Latin America and the United States: The Changing Political Realities.* Stanford, Calif., 1974.
Papers prepared for the conference of the Joint Committee on Latin American Studies of the Social Science Research Council and the American Council of Learned Societies. Sp. ed., B.A., 1974.

1003. Cuevas Mardones, G. *La C.I.A. Sin Máscara.* B.A., 1976.

1004. Davis, H. E., and L. C. Wilson. *Latin American Foreign Policies: An Analysis.* Baltimore, Md., 1975.

1005. ———, *et al. Revolutionaries, Traditionalists, and Dictators in Latin America.* N.Y., 1973.
A series of biographical sketches of Latin American leaders.

1006. Day, L. C. "United States Policy toward Pan-Americanism: A Decade of Shifting Emphasis, 1949–1959," U. of Pittsburgh Diss., 1965.

1007. Dimitrov, T. *Latinska Amerika Protiv Imperializma na SAST.* Sofia, Bulgaria, 1962.
Translated title: "Latin America versus U.S. Imperialism."

1008. Divine, R. A. *Foreign Policy and U.S. Presidential Elections.* 2 vols., N.Y., 1974.
First vol. covers 1940 to 1948; second vol. covers 1952 to 1960.

1009. ———. *Since 1945: Politics and Diplomacy in Recent American History.* N.Y., 1975.

1010. Dos Santos, T. *La Crisis Norteamericana y América Latina.* Bogotá, 1972.

1010a. Douglas, W. O. *Holocaust or Hemispheric Co-op: Cross Currents in Latin America.* N.Y., 1971.

1011. Einaudi, L. R. (ed.). *Beyond Cuba: Latin America Takes Charge of Its Future.* N.Y., 1974.
The volume was prepared for USDS.

1012. Fontaine, R. W., and J. D. Theberge (eds.). *Latin America's New Internationalism: The End of Hemispheric Isolation.* N.Y., 1976.

1013. Franco, P. *La Influencia de las Estados Unidos en América Latina.* Montevideo, 1967.

1014. Furtado, C. "U.S. Hegemony and the Future of Latin America," *WT* 22 (Sept., 1966) 375–385.

1015. Gil, F. "The Future of United States–Latin American Relations," *SECOLAS* 7 (Mar., 1976) 5–19.

1016. Goldhamer, H. *The Foreign Powers in Latin America.* Princeton, N.J., 1972.

1017. Gott, R. "Guevara, Debray and the CIA," *N* 205 (Nov., 1967) 521–530.

1018. Graziani, G. *América Latina: Imperialismo y Subdesarrollo.* Mexico, 1971.

1019. Greene, F. *El Enemigo: Lo que Todo Latinoamericano Debe Saber sobre el Imperialismo.* Mexico, 1973.
Concentrates on U.S. imperialism.

1020. Grieb, K. J. "Awakening Giants: Latin America Enters the World Arena," *NDQ* 15 (Spring, 1977) 73–83.

1021. Gurtuv, M. *The United States against the Third World: Antinationalism and Intervention.* N.Y., 1974.

1022. Hellman, R. G., and H. J. Rosenbaum (eds.). *Latin America: The Search for a New International Role.* N.Y., 1975.
Treats Latin American foreign policy in the 1970s.

1023. Herz, J. H. *International Politics in the Atomic Age.* N.Y., 1959.

1024. Hoffman, R. N. "Latin American Diplomacy: The Role of the Assistant Secretary of State, 1957–1969," Syracuse U. Diss., 1969.

1025. Horowitz, I. L. (ed.). *Latin American Radicalism.* N.Y., 1969.

1026. Ianni, O. *Imperialismo na América Latina.* Rio, 1972.
Demonstrates how the United States intervenes directly and indirectly in Latin America.

1027. ———. *Sociología del Imperialismo.* Mexico, 1974.

1028. Johnson, J. J. "Foreign Factors in Dictatorship in Latin America," *PHR* 20 (May, 1951) 127–141.

1029. ———. "The United States and the

Latin American Left Wings," *YR* 56 (Mar., 1967) 322–335.

1030. Julien, C. *El Imperio Norteamericano*. Havana, 1970.

1031. Jungbauer, R. *Latin America: A Survey of Post-War Development, 1945–1970*. Prague, Czechoslovakia, 1972.

1032. Kennan, G. F. *The Cloud of Danger: Current Realities of American Foreign Policy*. Boston, 1977.

Contains one section on Latin America emphasizing Cuba and the Panama Canal.

1033. Kim, C.-T. "Nammi-ui Hyonse-wa Migug-ui Chongch' aek," *SIN* 1 (Nov., 1962) 159–166.

Translated title: "The Present Condition of South America and the Policy of the United States."

1034. Kolko, G., and J. Kolko. *The Limits of Power*. N.Y., 1972.

1034a. Krieger Vasena, A., and J. Pasos. *Latin America: A Broader World Role*. London, 1973.

1035. Laredo, I. M. *Problemática de la Situación de Conflictos Intrabloques*. B.A., 1970.

Treats postwar controversies in Guatemala, Cuba, and the Dominican Republic.

1036. Lodge, G. C. *Engines of Change: United States Interests and Revolution in Latin America*. N.Y., 1970.

Contains a series of policy recommendations for government and the private sector.

1037. López Silveira, J. J. *Imperialismo Yanqui 1961 en América Latina*. Montevideo, 1962.

Published by a Fidelista group on the eve of the Punta del Este Conference.

1038. Mañach, J. *Frontiers in the Americas: A Global Perspective*. N.Y., 1975.

A series of lectures delivered at the U. of Puerto Rico in 1971 and originally published in Sp.

1039. Mann, T. C. "The Democratic Ideal in the Latin American Policy of the United States," *USDSB* 43 (Nov., 1960) 811–814.

1040. Marchetti, V., and J. D. Marks. *The CIA and the Cult of Intelligence*. N.Y., 1974.

1041. Movimiento Argentino Antimperialista de Solidaridad Latinoamericana. *La CIA,* ¿Qués Es? ¿Qué Hace en América Latina? B.A., 1974.

1042. Oliver, C. "Foreign and Human Relations with Latin America," *FA* 47 (Apr., 1969) 520–531.

1043. Olson, G. L. *U.S. Foreign Policy and the Third World Peasant: Land Reform in Asia and Latin America*. N.Y., 1974.

1043a. Pollock, J. C. "An Anthropological Approach to Mass Communication Research: The U.S. Press and Political Change in Latin America," *LARR* 13 (Spring, 1973) 158–172.

1044. Ramírez Necochea, H. *Los Estados Unidos y América Latina (1930–1965)*. Santiago, 1964.

Argues that the Alliance for Progress is a disguise for Dollar Diplomacy.

1045. Ramírez Novoa, E. *La Política Yanqui en América Latina*. 2 vols., Lima, 1962–1963.

1046. Renner, R. R. (ed.). *Universities in Transition: The U.S. Presence in Latin American Higher Education*. Gainesville, Fla., 1973.

1047. Rositzke, H. *The CIA's Secret Operations*. N.Y., 1977.

1048. Sampaio, N. de S. "Latin America and Neutralism," *AAAPSS* 362 (Nov., 1965) 62–70.

1049. Schneider, R. M. "The U.S. in Latin America," *CH* 48 (Jan., 1965) 1–8, 50.

1050. Scornik, F. "La Política de los Estados Unidos Hacia el Sector Agropecuario Latinoamericano," *DFA* 6 (1975) 31–52.

1051. Selser, G. *La CIA: Métodos, Logros y Pifias del Espionaje de Dulles a Raborn*. B.A., 1967.

1051a. Slater, J. "The United States and Latin America: The New Radical Orthodoxy," *FDCC* 25 (July, 1977) 747–762.

1052. Stanciu, A. "America Latina se Opune Imperialismului Yankeu," *PROBIN* 9 (1958) 47–54.

Translated title: "Latin America Opposes Yankee Imperialism."

1053. Stebbins, R. P. *The United States in World Affairs, 1967*. N.Y., 1968.

Published for the Council on Foreign Relations. Chapter 8 treats United States–Latin American relations.

1054. Suslow, L. A. "Democracy in Latin America–U.S. Plan," *SSC* 26 (Jan., 1951) 5–14.

1055. Szymanski, A. "Las Fundaciones Internacionales y América Latina," *RMS* 35 (Oct.–Dec., 1973) 801–817.

Argues that in spite of carefully articulated goals, the aim of the Ford and Rockefeller foundations is to thwart development in Latin America.

1056. Theberge, J. D. (ed.). *Soviet Seapower in the Caribbean: Political and Strategic Implications*. N.Y., 1972.

1057. Tucker, R. W. *The Radical Left and American Foreign Policy*. Baltimore, Md., 1971.

1058. Vasena, A. K., and J. Pazos. *Latin America: A Broader World Role*. Totowa, N.J., 1973.

1059. Wagner, R. H. *United States Policy toward Latin America*. Stanford, Calif., 1970.

Studies the domestic and foreign considerations which influence Latin American policy of the United States.

1060. West, R. *The Gringo in Latin America*. London, 1967.

Very critical of U.S. business community and diplomatic corps in Latin America.

X-A   cross references:
  a)   For post–World War II consultative conferences, see items 1868–1910.
  b)   For the ninth Inter-American Conference at Bogotá (1948), see items 1839–1842.
  c)   For the tenth Inter-American Conference at Caracas (1954), see items 1843–1848.
  d)   See also items 467, 551, 554, 569, 872, 875, 1400, 3244.
  e)   In the Trask, Meyer, and Trask *Bibliography* see items 3186, 3446, 3725–3790, 5064–5127a, 5256–5312, 5441.

B. EARLY POSTWAR PROJECTIONS

1061. Codovilla, V. *¿Será América Latina Colonia Yanqui?* B.A., 1947.

1062. Ferrero, R. A. *Perspectivas Económicas de la Post-Guerra*. Lima, 1943.

1063. Haya de la Torre, V. R. *Y Después de la Guerra Que?* Lima, 1946.

1064. Hudicourt, P. L. *Problémes d'Aprés Guerre*. Port-au-Prince, 1943.

1065. Nieves Ayala, A. *El Perú y la Inmigración de Post-guerra*. Lima, 1940.

1066. Sánchez Hernández, T. *México Frente a los Problemas de la Post-guerra*. Mexico, 1944.
A 17-page pamphlet.

X-B   cross references: In the Trask, Meyer, and Trask Bibliography *see items 3791–3838, 4159, 4774, 5222, 5255, 5478, 6343, 6349, 7985, 9770, 10136.*

C. THE TRUMAN AND EISENHOWER ADMINISTRATIONS, 1945–1961

1067. Acheson, D. *Present at the Creation: My Years in the State Department*. N.Y., 1969.
Memoirs of Truman's Secretary of State.

1068. ———. *Sketches from Life of Men I Have Known*. N.Y., 1961.

1069. Ádám, G. "A Truman-Elv Latin-amerikában," *GAZ* 2 (1947) 529–536.
Translated title: "The Truman Doctrine in Latin America."

1070. Alexander, C. C. *Holding the Line: The Eisenhower Era, 1952–1961*. Bloomington, Ind., 1975.

1071. Bernstein, B. J. (ed.). *Politics and Policies of the Truman Administration*. Chicago, 1970.

1072. ———, and A. J. Matusow (eds.). *The Truman Administration: A Documentary History*. N.Y., 1966.

1073. Branyan, R. L., and L. H. Larsen. *The Eisenhower Administration, 1953–1961: A Documentary History*. N.Y., 1971.

1074. Cochran, B. *Harry Truman and the Crisis Presidency*. N.Y., 1973.

1075. DiBacco, T. V. "Return to Dollar Diplomacy? American Business Reaction to the Eisenhower Foreign Aid Program, 1953–1961," American U. Diss., 1965.

1076. Freidell, T. D. "Truman's Point Four: Legislative Enactment and Development in Latin America," U. of Mo. Diss., 1965.

1077. Gerson, L. L. *John Foster Dulles*. N.Y., 1968.
A sympathetic biography of Eisenhower's Secretary of State.

1078. Guhin, M. *John Foster Dulles: A Statesman and His Times*. N.Y., 1972.

Eschews the moral issues of the period and concentrates on Dulles's diplomatic abilities.

1079. Hamby, A. L. *Beyond the New Deal: Harry S. Truman and American Liberalism*. N.Y., 1973.

1080. Harper, A. D. *The Politics of Loyalty: The White House and the Communist Issue, 1946–1952*. Westport, Conn., 1969.

1081. Hoopes, T. *The Devil and John Foster Dulles*. Boston, 1973.

Holds Dulles responsible for most of the Cold War policy of the United States.

1082. Larson, A. *Eisenhower: The President Nobody Knows*. N.Y., 1968.

1083. McLellan, D. S. *Dean Acheson: The State Department Years*. N.Y., 1976.

Secretary of State, 1949–1953.

1084. Noble, G. B. *Christian A. Herter*. N.Y., 1970.

Became Secretary of State on Dulles's illness in 1959.

1085. Parmet, H. S. *Eisenhower and the American Crusades*. N.Y., 1972.

1086. Paterson, T. G. (ed.). *Cold War Critics: Alternatives to American Foreign Policy in the Truman Years*. Chicago, 1971.

1087. Rovere, R. H. *Affairs of State: The Eisenhower Years*. N.Y., 1956.

1088. Smith, G. *Dean Acheson*. N.Y., 1972.

Secretary of State, 1949–1953.

1089. Tillapaugh, J. C. "From War to Cold War: U.S. Policies toward Latin America, 1943–1948," Northwestern U. Diss., 1973.

1089a. Trask, R. R. "George F. Kennan's Report on Latin America (1950)," *DH* 2 (Summer, 1978) 307–312.

1090. USCS. Committee on Foreign Relations. Subcommittee on American Republics Affairs. *United States–Latin American Relations: Compilation of Studies*. (88th Cong., 2d Sess.). Wash., 1960.

1091. USDS. *Foreign Relations of the United States. Diplomatic Paper, 1945*. Vol. IX: *The American Republics*. Wash., 1969.

1092. ———. *Foreign Relations of the United States, 1946*. Vol. XI: *The American Republics*. Wash., 1969.

1093. ———. *Foreign Relations of the United States, 1947*. Vol. III: *The American Republics*. Wash., 1972.

1094. ———. *Foreign Relations of the United States, 1948*. Vol. IX: *The Western Hemisphere*. Wash., 1972.

1095. ———. *Foreign Relations of the United States, 1949*. Vol. II: *The United Nations: The Western Hemisphere*. Wash., 1975.

1096. Walton, R. J. *Henry Wallace, Harry Truman and the Cold War*. N.Y., 1976.

X-C   *cross references:*

a) For various Inter-American conferences, consult items 1839–1848 and 1863–1876.

b) See also items 3109, 3304.

c) In the Trask, Meyer, and Trask *Bibliography* see items 3501, 3839–3921, 3972, 4646, 5064–5127a, 5230–5286b, 5395, 5410, 9814.

D. THE KENNEDY AND JOHNSON ADMINISTRATIONS, 1961–1968

1096a. Brauer, C. M. *John F. Kennedy and the Second Reconstruction*. N.Y., 1977.

1097. Cochrane, J. D. "Reconocimiento de Gobiernos Inconstitucionales: La Política de la Administración Johnson Hacia América Latina," *FI* 11 (1971) 481–489.

1098. Díaz Contini, M. "Política Exterior de Estados Unidos Hacia América Latina," *CDI* 9 (1968) 1–33.

1099. Duane, E. A. "Congress and Inter American Relations, 1961–1965," U. of Pa. Diss., 1969.

1099a. Fairlie, H. *The Kennedy Promise: The Politics of Expectation*. N.Y., 1973.

1100. Fitzsimons, L. *The Kennedy Doctrine*. N.Y., 1972.

Sees Kennedy's foreign policies, including the Cuban missile crisis, as an intensification of the Cold War.

1101. Forte, D. F. "The Policies and Principles of Dean Rusk," U. of Toronto Diss., 1974.

Secretary of State under Kennedy and Johnson.

1102. Franco, P. *La Influencia de los Estados Unidos en América Latina*. Montevideo, 1967.

1103. Geyelin, P. L. *Lyndon B. Johnson and the World*. N.Y., 1969.

1104. Goldman, E. F. *The Tragedy of Lyndon Johnson*. N.Y., 1969.

1105. Halberstam, D. *The Best and the Brightest*
N.Y., 1972.
Treats the Kennedy administration.

1106. Heath, J. F. *Decade of Disillusionment: Th
Kennedy Years*. Bloomington, Ind.,
1975.

1107. Hill, R. C. "U.S. Policy toward Latin
America," *OR* 10 (1966) 390–407.

1108. Johnson, L. B. *The Vantage Point: Perspectives of the Presidency, 1963–1969*. N.Y.,
1971.

1109. Kaufmann, W. W. *The McNamara Strategy*. N.Y., 1964.

1110. Kearns, D. *Lyndon Johnson and the American Dream*. N.Y., 1976.

1111. Lichtenstein, N., and E. W. Schoene-
baum (eds.). *Political Profiles: The Johnson
Years*. N.Y., 1976.

1112. ——— and ——— (eds.) *Political Profiles: The Kennedy Years*. N.Y., 1976.

1113. Lieuwen, E. "Neo-Militarism in Latin
America: The Kennedy Administration's
Inadequate Response," *IEA* 16 (Spring,
1963) 11–19.

1114. Linowitz, S. M. "The Nonshooting War
in Latin America," *USDSB* 58 (Apr.,
1968) 532–536.
By the U.S. representative to the OAS.

1115. Maher, T. J. "The Kennedy and Johnson
Responses to Latin American Coups
d'Etat," *WA* 131 (Oct.–Dec., 1968)
184–197.

1116. Miroff, B. *Pragmatic Illusions: The Presidential Politics of John F. Kennedy*. N.Y.,
1976.

1117. Needler, M. C. *The United States and the
Latin American Revolution*. Boston, 1972.
Emphasizes U.S. policies under Ken-
nedy and Johnson.

1118. Oliver, C. T. "Our Continuing Com-
mitment in the Home Hemisphere,"
USDSB 57 (Dec., 1967) 868–873.

1119. Paper, L. J. *The Promise and the Performance: The Leadership of John F. Kennedy*.
N.Y., 1975.

1120. Ross, D. "Urgent: A Realistic Latin
American Policy," *NR* 20 (Sept. 28,
1968) 23–26.

1121. Sidey, H. *John F. Kennedy: President*.
N.Y., 1964.

1122. Trewhitt, H. L. *McNamara*. N.Y.,
1971.
Secretary of Defense under Kennedy.

1123. Ulloa, J. *Carta a Mr. Lyndon Johnson,
Presidente de Los Estados Unidos*. Santiago,
1964.

1124. Walton, R. J. *Cold War and Counter-
revolution: The Foreign Policy of John F.
Kennedy*. N.Y., 1972.

1125. Whiteside, H. O. "Kennedy and the
Kremlin: Soviet-American Relations,
1961–1963," Stanford U. Diss., 1969.

X-D   cross references:

a) For the Eighth Consultative Conference at
Punta del Este (1962), see items 1882–
1887.

b) For works on the Alliance for Progress, see
items 1270–1298.

c) For works on the Peace Corps, see items
1299–1310.

d) See also items 2422, 2428.

e) In the Trask, Meyer, and Trask *Bibliography*
see items 3886, 3922–3942, 4096–4153,
5287–5311.

E. THE NIXON AND FORD ADMINISTRATIONS, 1968–1976

1126. Binning, W. C. "The Nixon Foreign Aid
Policy for Latin America," *IEA 25*
(Summer, 1971) 31–45.

1127. Bronheim, D. "Relations between the
United States and Latin America," *IAF*
46 (July, 1970) 501–516.
Argues that Latin America carries a
low priority.

1128. Cochrane, J. D. "Las Posiciones de
Humphrey y de Nixon Frente a América
Latina: Una Nota," *FI* 9 (Oct.–Dec.,
1968) 194–205.
Suggests that differences between the
candidates in the 1968 presidential campaign were insignificant.

1129. Evans, R., and R. D. Novak. *Nixon in the
White House: The Frustration of Power*.
N.Y., 1971.

1130. Fagen, R. R. "The 'New Dialogue' on
Latin America," *SO* 11 (Sept.–Oct.,
1974) 24–26, 28, 30.
Critical of the Kissinger policy.

1131. Graubard, S. R. *Kissinger: Portrait of a
Mind*. N.Y., 1973.
Studies Kissinger's published works.

1132. Gray, R. B. (ed.). *Latin America and the*

United States in the 1970's. Itasca, Ill., 1971.

1133. Henderson, C. P. *The Nixon Theology*. N.Y., 1972.

1134. Kissinger, H. A. "Good Partner Policy for the Americas," *SO* 11 (Sept.–Oct., 1974) 16–18, 21–22.

1135. Landau, D. *Kissinger: The Uses of Power*. Boston, 1972.

1136. Lehman, J. *The Executive, Congress and Foreign Policy: Studies of the Nixon Administration*. N.Y., 1976.

1137. Lowenthal, A. F. "The United States and Latin America: Ending the Hegemonic Presumption," *FA* 55 (Oct., 1976) 199–213.

1137a. Morris, R. *Uncertain Greatness: Henry Kissinger and American Foreign Policy*. N.Y., 1977.

1138. Nixon, R. M. *United States Foreign Policy for the 1970's: Building for Peace*. N.Y., 1971.

1139. Ojeda Gómez, M. "Hacia un Nuevo Aislacionismo de Estados Unidos? Posibles Consecuencias para América Latina," *FI* 12 (Apr.–June, 1972) 68–87.

1140. Pacheco, L. "La Filosofía Política de Kissinger y América Latina," *CA* 34 (Sept.–Oct., 1975) 7–23.

1141. Padilha, R. *O Presidente Nixon e a América Latina*. Brasília, 1969.
    A 26-page pamphlet.

1142. Peterson, G. H. "Latin America: Benign Neglect Is Not Enough," *FA* 51 (Apr., 1973) 598–607.

1143. Rockefeller, N. A. *The Rockefeller Report on the Americas: The Official Report of a United States Presidential Mission for the Western Hemisphere*. Chicago, 1969.

1144. Schilling, P. R. *El Imperio Rockefeller: América Latina; Documentos. La Estrategia Norteamericana en América Latina, de la Doctrina Monroe al Informe Rockefeller*. Montevideo, 1970.
    Strong attack on the Rockefeller report.

1145. Selser, G. *Los Cuatro Viajes de Cristóbal Rockefeller con su Informe al Presidente Nixon*. B.A., 1971.
    Very critical of the Rockefeller report.

1146. ———. *De la CECLA a la MECLA o la Diplomacia Panamericana de la Zanahoria*. B.A., 1972.

Argues that nothing much has changed in U.S.–Latin American relations except that the Nixon administration cares less about Latin America than his predecessors.

1147. Sloan, J. W. "Three Views of Latin America: President Nixon, Governor Rockefeller, and the Latin American Consensus of Viña del Mar," *OR* 14 (Winter, 1971) 934–950.

1148. USCH. Committee on International Relations. *Report of Secretary of State Kissinger on His Trip to Latin America . . . March 4, 1976*. Wash., 1976.

1149. USDS. Bureau of Public Affairs. *Secretary Kissinger Proposes New Program for the Americas*. Wash., 1974.

1150. Wills, G. *Nixon Agonistes*. Boston, 1970.

X-E cross references: 2292, 2419a, 2725, 3123, 3312.

F. HEMISPHERIC DEFENSE AND COLLECTIVE SECURITY

1511. Aliano, R. A. *American Defense Policy from Eisenhower to Kennedy: The Politics of Changing Military Requirements*. Athens, O., 1976.

1152. Baines, J. M. "U.S. Military Assistance to Latin America: An Assessment," *JIAS* 14 (1972) 469–487.

1153. Beaton, L., and J. Madday. *The Spread of Nuclear Weapons*. N.Y., 1962.

1154. Bedregal, G. *Algunos Aspectos para la Integración Defensiva de América Latina*. Caracas, 1966.

1155. Berkowitz, M., and P. G. Bock (eds.). *American National Security: A Reader in Theory and Policy*. N.Y., 1965.

1156. Bloomfield, L. P. (ed.). *International Military Force: The Question of Peacekeeping in an Armed and Disarming World*. Boston, 1964.

1157. Bobrow, D. B (ed.). *Components of Defense Policy*. Chicago, 1965.

1158. Bowett, D. *Self-Defense in International Law*. Manchester, Eng., 1958.

1159. Brown, T. A. *Statistical Indications of the Effect of Military Programs on Latin America, 1950–1965*. Santa Monica, Calif., 1969.

1160. Cocca, A. A. *Defensa Colectiva en América y Europa*. B.A., 1961.

1161. Davis, D. W. "The Inter-American Defense College: An Assessment of Its Activities," U. of Md. Diss., 1968.

1162. Deas, M. "Guerrillas in Latin America: A Perspective," *WT* 24 (Feb., 1968) 72–78.

1163. Dillon, J. W. *The Latin American Nuclear Free Zone.* Maxwell Air Force Base, Ala., 1967.

1164. Drier, J. C. "Organizing Security in the Americas," *USDSB* (May, 1954) 830–835.

1165. Edwards, D. V. *Arms Control in International Politics.* N.Y., 1969.

1166. Estep, R. *United States Military Aid to Latin America.* Maxwell Air Force Base, Ala., 1966.
   Air University documentary research study AU-206-65-AS1.

1167. Frank, L. A. *The Arms Trade in International Relations.* N.Y., 1969.

1168. Galula, D. *Counterinsurgency Warfare: Theory and Practice.* N.Y., 1964.

1169. Garrié Faget, R. *Organismos Militares Interamericanos.* B.A., 1968.

1170. Gebhardt, H. P. *Guerillas: Schicksal fur den Westen: Die Latein-Amerikanische Revolutions-Bewegung.* Stuttgart, 1961.

1171. Geller, W. E. *Defense of the Americas: Is There a Need for a Permanent Peace Keeping Force in the Organization of American States?* Maxwell Air Force Base, Ala., 1967.

1172. Glick, E. B. "Isolating the Guerrilla: Some Latin American Examples," *OR* 12 (Fall, 1968) 876–886.

1173. ———. *The Nonmilitary Use of the Latin American Military.* Santa Monica, Calif., 1963.

1174. Guillén, A. *Desafío al Pentágono: La Guerrilla Latinoamericana.* Montevideo, 1969.

1175. Heare, G. E. *Latin American Military Expenditures, 1967–1971.* Wash., 1973.

1176. Hersch, R. "The Transfer of Modern Weapons and Expertise," *SECOLAS* 8 (Mar., 1977) 38–47.

1177. Hyde, D. *The Roots of Guerrilla Warfare: A Background Book.* Chester Springs, Pa., 1968.

1178. Hyman, E. H. "Soldiers in Politics: New Insights on Latin American Armed Forces," *PSQ* 87 (Sept., 1972) 401–418.

1179. Inter-American Defense Board. *Inter-American Military Defense Council: Proposal for the Creation of a Permanent Military Agency of the American Republics.* Wash., 1946.

1180. Jordan, A. A. "Military Assistance and National Policy," *OR* 2 (Summer, 1958) 236–253.

1181. José, J. R. *An Inter-American Peace Force within the Framework of the Organization of American States: Advantages, Impediments, Implications.* Metuchen, N.J., 1970.

1182. Kemp, G. "Rearmament in Latin America," *WT* 22 (Sept., 1967) 375–384.

1183. ———. *Some Relationships between U.S. Military Training in Latin America and Weapons Acquisition Patterns, 1959–1969.* Cambridge, Mass., 1970.

1184. Kiessler, R. E. *Guerilla und Revolution: Parteikommunismus und Partisanenstrategie in Lateinamerika.* Bonn, 1975.

1185. Lamberg, R. F. *Die Guerilla in Lateinamerika: Theorie und Praxis e. Revolutionaren Modells.* Munich, 1972.

1186. ———. "La Guerrilla Urbana: Condiciones y Perspectivas de la Segunda Ola Guerrilla," *FI* 43 (Jan.–Mar., 1971) 421–443.

1187. Lazarev, M. I. *Voennye Bazy SShA v Latinskoi Amerike.* Moscow, 1972.
   Translated title: "United States Military Bases in Latin America: An International Offensive."

1188. Lerche, C. O., Jr. "Development of Rules Relating to Peacekeeping by the Organization of American States," *ASILP* 59 (Apr., 1965) 60–66.

1189. Loftus, J. E. *Latin American Defense Expenditures, 1938–1965.* Santa Monica, Calif., 1968.

1190. Lora, G. *Las Guerrillas: La Concepción Marxista Contra el Golpismo Aventurero.* La Paz, 1963.

1190a. Loveman, B. and T. M. Davies, Jr. (eds.). *The Politics of Antipolitics: The Military in Latin America.* Lincoln, 1978.
   A selection of readings by leading military specialists.

1191. Lozada, S. M. *Las Fuerzas Armadas en la Política Hispanoamericana.* B.A., 1967.

1192. Max, A. *Guerrillas in Latein-Amerika.* Zurich, 1970.

1193. McAlister, L. N. "Changing Concepts of

the Role of the Military in Latin America," *AAAPSS* 360 (1965) 85–98.

1194. McNamara, R. S. *The Essence of Security*. N.Y., 1968.

By the Secretary of Defense under Kennedy.

1195. Mercado Jorrín, E. *La Política y la Estrategia Militar en la Guerra Contrasubversiva en América Latina*. Lima, 1967.

1196. Mercier Vega, L. *Technique du Contre-Etat: Les Guerrillas en Amérique du Sud*. Paris, 1968.

1197. Mroziewecz, R. *Armie w Ameryce Lacińskiej: Historia i Dzień Dzisiejszy*. Warsaw, Poland, 1973.

Translated title: "The Army in Latin America: History and Today."

1198. Nunn, F. M. "Effects of European Military Training in Latin America," *MAF* 39 (Feb., 1975) 1–7.

1199. Orlov, A. *Handbook of Intelligence and Guerrilla Warfare*. Ann Arbor, Mich., 1963.

1200. Osanka, F. M. (ed.). *Modern Guerrilla Warfare: Fighting Communist Guerrilla Movements, 1941–1961*. N.Y., 1962.

1201. Pancake, F. R. "Military Assistance as an Element in U.S. Foreign Policy in Latin America, 1950–1968," U. of Va. Diss., 1969.

1202. Paret, P., and J. W. Shy. *Guerrillas in the 1960's*. N.Y., 1962.

1203. Porter, R. W. "Latin America: The Military Assistance Program," *VS* 34 (July, 1968) 573–576.

1204. Powell, J. D. "Military Assistance and Militarism in Latin America," *WPQ* 18 (June, 1965) 382–392.

1205. Radway, L. I. *Foreign Policy and National Defense*. Glenview, Ill., 1969.

1206. Redick, J. R. *Military Potential of Latin American Nuclear Energy Programs*. Beverly Hills, Calif., 1972.

1206a. ———. "U.S. Nuclear Policy and Latin America," *OR* 22 (Spring, 1978) 161–200.

1207. Robinson, D. R. "The Treaty of Tlateloco and the United States: Latin American Nuclear Free Zone," *AJIL* 64 (Apr., 1970) 282–309.

1208. Rostow, W. W. "Guerrilla Warfare in the Underdeveloped Areas: Address,

June 28, 1961," *USDSB* 45 (Aug., 1961) 233–238.

1209. Russett, B. M. *What Price Vigilance? The Burdens of National Defense*. New Haven, Conn., 1970.

1210. Saxe-Fernández, J. *Proyecciones Hemisféricas de la Pax Americana*. Lima, 1971.

Treats U.S. relations with the Latin American military.

1210a. Schmitter, P. C. (ed.). *Military Rule in Latin America*. Beverly Hills, Calif., 1973.

1211. Silva Herzog, J. "Reflexión sobre las Guerrillas," *CA* 27 (Jan.–Feb., 1968) 7–15.

1212. Spector, S. D. "United States Attempts at Regional Security and the Extension of the Good Neighbor Policy in Latin America, 1945–1952," NYU Diss., 1970.

1213. Staney, R. A. *The Inter-American Defense Board*. Wash., 1965.

1213a. Stöttleriie, M. G. "Measuring Foreign Policy: Determinants of U.S. Military Assistance to Latin America," Rice U. Diss., 1975.

1214. Tomasek, R. D. "Defense of the Western Hemisphere: A Need for Re-examination of United States Policy," *MJPS* 3 (Nov., 1959) 374–401.

1215. Toner, R. J. "The Latin American Military," *USNIP* 94 (Nov., 1968) 65–73.

1216. Torres Molina, R. H. *La Lucha Armada en América Latina*. B.A., 1968.

1217. United States Arms Control and Disarmament Agency. *Documents on Disarmament, 1967*. Wash., 1968.

Treats the Latin American nuclear-free zone.

1218. USDS. Bureau of Public Affairs. *Arms Sales to Latin America*. Wash., 1973.

1218a. Van Cleve, J. V. "The Political Use of Military Aid: The United States and the Latin American Military, 1945–1965," U. of Calif. Irvine Diss., 1976.

1219. Veneroni, H. L. *Estados Unidos y las Fuerzas Armadas de América Latina: La Dependencia Militar*. B.A., 1973.

1220. ———. *Fuerza Militar Interamericana*. B.A., 1966.

1221. Westlake, W. R. "An Institutional Approach to Inter-American Military Relations," Tufts U. Diss., 1968.

1222. Woiroe, W. S. *Is There a Requirement for a Defense Force within the OAS?* Maxwell Air Force Base, Ala., 1967.

1223. Wolf, C. "The Political Effects of Military Programs: Some Indications from Latin America," *EDCC* 14 (Oct., 1965) 1–20.

1224. Wyckoff, T. *The Defense of Latin America: The Changing Concept.* Tempe, Ariz., 1964.

X-F   cross references:
   a) For works on the Rio Pact (1947), see items 1868–1872.
   b) For works on the ninth Inter-American Conference at Bogotá (1948) and the tenth Inter-American Conference at Caracas (1954), see items 1839–1848.
   c) For collective hemispheric action against Cuba, see items 1882–1887.
   d) See also items 1560, 2417.
   e) In the Trask, Meyer, and Trask *Bibliography* see items 3758, 3942–3974a, 3990, 4249, 4352, 4815, 4828, 5064–5127a, 5242, 5256–5312.

G. COLD WAR AND SOCIAL REVOLUTION IN LATIN AMERICA

1224a. Aronson, J. *The Press and the Cold War.* N.Y., 1970.

1225. Halle, L. J. *The Cold War as History.* N.Y., 1967.

1226. Herz, M. F. *Beginnings of the Cold War.* Bloomington, Ind., 1966.

1227. LaFeber, W. *America, Russia and the Cold War, 1945–1971.* N.Y., 1972.

1228. Langley, L. D. (ed.). *The United States, Cuba and the Cold War: American Failure or Communist Conspiracy.* Lexington, Mass., 1970.

1229. Miller, L. H., and R. W. Pruessen (eds.). *Reflections on the Cold War: A Quarter Century of American Foreign Policy.* Philadelphia, Pa., 1974.
   The selections are primarily from revisionist historians.

1230. Parkinson, F. *Latin America, the Cold War, and the World Powers, 1945–1973.* Beverly Hills, Calif., 1974.

1231. Paterson, T. G. "The Economic Cold War: American Business and Economic Foreign Policy, 1945–1950," U. of Calif. Diss., 1968.

1232. Sau Aguayo, J. *La Guerra Fría.* Santiago, 1968.

1233. Seabury, P. *The Rise and Decline of the Cold War.* N.Y., 1967.

1234. Wilson, L. C. "The Monroe Doctrine Cold War Anachronism: Cuba and the Dominican Republic," *JP* 28 (May, 1966) 322–346.

1235. Yergin, D. *Shattered Peace: The Origins of the Cold War and the National Security State.* Boston, 1977.

X-G   cross references:
   a) For the Punta del Este Conference (1962), see items 1882–1887.
   b) For the Alliance for Progress, see items 1270–1298.
   c) See also items 1593, 2946.
   d) In the Trask, Meyer, and Trask *Bibliography* see items 3758, 3764, 3787, 3975–4043, 4096–4147, 4236, 4356, 5287–5311, 6337, 6371, 8474, 8484, 8486, 8669, 9777, 10097, 10174, 10176.

H. COMMUNISM IN LATIN AMERICA

1236. Aguilar, L. E. *Marxism in Latin America.* N.Y., 1968.

1237. Alba, V. *La América Latina y los Congresos del Partido Comunista Ruso.* San José, C.R., n.d.

1238. Albertini, G. "Progresos del Comunismo en América Latina," *EYO* 2 (1963) 1–6.

1239. Alexander, R. J. "Latin America and the Communist Bloc," *CH* 44 (Feb., 1963) 73–77.

1240. ———. *Trotskyism in Latin America.* Stanford, Calif., 1973.

1241. Arico, J. *El Comunismo Latinoamericano.* B.A., 1974.

1242. Cheston, T. S., and B. Loeffke. *Aspects of Soviet Policy toward Latin America.* N.Y., 1974.

1243. Clissold, S. (ed.). *Soviet Relations with Latin America, 1918–1968: A Documentary Survey.* London, 1970.

1244. Confederación Interamericana de Defensa del Continente. *Resoluciones del Tercer Congreso contra la Infiltración Soviética en América Latina.* Lima, 1957.

1245. Dinnerstein, H. "Soviet Policy in Latin

America," *APSR* 61 (Mar., 1967) 80–90.

1246. Duncan, W. R. "Soviet Policy in Latin America Since Khruschev," *OR* 15 (Summer, 1971) 643–669.

1247. Einaudi, L. R. "Marxism in Latin America: From Aprismo to Fidelismo," Harvard U. Diss., 1967.

1248. Faleroni, A. D. "Breve Informe sobre Actividades del Comunismo en América Latina y en la República Argentina," *ESC* 9 (Jan.–Mar., 1961) 114–134.

1249. Garner, W. R. "The Sino-Soviet Ideological Struggle in Latin America," *JIAS* 10 (Apr., 1968) 244–255.

1250. Gouré, L., and M. Rothenberg. *Soviet Penetration of Latin America*. Coral Gables, Fla., 1975.

Treats all of Latin America but with heavy emphasis on Cuba and Chile.

1251. Hamburg, R. P. "The Soviet Union and Latin America, 1953–1963," U. of Wis. Diss., 1956.

1252. Herman, D. L. *The Communist Tide in Latin America: A Selected Treatment*. Austin, Tex., 1973.

Offers examples of communist activities rather than comprehensive treatment.

1253. "Intervention of International Communism in the Americas," *USDSB* 30 (Mar., 1954) 419–426.

1254. Johnson, C. *Communist China and Latin America, 1959–1967*. N.Y., 1970.

Heavy concentration on Chinese-Cuban relations.

1255. Joxe, A. *El Conflicto Chino-Soviético en América Latina*. Montevideo, 1967.

1256. Kanet, R. E. (ed.). *The Soviet Union and the Developing Nations*. Baltimore, Md., 1974.

Roger Hamburg prepared the essay on the Soviet Union and Latin America.

1257. *Komunističke Partije Latinske Amerike*. Belgrade, Yugoslavia, 1962.

Translated title: "The Communist Parties of Latin America."

1258. Oswald, J. G. (comp.). *Soviet Image of Contemporary Latin America: A Documentary History, 1960–1968*. Austin, Tex., 1970.

1259. Pope, R. R. "Soviet Foreign Policy toward Latin America," *WA* 50 (Fall, 1972) 139–170.

1260. Ramos Alva, A. *7 Tesis Equivocadas del Marxismo-Leninismo sobre Indoamérica*. Lima, 1977.

1261. Ratliff, W. E. (ed.). *Yearbook on Latin American Communist Affairs, 1971*. Stanford, Calif., 1971.

1262. Rowntree, M. E. "Spanish American Marxian Political Theory," U. of Calif. Diss., 1968.

1263. Smith, W. S. "Soviet Policy and Ideological Formulations for Latin America," *OR* 15 (Winter, 1972) 1122–1146.

1264. Staar, R. F. (ed.). *Yearbook on International Communist Affairs, 1969*. Stanford, Calif., 1970.

1265. ——— (ed.). *Yearbook on International Communist Affairs, 1973*. Stanford, Calif., 1973.

One hundred twenty pages are devoted to the Western Hemisphere.

1266. Thorton, T., and C. E. Black. *Communism and the Strategic Use of Political Violence*. Princeton, N.J., 1965.

1267. Tretiak, D. "Latin America: The Chinese Drive," *CR* 205 (Nov., 1964) 571–576.

1268. USCH. Committee on Foreign Relations. Subcommittee on Inter-American Affairs. *Soviet Naval Activities in Cuba: Hearings . . . .* (91st Cong., 2d Sess.) Wash., 1971.

1269. USCS. Judiciary Committee. *Communist Threat to the United States through the Caribbean*. (86th Cong., 2d Sess.) Wash., 1960.

X-H   *cross references:*

a) For pertinent studies on Mexican communism, see items 2390–2395.

b) For the pledge of unity against communist penetration of the hemisphere at the Fourth Consultative Conference (Washington, 1951), see items 1873–1874.

c) For the anti-communist resolution adopted at the Caracas Conference (1954), see items 1843–1848.

d) See also items 1056, 1184, 2519, 2521, 2627, 2686, 2687, 2713, 2714, 2720, 2732, 2766, 2945, 2988, 3010, 3119, 3141, 3297, 3346, 3409, 3422, 3513.

e) In the Trask, Meyer, and Trask *Bibliography* see items 3180a, 3467, 4044–4095, 4096a, 4813, 5064a, 5104a–5127a, 5270–5280, 6611–6629, 6864–6868, 6871–6874, 6876, 6879–6882, 6885,

6887, 6891, 6895–6897, 6900, 6902–
6903, 6906, 6908, 6911, 6912, 6914,
6917, 6920, 6923, 6925, 7214, 7218,
7674, 7944, 7950, 7983, 8400, 8713,
8946a, 8947, 8950a, 9004, 9008, 9012,
9167, 9168, 9181a, 9441, 9446, 9447,
9456, 9462, 9465a, 9467–9469, 9472,
9472a, 9475, 9481, 9528, 9722, 9723,
9807, 10093, 10099, 10120a, 10122,
10158.

I. THE ALLIANCE FOR PROGRESS

1270.   Agudelo Villa, H. *La Alianza para el Progreso: Esperanza y Frustración*. Bogotá, 1966.

1271.   ———. *La Revolución del Desarrollo: Orígen y Evolución de la Alianza para el Progreso*. Mexico, 1966.

1272.   Aguilar, A. *Latin America and the Alliance for Progress*. N.Y., 1966.

1273.   Alba, V. *Parásitos, Mitos y Sordomudos: Ensayo sobre la Alianza para el Progreso y el Colonialismo Latinoamericano*. Mexico, 1964.
        Published in Eng. under the title *Alliance without Allies*.

1274.   Anderson, M. I. "New Era for the Alliance: The Inter-American Committee on the Alliance for Progress," *TA* 16 (June, 1964) 1–7.

1275.   Butler, D. J. "Social Reform and Foreign Policy: A Critique of the Alliance for Progress," Harvard U. Diss., 1966.

1275a. Davidson, J. R. "The Implementation of the Political Development Goals of the Alliance for Progress," U. of Wis. Diss., 1976.

1276.   Feder, E. "Land Reform under the Alliance for Progress," *JFE* 47 (Aug., 1965) 652–668.

1277.   Grunwald, J. "The Alliance for Progress," *PAPS* 27 (May, 1964) 78–93.

1278.   Hanson, S. G. "The Alliance for Progress: The Sixth Year," *IEA* 22 (1968) 1–95.

1279.   ———. *Dollar Diplomacy Modern Style: Chapters in the Failure of the Alliance for Progress*. Wash., 1970.

1280.   ———. *Five Years of the Alliance for Progress*. Wash., 1967.
        A pessimistic analysis.

1281.   Hillabold, A. B. "The Alliance for Progress," Stanford U. Diss., 1965.

1282.   Inter-American Economic and Social Council. *La Alianza para el Progreso y las Perspectivas de Desarrollo de América Latina, 1961–1965*. Wash., 1967.

1283.   Krátký, K. *Program Spojenectvi Pro Pokrok*. Prague, Czechoslovakia, 1965.
        Translated title: "Program of the Alliance for Progress."

1284.   La Rocque, J. N. "The Alliance for Progress: A Conceptualization and Policy Critique," Ia. State U. Diss., 1964.

1285.   Latimer, P. D. "The Formation of the Alliance for Progress," Tufts U. Diss., 1966.

1286.   Levinson, J., and J. de Onís. *The Alliance That Lost Its Way: A Critical Report on the Alliance for Progress*. Chicago, 1970.

1287.   May, H. K. *Problems and Prospects of the Alliance for Progress: A Critical Examination*. N.Y., 1968.
        Views the alliance more favorably than most studies, but recognizes some of the problems.

1288.   Montenegro, A. F. da. *"Aliançā para o Progresso" à "Ação para o Progresso."* Fortaleza, Brazil, 1971.

1289.   Moreira, M. M. "A América Latina entre a Revolução e a Aliança," *CB* 6 (Nov.–Dec., 1964) 19–35.

1290.   Perloff, H. S. *Alliance for Progress: A Social Invention in the Making*. Baltimore, Md., 1969.

1291.   "Problems Facing the Alliance for Progress in the Americas," *USDSB* 45 (July, 1961) 139–144.

1292.   Réti, E. "Szövetség a Haladás Ellen: Az Egyesult Államk Uj Latinamerikai Politikójának Ellentmondásai," *TAR* 21 (1966) 62–72.
        Translated title: "Alliance against Progress: Contradictions of the U.S.A.'s New Latin American Policy."

1293.   Rogers, W. D. *The Twilight Struggle: The Alliance for Progress and the Politics of Development in Latin America*. N.Y., 1967.
        The author was deputy U.S. coordinator for the alliance.

1294.   Selser, G. *Alianza para el Progreso*. B.A., 1964.

1295. Sepúlveda, C. "Reflexiones sobre la Alianza para el Progreso." *FI* 8 (July–Sept., 1967) 68–79.

1296. Sommerfeld, R. M. *Tax Reform and the Alliance for Progress*. Austin, Tex., 1966.

1297. Ubertalli, R. *Alianza contra el Progreso*. B.A., 1974.

1298. USCS. Committee on Foreign Relations. *Survey of the Alliance for Progress*. Wash., 1968.

X-I cross references:

a) For the planning of the Alliance for Progress at the Punta del Este Conference, see items 1882–1887.

b) See also items 3097, 3118, 3514.

c) In the Trask, Meyer, and Trask *Bibliography* see items 4096–4147, 4236, 4282, 4360, 5287–5311, 6352, 7169, 8668, 9250, 10131.

J. THE PEACE CORPS IN LATIN AMERICA

1299. Carey, R. C. *The Peace Corps*. N.Y., 1970.

1300. Cornell University. Peru Project. *Peace Corps Program Impact in the Peruvian Andes*. Ithaca, N.Y., 1965
A report prepared by Henry Dobyns, Paul Doughty, and Allen Holmberg.

1301. Cowan, P. *The Making of an Un-American*. N.Y., 1967.
Author served in the Peace Corps in Ecuador. Account is very critical.

1302. Hoopes, R. *The Complete Peace Corps Guide*. N.Y., 1965.

1303. ———. *The Peace Corps Experience*. N.Y., 1968.

1304. Luce, I. (ed.). *Letters from the Peace Corps*. N.Y., 1964.
Selected letters from 28 Peace Corps volunteers.

1305. Stein, M. I. *Volunteers for Peace*. N.Y., 1966.
A study of the first group of volunteers to Colombia.

1306. Textor, R. B. *Cultural Frontiers in the Peace Corps*. Cambridge, Mass., 1966.
Contains sections on Peace Corps activities in Peru and Bolivia.

1307. Thomsen, M. *Living Poor: A Peace Corps Chronicle*. Seattle, Wash., 1969.
Experiences of a volunteer in rural Ecuador from 1965 to 1968.

1308. USCH. *Hearings before the Committee on Foreign Affairs, House of Representatives . . . a Bill to Amend Further the Peace Corps Act*. (89th Cong., 1st Sess.) Wash., 1965.

1309. USCS. *Hearings before the Committee on Foreign Relations . . . a Bill to Amend Further the Peace Corps Act as Amended*. (89th Cong., 1st Sess.) Wash., 1965.

1310. Windmiller, M. *The Peace Corps and Pax Americana*. Wash., 1970.

X-J cross references: In the Trask, Meyer, and Trask Bibliography see items 4148–4153.

K. LATIN AMERICA AND THE UNITED NATIONS

1311. Abellán, V. *Las N.U. y el Tercer Mundo: La Cooperación Internacional para el Desarrollo*. Barcelona, 1971.

1312. Alker, H. R., Jr. "Dimensions of Conflict in the General Assembly," *APSR* 58 (Sept., 1964) 642–657.

1313. ———, and B. M. Russett. *World Politics in the General Assembly*. New Haven, Conn., 1965.

1314. Amerikan Haberler Merkezi. *Birlesmis Devletler Istikbali Kuruyor. Unicef Latin Amerika'da*. Ankara, Turkey, 1973.
Translated title: "The United Nations Plans the Future: UNICEF in Latin America."

1315. Argentina. Ministerio de Relaciones Exteriores y Culto. *Argentina y las Actividades de las Naciones Unidas en el Campo Económico*. B.A., 1966.

1316. Arteaga, R. *México y la UNCTAD*. Mexico, 1974.

1317. Bailey, S. D. *The General Assembly of the United Nations, a Study of Procedure and Practice*. Rev. ed., N.Y., 1964.

1318. Ball, M. M. "Bloc Voting in the General Assembly," *IO* 5 (Feb., 1951) 3–31.

1319. Belaúnde, V. A. *20 Años de Naciones Unidas*. Madrid, 1966.
The author, president of the 14th General Assembly, stresses the Latin American role in the UN.

1320. Bohórquez Ramírez, R. *La Conferencia de San Francisco*. Potosí, Bolivia, 1946.

1321. Campbell, T. M. *Masquerade Peace: America's U.N. Policy, 1944–1945*. Tallahassee, Fla., 1973.

1322. Carrillo Salcedo, J. A. *La Crisis Constitucional de las Naciones Unidas*. Madrid, 1964.

1323. Cavalcanti, T. B., *et al. As Nações Unidas e os Problemas Internacionais*. Rio, 1974. A series of essays by Brazilian scholars.

1324. Claret de Voogd, L. *La Organización Mundial y la Paz*. Rosario, Arg., 1970.

1325. Clark, W. "New Forces in the United Nations," *IAF* 36 (July, 1960) 322–329.

1326. Claude, I. L. *The Changing United Nations*. N.Y., 1967.

1327. Coyle, D. C. *The United Nations and How It Works*. N.Y., 1964.

1328. Cruz, R. *La Crisis Finaciera de la NU y el Art. 19 de la Carta*. Santiago, 1967.

1329. De Camp, W. S. "The Latin American Group in a Changing United Nations, 1955–1965," Tulane U. Diss., 1971.

1330. Diniz, A. J. Almeida. "A ONU e a Realidade Internacional," *RBEP* 36 (July, 1973) 83–103.

1330a. Echeverría, L. "La Posición de México ante la Organización de las Naciones Unidas," *COM* 25 (Oct., 1975) 1076–1082.

1331. Elmandjra, M. *The United Nations System: An Analysis*. London, 1973.

1332. Esser Braun, E. "La Desnuclearización de América Latina: Discusiones en la 22ª Sesión de la Asamblea General," *FI* (Oct.–Dec., 1967) 203–215.

1332a. ———. "La XXI Sesión de la Asamblea General de las Naciones Unidos: Actitudes y Decisiones Mexicanas," *FI* 12 (Oct.–Dec., 1971) 221–228.

1333. ———. "Mexico's Attitude toward Political and Security Matters in the United Nations, 1945–1960," U. of Ky. Diss., 1963.

1334. Finkelstein, L. S. (ed.). *The United States and International Organization: The Changing Setting*. Cambridge, Mass., 1969.

1335. Fuentes-Mohr, A. "Latin American Policies in the United Nations," U. of London Diss., 1956.

1336. García Robles, A. *México en las Naciones Unidas*. 2 vols., Mexico, 1970.

Discusses the positions taken by Mexico from the founding of the UN until the date of publication.

1337. Gilbert, J. H. "The Argentine Role in the United Nations, 1946–1962," U. of Va. Diss., 1969.

1338. Gondi, O. *Las Batallas de Papel en la Casa de Cristal: ONU Los Años Decisivos*. Mexico, 1971.

1339. Goodrich, L. M. *The United Nations in a Changing World*. N.Y., 1974.

1340. ———, and A. P. Simons. *The United Nations and the Maintenance of International Peace and Security*. Wash., 1962.

1341. Green, M. del Rosario, and B. Sepúlveda Amor (eds.). *La ONU: Dilema a los 25 Años*. Mexico, 1970.

1342. Gutiérrez Gutiérrez, M. R. *La Palabra de Bolivia en la Asamblea de Naciones Unidas*. La Paz, 1971.

1343. Jacobson, H. K. "The United Nations and Colonialism: A Tentative Appraisal," *IO* 16 (Winter, 1962) 37–56.

1344. Jiménez de Aréchaga, E. *Derecho Constitucional de las Naciones Unidas*. Madrid, 1958.

1345. Kelly, P. L. "The Consistency of Voting by the Latin American States in the United Nations General Assembly," U. of Nebr. Diss., 1971.

1346. Kotschnig, W. M. "The United Nations as an Instrument of Economic and Social Development," *IO* 22 (Winter, 1968) 16–43.

1347. Laredo, I. M. "Latinoamérica en las Naciones Unidas," *FI* 4 (Apr.–June, 1964) 571–611.

1348. Lijphart, A. "The Analysis of Bloc Voting in the General Assembly: A Critique and a Proposal," *APSR* 57 (Dec., 1963) 902–917.

1349. Maúrtua, M. F. "El Grupo Latino-Americano en las Naciones Unidas y Algunos Problemas Jurídicos," *RPDI* 16 (Jan.–June, 1956) 10–43.

1350. México. Secretaría de la Presidencia. *México en las Naciones Unidas: La Visita del Presidente Echeverría*. Mexico, 1971.

1351. Moore, R. A., Jr. (ed.). *The United Nations Reconsidered*. Columbia, S.C., 1963.

1352. Moreno, J. V. *Las Naciones Unidas en el Ambito Centro Americano*. San Salvador, 1972.

1353. Navia Varón, H. *Política Internacional: Colombia en la ONU*. Cali, Colombia, 1966.

1354. Padelford, N. J. *Elections in the United Nations General Assembly: A Study in Political Behavior*. Cambridge, Mass., 1959.

1355. ———, and L. M. Goodrich (eds.). *The United Nations in the Balance*. N.Y., 1965.
    Contains a chapter by Bryce Wood and Minerva Morales on the role of Latin America in the UN.

1356. Pederson, R. F. "National Representation in the United Nations," *IO* 15 (Spring, 1961) 256–266.

1357. Pellicer de Brody, O. "¿Un Nuevo Derecho Internacional? El Comité de la ONU para los Principios de la Coexistencia Pacífica," *FI* 8 (Oct.–Dec., 1967) 128–154.

1358. Pérez Venero, A., Jr. *La Posición de Panamá antes las Naciones Unidas*," *L* 202 (Sept., 1972) 24–40.

1359. Prat Gay, G. de. *Política Internacional del Grupo Latinoamericano*. B.A., 1967.

1360. Ruda, J. M. "Latinoamérica en las Naciones Unidas," *FI* 11 (Oct.–Dec., 1970) 362–377.

1361. Russell, R. B. *United Nations' Experience with Military Forces: Political and Legal Aspects*. Wash., 1964.

1362. Sady, E. J. *The United Nations and Dependent Peoples*. Wash., 1956.

1363. Sáenz de Miera Camino, C. "México y las Naciones Unidas," UNAM Diss., 1965.

1364. United Nations. Development Program. *Acción de las Naciones Unidas en Argentina, 1959–1972*. B.A., 1972.

1365. Uruguayan Institute of International Law. *Uruguay and the United Nations*. N.Y., 1958.

1366. Vincent, J. E. *A Handbook of the United Nations*. Woodbury, N.J., 1969.

1367. Woods, R. B. "Conflict or Community? The United States and Argentina's Admission to the United Nations," *PHR* 46 (Aug., 1977) 361–386.

X-K   cross references:
  a) For works referring to the Inter-American system and the United Nations, see items 1752–1762.
  b) See also items 1095, 2996, 3210.
  c) In the Trask, Meyer, and Trask *Bibliography* see items 4154–4196, 4752–4786, 4981, 7411, 7721, 7952, 9046.

L. ECONOMIC RELATIONS

1. GENERAL WORKS AND SPECIAL STUDIES

1368. Baldwin, D. *Economic Development and American Foreign Policy*. Chicago, 1966.

1369. Besada Ramos, B. A. "La Política Económica Norteamericana en Latinoamérica: Epoca de la Posguerra," *POI* 11–12 (1965) 147–157.

1370. Carranza, J. E. *Latin America in the World Economy: Recent Development and Trends*. Wash., 1975.

1371. Clark, P. G. *American Aid for Development*. N.Y., 1972.

1372. Espinosa García, M. *La Política Económica de los Estados Unidos Hacia América Latina entre 1945 y 1961*. Havana, 1971.

1373. Fishlow, A. *The Mature Neighbor Policy: A New United States Economic Policy for Latin America*. Berkeley, Calif., 1977.

1373a. Fontaine, P. M. "Regionalism and Functionalism in International Organization: The United States Economic Commission for Latin America," U. of Denver Diss., 1968.

1374. Francis, M. J. "La Ayuda Económica de Estados Unidos a América como Instrumento de Control Político," *FI* 12 (Apr.–June, 1972) 433–452.

1375. Groves, R. T. "Expropriation in Latin America: Some Observations," *IEA* 23 (Winter, 1969) 47–66.

1376. Haberleri, G., and T. D. Willett. *Una Estrategia para la Política de Balanza de Pagos de los Estados Unidos*. Mexico, 1971.

1377. Hansen, R. D. *United States–Latin American Economic Policy: Bilateral, Regional or Global*. Wash., 1975.

1378. Hayter, T. *Aid as Imperialism*. Middlesex, Eng., 1971.

1379. Ingram, G. M. *Expropriation of U.S. Property in South America: Nationalization of Oil and Copper Companies in Peru, Bolivia, and Chile*. N.Y., 1974.

1380. Karst, K. L., and K. S. Rosenn. *Law and Development in Latin America*. Berkeley, Calif., 1976.

1381. Kingsley, R. E. "The Public Diplomacy of U.S. Business Abroad: The Experience of Latin America," *JIAS* 9 (July, 1967) 413–428.

1382. Magdoff, H. *The Age of Imperialism: The Economics of U.S. Foreign Policy.* N.Y., 1969.
The chapters comprise articles which originally appeared in *Monthly Review*.

1383. McGrath, M. G. "Ariel or Caliban," *FA* 52 (Oct., 1973) 75–95.
The Bishop of Panama criticizes U.S. business practices in Latin America.

1384. Russett, B. M. (ed.) *Economic Theories of International Politics.* Chicago, 1968.

1385. Schreiber, A. P. "Economic Coercion as an Instrument of Foreign Policy: U.S. Economic Measures against Cuba and the Dominican Republic," *WP* 25 (Apr., 1973) 387–413.

1386. Swansborough, R. H. *The Embattled Colossus: Economic Nationalism and the United States Investors in Latin America.* Gainesville, Fla., 1976.

1387. Tancer, S. *Economic Nationalism in Latin America: The Quest for Economic Independence.* N.Y., 1976.
Essays on Latin America's economic relations with other countries including treatment of investment and natural resources.

1388. Torrence, D. R. "American Imperialism and Latin American Labor, 1959–1970: A Study in the Role of the Organización Regional Interamericana de Trabajadores in the Latin American Policy of the U.S.," Northern Ill. U. Diss., 1975.

1389. USCH. Committee on Foreign Affairs. Subcommittee on Inter-American Affairs. *Foreign Policy Implications of the U.S. Participation in the Inter-American Development Bank: Hearings.* Wash., 1970.

1390. USCS. Committee on Banking and Currency. *Study of Latin American Countries: Interim Report of the Senate Committee on Banking and Currency.* (83d Cong., 2d Sess.). Wash., 1954.

1391. Williamson, R. B., W. P. Glade, Jr., and K. M. Schmitt. *Latin American–U.S. Economic Interactions: Conflict, Accommodation, and Policies for the Future.* Wash., 1974.

X-L-1   cross references:
a) See item 56.
b) In the Trask, Meyer, and Trask *Bibliography* see items 209, 328a, 3418, 4019, 4197–4245.

2. Economic Development

1392. Bradford, C. I., *et al. New Directions in Development: Latin America, Export Credit, Population, Growth and U.S. Attitudes.* N.Y., 1974.

1393. Dell, S. S. *The Inter-American Development Bank: A Study in Development Financing.* N.Y., 1972.
Studies the policies of the bank and its role in development.

1394. Farley, R. *The Economics of Latin America: Development Problems in Perspective.* N.Y., 1972.

1395. Ferguson, Y. H. "United States Policy and Development in Latin America," *SCID* 7 (Summer, 1972) 156–180.

1396. Hirshman, A. O. *A Bias for Hope: Essays on Development in Latin America.* New Haven, Conn., 1971.

1397. Nisbett, C. T. *Latin America: Problems in Economic Development.* N.Y., 1969.

1398. Prebisch, R. *Change and Development, Latin America's Great Task: Report Submitted to the Inter-American Development Bank.* N.Y., 1971.

1399. "Small-Scale Industry in the Development of Latin America," *EBLA* 12 (May, 1967) 63–103.

X-L-2   cross references:
a) See items 73, 421, 1453, 3118, 3492, 3566.
b) In the Trask, Meyer, and Trask *Bibliography* see items 4246–4278.

3. Foreign Assistance

1400. Beaulac, W. L. *A Diplomat Looks at Aid to Latin America.* Carbondale, Ill., 1970.
Author served as U.S. ambassador to five Latin American countries.

1401. Black, L. D. *The Strategy of Foreign Aid.* N.Y., 1968.

1402. Chasteen, R. J. "American Foreign Ai

and Public Opinion, 1945–1952," U. of N.C. Diss., 1958.

1403. Feis, H. *Foreign Aid and Foreign Policy*. N.Y., 1964.

1404. Loehr, W. *A Comparison of U.S. and Multilateral Aid Recipients in Latin America, 1957–1971*. Beverly Hills, Calif., 1976.

1405. Malpica S. S., C. *El Mito de la Ayuda Exterior*. Lima, 1967.

1406. Mason, E. S. *Foreign Aid and Foreign Policy*. N.Y., 1964.

1407. Millikan, M. F. *American Foreign Aid: Strategy for the 1970's*. N.Y., 1969.

1408. Montgomery, J. N. *Foreign Aid in International Politics*. Englewood Cliffs, N.J., 1967.

1409. Nelson, J. M. *Aid, Influence and Foreign Policy*. N.Y., 1968.

1410. Pearson, N. M. *Fact and Fantasy in Aid to Latin America: Adjusting United States Policy to the Realities*. Rockville, Md., 1976.

1411. Seno, M. "Beikoku no tai Raten Amerika Enjo Seisaku," *RAK* 3 (Nov., 1963) 88–106.

Translated title: "U.S. Aid Policy toward Latin America."

1412. Sestrimski, V. *Tajnite na Imperialisticeskata "Pomost."* Sofia, Bulgaria, 1973.

Translated title: "The Secrets of Imperialistic 'Assistance.'"

1413. Smetherman, R. M. "U.S. Aid to Latin America, 1945–1960," Claremont U. Diss., 1967.

1414. Weissman, S. *The Trojan Horse: A Radical Look at Foreign Aid*. San Francisco, 1974.

X-L-3 cross references: *In the Trask, Meyer, and Trask Bibliography see items 3908, 3969–3971, 4279–4320, 5414a, 6790, 9047, 10116, 10117, 10186, 10203.*

4. TRADE, COMMERCE, AND FOREIGN INVESTMENT

1415. Arcila Farías, E. *El Capital Extranjero: Limitaciones a la Inversión de Capital Extranjero en Países Americanos*. Caracas, 1950.

1416. Baklanoff, E. N. "The Expropriation of United States Investment in Latin America, 1959–1974: A Study of International Conflict and Accommodation," *SECOLAS* 8 (Mar., 1977) 48–60.

1416a. Behrman, J. N. *Decision Criteria for Foreign Investment in Latin America*. N.Y., Treats threats to U.S. investments.

1417. Bernstein, M. D. *Foreign Investment in Latin America: Cases and Attitudes*. N.Y., 1966.

1417a. Bonnington, R. L. "Foreign Investment Inducements in Latin America," U. of Ia. Diss., 1968.

1418. Centro Interamericano de Promoción de Exportaciones. *El Comercio de América Latina con Estados Unidos, 1967–1970*. Bogotá, 1972.

1418a. Contreras, A. H. "U.S. Investment in the Forest-Based Sector in Latin America," U. of Minn. Diss., 1976.

1419. Council for Latin America. *The Effects of United States and Other Foreign Investment in Latin America*. N.Y., 1970.

1419a. Farrar, R. A. "Changes in Concentration of Latin American Trade, 1953–1965," NYU Diss., 1969.

1420. Gregersen, H. M., and A Contreras. *U.S. Investment in the Forest-Based Sector in Latin America*. Baltimore, Md., 1975.

1420a. Guisinger, S. E. (ed.). *Trade and Investment Policies in the Americas*. Dallas, Tex., 1973.

Emphasizes petroleum and copper companies.

1421. Márquez, J. *Inversiones Internacionales en América Latina: Problemas y Perspectivas*. Mexico, 1945.

1422. Mikesell, R. F. *Foreign Investment in the Petroleum and Mineral Industries: Case Studies of Investor-Host Country Relations*. Baltimore, Md., 1971.

Ten of the twelve case studies treat Latin America.

1423. Montenegro, C. *Las Inversiones Extranjeras en América Latina*. B.A., 1962.

1424. Moore, J. R., and F. A. Padovano. *U.S. Investment in Latin American Food Processing*. N.Y., 1967.

More of a general study of U.S. investment opportunities than the title would suggest.

1425. Postweeler, R. A. "Problems Concerning the Supply and Demand for Direct United States Private Investment in Latin America for the Years 1957–1965," U. of Wis. Diss., 1969.

1426.   USC. Joint Economic Committee. Sub-
        committee on Inter-American Economic
        Relationships. *Private Investment in Latin
        America: Hearings.* (88th Cong., 2d
        Sess.). Wash., 1963.

X-L-4   cross references:
  a)   See items 1736, 2646a, 2941, 2988a,
        2997a, 2998, 3000, 3003, 3086, 3438,
        3514a, 3516a, 3526a.
  b)   In the Trask, Meyer, and Trask *Bibliography*
        see items 3408, 4058, 4321–4363a,
        5414a.

5. LATIN AMERICAN COMMON MARKETS

1427.   Agostino, V. *Integración Económica: El
        Mercado Andino.* Lima, 1970.
1428.   Alcantara Pons, E. O. "The Central
        American Common Market: Integration
        as an Instrument of Economic Develop-
        ment," Harvard U. Diss., 1966.
1429.   Aleixo, J. C. B. *A Integração Latino-
        Americana: Considerações Políticas e His-
        tóricas sobre suas Bases, Processo e Sig-
        nificado.* Brasília, 1970.
1430.   Bachmura, F. T. "Toward Economic
        Reconciliation in Central America," *WA*
        133 (Mar., 1971) 283–292.
1431.   Barceló R., V. M. *¿América Latina, Inte-
        gración, o Dependencia?* Bogotá, 1973.
1432.   Bernales B., E. *Actores Políticos de la Inte-
        gración Andina.* Lima, 1974.
1433.   Business International. *LAFTA: Key to
        Latin America's 200 Million Consumers.*
        N.Y., 1966.
        A 68-page pamphlet prepared for
        businessmen.
1434.   Cale, E. G. *Latin American Free Trade
        Association.* Wash., 1969.
1435.   El Salvador. Cámara de Comercio y In-
        dustria. *Algunos Datos sobre la Integración
        de Centroamérica.* San Salvador, 1961.
1436.   *Evropa i SAD u Borki Tržišta Latinske
        Amerike.* Zagreb, Yugoslavia, 1965.
        Translated title: "Europe and the
        United States in the Struggle for the
        Latin American Common Market."
1437.   Fernández Shaw, F. *La Integración de Cen-
        tro América.* Madrid, 1965.
        Contains correspondence and minutes
        of all the conferences from 1951 to 1965.

1438.   Ferrero, R. A. *Los Problemas de la ALALC
        y sus Posibles Soluciones.* Lima, 1968.
1439.   Ferris, E. G. "National Support for the
        Andean Pact: A Comparative Study of
        Latin American Foreign Policy," U. of
        Fla. Diss., 1976.
1440.   Fuentes Irurozqui, M. *La Integración
        Económica de América Latina.* Madrid,
        1967.
1441.   Furnish, D. B. *The Andean Common Mar-
        ket and Latin American Development.*
        Tempe, Ariz., 1974.
1442.   Gálvez, J. L., and A. Llosa. *Dinámica de
        la Integración Andina.* La Victoria, Peru,
        1974.
1442a. García-Amador, F. V. *The Andean Legal
        Order: A New Community Law.* Dobbs
        Ferry, N.Y., 1978.
1443.   Gómez Vanegas, J. *Régimen del Mercado
        Andino.* Bogotá, 1975.
1444.   Grunwald, J., M. Wioncek, and M.
        Carnoy. *Latin American Integration and the
        United States.* Wash., 1972.
1445.   Hansen, R. D. *Central America: Regional
        Integration and Economic Development.*
        Wash., 1967.
1446.   Jarque, A. *Oportunidades y Ventajas del
        Grupo Andino.* Lima, 1974.
1447.   Jiménez Lazcano, M. *Integración,
        Económica e Imperialismo.* Mexico, 1968.
1448.   Karcag, G. "A Latin-Amerikai 'Közös
        Piac' Problémája," *TAR* 15 (1960)
        103–109.
        Translated title: "The Problem of the
        Latin America Common Market."
1449.   Kearns, K. C. "The Andean Common
        Market," *JIAS* 14 (May, 1972) 225–249.
1450.   Krause, W., and F. J. Mathis. *Latin
        America and Economic Integration: Regional
        Planning for Development.* Iowa City, Ia.,
        1970.
1451.   Landry, D. M. "United States Interests
        in Central America: A Case Study of
        Policies toward Economic Integration
        and Development from 1952 to 1968,"
        U. of Notre Dame Diss., 1972.
1452.   Lanús, J. A. *Sobre la Integración Económica
        en América Latina: El Caso de la ALALC.*
        B.A., 1970.
1453.   Linares, A. *La Integración como Factor del
        Desarrollo en América Latina.* Caracas,
        1975.

1454. Lozano, E. F. *Integración Económica Centro Americana*. Mexico, 1975.

1454a. McConnell, J. E. "An Analysis of International Trade Networks: The Examples of ERTA and LAFTA," O. State U. Diss., 1969.

1455. Milenky, E. S. *The Politics of Regional Organization in Latin America: The Latin American Free Trade Association*. N.Y., 1973.

1456. Morawetz, D. *The Andean Group: A Case Study in Economic Integration among Developing Countries*. Cambridge, Mass., 1974.

1457. Naleszkiewcz, W. "The Central American Common Market and the European Economic Community," *CB* 2 (Jan., 1964) 34–45.

1458. Nugent, J. B. *Economic Integration in Central America: Empirical Investigations*. Baltimore, Md., 1974.
Methodological exercise.

1459. Ocampo Rodríguez, E. *Imperialismo y Pacto Andino*. Lima, 1973.

1460. ———. *El Pacto Andino o Acuerdo de Cartagena*. Lima, 1974.

1461. Oemubu, T. *Latin America Chayumuyok Yonhap*. Seoul, Korea, 1965.
Translated title: "The Latin American Free Trade Association."

1462. Orantes, I. C. *Regional Integration in Central America*. Lexington, Mass., 1972.

1463. Pereira Pinto, J. C. *El Mercado Común Centroamericano*. B.A., 1969.

1464. Pfirter de Armas, F. M. *La Integración Fronteriza y la Asociación Latinoamericana de Libre Comercio*. Rosario, Arg., 1970.

1465. Rizo Otero, H. J. *Colombia y el Grupo Andino en el Proceso de Integración de América Latina*. Cali, Colombia, 1975.

1466. Rodríguez, L. A. "LAFTA: An Experiment in Economic Integration," Catholic U. Diss., 1965.

1467. Schmitter, P. C. *Autonomy or Dependence as Regional Outcomes: Central America*. Berkeley, Calif., 1972.
Argues that the Central American common market has not slowed down U.S. economic penetration.

1468. Solomon, A. M. "The Economic Integration of Latin America," *USDSB* 57 (Oct., 1967) 534–540.

1469. Switzer, K. A. "The Andean Group," *IEA* 26 (Spring, 1973) 69–81.

1469a. Tepperberg, A. G. "Trade Creation and Trade Diversion in the Latin American Free Trade Area," U. of Cincinnati Diss., 1975.

1470. Trucco Padin de Maniscri, E. *El Pacto Andino*. B.A., 1975.

1471. Valentino Sobrinho, R. *A Função da Empresa na Integração Latino Americana*. Rio, 1975.

1472. Villagran Kramer, F. *Integración Económica Centroamericana*. Guatemala, 1967.

1473. Wionczek, M. S. (ed.). *Integración de América Latina: Experiencias y Perspectivas*. Mexico, 1972.
Contains 18 essays.

X-L-5   *cross references:*
a) See items 1700, 1717, 1722, 2415.
b) In the Trask, Meyer, and Trask *Bibliography* see items 4223, 4229, 4233b, 4242, 4354–4357, 4364–4384a, 5438, 6764, 6766, 6770, 6775, 6785, 6789, 6790, 6797–6799, 9021.

6. DEPENDENCY AND MULTINATIONAL CORPORATIONS

1474. *Abad Arango, D. "Tecnología y Dependencia," TE* 40 (1973) 371–392.
(1973) 371–392.

1475. Anaya Franco, E. *Imperialismo, Industrialización y Transferencia de Tecnología en el Perú*. Lima, 1975.

1475a. Apter, D., and L. W. Goodman (eds.) *The Multinational Corporation and Social Change*. N.Y., 1976.
A disparate series of essays.

1476. Barber, R. J. *The American Corporation*. N.Y., 1970.

1477. Barceló R., V. M. *La Empresa Multinacional en Países del Tercer Mundo*. Mexico, 1975.

1478. Barnet, R. S., and R. E. Muller. *Global Reach: The Power of the Multinational Corporations*. N.Y., 1975.

1479. Bath, C. R., and D. D. James "Dependency Analysis of Latin America," *LARR* 11 (1976) 3–54.

1480. Behrman, J. N. *Conflicting Constraints on Multinational Enterprise: Potential for Resolution.* N.Y., 1974.
——. *The Role of International Companies in Latin American Integration: Auto and Petro-Chemicals.* Lexington, Mass., 1972.

1480b. ——. *Some Patterns in the Rise of the Multinational Enterprise.* Chapel Hill, N.C., 1969.

1481. Bertin, G. Y. *Les Sociétés Multinationales.* Paris, 1975.

1482. Biocca, S. M. *Sociedades Extranacionales y Multinacionales.* B.A., 1974.

1483. Bonilla, F., and R. Girling (eds.). *Structures of Dependency.* Stanford, Calif., 1973.

1484. Bortnik, R. *Dependencia y Revolución en América Latina.* B.A., 1972.

1485. Buckley, P. J., and M. Casson. *The Future of the Multinational Enterprise.* N.Y., 1976.

1486. Camacho Miste, E. *La Integración Andina: Fundamentos Políticos y Perspectivas.* La Paz, 1975.

1487. Cambre Mariño, J. "La Compañía Transnacional: Evolución de la Gran Empresa Capitalista," *CA* 34 (July–Aug., 1975) 26–49.

1488. Caputo, O. *Imperialismo, Dependencia y Relaciones Económicas Internacionales.* B.A., 1975.

1489. Cárdenas, G. H. *Las Luchas Nacionales contra la Dependencia.* B.A., 1969.

1490. Cardoso, F. H., and E. Faleto. *Dependencia y Desarrollo en América Latina.* Mexico, 1969.

1491. Carretero, A. M. *Liberalismo y Dependencia.* B.A., 1975.

1492. Casas, J. C. *Las Multinacionales y el Comercio Latinoamericano.* Mexico, 1973.

1493. Cecena, J. L. *El Imperio del Dólar.* Mexico, 1972.

1494. Centro de Estudos e Ação Social, Salvador, Brasil. *Dependencia e Marginalização: Nova Fase do Capitalismo.* São Paulo, 1972.

1495. Chilcote, R. H., and J. C. Edelstein (eds.). *Latin America: The Struggle with Dependency and Beyond.* Cambridge, Mass., 1974.

1496. Cholvis, F. *La Dependencia Exterior.* B.A., 1974.

1497. Chudnovsky, D. *Empresas Multicionales y Ganancias Monopólicas en una Economía Latinoamericana.* B.A., 1974.

1498. Cockcroft, J. D., A. G. Frank, and D. L. Johnson. *Dependence and Underdevelopment: Latin America's Political Economy.* N.Y., 1972.

1499. Cohen, B. *The Question of Imperialism: The Political Economy of Dominance and Dependence.* N.Y., 1973.

1500. Cooke, J. W. *La Prensa, los Monopolios, la Dependencia Extranjera.* B.A., 1974.

1501. Cueva, A. "A Summary of Problems and Perspectives of Dependency Theory," *LAP* 3 (Fall, 1976) 12–16.

1502. Davenport, G. W. "Controlling the Multi-National Corporations: A Challenge for International Law and the International Community," Duke U. Diss., 1976.

1503. Dos Santos, T. *Dependencia y Cambio Social.* Santiago, 1970.

1504. ——. "Dependencia Económica y Alternativas de Cambio en América Latina," *RMS* 32 (1970) 416–463.

1505. Dussel, E. D. *América Latina: Dependencia y Liberación.* B.A., 1973.

1506. Eells, R. *Global Corporations: The Emerging System of World Economic Power.* N.Y., 1976.

1507. Fagen, R. R. "Studying Latin American Politics: Some Implications of a Dependencia Approach," *LARR* 12 (1977) 3–26.

1508. Fajnzyller, F., *et al. Corporaciones Multinacionales en América Latina.* B.A., 1973.

1509. Fernández Serña, G., and O. Vite Bonilla. *Monopolios Transnacionales y la Escala Inflacionaria.* Mexico, 1975.

1510. Frank, A. G. *Lumpenbourgeoisie: Lumpendevelopment, Dependence, Class and Politics in Latin America.* N.Y., 1972.

1511. Green, M. del Rosario. "Inversión Extranjera, Ayuda y Dependencia en América Latina," *FI* 12 (1971) 1–26.

1512. ——. "Las Relaciones de Estados Unidos y América Latina en el Marco de la Dependencia," *FI* 13 (Jan.–Mar., 1973) 327–347.

1513. Hartshorn, J. E. *Oil Companies and Governments.* N.Y., 1968.

1514. Hellman, R. *The Challenge to U.S. Domi-*

nation of the International Corporation. N.Y., 1970.

1515.   Huntington, S. P. "Transnational Organizations in World Politics," *WP* 25 (Apr., 1973) 333–369.

1515a. Irish, D. P. (ed.) *Multinational Corporations in Latin America: Private Rights and Public Responsibilities.* Athens, O., 1978.

1515b. Jenkins, R. O. *Dependent Industrialization in Latin America.* New Haven, Conn., 1971.

1516.   Kane, W. E. *Civil Strife in Latin America: A Legal History of U.S. Involvement.* Baltimore, Md., 1972.

1517.   Kindelberger, C. P. (ed.). *The International Corporation.* Cambridge, Mass., 1970.

1517a. Krause, W. "The Implications of UNCTDAD III for Multinational Enterprise," *JIAS* 15 (Feb., 1973) 46–59.

1518.   Ledogar, R. J. *Hungry for Profit: U.S. Food and Drug Multinationals in Latin America.* N.Y., 1975.

1519.   Lozada, S. M. *Las Corporaciones Multinacionales en el Desarrollo Mundial.* B.A., 1974.

1520.   ———. *Dependencia y Empresas Multinacionales.* B.A., 1974.

1521.   ———. *Las Empresas Multinacionales.* B.A., 1973.

1522.   Marini, R. *Dialéctica de la Dependencia.* Mexico, 1973.

1523.   Márquez, P. *Imperialismo, Dependencia, Latifundismo.* Caracas, 1958.

1524.   Maza Zavala, D. F. *Los Mecanismos de la Dependencia.* Caracas, 1973.
          Ten essays treating different aspects of dependency.

1524a. McCann, T. *An American Company.* N.Y., 1976.
          Treats activities of the United Fruit Company in Central America.

1525.   Moore, R. M. "Imperialism and Dependency in Latin America: A View of the New Reality of Multi-National Investment," *JIAS* 15 (Feb., 1973) 21–35.

1526.   Para-Peña, I. "Subdesarrollo: Dualismo, Marginalización y Dependencia," *TE* 40 (1973) 663–678.

1527.   Penrose, E. T. *The Large International Firm in Developing Countries: The International Petroleum Industry.* London, 1968.

1527a. Pérez Alfonzo, J. P. *Petróleo y Dependen-*

cia. Caracas, 1971.

1528.   Petras, J. (ed.). *Latin America from Dependence to Revolution.* N.Y., 1973.

1529.   Preito, C. *Radiografia das Multinacionais.* Rio, 1975.

1530.   Puig, J. C. *De la Dependencia a la Liberación: Política Exterior de América Latina.* B.A., 1973.

1531.   Ramírez Rancaño, M. "Imperialismo y Sectores Empresariales," *RMS* 35 (July–Sept., 1973) 527–567.

1532.   Ray, D. "The Dependency Model of Latin American Underdevelopment: Three Basic Fallacies," *JIAS* 15 (Feb., 1973) 4–20.

1533.   Roel, V. *El Imperialismo de las Corporaciones Transnacionales.* Lima, 1974.

1534.   Rolfe, S. E., and W. Damm (eds.). *The Multinational Corporation in the World Economy: Direct Investment in Perspective.* N.Y., 1970.
          Special ed., Mexico, 1971.

1535.   Rosak, A. *Comercio Mundial y Explotacion: Como nos Compran y Como nos Venden las Empresas Multinacionales.* B.A., 1974.

1536.   Sampay, A., *et al. Empresas Multinacionales.* B.A., 1974.

1537.   Sampson, A. *The Sovereign State of ITT.* N.Y., 1973.

1538.   San Vicente, A. Z. *Empresas Multinacionais: Estrutura Administrativa e Administração Financeira.* Rio, 1975.

1538a. Silverman, M. *The Drugging of the Americas.* Berkeley, Calif., 1976.
          A scathing indictment of the multinational drug companies.

1539.   Sunkel, O. "Big Business and 'Dependencia': A Latin American View," *FA* 50 (Apr., 1972) 517–531.

1540.   ———. *A Critical Commentary on the United Nations' Report on Multinational Corporations in World Development.* Sussex, Eng., 1974.

1541.   Szymanski, A. J. "The Dependence of South America on the United States," Columbia U. Diss., 1971.

1542.   Tanzer, M. *The Political Economy of International Oil and the Underdeveloped Countries.* Boston, 1969.

1543.   Torres-Rivas, E. *Procesos y Estructuras de Una Sociedad Dependiente.* Santiago, 1969.

1544.   Turner, L. *Multinational Companies and*

the Third World. N.Y., 1973.

1545.   USCS. Committee on Foreign Relations. Subcommittee on Multinational Corporations. *Multinational Corporations and United States Foreign Policy: Hearings* . . . . (93d Cong., 2d Sess.) Wash., 1973.

1546.   Vernon, R. *Multinational Enterprise and National Security*. London, 1971.

1547.   ———. "Storm over the Multinationals: Problems and Prospects," *FA* 55 (Jan., 1977) 243–264.

X-L-6   *cross references: See items 55a, 1431, 1471, 2236, 2260, 2558, 2628a, 2947, 3005, 3082, 3089, 3089a, 3100, 3110, 3142, 3321, 3408, 3497a, 3535, 3567.*

Chapter XI The New Pan Americanism Since 1889

A. GENERAL ACCOUNTS AND INTERPRETATIONS

1548. Aguilar, A. *Pan Americanism from Monroe to the Present: A View from the Other Side.* N.Y., 1968.
Sp. ed., Mexico, 1965.

1549. Barbosa, F. de Assis. "Flutuações do Pan-Americanismo," *RIHGB* 263 (Apr.–June, 1964) 94–128.

1550. Bayona Ortiz, A. *Aspectos Politico-Jurídicos de la Organización Internacional Americana.* Bogotá, 1953.

1551. Bradshaw, J. S. "The 'Lost' Conference: The Economic Issue in United States–Latin American Relations, 1945–1957," Mich. State U. Diss., 1972.

1552. Briggs, E. O. "The Inter-American System: A Solid Foundation for the Future," *USDSB* 16 (Apr., 1947) 769–770.

1553. Bustamante, D. S. *Los Conflictos Internacionales y el Panamericanismo.* La Paz, 1917.

1554. Connell-Smith, G. *The Inter-American System.* London, 1966.

1555. Davis, C. D. *The United States and the Second Hague Peace Conference: American Diplomacy and International Organization, 1899–1914.* Durham, N.C., 1976.
Treats several of the early Inter-American conferences.

1556. Ferguson, Y. H. "The Inter-American System, the United States, and the Promotion of Hemispheric Diplomacy: Perspectives on Intervention and Collective Security in the Americas," Columbia U. Diss., 1967.

1557. Gannaway, R. M. "United States Representation at the Inter-American Conferences, 1889–1928," U. of S.C. Diss., 1968.

1558. García Bauer, C. *Universalismo y Panamericanismo.* Guatemala, 1968.

1559. Gregg, R. W. (ed.). *International Organization in the Western Hemisphere.* Syracuse, N.Y., 1968.
Articles by John C. Drier, Gordon Connell-Smith, Miguel S. Wionczek, and Michael K. O'Leary.

1560. José, J. R. *An Inter-American Peace Force within the Framework of the Organization of American States: Advantages, Impediments, Implications.* Metuchen, N.J., 1970.
Argues against such an organization.

1561. López M., U. *Del Congreso de Panamá a la Conferencia de Caracas, 1826–1954.* Quito, 1954.

1562. Murphy, D. J. "Professors, Publicists and Pan-Americanism, 1905–1917: A Study in the Origins of the Use of 'Experts' in Shaping American Foreign Policy," U. of Wis. Diss., 1970.

1563. OAS. General Secretariat. *Estado de los Tratados y Convenciones Interamericanos.* Wash., 1976.

1564. ———. ———. *Inter-American Treaties and Conventions: Signatures, Ratifications, and Deposits with Explanatory Notes.* Wash., 1976.

1565. PAU. Department of Legal Affairs. *Inter-American Treaty of Reciprocal Assistance: Applications, 1948–1970.* 2 vols., Wash., 1974.

1566. Seidel, R. N. "Progressive Pan Americanism: Development and U.S. Policy toward South America, 1906–1931," Cornell U. Diss., 1973.

1567. Sepúlveda, C. *El Sistema Interamericano: Génesis, Integración, Decadencia.* Mexico, 1974.
Survey study with useful appendices

including the Rio Pact, the Pact of Bogotá, and the Protocol of Buenos Aires.

1568. Tomic Romero, R. *Sobre el Sistema Interamericano*. Santiago, 1963.

1569. Vukusić, B. *Panamerikanizam i Latinska Amerika*. Belgrade, Yugoslavia, 1960.
Translated title: "Panamericanism and Latin America."

XI-A   cross references:
a) See item 1006.
b) In the Trask, Meyer, and Trask *Bibliography* see items 1416, 1596, 1600, 1614, 1743, 3056, 3186, 3488, 3509, 3537, 3789, 3956, 4385–4506, 4884, 5501, 9659.

B. THE INTER-AMERICAN SYSTEM AND THE MONROE DOCTRINE

XI-B   cross references: In the Trask, Meyer, and Trask Bibliography see items 4507–4519, 4942, 5028.

C. INTER-AMERICAN JURISPRUDENCE

1. GENERAL WORKS

1570. Acosta, C. *Estudios de Derecho Internacional*. Madrid, 1908.

1571. Armas Barea, C. A. *Temas de Derecho Internacional*. 2 vols., Rosario, Arg., 1970.

1572. Barberis, J. A. *Fuentes del Derecho Internacional*. B.A., 1973.

1573. Caicedo Castilla, J. J. *El Derecho Internacional en el Sistema Interamericano*. Madrid, 1970.

1574. ———. *La Obra del Comité Jurídico Interamericano*. Wash., 1962.

1575. Camargo, P. P. *Derecho Internacional*. 3 vols., Bogotá, 1974–1975.

1576. Corbett, P. E. *Law in Diplomacy*. Princeton, N.J., 1959.

1577. Cox Urrejola, S. *América Latina: Sujeto del Derecho Internacional*. Santiago, 1970.

1578. De Visscher, C. *Théories et Réalites en Droit International Public*. 3d ed., Paris, 1960.

1579. Finch, G. A. *The Sources of Modern International Law*. Wash., 1937.

1580. Friedman, W. *The Changing Structure of International Law*. N.Y., 1964.

1581. Hammanberg, H. V. "Theory of an American International Law," U. of Calif. Diss., 1944.

1582. Kaplan, M. A., and N. de B. Katzenbach. *The Political Foundations of International Law*. N.Y., 1961.

1583. Korovin, Y. *Derecho Internacional Público*. Mexico, 1963.

1584. Maúrtua, M. F. "Observaciones a la Declaración del Comité Jurídico Interamericano sobre Reafirmación de los Principios Fundamentales del Derecho Internacional," *RPDI* 4 (1944) 187–204.

1585. McDougal, M. S., and W. T. Burke. *The Public Order of the Oceans*. New Haven, Conn., 1962.

1586. Nucete-Sardi, J. "Doctrinas Internacionales en América," *RNC* 26 (Nov.–Dec., 1963) 52–70.

1587. Rodríguez Guerrero, I. *Existencia del Derecho Internacional Americano e Importancia de su Estudio*. Bogotá, 1953.

1588. Sánchez y Sánchez, C. *Curso de Derecho Internacional Público Americano*. Cd. Trujillo, D.R., 1943.

1589. Sepúlveda, C. *Las Fuentes del Derecho Internacional Americano*. Mexico, 1969.

1590. Sereni, A. P. *Diritto Internazionale*. 4 vols., Milan, Italy, 1957–1965.

1591. Silva, G. E. do Nascimento. *Diplomacy in International Law*. Leiden, 1972.

1592. Strupp, K. *Droit International Public Universel, Européen et Américain*. 3 vols., Paris, 1930.

1593. Tercero Castro, D. *Contribución de la O.E.A. al Derecho Internacional*. Guatemala, 1955.

1594. Tunkin, G. I. *Theory of International Law*. Cambridge, Mass., 1974.

1595. Ulloa, A. "Los Principios Fundamentales del Derecho Internacional y la Política de Nuestro Tiempo," *RPDI* 2 (1942) 391–401.

1595a. Vallejo y Arizmendi, J. *Derecho Constitucional y Derecho Internacional*. Mexico, 1977.

1596. Wright, Q. *Contemporary International Law: A Balance Sheet*. Garden City, N.Y., 1955.

XI-C-1   cross references:
a) See items 536, 891, 2020.
b) In the Trask, Meyer, and Trask *Bibliography* see items 3298, 4520–4556, 5323.

2. RECOGNITION

1597. Arechaga, E. J. de. *Reconocimiento de Gobiernos*. Montevideo, 1947.

1598. Bode, K. A. "An Aspect of United States Policy in Latin America: The Latin American Diplomats' View," *PSQ* 85 (Sept., 1970) 471–491.
Treats inconsistencies in U.S. recognition of Latin American governments.

1599. Cochrane, C. L. "The Development of an Inter-American Policy for the Recognition of De Facto Governments," *AJIL* 62 (Apr., 1968) 460–464.

1600. Dozer, D. M. "Recognition in Contemporary Inter-American Relations," *JIAS* 8 (Apr., 1966) 318–335.

1601. Gueron, C. "La 'Doctrina Betancourt' y el Papel de la Teoría en Política Exterior," *POL* 1 (1972) 231–243.
The Betancourt Doctrine calls for the nonrecognition of governments coming to power by a coup.

1602. Houghton, N. D. "Defacto Governments: A Study in International Law and American Policy," U. of Ill. Diss., 1927.

1603. Sepúlveda, C. *La Teoría y la Práctica del Reconocimiento de Gobiernos*. Mexico, 1954.

XI-C-2   cross references:
a) See items 1097, 2182, 2215, 2224, 2225, 2231, 2543.
b) In the Trask, Meyer, and Trask *Bibliography* see items 1579, 1586, 1590, 3304, 4557–4565, 4812, 5539, 6168, 6707, 6754, 7108, 7223b, 7224, 7241, 8946b.

3. EXILE AND ASYLUM

1604. Espona, C. C. "El Asilo Diplomático Americano," *RDICD* 6 (1954) 151–169.

1605. García Velutini, O. *El Asilo: Lugar de Protección*. Caracas, 1972.

1606. Helfant, H. *The Trujillo Doctrine of the Humanitarian Diplomatic Asylum*. Mexico, 1947.
Contains some documents.

1607. Ituaçu, O. C. "O Direito de Asilo e sua Repercussão nas Relações Internacionais," *RFOR* 206 (Apr.–June, 1964) 27–34.

1608. López Jiménez, R. "Las Instituciones del Asilo Diplomático y del Asilo Territorial

Desaparecerán de la América Latina," *RDCSP* 30 (Apr.–June, 1962) 51–74.

1609. Moncada, H. Cabral de. *O Asilo Interno em Direito Internacional Público*. Coimbra, Portugal, 1946.

1610. Rodríguez Araya, R. "Derecho de Asilo," *RDICD* 6 (1957) 7–34.

1611. Torres Gigena, C. *Asilo Diplomático: Su Práctica y Teoría*. B.A., 1960.

1612. Vásquez Carrizosa, A. *El Derecho de Asilo y los Derechos Humanos*. Bogotá, 1974.

1613. Vieira, M. A. *Derecho de Asilo Diplomático*. Montevideo, 1961.

XI-C-3   cross references: In the Trask, Meyer, and Trask Bibliography *see items 4566–4585, 8125.*

4. CODIFICATION OF INTERNATIONAL LAW

1614. Alvarez Tabio, F. "La Codificación de los Principios de Derecho Internacional," *POL* 6 (1968) 7–26.

1615. International American Conference. Fifth. *La Codificación del Derecho Internacional de América*. Santiago, 1923.

1616. Kawakami, T. "Raten Amerika to Kokusai Shihô no Hôtenka," *KKKN* 10 (Jan., 1960) 169–194.
Translated title: "Codification of International Private Law in Latin America."

1617. Ortiz Urquidi, R. *Oaxaca, Cuna de la Codificación Iberoamericana*. Mexico, 1974.

1618. PAU. *Codification of American International Law*. Wash., 1925.

XI-C-4   cross references: In the Trask, Meyer, and Trask Bibliography *see items 4586–4594, 4958.*

5. INTERVENTION AND NONINTERVENTION

1619. Alfaro, R. J. "La Intervención Colectiva de las Repúblicas Americanas," *RDI* 24 (Dec., 1945) 153–162.

1620. Elmore, A. A. *Ensayo sobre la Doctrina de la Intervención Internacional*. Lima, 1896.

1621. Fenwick, C. G. "Intervention: Individual and Collective," *AJIL* 39 (Oct., 1945) 645–663.

1622. ———. "Intervention and the Inter-American Rule of Law," *AJIL* 53 (Oct., 1959) 873–876.

1623. Ferguson, Y. H. "Reflections on the Inter-American Principle of Nonintervention: A Search for Meaning in Ambiguity," *JP* 32 (Aug., 1970) 628–654.

1624. Fuerra Iñíguez, D. "El Principio de la no Intervención en América," *RFDCS* 14 (Feb., 1958) 9–40.

1625. García Robles, A. *La Cláusula Calvo ante del Derecho Internacional*. Mexico, 1939.

1626. Halpern, M. *The Morality and Politics of Intervention*. N.Y., 1963.

1627. Haya de la Torre, V. R. "Intervención e Imperialismo," *CA* 10 (July–Aug., 1943) 7–12.

1628. Hoopes, T. W. *The Limits of Intervention*. N.Y., 1969.

1629. Inter-American Juridicial Committee. *Instrument Relating to Violations of the Principle of Non-Intervention*. Wash., 1959.

1630. ————. *Opinion on the Legal Aspects of the Draft Declaration on Non-Intervention Presented by the Mexican Delegation*. Wash., 1961.

1631. Lépervanche Parparcén, R. *Intervencionismo: Dos Cartas sobre la "Doctrina Betancourt" o Doctrina Tobar Revivida*. Caracas, 1963.

1632. Lima, F. R. "El Principio de no Intervención en el Derecho Internacional de América Latina," *UES* 93 (Sept.–Oct., 1968) 27–39.

1633. López González, F. *México y la Cláusula Calvo*. Mexico, 1936.

1634. Martínez Rios, J. "Intervención y Conflicto en los Sistemas Sociales: La Orientación Funcional de la Fuerza Interamericana de Paz," *BJV* (Jan.–Feb., 1966) 49–80.

1635. Morgenthau, H. J. "To Intervene or Not to Intervene," *FA* 45 (Apr., 1967) 425–536.

1636. Nakaya, K. "Kanshô to Fukanshô no Shiteki Gaikan-Beikoku no tai Raten Amerika Seisaku," *RAK* 7 (Jan., 1966) 1–30.

Translated title: "General Survey of a History of Intervention and Non-Intervention in U.S. Policy toward Latin America."

1637. OAS. *Differences between Intervention and Collective Action*. Wash., 1966.

1638. Ronning, C. N. (ed.). *Intervention in Latin America*. N.Y., 1970.

Selected readings by Latin American and U.S. scholars.

1639. Sepúlveda Gutiérrez, C. *La Responsabilidad Internacional del Estado y la Validez de la Cláusula Calvo*. Mexico, 1944.

1640. Starger, R. T. (ed.). *Essays on Intervention*. Columbus, O., 1964.

1641. Vaca Romero, D. *Limitaciones Ethicas de la No Intervención*. Quito, 1966.

1642. Vicent, R. J. *No Intervención y Orden Internacional*. B.A., 1976.

XI-C-5　cross references:

a) For the initial qualified endorsement of nonintervention by the United States at the Montevideo conference (1933), see items 1832–1835.

b) For a more comprehensive endorsement of the principle at the Buenos Aires Conference (1936), see items 1850–1853.

c) For the Venezuelan debt controversy of 1902–1903, which involved the forced collection of debts by European countries, see items 2971–2981.

d) For the heyday of interventionism, consult appropriate sections of Chapter VI; for the decline of interventionism, consult appropriate sections of Chapter VIII.

e) For intervention in the Dominican Republic, see items 2796–2824.

f) See also items 819, 1556, 1776, 2158.

g) In the Trask, Meyer, and Trask *Bibliography* see items 1608, 2143, 2687, 2949, 2949a, 2956a, 2957a, 4302, 4595–4650, 4791, 4801, 4824, 4836, 4963, 4966, 4976–5012a, 5114, 5150–5181h, 5294, 6847b—6925, 7598, 7696a—7852 7994a–8004a, 8605b–8627.

6. ARBITRATION, MEDIATION, AND CONCILIATION

1643. Acrement, A. *La Procédure dans les Arbitrages Internationaux*. Paris, 1905.

1644. Barrios de Angeles, D. *Manual del Arbitraje*. Montevideo, 1973.

1645. Bernal Jiménez, R. *El Arbitraje y la Política Internacional Americana*. Bogotá, 1927.

1646. Bishop, C. M. *International Arbitral Procedure*. Baltimore, Md., 1930.

1647. Brum, B. *La Doctrina del Arbitraje Amplio*. Montevideo, 1915.

1648. Carlston, K. S. *The Process of International Arbitration*. Westport, Conn., 1972.

1649. Di Meglio, P. M. "The United States and the Second Hague Peace Conference: The Extension of the Use of Arbitration," St. Johns U. Diss., 1968.

1650. Katz, M. *The Relevance of International Adjudication*. Cambridge, Mass., 1968.

1651. Malca B., C. "El Arbitraje Internacional," *RPDI* 5 (1945) 157–187, 306–340.

1652. Nelson, L. D. M. "The Arbitration of International Disputes in Latin America," U. of London Diss., 1969.

1653. OAS. General Secretariat. *Convención Interamericana sobre Arbitraje Comercial Internacional*. Wash., 1975.

1654. Paredes, J. F. *Arbitraje Amplio y Obligatorio*. San Salvador, 1924.

1655. Root, E. "The Relations between International Tribunals of Arbitration and Jurisdiction of National Courts," *AJIL* 3 (July, 1909) 529–536.

1656. Sansón-Terán, J. *El Arbitraje Internacional*. Barcelona, 1959.

1657. Teyssaire, J., and P. Solere. *Les Tribunaux Arbitraux Mixtes*. Paris, 1931.

XI-C-6 cross references:
  a) Proceedings associated with various Latin American boundary disputes are listed in appropriate country chapters (XIII-XXIV).
  b) For works on the attempted A.B.C. mediation of the United States–Mexican dispute of 1914–1916, see items 2196–2200.
  c) In the Trask, Meyer, and Trask *Bibliography* see items 1615, 1616, 4651–4671, 4778, 4790, 4902b, 4966, 5144–5149, 6205–6225, 9062a, 9495.

7. LAW OF THE SEA

1658. Aja Espil, J. A. *El Derecho del Mar: Las Nuevas Cuestiones del Derecho Internacional Marítimo*. Bogotá, 1974.
By an Argentine legal specialist.

1659. Alvarado Garaicoa, T. *Derecho Internacional Marítimo*. Guayaquil, Ecuador, 1970.

1660. ———. *El Dominio del Mar*. Guayaquil, Ecuador, 1968.

1661. Amacher, R. C., and R. J. Sweeney (eds.). *The Law of the Sea: U.S. Interests and Alternatives*. Wash., 1976.

1662. Bath, C. R. "Latin American Claims on the Living Resources of the Sea." *IEA* 27 (Spring, 1974) 59–85.

1663. Brazil. Ministerio da Marinha. *Mar Territorial*. 2 vols., Brasília, 1972.

1664. Bustamante y Rivero, J. L. *Derechos del Mar: La Doctrina del Mar Peruano y el Proceso de Expansión de los Mares Territoriales*. Lima, 1974.

1665. Cervantes Ahumada, R. *Derecho Marítimo*. Mexico, 1970.

1666. García Amador, F. V. *América Latina y el Derecho del Mar*. Santiago, 1976.

1666a. ———. "The Latin American Contribution to the Development of the Law of the Sea," *AJIL* 68 (Jan., 1974) 33–50.

1667. Holguín Peláez, H. *Proyecciones de un Límite Marítimo entre Colombia y Venezuela*. Bogotá, 1971.

1668. Illanes Fernández, J. *El Derecho del Mar y sus Problemas Actuales*. B.A., 1974.

1669. Luna Tobar, A. *La Doctrina Marítima Latinoamericana*. Quito, 1972.

1670. Mattos, A. M. "A Declaração de Santo Domingo e o Dereito do Mar," *RBEP* 39 (July, 1974) 171–191.

1671. Orrego Vicuña, G. *Chile y el Derecho del Mar*. Santiago, 1972.

1672. Perú. Ministerio de Relaciones Exteriores. *Instrumentos Nacionales e Internacionales sobre Derecho del Mar*. Lima, 1971.

1673. Rangel, V. M. "A Próxima Confêrencia sobre Direito do Mar e seus Antecedentes," *PB* 10 (Sept., 1972) 6–16.

1674. Rivera, J. *La Declaración sobre Zona Marítima de 1952*. Santiago, 1968.
Treats the agreement reached by Chile, Peru, and Ecuador.

1675. Romero, G. *¿De Quien Es el Mar?* Lima, 1975.

1676. Ruiz Eldredge, A. *El Nuevo Derecho del Mar*. Lima, 1973.

1677. Sepúlveda Amor, B. "Derecho del Mar: Apuntes sobre el Sistema Legal Mexicana," *FI* 13 (Oct.–Dec., 1972) 232–271.

1678. Smetherman, B. B., and R. M. Smetherman. *Territorial Seas and Inter-American Relations: With Case Studies of the Peruvian and U.S. Fishing Industries*. N.Y., 1974.

Study written before the 1974 Caracas Conference on Law of the Sea.

1679. Teitelboim, S. V. *Chile y la Soberanía en el Mar*. Santiago, 1966.

1680. Uruguay. Presidencia del la República. *América Latina y la Extensión del Mar Territorial*. Montevideo, 1971.

1681. ———. Secretaría de la Presidencia. *América Latina y la Extensión del Mar Territorial: Régimen Jurídico*. Montevideo, 1971.

1682. USCH. Subcommittee on Inter-American Affairs. *Fishing Rights and United States–Latin American Relations: Hearings. . . .* (92d Cong., 2d Sess.) Wash., 1972.

1683. USDS. *Law of the Sea: Third United Nations Conference*. Wash., 1974.

The conference was held in Caracas in the summer of 1974.

1684. Vargas, J. A., and E. Vargas C. (eds.). *Derecho del Mar: Una Visión Latinoamericana*. Mexico, 1976.

Contains 13 articles.

1685. Vargas Carreño, E. *América Latina y el Derecho del Mar*. Mexico, 1973.

1686. ———. *América Latina y los Problemas Contemporáneos del Derecho del Mar*. Santiago, 1974.

1687. Vásquez Carrizosa, A. *Colombia y los Problemas del Mar*. Bogotá, 1971.

XI-C-7 cross references: See items 1585, 2474, 3324, 3336.

8. SPECIAL ASPECTS

1688. Antelo, M. *La Técnica Consultiva en el Derecho de Gentes*. Rosario, Arg., 1938.

1689. Argentina. *La República Argentina en la Segunda Conferencia Internacional de la Paz, Haya, 1907*. B.A., 1908.

1690. Artigas Villaroel, E. *Los Delitos Internacionales y su Tratamiento Jurídico-Político*. Santiago, 1969.

1691. Barceló, S. (comp.). *Manual Diplomático y Consular Hispano-Americano*. Barcelona, 1909.

1692. Bassiouni, M. C. *International Extradition and World Public Order*. Dobbs Ferry, N.Y., 1974.

1693. Boffi Boggero, L. M. *¿Está en Crisis la Corte Internacional de Justica?* B.A., 1975.

1694. Boggiano, A. *La Doble Nacionalidad en Derecho Internacional Privado*. B.A., 1972.

1695. Caicedo Castilla, J. J. *La Obra del Comité Jurídico Interamericano*. Rio, 1966.

1696. Caicedo Perdomo, J. J. *Textos y Documentos de Derecho Internacional Público*. Bogotá, 1975.

1697. Camargo, P. P. *La Dictadura Constitucional y la Suspensión de Derechos Humanos*. Bogotá, 1975.

1698. Chayes, A. *The Cuban Missile Crisis: International Crisis and the Role of Law*. N.Y., 1974.

Discusses the legal aspects of the selective quarantine on Cuba.

1699. Conil Paz, A. L. *Historia de la Doctrina Drago*. B.A., 1975.

1700. Copete Saldarriaga, I. *Acotaciones sobre Algunos Problemas Jurídicos de la Integración Latinoamericana*. Bogotá, 1971.

1701. Cruchaga, V. *La Igualdad Jurídica de los Estados*. Santiago, 1968.

1702. Doxey, M. P. *Economic Sanctions and Internatinal Enforcement*. London, 1971.

Chapter 3 treats OAS sanctions.

1703. Essen, J. L. F. van. *Immunities in International Law*. Leiden, 1955.

1704. Foglia, R. A., and A. R. Mercado. *Derecho Aeronaútico*. B.A., 1968.

1705. Gaete, E. *La Extradición ante la Doctrina y la Jurisprudencia (1935–1965)*. Santiago, 1972.

1706. Gómez de la Torre, M. *Derecho Constitucional Interamericano*. 2 vols., Quito, 1964.

1707. Hara, M. "Karubo Jâkô no Kôka," *RAK* 5 (Dec., 1964) 59–73.

Translated title: "The Effect of the Calvo Clause."

1708. Instituto Argentino de Derecho Internacional. *La Nacionalidad en las Repúblicas Americanas*. B.A., 1936.

1709. Instituto de Derecho Comparado. *Primeras Jornadas Latinoamericanas de Derecho Aeronaútico*. B.A., 1962.

1710. Inter-American Bar Association. *Anales de la VII Conferencia Interamericana de Abogados*. 2 vols., Montevideo, 1952.

The meeting was held in Montevideo in 1951.

1711. ———. *Cuarta Conferencia, Federación*

Interamericana de Abogados. 3 vols., Santiago, 1946.
The meeting was held in Santiago in 1945.

1712. ———. *Federação Interamericana de Advogados. Anais da Segunda Conferência*. 6 vols., Rio, 1950.
The meeting was held in Rio in 1943.

1713. ———. *Inter-American Bar Association. Organization of the Association and Proceedings of the First Conference*. Baltimore, Md., 1942.
The meeting was held in Havana in 1941.

1714. ———. *Memoria de la Tercera Conferencia de la Federación Interamericana de Abogados*. 3 vols., Mexico, 1945.
The meeting was held in Mexico City in 1944.

1715. ———. *Proceedings of the Sixth Conference, Inter-American Bar Association*. Wash., 1952.
The meeting was held in Detroit, Mich., in 1949.

1716. ———. *Quinta Conferencia de la Federación Interamericana de Abogados*. Lima, 1947.
The meeting was held in Lima in 1947.

1717. Inter-American Development Bank. *La Dimensión Jurídica de la Integración*. B.A., 1973.

1718. Kelsen, H. *Derecho y Paz en las Relaciones Internacionales*. Mexico, 1975.

1719. La Fontaine, H. *Pasicrise Internationale: Histoire Documentaire des Arbitrages Internationaux*. Berne, Switzerland, 1902.

1720. Lindo, J. *La Integración Centroamerica ante el Derecho Internacional*. San Salvador, 1969.

1721. Lion Depetre, J. *Derecho Diplomático*. Mexico, 1974.

1721a. Lorenz, L. "Origins of Pan American Copyright Protection: 1889–1910," *JQ* 49 (Winter, 1972) 717–721.

1722. Luard, E. (ed.). *The International Regulation of Frontier Disputes*. London, 1970.

1723. OAS. General Secretariat. *American Convention on Human Rights—Pact of San José*. Wash., 1970.

1724. ———. ———. *Copyright Protection in the Americas*. Wash., 1967.

1725. ———. ———. *La Organización de los Estados Americanos y los Derechos Humanos, 1960–1967*. Wash., 1972.

1726. ———. ———. *Trabajos Realizados por el Comité Jurídico Interamericano durante su Período Extraordinario de Sesiones*. Wash., 1971.
Treats work accomplished during the meetings of Aug. to Oct., 1971.

1727. ———. ———. *Trabajos Realizados por el Comité Jurídico Interamericano durante el Período Ordinario de Sesiones*. Wash., 1971.
Treats accomplishments of the meetings held from Mar. to Apr., 1971.

1728. ———. ———. *Trabajos Realizados por el Comité Jurídico Interamericano durante el Período Ordinario de Sesiones Celebrado del 15 de Enero al 16 de Febrero de 1973*. Wash., 1973.

1729. ———. ———. Inter-American Commission on Human Rights. *Handbook of Existing Rules Pertaining to Human Rights*. Wash., 1970.

1730. Ogdon, M. *Juridical Bases of Diplomatic Immunity*. Wash., 1936.

1731. Oliveira Franco Sobrinho, M. de *Desapropriação na Doutrina, no Direito Brasileiro na Legislação Comparada*. São Paulo, 1973.

1732. Parra Aranguren, G. "El Tratamiento Procesal del Derecho Extranjero en los Países de la América del Sur," *BACPS* 32 (Oct.–Dec., 1971) 41–72.

1733. PAU. *Handbook. First Meeting of the Inter-American Council of Jurists*. Wash., 1950.

1734. ———. Department of Legal Affairs. *Brief Review of the Legal System of Free Zones in Latin America*. Wash., 1968.

1735. ———. Juridical Division. *Informes y Proyectos sobre el Establecimiento de la Corte Interamericana de Justicia Internacional*. Wash., n.d.

1736. Ricci, D. de. *Investissements en l'Amerique Latine: Aspect Juridique et Fiscal*. 2 vols., Paris, 1955.

1737. Ruzié, D. *Organisations Internationales et Sanctions Internationales*. Paris, 1971.

1738. Schreiber, A. P. "The Inter-American Commission on Human Rights," Columbia U. Diss., 1969.

1739.   ———. *The Inter-American Commission on Human Rights*. Leiden, 1970.

1740.   Staley, E. "Une Critique de la Protection Diplomatique des Placements á l'Etranger," *RGDIP* 42 (1935) 541–558.

1741.   Ténékidès, C. G. "Considérations sur la Clause Calvo: Essai de Justification dy Système de la Nullité Intégrale," *RGDIP* 43 (1936) 270–284.

XI-C-8   cross references:

a)   See items 2705, 2798, 2812, 2819, 3016, 3564.

b)   In the Trask, Meyer, and Trask *Bibliography* see items 1600, 3255, 4672–4707a, 4869, 4920, 4952, 4961, 4975a, 5023, 5044, 5323, 6722, 6727, 7310, 7366, 7730, 7732, 7754, 7766, 7790, 7792, 7850, 8338, 8613, 9452.

D. PAN AMERICAN UNION

1742.   Alvarez, A. *L'Union Internationale Européenne et l'Union Panaméricaine*. Paris, 1930.

1743.   Fox, W. C. *International Bureau of American Republics*. Wash., 1906.

1744.   Martínez, C. M. *La Unión Americana*. Santiago, 1919.

1745.   OAS. Council. *Report on Amendments to the Regulations of the Pan American Union*. Wash., 1967.

1746.   Pinto, R. W. "The Pan American Union," U. of Wis. Diss., 1927.

1747.   Prisco III, S. *John Barrett, Progressive Era Diplomat: A Study of a Commercial Expansionist, 1887–1920*. University Ala., 1973.

Barrett was director general of the Pan American Union from 1907 to 1920.

1748.   Tsui, T. H. "The Pan American Union as an Agency of Cooperation for the American Nations," Stanford U. Diss., 1927.

1749.   Waller, A. "John Barrett: Pan-American Promoter," *MA* 53 (July, 1971) 170–189.

XI-D   cross references:

a)   See item 3193.

b)   In the Trask, Meyer, and Trask *Bibliography* see items 4509, 4708–4728, 4992.

E. THE INTER-AMERICAN SYSTEM AND WORLD WAR II

1750.   Guani, A. *La Solidaridad Internacional en América*. Montevideo, 1942.

1751.   Holly, D. A. "The United States and the Inter-American System, 1939–1945," U. of Denver Diss., 1966.

XI-E   cross references:

a)   For works on the Panama Conference (1939), see items 1855–1858.

b)   For the Havana Conference (1940), see item 1859.

c)   For the Rio Conference (1942), see items 1860–1862.

d)   For the Chapultepec Conference (1945), see items 1863–1867.

e)   In the Trask, Meyer, and Trask *Bibliography* see items 3538. 3832, 4423, 4729–4751, 4844, 4862, 5189a–5255a.

F. THE INTER-AMERICAN SYSTEM AND THE UNITED NATIONS

1752.   Allen, W. P. "Regional Arrangements and the United Nations," *USDSB* 14 (June, 1946) 923–927.

1753.   Claude, I. L. "The OAS, the UN, and the United States," *IC* 547 (Mar., 1964). Part of *IC* pamphlet series.

1754.   Conferencia Interamericana sobre Problemas de la Guerra y de la Paz. *Resolución XXX sobre Establecimiento de una Organización Internacional General*. Mexico, 1945.

1755.   Halderman, J. W. "Regional Enforcement Measures and the United Nations," *GLJ* 52 (Fall, 1963) 89–118.

1756.   Letts, S. E. "Los Sistemas Regionales y la Organización Mundial de la Paz," *RPDI* 11 (1951) 339–378.

1757.   PAU. *The United Nations Conference on International Organizations: Report on the Actions of the Conferences on Regional Arrangements*. Wash., 1945.

1758.   ———. Governing Board. *Report on the Relations between Specialized Inter-American Organizations and World Organizations of the Same Nature*. Wash., 1946.

1759.   Penna Marinho, I. *O Funcionamento do Sistema Interamericano Dentro do Sistema Mondial*. Rio, 1959.

1760. Wilcox, F. O. "Regionalism and the United Nations," *IO* 19 (Summer, 1965) 789–811.

1761. Wood, B., and M. M. Morales. "Latin America and the United Nations," *IO* 19 (Summer, 1965) 714–727.

1762. Yalem, R. *Regionalism and World Order*. Wash., 1965.

Among other topics treats the relationship of the Inter-American system and the United Nations.

XI-F   cross references:

a) For early views on the relationship between the Inter-American system and the world organization, see works on the Chapultepec Conference (1945), items 1863–1867.

b) In the Trask, Meyer, and Trask *Bibliography* see items 3524, 4166, 4181, 4417, 4752–4786, 5067, 5230–5255a.

G. THE ORGANIZATION OF AMERICAN STATES (OAS)

1763. Ball, M. M. *The OAS in Transition*. Durham, N.C., 1969.

1764. Barrera Reyes, A. *O.E.A., la Organización de Estados Americanos, Medios Pacíficos para la Solución de Conflictos Interamericanos*. Mexico, 1955.

1765. Buergenthal, T. "The Revised OAS Charter and the Protection of Human Rights," *AJIL* 69 (Oct., 1975) 828–832.

1766. Carrión, B. "Con OEA o sin OEA, Ganaremos la Pelea," *CA* 34 (Jan.–Feb., 1975) 15–23.

1767. Cuba. Ministerio de Relaciones Exteriores. *¿Que Es la OEA?* Havana, 1968.

1768. Drier, J. C. "New Wine in Old Bottles: The Changing Inter-American System," *IO* 22 (Spring, 1968) 477–493.

Treats some of the structural reforms of the OAS.

1769. Fischlowitz, E. "A O.E.A. no Sistema Polítema Político Interamericano," *RDCPB* 4 (May–Aug., 1961) 62–80.

1770. Freeman, A. V. "La Competencia General del Consejo de Organización de los Estados Americanos con Respecto a Cuestiones de Indole Política," *RPDI* 10 (Jan.–Apr., 1950) 3–35.

1771. Freitas, J. J. de Oliveira. *Carta da Organização dos Estados Americanos*. Pôrto Alegre, Brazil, 1973.

Discusses the revisions of the OAS charter in 1967.

1772. Gerold, R. *Die Sisherung des Friedens durch die Organisation dere Amerikanischen Staaten*. Berlin, 1971.

1773. Inter-American Institute of International Legal Studies. *The Inter-American System: Its Development and Strengthening*. Dobbs Ferry, N.Y., 1966.

1774. Kim, J. G. "Non-Member Participation in the Organization of American States," *JIAS* 10 (Apr., 1968) 194–212.

1775. Kutzner, G. *Die Organisation der Amerikanischen Staaten*. Hamburg, 1970.

1775a. Le Blanc, L. J. *The OAS and the Protection of Human Rights*. The Hague, Netherlands, 1977.

1776. Manger, W. "The Inter-American Regional System. The Dilemma of Contradictional Multilateralism, Collective Intervention and Unilateral Nonintervention," *WA* 124 (Fall, 1961) 83–86.

1777. ———. "Reform of the OAS, the 1967 Buenos Aires Protocol of Amendment to the 1948 Charter of Bogotá: An Appraisal," *JIAS* 10 (Jan., 1968) 1–14.

1778. Mariz, V. "A Ampliação do Papel da OEA," *RBEP* 32 (July, 1971) 45–55.

1779. Martz, M. J. R. "OAS Reforms and the Future of Pacific Settlements," *LARR* 12 (1977) 170–186.

1780. Meek, G. "U.S. Influence in the Organization of American States," *JIAS* 17 (Aug., 1975) 311–325.

1781. OAS. *Annual Report of the Secretary-General: 1964–1965*. Wash., 1965.

1782. ———. *Annual Report of the Secretary-General: 1965–1966*. Wash., 1966.

1783. ———. *Organizations with Which the Organization of American States Has Established Relations as of June, 1959*. Wash., n.d.

1784. ———. General Secretariat. *Charter of the Organization of American States as Amended by the Protocol of Buenos Aires in 1967*. Wash., 1967.

1785. Pak, B. K. "The Cuban Problem in the Organization of American States: A

Model for Collective Decision-Making," Fla. State U. Diss., 1965.

1786.   PAU. *Agreement between the Council of the OAS and the International Labour Organization*. Wash., 1951.

1787.   ———. *The Organization of American States: What It Is and How It Works*. Wash., 1959.

1788.   Plaza, G. *1968–1975: Seven Years of Change*. Wash., 1975.

1789.   Remiro Brotons, A. *Le Hegemonía Norteamericana: Factor de Crisis de la OEA*. Bologna, 1970.

1790.   Silva, G. E. do Nascimento. "Estructura e Funcionamento da Organização dos Estados Americanos," *BSBDI* 12 (1956) 38–61.

1791.   Slater, J. "The Decline of the OAS," *IJ* 24 (Summer, 1969) 497–506.

1792.   Tomask, R. D. "The Chilean-Bolivian Lauca River Dispute and the OAS," *JIAS* 9 (July, 1967) 351–366.

1793.   USCS. Committee on Foreign Relations. *Amendments to the OAS Charter: Hearings*. Wash., 1968.

1794.   Vukusić, B. *Organizacĳa Američkih Država*. Belgrade, Yugoslavia, 1958.
        Translated title: "Organization of American States."

XI-G   cross references:
a)   For creation of the OAS at Bogotá in 1948, see items 1839–1842.
b)   See also items 1071, 1181, 1222, 1560, 1702, 2821.
c)   In the Trask, Meyer, and Trask *Bibliography* see items 4234, 4700, 4787–4830, 4841, 5064—5104, 7995c.

H. NATIONAL AND REGIONAL RELATIONS WITH THE INTER-AMERICAN SYSTEM

1. MEXICO

1795.   Koslow, L. E. *Mexico and the Organization of American States*. Tempe, Ariz., 1969.

1796.   Ramírez Reyes, M. *La Posición de México ante la OEA*. Mexico, 1965.
        A 46-page pamphlet.

XI-H-1   cross references:
a)   See item 1814.

b)   In the Trask, Meyer, and Trask *Bibliography* see items 3156, 4831–4836, 4906, 4922, 4967, 4995, 4996, 5001, 5003, 5004, 5034, 5074, 5088, 5112, 5119, 5120, 5282.

2. THE CENTRAL AMERICAN–CARIBBEAN REGION

1797.   D'Angelo Evans, A. "Los Conflictos del Caribe y el Sistema Interamericano de Paz," *RDICD* 6 (Jan.–Dec., 1954) 133–149.

1798.   Portell Vilá, H. *Cuba y la Conferencia de Montevideo*. Havana, 1934.

XI-H-2   cross references:
a)   For the explusion of Cuba from the Inter-American system, see items 1882–1887.
b)   In the Trask, Meyer, and Trask *Bibliography* see items 2520, 2538, 4832, 4837–4847, 4981, 5007, 5070, 5111, 5152, 5163, 5174, 5175, 5273, 5287–5311.

3. SPANISH SOUTH AMERICA

1799.   Argentina. Ministerio de Relaciones Exteriores y Culto. *Reuniones de Consulta entre Ministros de Relaciones Exteriores de las Repúblicas Americanas . . . Participación Argentina*. B.A., 1941.

1800.   *Condensed Minutes*. Rio, 1906.

1801.   Conil Paz, A. *La Argentina y los Estados Unidos en la Sexta Conferencia Panamericana*. B.A., 1965.

1802.   Jiménez de Aréchaga, J. "El Uruguay en las Conferencias Internacionales Americanas," *RFDCSU* 1 (July, 1936) 233–264, 285–298.

1803.   Ramírez Echeverría, F. "La República del Ecuador y el Sistema Interamericano," *AUC* 17 (Oct.–Dec., 1961) 625–684.

XI-H-3   cross references:
a)   See items 1813, 1836, 1839, 1850, 1869, 1889, 3325.
b)   In the Trask, Meyer, and Trask *Bibliography* see items 2524, 2527–2529, 2534, 2602, 2603, 2616, 2617, 3690, 4109, 4848–4868, 4908, 4918, 4930, 4948, 4957, 4971, 4991, 4994, 5014, 5016, 5085, 5105, 5189b, 5221, 5234, 5235, 5240, 5248, 5259, 5272, 5293, 9175, 9659.

4. BRAZIL

1804. Kenyon, R. G. B. "The Pan American-
       ism of Joaquím Nabuco," U. of N.M.
       Diss., 1952.
1805. Rodrigues, J. A. "A Diplomácia Bra-
       sileira e a 'Crise' do Sistema Americana,"
       PEI 1 (May, 1965) 157–174.

XI-H-4   cross references:
  a) See items 1820, 1840, 1875.
  b) In the Trask, Meyer, and Trask *Bibliography*
        see items 2540, 2601, 2611, 3716, 4869–
        4876, 5025, 5292, 5299, 9878.

5. CANADA

1806. Anglin, D. G. "United States Opposi-
       tion to Canadian Membership in the Pan
       American Union: A Canadian View," *IO*
       15 (Winter, 1961) 1–20.
1806a. Guy, J. J. "Canada's External Relations
       with Latin America: Environment, Pro-
       cesses and Prospects," St. Louis U. Diss,
       1975.
1807. Holmes, J. W. "Canada and Pan
       America," *JIAS* 10 (Apr., 1968) 173–
       184.
1808. Lyon, P. W., and T. Y. Ismael. *Canada
       and the Third World*. Toronto, 1976.
1808a. Murray, D. H. "Canada's First Diplo-
       matic Missions in Latin America," *JIAS*
       16 (May, 1974) 153–172.
       Treats the World War II period.
1808b. Ogelsby, J. C. M. *Gringos from the Far
       North: Essays in the History of Canadian–
       Latin American Relations, 1866–1968*.
       Toronto, 1976.
1809. Wood, B. M. "La Nueva Política de
       Canadá Hacia América Latina," *FI* 12
       (July–Sept., 1971) 27–45

*XI-H-5   cross references: In the Trask, Meyer, and
Trask* Bibliography *see items 4738, 4876a–4902*.

I. REGULAR INTER-AMERICAN
CONFERENCES

1. WASHINGTON, 1889

1810. Flint, C. R. *Memories of an Active Life*.
       N.Y., 1923.
       Flint was a member of the U.S. delega-
       tion to the Washington Conference.

1810a. Karras, B. J. "José Martí and the Pan
       American Conference, 1889–1891,"
       RHA 77–78 (Jan.–Dec., 1974) 77–99.

XI-I-1   cross references:
  a) For accounts of the role of Secretary of State
        James G. Blaine, see items 663 and 666.
  b) In the Trask, Meyer, and Trask *Bibliography*
        see items 2063a, 2081, 2091, 2111,
        2120a, 2131, 2141, 2145, 2146, 2547,
        2605, 2606, 4902a–4916.

2. MEXICO CITY, 1901

1811. Inter-American Conference. Second. *Or-
       ganización de la Conferencia, Proyectos, In-
       formes, Dictámenes, Debates y Resoluciones*.
       Mexico, 1901.
1812. *La Conferencia Internacional de México*.
       Mexico. 1902.
1813. Perú. *El Perú en la Conferencia Interna-
       cional de México, 1901–1902*. Lima,
       1903.
1814. *Report Which the Mexican Delegation Sub-
       mits to the Second Pan American Conference*.
       Mexico, 1901.

*XI-I-2   cross references: In the Trask, Meyer, and
Trask* Bibliography *see items 4663, 4916a–4926*.

3. RIO DE JANEIRO, 1906

1815. Brazil. Ministerio das Relações Ex-
       teriores. *3ª Conferência Internacional
       Americana*. Rio, 1918.
1816. *Extracto de las Ideas de los Países de América
       con Relación al Programa de la Tercera Con-
       ferencia Pan Americana de Rio de Janeiro,
       1906*. Rio, 1906.
1817. Inter-American Conference, 1906. *Min-
       utes, Resolutions, Documents*. Rio, 1907.
1818. *Lista e Actas das Sessões de 23 de Julho de
       1906 a 27 de Agosto de 1906*. Rio, 1906.
1819. *Report of the Delegates of the U.S. to the 3rd
       International Conference of the American
       States*. Wash., 1907.
1820. *Trabalhos do Dr. Amaro Cavalcanti, De-
       legado do Brasil*. Rio, 1906.
1821. United States. *Report of the Delegates of the
       United States to the Third International Con-
       ference of American States Held at Rio de
       Janeiro, Brazil July 21 to August 26, 1906*.
       Wash., 1907.

XI-1-3   cross references: In the Trask, Meyer, and Trask Bibliography *see items 4927–4935.*

4. BUENOS AIRES, 1910

1822.   Chile. Ministerio de Relaciones Exteriores. *La Conferencia Pan-Americana de Buenos Aires. Informe Presentado por los Delegados Plenipoteciarios de Chile.* Santiago, 1911.

1823.   *Diario de las Sesiones.* B.A., 1911.

1824.   *Fourth International Conference of American States. Delegation from the United States.* Wash., 1911.

1825.   Inter-American Conference, 1910. *Fourth American International Conference. Daily Account of the Sessions.* B.A., 1911.

XI-1-4   cross references: In the Trask, Meyer, and Trask Bibliography *see items 4936–4944.*

5. SANTIAGO, 1923

1826.   *Informe de la Delegación de Chile, Presentado en Complimiento del Tema 1 del Programa.* Santiago, 1923.

1827.   Moreno Quintana, L. M. "La Quinta Conferencia Panamericana," *RFDCS* 8 (July–Sept., 1924) 672–702.

1828.   Uribe Echeverri, C. *La Conferencia de Santiago.* B.A., 1923.

XI-1-5   cross references: In the Trask, Meyer, and Trask Bibliography *see items 4719, 4945–4954, 9253.*

6. HAVANA, 1928

1829.   Inter-American Conference. Sixth. *Diario de la Sexta Conferencia Internacional Americano.* Havana, 1928.

1830.   ———. ———. *Final Act. Motions, Agreements, Resolutions and Conventions.* Havana, 1928.

1831.   Stitzel, J. A. "The Evolution of Improved Inter-American Relations as Seen in the Speeches of Two Inter-American Conferences—1928 and 1933," Northwestern U. Diss., 1956.

XI-1-6   cross references: In the Trask, Meyer, and Trask Bibliography *see items 3295, 4714, 4955–4975a.*

7. MONTEVIDEO, 1933

1832.   Harris, S. A. "The Inter-American Conferences of the 1930's," U. of Mo. Diss., 1967.

1833.   International American Conference. Seventh. *Minutes and Antecedents with General Index.* Montevideo, 1933.

1834.   PAU. *Special Handbook for the Use of Delegates.* Wash., 1938.

1835.   Perú. *Informe sobre la Séptima Conferencia Internacional Americana de Montevideo.* Lima, 1935.

XI-1-7   cross references:
a)   See items 1798, 1831, 2668.
b)   In the Trask, Meyer, and Trask *Bibliography* see items 3340, 3359, 3362, 3377, 4975b–5012a.

8. LIMA, 1938

1836.   Argentina. Ministerio de Relaciones Exteriores y Culto. *La República Argentina en la Octava Conferencia Internacional Americana.* B.A., 1939.

1837.   Finch, G. L. "Eighth International Conference of American States," *IC* 349 (Apr., 1938) 141–249.

1838.   Hull, C. *Address and Statements by the Honorable Cordell Hull . . . in Connection with the Eighth International Conference of American States.* Wash., 1940.

XI-1-8   cross references:
a)   For a discussion of emergency procedures, see item 1854.
b)   See also item 1832.
c)   In the Trask, Meyer, and Trask *Bibliography* see items 3340, 3388, 4512, 5012b–5063, 5451, 5477.

9. BOGOTÁ, 1948

1839.   Argentina. Ministerio de Relaciones Exteriores y Culto. *La República Argentina en la IX Conferencia Internacional Americana.* B.A., 1949.

1840.   Brazil. Ministerio das Relações Exteriores. *IX Conferência Internacional Americana: Relatório de Chefe da Delegação do Brasil. Embaixador João Neves da Fontoura.* Rio, 1948.

1841. *Documentos Presentados a la Novena Conferencia Internacional Americana.* Bogotá, 1948.

    Selected documents treating the major issues discussed.

1842. Lleras, A. "Report on the Ninth International Conference of American States," *AOAS* 1 (1949) 1–75.

XI-I-9   cross references: In the Trask, Meyer, and Trask Bibliography *see items 5064–5104, 5263, 9842, 9853.*

10. CARACAS, 1954

1843. Argentina. Ministerio de Relaciones Exteriores y Culto. "Organismos y Reuniones Internacionales: X Conferencia Interamericana," *BMREC* 3 (Apr.–June, 1954) 305–348.

1844. Falconi, G. "El Sistema Interamericano Frente a los Casos de Guatemala y Costa Rica," *BJ* 1 (Jan. June, 1955) 45–56.

1845. García Silva, E. *Bosquejo Panorámico de la X Conferencia Interamericana Celebrada en Caracas en 1954.* Quito, 1954.

1846. Goncal, G. "A Latinamerikai Népek Harca a Wall Street Gyarmatositó Politikája Ellen: A Caracasi Panamerikai Ertekezlet," *TAR* 9 (1954) 148–156.

    Translated title: "The Struggle of Latin American Peoples against the Colonizing Policy of Wall Street: The Pan American Conference in Caracas."

1847. PAU. *Final Act.* Wash., 1954.

1848. ———. Department of International Law. *Tenth Inter-American Conference . . . Report of the Pan American Union on the Conference.* Wash., 1954.

XI-I-10   cross references:
a) For studies on John F. Dulles, see items 1073, 1077, 1078, 1081.
b) In the Trask, Meyer, and Trask *Bibliography* see items 3849, 3851, 3865, 3874, 3878, 3919, 5104a–5127a.

J. SPECIAL AND CONSULTATIVE CONFERENCES

1. CENTRAL AMERICAN PEACE CONFERENCE—WASHINGTON, 1907

1849. Martínez Moreno, A. "La Conferencia de Washington de 1907 y la Carta de Justicia Centroamericana," *UES* 90 (Sept.–Oct., 1965) 73–98.

XI-J-1   cross references: In the Trask, Meyer, and Trask Bibliography *see items 5128–5135.*

2. SECOND CONFERENCE ON CENTRAL AMERICAN AFFAIRS—WASHINGTON, 1922–1923

XI-J-2   cross references: In the Trask, Meyer, and Trask Bibliography *see items 5136–5143.*

3. CONFERENCE ON CONCILIATION AND ARBITRATION—WASHINGTON, 1928–1929

XI-J-3   cross references: In the Trask, Meyer, and Trask Bibliography *see items 4966, 5144–5149.*

4. CONFERENCE ON MAINTENANCE OF PEACE—BUENOS AIRES, 1936

1850. "Conferencia Interamericana de Consolidación de la Paz . . . Informe de la Delegación del Uruguay," *BMRE* 5 (Feb., 1938) 51–144.

1851. *Conferencia Interamericana de Consolidación de la Paz que se Reunirá en Buenos Aires, República Argentina. 1 de Diciembre de 1936. Manual Especial para Uso de los Delegados.* Wash., 1936.

1851a. Toro Jiménez, F. *La Política de Venezuela en la Conferencia Interamericana de Consolidación de la Paz.* Caracas, 1977.

1852. Uruguay. Cámara de Representantes. *Conferencia Interamericana de Consolidación de la Paz.* Montevideo, 1938.

1853. USDS. *Addresses and Statements by . . . Cordell Hull . . . in Connection with . . . the Inter-American Conference for the Maintenance of Peace . . . Buenos Aires.* Wash., 1937.

XI-J-4   cross references:
a) See item 1832.
b) In the Trask, Meyer, and Trask *Bibliography* see items 3340, 4519, 5150–5181h, 9107.

5. ESTABLISHMENT OF EMERGENCY PROCEDURES

1854. Comité Consultativo de Emergencia para

la Defensa Política. *Informe Anual Sometido a los Gobiernos de las Repúblicas Americanas. Julio de 1943*. Montevideo, 1943.

XI-J-5   cross references: In the Trask, Meyer, and Trask Bibliography *see items 5013–5063, 5181i–5189.*

6. FIRST CONSULTATIVE CONFERENCE— PANAMA, 1939

1855.   *Actas de las Sesiones Preliminares y Reglamentarias Privadas*. Panama, 1939.

1856.   *Actas de las Sesiones de las Sub-Comisiones de Mantenimiento de Paz y de Cooperación Económica*. Panama, 1939.

1857.   PAU. *Acta Final de la Reunión de Consulta entre los Ministros de Relaciones Exteriores de las Repúblicas Americana en Panamá*. Panama, 1939.

1858.   ———. Director General. *Report of the Meeting of the Ministers of Foreign Affairs of the American Republics. Panama, September 23 . . . October 3, 1939*. Wash., 1939.

XI-J-6   cross references:
a)   See item 1832.
b)   In the Trask, Meyer, and Trask *Bibliography* see items 5189a–5201.

7. SECOND CONSULTATIVE CONFERENCE— HAVANA, 1940

1859.   *Diario de Sessiones*. Havana, 1940.

XI-J-7   cross references: In the Trask, Meyer, and Trask Bibliography *see items 3493, 5189b, 5202–5215.*

8. THIRD CONSULTATIVE CONFERENCE— RIO DE JANEIRO, 1942

1860.   Concheso, A. F. *Discurso de Clausura: III Reunión de Consulta entre los Ministros de Relaciones Exteriores de las Repúblicas Americanas*. Wash., 1942.

1861.   Francis, M. J. "The United States at Rio, 1942: The Strains of Pan-Americanism," *JLAS* 6 (May, 1974) 77–95.

1862.   PAU. *Manual Especial Preparada por la Unión Panamericana*. Wash., 1941.

XI-J-8   cross references: In the Trask, Meyer, and

Trask Bibliography *see items 3444, 5216–5229.*

9. CONFERENCE ON PROBLEMS OF WAR AND PEACE—MEXICO CITY (CHAPULTEPEC), 1945

1863.   Confederación de Trabajadores de América Latina. *Balance de la Conferencia Interamericana de Chapultepec*. Mexico, 1945.
Contains the ideas of Lombardo Toledano.

1864.   Inter-American Conference for the Maintenance of Continental Peace and Security. *Final Act*. Wash., 1947.

1865.   López, R. P. "The Inter-American Conference on Problems of War and Peace," *ILR* 11 (May, 1945) 564–588.

1866.   PAU. *Handbook for the Use of Delegates*. Wash., 1945.

1867.   ———. Director General. *Conferencia Interamericana sobre Problemas de Guerra y de Paz . . . Informe sobre los Resultados de la Conferencia*. Wash., 1945.

XI-J-9   cross references:
a)   See item 1754.
b)   In the Trask, Meyer, and Trask *Bibliography* see items 3821, 5230–5255a.

10. CONFERENCE ON MAINTENANCE OF CONTINENTAL PEACE AND SECURITY— RIO DE JANEIRO, 1947

1868.   Accioly, H. "A Evolução do Pan-Americanismo e o Tratado Interamericano do Assistência Recíproca," *BSBDI* 3 (1947) 11–23.

1869.   Argentina. Ministerio de Relaciones Exteriores y Culto. *La República Argentina ante la Conferencia Interamericana para el Mantenimiento de La Paz y Seguridad del Continente*. B.A., 1947.

1870.   Inter-American Conference for the Maintenance of Continental Peace and Security. *Diário das Sessões*. Rio, 1947.

1871.   PAU. Director General. *Inter-American Conference for the Maintenance of Continental Peace and Security: Report on the Results of the Conference*. Wash., 1947.

1872.   Uruguay. Ministerio de Relaciones Exteriores. *Conferencia Interamericana para el Mantenimiento de la Paz y la Seguridad del Continente*. Montevideo, 1947.

XI-J-10   cross references: In the Trask, Meyer, and Trask Bibliography see items 5256–5269.

11. FOURTH CONSULTATIVE CONFERENCE—WASHINGTON, 1951

1873. Bellegarde, D. "La Quatrièmme Réunion Consultative des Ministres des Relations Extérieures de Amérique," *JIAS* 4 (Jan., 1962) 1–21.

1874. "Fourth Meeting of Consultation of Ministers of Foreign Affairs of American States: Final Act," *USDSB* 24 (Apr., 1951) 606–613.

XI-J-11   cross references: In the Trask, Meyer, and Trask Bibliography see items 5270–5280.

12. FIFTH CONSULTATIVE CONFERENCE—SANTIAGO, 1959

1875. Brazil, Ministerio das Relações Exteriores. *V Reunião de Consulta dos Ministros das Relações das Repúblicas Americanas: Relatório do Ministro Horacio Lafer. Chefe da Delegação do Brasil.* Rio, 1960.

1876. OAS. Council. *Report of the Special Committee to Study Resolutions IX and X of the Fifth Meeting of Consultation of Ministers of Foreign Affairs.* Wash., 1959.

XI-J-12   cross references: In the Trask, Meyer, and Trask Bibliography see items 5280a–5283.

13. SIXTH AND SEVENTH CONSULTATIVE CONFERENCES—SAN JOSÉ, C.R., 1960

1877. *Actas de la Segunda Reunión Extraordinaria. Celebrada en San José, Costa Rica, del 22 al 23 de Junio de 1961.* San Salvador, 1962.

1878. Costa Rica. Dirección General de Estadística y Censos. *Sexta y Séptima Conferencias de Consulta de los Cancilleres Americanos: Discursos.* San José, C.R., 1960.

1879. Guerrero, G. *La Delegación Salvadoreña en la VI Conferencia Panamericana.* San Salvador, 1949.

1880. Moreno, I. "Las Reuniones de San José," *FI* 1 (Jan.–Mar., 1961) 431–459.

1881. PAU. *Final Act: Seventh Meeting of Consultation of Ministers of Foreign Affairs, San José, Costa Rica, August 22–29, 1960.* Wash., 1960.

XI-J-13   cross references:
 a) See item 1801.
 b) In the Trask, Meyer, and Trask *Bibliography* see items 4840, 5283a–5286b.

14. EIGHTH CONSULTATIVE CONFERENCE—PUNTA DEL ESTE, 1962

1882. Lentin, A. P. "Punta del Este y Boinas Verdes," *UES* 93 (Sept.–Oct., 1968) 81–99.

1883. OAS. *Reunión Extraordinaria del Consejo Interamericano Económico y Social al Nivel Ministerial, Punta del Este, Uruguay, del 5 a 17 de Agosto de 1961: Actas y Documentos.* Wash., 1962.

1884. Ortega, E. *La Carta de Punta del Este y la Alianza para el Progreso.* Santiago, 1967.

1885. PAU. *Final Act: Eighth Meeting of Consultation of Ministers of Foreign Affairs, Punta del Este, Uruguay, January 22–31, 1962.* Wash., 1962.

1886. Ramírez Novoa, E. *Escándalo en Punta del Este: Alianza para el Retroceso.* Lima, 1962.

1887. Selser, G. *Punta del Este contra Sierra Maestra.* B.A., 1968.

XI-J-14   cross references:
 a) For specialized materials relating to the Alliance for Progress, see items 1270–1298.
 b) See also item 3079.
 c) In the Trask, Meyer, and Trask *Bibliography* see items 4096–4147, 5287–5311, 10175.

15. NINTH CONSULTATIVE CONFERENCE—WASHINGTON, 1964

1888. Cárdenas Salas, Y. *La Novena Reunión de Consulta de los Ministros de Relaciones Exteriores y el Asunto de Cuba.* Mexico, 1967.

1889. Escudero, G. *El Ecuador en la Novena Reunión de Consulta de Ministros de Relaciones Exteriores: Wash., D.C., 21–26 de Julio de 1964.* Quito, 1964.

1890. Seara Vásquez, M. "La IX Reunión de Consulta de los Ministros de Relaciones Exteriores y el Asunto de Cuba," *RFDM* 15 (Apr.–June, 1965) 419–435.

XI-J-15   cross references: In the Trask, Meyer, and

Trask Bibliography *see items 5311a–5312.*

16. SPECIAL AND CONSULTATIVE CONFERENCES
SINCE 1964

1891. "American Chiefs of State Meet at Punta del Este," *USDSB* 56 (May, 1967) 706–720.

1892. Conferencia Especializada Interamericana sobre Derechos Humanos, San José, 1969. *Convención Americana sobre Derechos Humanos: Pacto de San José de Costa Rica.* Wash., 1970.

1893. "Foreign Ministers of the American Republics Meet at Buenos Aires," *USDSB* 56 (Mar., 1967) 72–476.

Treats the Third Special Inter-American Conference and the Eleventh Meeting of Consultation.

1894. Gordon, L. "Punta del Este Revisited," *FA* 45 (July, 1967) 624–638.

1894a. Iriarte González, R. "La Conferencia de Quito: Un Fracaso de la OEA," *NS* 16 (Jan., 1975) 5–12.

1895. Manger, W. "Reform of the OAS: The 1967 Buenos Aires Protocol of Amendment to the 1948 Charter of Bogotá: An Appraisal," *JIAS* 10 (Jan., 1968) 1–14.

1896. "OAS Foreign Ministers Take Steps against Cuban Subversion," *USDSB* 57 (Oct., 1967) 490–498.

Treats the Twelfth Meeting of Consultation.

1897. OAS. Asamblea General. *Actas y Documentos.* 2 vols., Wash., 1970.

Full texts from the first special session.

1898. ———. ———. *Eleventh Inter-American Conference. Agenda.* Wash., 1959.

1899. ———. ———. *American Convention on Human Rights: The Pact of San José, Costa Rica.* Wash., 1970.

1900. ———. ———. *Cuarto Período Ordinario de Sesiones: Actas y Documentos.* Wash., 1974.

Meetings held in Atlanta, Ga.

1901. ———. ———. *Duodécima Reunión de Consulta.* Wash., 1967.

1902. ———. ———. *Fifteenth Meeting of Consultation.* Wash., 1974.

The fifteenth meeting was held in Quito, Ecuador.

1903. ———. ———. *Primer Período Extraordinario de Sesiones: Actas y Documentos.* Wash., 1970.

1904. ———. ———. *Quinto Período Ordinario de Sesiones. Actas y Documentos.* Wash., 1975.

Meetings held in Washington.

1905. ———. ———. *Segundo Período Extraordinario de Sesiones: Actas y Documentos.* Wash., 1970.

1906. ———. ———. *Sixteenth Meeting of Consultation.* Wash., 1975.

The sixteenth meeting was held in San José, C.R.

1907. ———. ———. *Tercer Período Extraordinario de Sesiones: Actas y Documentos.* Wash., 1971.

1908. ———. Tenth Meeting of Consultation of Ministers of Foreign Affairs. *Amendments to U.S. Draft Resolution (Doc. 7 Rev. 3).* Wash., 1965.

1909. Perú. Ministerio de Relaciones Exteriores. *El Perú en la XIV Reunión de Consulta de Ministros de RR. EE. en la O.E.A.* Lima, 1971.

A speech by the Peruvian Minister of Foreign Relations.

1910. Villaverde, J. "A Year of Meditation: The OAS General Assembly," *APAU* 25 (May, 1973) 10–16.

Chapter XII   Pan Hispanism, Yankeephobia, and Aprismo

A. PAN HISPANISM

1911. Artajo, M. *Hacia la Comunidad Hispánica de Naciones*. Madrid, 1956.

1912. Barcía Trelles, C. *Puntos Cardinales de la Política Internacional*. Barcelona, 1939.

1913. Barquín y Ruiz, A. *Agustín de Iturbide, Campeón del Hispanoamericanismo*. Mexico, 1968.

1914. Barrios Carrión, L. *El Porvenir de las Naciones Iberoamericanas*. Madrid, 1896.
    Advocates a Catholic Pan Hispanism.

1914a. Boixados, A. *España entre Europa e Hispanoamérica*. B.A., 1973.
    Treats the conflict between Hispanism and utilitarianism.

1915. Bonilla y San Martín, A. *Nuestra Raza Española*. Madrid, 1926.

1916. Briceño-Iragorry, M. *Tradición, Nacionalidad y Americanidad*. Santiago, 1955.

1917. Coloma Silva, L. "Iberoamericanismo; Panamericanismo," *BINM* 2 (Nov.– Dec., 1934) 544–563.

1918. Conangla Fontanilles, J. *Del Hispanismo Ingenuo a la Cubanía Práctica*. Havana, 1950.

1919. Conte y Lacave, A. J. *El Día de la Hispanidad*. Madrid, 1941.

1920. ———. *La Leyenda Negra en la Primer Mitad el Siglo XIX*. Madrid, 1923.

1921. Fabra Rivas, A. "Concepto del Iberoamericanismo," *RE* 5–6 (Jan.– Feb., 1927) 58–66.

1922. Fernández Pesquero, J. *España en Chile*. Cádiz, Spain, 1910.

1923. ———. *El Iberoamericanismo y su Influencia en la Grandeza de la Raza Latina*. Cádiz, Spain, 1908.

1924. Ferrer de Couto, J. *América y España Consideradas en sus Intereses de Raza ante la República de los Estados Unidos del Norte*. Cádiz, Spain, 1859.

1925. Galasso, N. *Manuel Ugarte y la Unidad de Latinoamerica*. B.A., 1974.

1926. García Caminero, J. *El Problema Hispano-Americano*. Madrid, 1926.
    Argues that economic ties are more significant than spiritual ones.

1927. García Morente, M. *Idea de la Hispanidad*. Madrid, 1947.

1928. Goicoechea, A. *La Obra Pasada y Actual de España en América*. Montevideo, 1928.

1929. Gómez de Baquero, E. *Nacionalismo e Hispanismo*. Madrid, 1928.

1929a. Guevara Bazán, R. "Meditaciones sobre la Hispanidad, la Arabidad y la Peruanidad," *BANHC* 42 (Sept., 1976) 460–482.

1930. Gutiérrez Lasanta, F. *Juan Vásquez de Mella: El Verbo de Hispanidad*. Madrid, 1961.

1931. ———. *Rubén Darío: El Poeta de la Hispanidad*. Zaragoza, Spain, 1962.

1932. Gutiérrez Solana, V. *La Gran Familia Hispano-Americana*. Madrid, 1924.

1933. ———. *Hispanoamericanismo Práctico*. Madrid, 1925.

1934. ———. *Optimismo Hispanoamericano*. Madrid, 1929.

1935. Labra, R. M. de. *El Problema Hispano-Americano*. Madrid, 1906.

1936. Lianos Alcaraz, A. *El Porvenir de España en América*. Mexico, 1878.

1937. López Moreno, J. *En Busca de Latinoamérica: Un Proyecto de Integración Latinoamericana*. Mexico, 1975.

1938. Mañas Jiménez, J. *Esquemas Ideológicos sobre Hispano-Americanismo*. Cádiz, Spain, 1928.

Roman Catholicism is the basis for a lasting Pan Hispanism.

1939. Méndez Bejarano, M. *Poetas Españoles que Vivieron en América: Recopilación de Artículos Biográficos-Críticos*. Madrid, 1929.

1940. Moreno Herrera, F. *El Ser de la Hispanidad*. Jérez de la Frontera, Spain, 1966.

1941. Moya y Jiménez, F. J. de. *Exégisis de la Nacionalidad Hispanoamericana*. Cádiz, Spain, 1912.

1942. Onís, J. de. "Panhispanismo," *BANH* 46 (1964) 66–70.

1943. Orbea, R. *La Reconquista de América*. Madrid, 1905.

1944. Ortíz, F. *La Reconquista de América*. Paris, 1910.

Cuban historian argues against a "spiritual" reconquest of Spanish America led by Spain.

1945. Peman, J. M. *Valor del Hispanoamericanismo en el Progreso Total Humano Hacia la Unificación y la Paz*. Madrid, 1927.

1946. Pike, F. B. "Hispanismo and the Non-Revolutionary Spanish Immigrant in Spanish America (1900–1930)," *IEA* 25 (Autumn, 1971) 3–30.

1947. ———. *Hispanismo, 1898–1936: Spanish Conservatives and Liberals and Their Relations with Spanish America*. Notre Dame, Ind., 1971.

1948. ———. "Making the Hispanic World Safe from Democracy," *RP* 33 (July, 1971) 307–322.

1949. Ras, A. *Panhispania*. Barcelona, 1922.

1950. Sánchez de Toca, J. *Del Poder Naval en España y su Política Económica para la Nacionalidad Ibero-Americano*. Madrid, 1908.

1951. Sangroniz, J. A. *Nuevas Orientaciones para la Política Internacional de España: La Expansión Cultural en España con el Extranjero y Principalmente en Hispano América*. Madrid. 1925.

1952. Santos Chocano, J. *Alma América: Poemas Indo-Españoles*. Madrid, 1908.

1953. Sepúlveda, A. A. "La Nueva Política Exterior de Chile," *RPI* 121 (May–June, 1972) 71–97.

Calls for a new Pan Hispanism to offset the influence of the United States.

1954. Suárez, A. *Supremo Ideal Hispanoamericano*. Cádiz, Spain, 1928.

1955. Ugarte, M. *El Porvenir de la América Española*. Valencia, Spain, 1920.

1956. ———. *Mi Campaña Hispanoamericana*. Barcelona, 1922.

1957. Unión Ibero-Americano en México. *Compilación de Actas, Reglamentos, Bases Constitucionales y Demás Documentos Referente a Dicha Sociedad*. Mexico, 1886.

1958. Valdivia, V. de. *El Imperio Iberoamericano*. Santiago, 1930.

1959. Wagner de Reyna, A. *Destino y Vocación de Iberoamérica*. Madrid, 1954.

1960. Zaldumbide, G. *Significado de España en América*. N.Y., 1933.

1961. Zurano Muñoz, E. *España: Madre de América*. Madrid, 1935.

1962. ———. *Valor y Fuerza de España como Potencia en el Concierto Internacional*. Madrid, 1922.

Argues the necessity of the union of Spain and Spanish America.

XII-A cross references:
  a) Latin American attempts at union are considered in items 771–773.
  b) See also items 860, 3044.
  c) In the Trask, Meyer, and Trask *Bibliography* see items 2545, 2560, 2562, 2599–2622, 3110, 5313–5384.

B. YANKEEPHOBIA: APPRAISALS

1963. Agramonte y Pichardo, R. D. *Martí y su Concepción del Mundo*. Río Piedras, P.R., 1971.

1964. Barra, E. de la. *Francisco Bilbao: Sociabilidad Chilena*. Valparaíso, 1913.

1965. Castellanos, R. *Rufino Blanco Fombona y sus Coterráneos*. Bogotá, 1970.

1966. Donoso, A. *Bilbao y su Tiempo*. Santiago, 1913.

1967. ———. *El Pensamiento Vivo de Bilbao*. Santiago, 1940.

1968. Figueroa, P. P. *Historia de Francisco Bilbao: Su Vida, sus Obras*. 3 vols., Santiago, 1897–1898.

1969. Galasso, N. *Manuel Ugarte*. B.A., 1974.

Studies his anti-imperialist and anti-Yankee views.

1970. González y Contreras, G. *Radiografía y Disección de R. Blanco-Fombona*. Havana, 1944.

1971. Lipp, S. *Three Chilean Thinkers*. Waterloo, Canada, 1975.
The three are Francisco Bilbao, Valentín Letelier, and Enrique Molina.

1972. Oribe, E. *Rodó: Estudio Crítico y Antología*. B.A., 1974 (?).

1973. Torrano, H. *Rodó—Acción y Libertad: Restauración de su Imagen*. Montevideo, 1973.

1974. Ugarte Figueroa, E. *Francisco Bilbao, Agitador y Blásfemo*. Santiago, 1965.

1975. Varona, A. *Francisco Bilbao, Revolucionario de América*. B.A., 1973.

1976. Wolfe, W. "Attitudes toward the United States as Revealed in the Latin American Press," Ind. U. Diss., 1961.

XII-B cross references:
a) See item 1925.
b) In the Trask, Meyer, and Trask *Bibliography* see items 1414, 5328, 5385–5416a, 6336, 9460, 9461a, 9480a, 9480b, 9481a, 9649, 9826.

C. YANKEEPHOBIA: MANIFESTATIONS

1977. Araquistain, L. *La Agonía Antillana*. Madrid, 1928.

1978. ———. *El Peligro Yanqui*. Madrid, 1919.

1979. Bilbao, F. *El Evangelio Americano y Páginas Selectas*. Barcelona, 1920.

1980. ———. *El Pensamiento Vivo de Francisco Bilbao*. Santiago, 1940.

1981. Blanco Fombona, R. *La Americanización del Mundo*. Amsterdam, 1902.
A review of W. T. Steads's *The Americanization of the World*.

1982. ———. *Diario de Mi Vida, 1904–1905*. Madrid, 1929.

1983. ———. *La Espada del Samuray*. Madrid, 1924.
A series of political essays.

1984. Clulow, C. A. *El Oro Yanqui en Latinoamérica*. Montevideo, 1928.

1984a. Falcón Briceño, M. (ed.). *Cartas de Blanco-Fombona a Unamuno*. Caracas, 1968.

1985. Gil de Oto, M. *Los Enemigos de América: Los Yanquis Vistos de Prisa por un Tratamundos Madrileño*. Barcelona, 1924.

1986. Martí, J. *Cuba, Nuestra América, los Estados Unidos*. Mexico, 1973.
Treats the dangers the United States presents to Latin America.

1987. ———. *Inside the Monster: Writings on the United States and American Imperialism*. N.Y., 1975.
A collection of Martí's critical writings on the United States.

1988. Rodó, J. E *Ideario*. Santiago, 1944.

1989. ———. *Obras Completas*. Madrid, 1957.

1990. ———. *El Pensamiento Vivo de Rodó*. B.A., 1944.

1991. ———. *Rodó: Su Americanismo*. Montevideo, 1970.

1992. Ugarte, M. *The Destiny of a Continent*. N.Y., 1970.
New ed. of the 1925 translation.

1993. ———. *Las Mejores Páginas de Manuel Ugarte*. Barcelona, 1924.

XII-C cross references: In the Trask, Meyer, and Trask Bibliography *see items 1738, 2137, 2293, 2910, 2915, 2931, 2968, 2969, 3182, 3740, 4609, 5342, 5375, 5417–5445, 5768, 6614, 7536, 8355, 9424, 10072, 10202.*

D. APRISMO

1994. Aguirre Gamio, H. *Mariátegui: Destino Polémico*. Lima, 1975.

1995. Alexander, R. J. (ed.) *Aprismo: The Ideas and Doctrines of Víctor Raúl Haya de la Torre*. Kent, O., 1973.
A selection of Haya's writings.

1996. Baines, J. M. "José Carlos Mariátegui and the Development of the Ideology of Revolution in Peru," U. of Wis. Diss., 1968.

1997. ———. *Revolution in Peru: Mariátegui and the Myth*. University, Ala., 1972.

1998. Carrión, B. *José Carlos Mariátegui: El Precursor, el Anticipador, el Suscitador*. Mexico, 1976.

1999. Chavarría, J. "The Intellectuals and the Crisis of Modern Peruvian Nationalism, 1870–1919," *HAHR* 50 (May, 1970) 257–278.

2000. ———. "José Carlos Mariátegui, Revolutionary Nationalist," UCLA Diss., 1967.

2001. Choy, E., *et al. Lenín y Mariátegui*. Lima, 1970.

2002. Ferreira, O. S. *Nossa-América: Indo-América, a Ordem e a Revolução no Pensamento de Haya de la Torre*. São Paulo, 1971.

2003. Gil, B. *El Aprismo y el Movimiento Sindical Chimbotano*. Lima, 1974.
A 33-page pamphlet.

2004. González Prada, M. *Antología: Páginas Libertarias*. Lima, 1975.

2005. ———. *Horas de Lucha*. Lima, 1969.

2006. Haya de la Torre, V. R. *Obras Completas*. 7 vols., Lima, 1977.

2007. Klarén, P. F. *Modernization, Dislocation and Aprismo: Origins of the Peruvian Aprista Party, 1870–1932*. Austin, Tex., 1973.

2008. Luna Vigas, R. *Introducción a Mariátegui*. Lima, 1975.

2009. Mariátegui, J. C. *Facismo Sudamericano: Los Intelectuales y la Revolución y Otros Artículos Inéditos*. Lima, 1975.

2010. Mercado, R. *Vida, Traición y Muerte del Movimiento Aprista*. Lima, 1970.

2011. Meseguer Illán, D. *José Carlos Mariátegui y su Pensamiento Revolucionario*. Lima, 1974.

2012. Moretic, Y. *José Carlos Mariátegui: Su Vida, e Ideario, su Concepción del Realismo*. Santiago, 1970.

2013. Murillo Garaycochea, P. *Historia del Apra, 1919–1945*. Lima, 1976.

2014. Obelson, W. *Funerales del APRA y el Fraude Electoral y Fiscal*. Lima, 1962.

2015. Partido Aprista Peruano. *No Más Impuestos que Agraven al Pueblo ha Dicho Haya de la Torre Transmitiendo el Planteamiento del Partido Aprista Peruano*. Lima, 1966.

2016. Peláez Bazán, M. *Haya de la Torre y la Unidad de América Latina*. Lima, 1977.

2017. Podesta, B. *Pensamiento Político de González Prada*. Lima, 1975.

2018. Silva Villacorta, P. *¿A Dónde van las Ideas de Haya de la Torre?* Lima, 1966.

2019. Vanden, H. E. *Mariátegui: Influencias en su Formación Ideológica* Lima, 1975.

XII-D cross references: In the Trask, Meyer, and Trask Bibliography *see items 1518, 5055, 5077, 5446–5515a, 8835, 8955a.*

Chapter XIII   The United States and Mexico

A. GENERAL WORKS AND SPECIAL STUDIES

2020. Bayitch, S. A., and J. L. Siqueiros. *Conflict of Laws: Mexico and the United States, a Bilateral Study*. Coral Gables, Fla., 1968.

2021. Bazant, J. *A Concise History of Mexico: From Hidalgo to Cárdenas, 1805–1940*. Cambridge, Eng., 1977.

2022. ———. *Historia de la Deuda Exterior de México, 1823–1946*. Mexico, 1968.

2023. Cabra Ybarra, J. *México en el Derecho Convencional*. 2 vols., Mexico, 1970.
Reproduces international conventions to which Mexico is a party.

2024. Calvert, P. *Mexico*. N.Y., 1973.
Survey history of the twentieth century.

2025. Camarillo, T. *Representantes Diplomáticos de México en Washington*. Mexico, 1974.
Biographical treatment of Mexican representatives in Washington from 1822 to 1973.

2026. Cue Cánovas, A. *Los Estados Unidos y el México Olvidado*. Mexico, 1970.
Heavy concentration on the nineteenth century.

2027. Cumberland, C. C. *Mexico: The Struggle for Modernity*. N.Y., 1968.
Emphasizes socioeconomic themes rather than political history.

2028. Fehrenbach, T. R. *Fire and Blood: A History of Mexico*. N.Y., 1973.
Emphasizes the negative aspects of Mexican history.

2029. Flores Caballero, R. *La Frontera entre México y los Estados Unidos*. Monterrey, Mexico, 1976.
Studies how the border has influenced relations between the two countries from the colonial period to the date of publication.

2030. García Cantú, G. *Las Invasiones Norteamericanas en México*. Mexico, 1971.

2031. Koslow, L. E. "Mexican Foreign Policy Decision-Making: The Mutual Adjustment of Needs and Independence," U. of Calif. Riverside Diss., 1969.

2032. Levenstein, H. A. *Labor Organization in the United States and Mexico: A History of Their Relations*. Westport, Conn., 1971.

2033. López Romero, A. *Comercio y Servicio Exterior Mexicanos*. Mexico, 1957.

2034. Machado, M. A. *Aftosa: A Historical Survey of Foot-and-Mouth Disease and Inter-American Relations*. Albany, N.Y., 1969.

2035. McChesney, R. M. "International Law and Mexican Foreign Policy," U. of Va. Diss., 1969.

2036. Mexico. Secretaría de Relaciones Exteriores. *Secretarios y Encargados del Despacho de Relaciones Exteriores, 1821–1973*. Mexico, 1974.

2036a. Meyer, M. C. and W. L. Sherman. *The Course of Mexican History*. N.Y., 1979.
Covers both the colonial and national periods.

2037. Quirk, E. *Mexico*. Englewood Cliffs, N.J., 1971.
A brief but excellent survey history.

2038. Schmitt, K. M. *Mexico and the United States, 1821–1973: Conflict and Coexistence*. N.Y., 1974.
A comprehensive survey of the topic.

2039. Zelman, D. L. "American Intellectual Attitudes toward Mexico 1908–1940," O. State U. Diss., 1969.

2040. Zorrilla, L. G. *Historia de las Relaciones*

93

entre México y los Estados Unidos de América, 1800–1958. 2 ⅼs., Mexico, 1965–1966.

XIII-A   cross references:

a) For works on Mexico and the Inter-American system, see items 1795–1796.

b) In the Trask, Meyer, and Trask *Bibliography* see items 4831–4836, 5516–5559.

B. THE UNITED STATES AND MEXICAN INDEPENDENCE

2041.   Bell, T. W. *A Narrative of the Capture and Subsequent Suffering of the Mier Prisoners in Mexico.* Waco, Tex., 1964.

Reprint of work originally published in 1845.

2042.   Guzmán, J. R. "La Correspondencia de Don Luis Onís sobre la Expedición de Javier Mina," *BAGNM* 9 (July–Dec., 1968) 509–544.

2043.   ———. "Francisco Javier Mina en la Isla de Galveston y Soto la Marina," *BAGNM* 7 (Oct.–Dec., 1966) 891–1082.

2044.   ———. "John Galvin en la Guerra de Independencia de México," *BAGNM* 10 (1969) 557–587.

Galvin fought in the independence wars and arranged for arms shipments from the United States.

2045.   ———. "La Misión de José Manuel Herrera en Estados Unidos," *BAGNM* 10 (Jan.–June, 1969) 253–288.

Morelos sent Herrera to the United States to seek aid for the revolutionaries.

2045a.   Hruneni, G. A. "Palmetto Yankee: The Public Life and Times of Joel Roberts Poinsett: 1824–1851," U. of Calif. Santa Barbara Diss., 1972.

2046.   Lewis III, W. F. "Francisco Xavier Mina, Guerrilla Warrior for Romantic Liberalism," U. of Calif. Santa Barbara Diss., 1967.

2047.   ———. "Xavier Mina and Fray Servando Mier: Romantic Liberals of the Nineteenth Century," *NMHR* 44 (Apr., 1969) 119–136.

2048.   Salado Alvarez, V. *Poinsett y Algunos de su Discípulos.* Mexico, 1968.

2049.   Torre Villar, E. de la. *Labor Diplomática de Tadeo Ortíz.* Mexico, 1974.

XIII-B   cross references:

a) See item 1913.

b) In the Trask, Meyer, and Trask *Bibliography* see items 5560–5593, 9326a.

C. UNITED STATES–MEXICAN RELATIONS, 1821–1836

2050.   Barnard, J. G. *The Isthmus of Tehuantepec: Being the Results of a Survey for a Railroad to Connect the Atlantic.* N.Y., 1852.

2051.   Bosch García, C. "Discusiones Previas al Primer Tratado de Comercio entre México y los Estados Unidos: 1821–1838," *TE* 13 (Apr.–June, 1946) 329–345.

2052.   Brack, G. M. "Imperious Neighbor: The Mexican View of the United States, 1821–1846," U. of Tex. Diss., 1967.

2052a.   Campbell, R. "Henry Clay and the Poinsett Pledge Controversy of 1826," *TA* 28 (Apr., 1972) 429–440.

2053.   Carnes, Sister M. L. "The American Occupation of New Mexico, 1821–1852," U. of Calif. Diss., 1925.

2054.   Chávez Orozco, L. (ed.). *Colección de Documentos para la Historia del Comercio Exterior en México.* 3 vols., Mexico, 1965–1966.

Covers foreign commerce in the first years after independence.

2055.   Crawford, A. F. (ed.). *The Eagle: The Autobiography of Santa Anna.* Austin, Tex., 1967.

First Eng. trans.

2056.   Donathan, C. D. "Lucas Alamán and Mexican Foreign Relations, 1821–1833," Duke U. Diss., 1968.

2057.   Gaxiola, F. J. *Poinsett en México (1822–1828).* Mexico, 1936.

First U.S. minister to Mexico.

2058.   Green, S. C. "Lucas Alamán," Tex. Christian U. Diss., 1970.

2059.   Lamar, Q. C. "The Role of Lucas Alamán in Mexican–United States Relations, 1824–1853," La. State U. and Agricultural and Mechanical College Diss., 1971.

2060.   Leary, D. T. "The Attitudes of Certain United States Citizens toward Mexico, 1821–1846," U.S.C. Diss., 1970.

2061.   Moyanho Phissa, A. "El Significado del

Comercio de Santa Fe en las Relaciones entre México y los Estados Unidos," UNAM Diss., 1975.

2062. Winn, W. B. "The Efforts of the United States to Secure Religious Liberty in a Commercial Treaty with Mexico, 1825–1831," *TA* 28 (Jan., 1972) 311–332.

Anthony Butler succeeded after Joel Poinsett failed.

XIII-C cross references:

a) See item 707.

b) In the Trask, Meyer, and Trask *Bibliography* see items 2340, 5560, 5565, 5578, 5580, 5583, 5593–5631, 5888, 9316, 9326a.

D. THE TEXAS ISSUE, 1836–1845

2063. Brack, G. *Mexico Views Manifest Destiny, 1821–1846.* Albuquerque, N.M., 1975.

2064. Crisp, J. E. "Anglo-Texan Attitudes toward the Mexican, 1821–1845," Yale U. Diss., 1976.

2065. Downs, F. "The History of Mexicans in Texas, 1820–1845," Tex. Technical U. Diss., 1970.

2066. Gamble, S. G. "James Pinckney Henderson in Europe: The Diplomacy of the Republic of Texas, 1837–1840," Tex. Technical U. Diss., 1976.

2067. Jones, O. L. *Santa Anna.* N.Y., 1968.

2068. Merk, F. *Fruits of Propaganda in the Tyler Administration.* Cambridge, Mass., 1971.

2069. ———. *Slavery and the Annexation of Texas.* Cambridge, Mass., 1972.

2070. Pierce, G. S. *Texas under Arms: The Camps, Posts, Forts, Military Towns of the Republic of Texas, 1836–1846.* Austin, Tex., 1969.

A military history of the Republic of Texas from the battle of San Jacinto to annexation by the United States.

2071. Pletcher, D. M. *The Diplomacy of Annexation: Texas, Oregon and the Mexican War.* Columbia, Mo., 1973.

2072. Rohrs, R. C. "George Bancroft and American Foreign Relations," U. of Nebr. Diss., 1976.

Bancroft was Secretary of the Navy at the time of the annexation of Texas and the beginning of the Mexican War.

2073. Sánchez Lamego, M. A. *The Siege and Taking of the Alamo.* Santa Fe, N.M., 1968.

One of the few English-language accounts by a professional Mexican historian.

2074. Urbina, M. "The Impact of the Texas Revolution on the Government, Politics, and Society of Mexico, 1836–1846," U. of Tex. Diss., 1976.

2075. Webster, M. G. "Texan Manifest Destiny and the Mexican Border Conflict, 1865–1880," Ind. U. Diss., 1972.

2076. Weems, J. E., and J. Weems. *Dream of an Empire: A Human History of the Republic of Texas, 1836–1846.* N.Y., 1971.

XIII-D cross references:

a) For works on the Pastry War (1838), see item 675.

b) See also items 2052, 2059, 2060.

c) In the Trask, Meyer, and Trask *Bibliography* see items 2070, 2097a, 2110, 2177a–2182b, 5560, 5601, 5606, 5615a, 5615b, 5622, 5623, 5624b, 5627, 5630, 5632–5745, 5810, 5888.

E. THE MEXICAN WAR, 1846–1848

2077. Balbontin, M. *La Invasión Americana, 1846 a 1848: Apuntes del Subteniente de Artillería.* Mexico, 1883.

A Mexican war diary.

2078. Bauer, K. J. *Surfboats and Horse Marines: U.S. Naval Operations in the Mexican War, 1846–48.* Annapolis, Md., 1969.

2078a. Bochin, H. W., "Western Whig Opposition to the Mexican War: A Rhetoric of Dissent," Indiana U. Diss., 1970.

2079. Bodson, R. L. "A Description of the United States Occupation of Mexico as Reported by American Newspapers Published in Vera Cruz, Puebla and Mexico City, September 14, 1847 to July 31, 1848," Ball State U. Diss., 1971.

2080. Connor, S. V., and O. B. Faulk. *North America Divided: The Mexican War 1846–1848.* N.Y., 1971.

2081. Cutts, J. M. *The Conquest of California and New Mexico by the Forces of the United States in the Years 1846 and 1847.* Albuquerque, N.M., 1965.

2082.   Dufour, C. L. *The Mexican War: A Compact History*. N.Y., 1968.

2083.   Farnham, T. J. "Nicholas Trist and James Freaner and the Mission to Mexico," *AAW* 99 (Autumn, 1969) 247–260.

Trist followed Freaner's advice in negotiating the Treaty of Guadalupe-Hidalgo.

2084.   Harstad, P. T., and R. W. Resh. "The Causes of the Mexican War: A Note on Changing Interpretations," *AAW* 6 (1964) 289–302.

2084a. Katcher, P. R. *The Mexican-American War, 1846–1848*. London, 1976.

Profusely illustrated.

2085.   Lofgren, C. A. "Force and Diplomacy, 1846–1848: The View from Washington," *MAF* 31 (Summer, 1967) 57–64.

Argues that President Polk used a combination of force and diplomatic pressure to achieve U.S. objectives.

2086.   López y Rivas, G. *La Guerra del 47 y la Resistencia Popular a la Ocupación*. Mexico, 1976.

2086a. Mawn, B. P. "A Land Grant Guarantee: The Treaty of Guadalupe-Hidalgo or the Protocol of Querétaro?" *JW* 14 (Oct., 1975) 49–63.

2087.   McDonald, A. P. (ed.). *The Mexican War: Crisis for American Democracy*. Lexington, Mass., 1969.

Selected readings.

2088.   Mullins, W. H. "The British Press and the Mexican War: Justin Smith Revised," *NMHR* 52 (July, 1977) 207–228.

2089.   Nelson, A. L. K. "The Secret Diplomacy of James K. Polk during the Mexican War, 1846–1847," George Washington U. Diss., 1972.

2090.   O'Neil, D. J. "The United States Navy in the Californias, 1840–1850," U.S.C. Diss., 1969.

2091.   Price, G. W. *Origins of the War with Mexico: The Polk-Stockton Intrigue*. Austin, Tex., 1967.

Argues that Polk was using Commodore Stockton for his own purposes. Sp. ed., Mexico, 1974.

2092.   Ramsey, A. C. *The Other Side: Or a Mexican History of the War in Mexico*. N.Y., 1850.

2092a. Reilly, T. W. "American Reporters and the Mexican War, 1846–1848," U. of Minn. Diss., 1975.

2093.   Schroeder, J. H. *Mr. Polk's War: American Opposition and Dissent, 1846–1848*. Madison, Wis., 1973.

2094.   ———. "To Give Aid and Comfort: American Opposition to the Mexican War, 1846–1848," U. of Va. Diss., 1971.

2095.   Smith, G. W. (comp.). *Chronicles of the Gringos: The U.S. Army in the Mexican War, 1846–1848*. Albuquerque, N.M., 1968.

Selections from contemporary writings.

2096.   Tennery, T. D. *The Mexican War Diary of Thomas D. Tennery*. Norman, Okla., 1970.

The author was a member of the Illinois volunteers who went to Mexico with General Scott.

2097.   Tuturow, R. E. "Whigs of the Old Northwest and the Mexican War," Stanford U. Diss., 1968.

2098.   Weems, J. E. *To Conquer a Peace: The War between the United States and Mexico*. Garden City, N.Y., 1974.

XIII-E   cross references:
a)   See items 2063, 2067, 2071, 2072.
b)   In the Trask, Meyer, and Trask *Bibliography* see items 2092, 2103b, 2104, 2113, 2128, 5601, 5603, 5610, 5623, 5710a, 5746–5844.

F. UNITED STATES–MEXICAN RELATIONS, 1848–1876

2099.   Andrade, A. R. "Mexican Liberalism and the United States during the Era of La Reforma: A History of Attitudes and Policy, 1855–1861," U. of Okla. Diss., 1975.

2100.   Auer, J. J. "Lincoln's Minister to Mexico," *OSAHQ* 59 (Apr., 1950) 115–128.

Treats Thomas Corwin's career from 1861 to 1864.

2100a. Berbusse, E. J. "Two Kentuckians Evaluate the Mexican Scene from Vera

Cruz, 1853–1861," *TA* 31 (Apr., 1975) 501–512.
Both were U.S. consuls.

2101. Broussard, R. F. "Vidaurri, Juárez and Comonfort's Return from Exile," *HAHR* 49 (May, 1969) 268–280.

2101a. Casellas, R. "Confederate Colonists in Mexico," *APAU* 27 (Sept., 1975) 8–15.

2101b. Cortada, J. W. "España y los Estados Unidos ante la Cuestión Mexicana, 1855–1868," *HM* 27 (Jan.–Mar., 1978) 387–426.

2102. Cué Canovas, A. *Juárez, los E.E.U.U. y Europa: El Tratado McLane-Ocampo*. Mexico, 1970.

2103. Daddysman, J. W. "The Matamoros Trade, 1861–1865," W.Va. U. Diss., 1976.

2104. Farnell, E. W. "Texas and the Filibusters in the 1850's," *SHQ* 59 (Apr., 1956) 411–428.

2105. Goldstein, M. G. "Americanization and Mexicanization: The Mexican Elite and Anglo-Americans in the Gadsden Purchase Lands, 1853–1880," Case Western Reserve U. Diss., 1977.

2106. González Fernández, A. R. *La Servidumbre de Tránsito sobre el Istmo de Tehuantepec en Favor de los Estados Unidos y su Abrogación Definitiva*. Mexico, 1958.

2107. Gordon, L. "Lincoln and Juárez: A Brief Reassessment of Their Relationship," *HAHR* 48 (Feb., 1968) 75–80.
Concludes that the close relationship between the two presidents has been exaggerated.

2108. Irby, J. A. "Line of the Rio Grande: War and Trade on the Confederate Frontier, 1861–1865," U. of Ga. Diss., 1969.

2109. Kaiser, C. C. "John Watson Foster: United States Minister to Mexico, 1873–1880," American U. Diss., 1954.

2110. Miller, R. R. *Arms across the Border: United States Aid to Juárez during the French Intervention*. Philadelphia, Pa., 1973.
Vol. 63 of the publications of the American Philosophical Society.

2111. ———. "Californians against the Emperor," *CHSQ* 37 (Sept., 1958) 193–214.
Treats Plácido Vega's recruitment efforts in California and Nevada.

2112. Oliff, D. C. "Economics of Mexican-U.S. Relations during the Reforma, 1851–1861," U. of Fla. Diss., 1974.

2112a. Ruibal Corella, J. A. *Y Caborca se Cubrió de Gloria: La Expedición Filubustera de Henry Alexander Crabb a Sonora*. Mexico, 1976.

2113. Salado Alvarez, V. *Como Perdimos California y Salvamos Tehuantepec*. Mexico, 1968.

2114. Schoonover, T. D. "El Algodón Mexicano y la Guerra Civil Norteamericana," *HM* 23 (Jan.–Mar., 1974) 483–506.

2114a. ———. *Dollars over Dominion: The Triumph of Liberalism in Mexican–United States Relations, 1861–1867*. Baton Rouge, La., 1978.

2115. ———. "Mexican–United States Relations, 1861–1867," U. of Minn. Diss., 1970.

2116. Southerland, J. E. "Mexican–United States Relations, 1857–1860: The Failure of Manifest Destiny," U. of Ga. Diss., 1976.

2117. Stevens, S. *Tehuantepec Railway Company*. N.Y., 1869.

2118. Stout, J. A., Jr. "The Last Years of Manifest Destiny: Filibustering in Northwestern Mexico, 1848–1862," Okla. State U. Diss., 1971.

2119. Tamayo, J. L. "El Tratado McLane-Ocampo," *HM* 21 (Apr.–June, 1972) 573–614.

2120. Tyler, R. C. *Santiago Vidaurri and the Southern Confederacy*. Austin, Tex., 1973.

2121. USCS. *Reports of Explorations and Surveys to Ascertain the Practicability of a Ship Canal between the Atlantic and Pacific Oceans by Way of the Isthmus of Tehuantepec*. (42d Cong., 2d Sess., Sen. Exec. Doc. 6.) Wash., 1872.

2122. ———. Committee on Foreign Relations. *Report . . . Communicating the Correspondence between the Government of the United States and the Republic of Mexico, Respecting the Right of War across the Isthmus of Tehuantepec*. (32d Cong., 1st Sess.) Wash., 1852.

2123. Ysunza Uzeta, S. *La Verdad sobre la Supuesta Ayuda de los Estados Unidos a Juárez durante la Intervención Francesa*. Mexico, 1966.

2124. Zertucker Muñoz, F. *La Primera Presiden-

cia de Benito Juárez. Mexico, 1972.
   Narrative history covering the period
   1858 to 1861.

XIII-F   cross references:
   a)   For works relating to the McLane-Ocampo
         Treaty and other questions concerning
         transit rights across the Isthmus of Tehuan-
         tepec, see items 2102, 2106, 2117, 2119,
         2121, 2122.
   b)   For works relating to the French interven-
         tion of 1862–1867, see items 687–705.
   c)   See also items 148, 736, 2402.
   d)   In the Trask, Meyer, and Trask *Bibliography*
         see items 2233–2337a, 2352, 2400, 2406,
         2413, 2414, 2416–2418, 2422–2424,
         2428, 2429, 2446, 5603, 5663, 5693,
         5845–5930, 5963, 9989.

G.   THE UNITED STATES AND THE DÍAZ DICTATORSHIP, 1876–1910

2125.   Albro, W. S. "Ricardo Flores Magón and
        the Liberal Party: An Inquiry into the
        Origins of the Mexican Revolution of
        1910," U. of Ariz. Diss., 1967.
2126.   Ammen, D. "Objections to the Isthmus
        of Tehuantepec as a Canal Route," *JAGS*
        11 (Dec., 1879) 297–300.
2127.   Anderson, A. D. *The Tehuantepec Inter-
        Ocean Railroad: A Commercial and Statisti-
        cal Review Showing Its Local, National,
        International Features, and Advantages.*
        N.Y., 1881.
2128.   Clendenen, C. C. *Blood on the Border: The
        United States Army and the Mexican Irregu-
        lars.* N.Y., 1969.
           In spite of the title the work also treats
        the intervention in Veracruz.
2129.   Forest, J. L. "United States Recognition
        of the Government of Porfirio Díaz," U.
        of Okla. Diss., 1967.
2130.   Gibbs, W. E. "Díaz Executive Agents
        and United States Foreign Policy," *NDQ*
        45 (Spring, 1977) 36–53.
2131.   ————. "Spadework Diplomacy: U.S.-
        Mexican Relations during the Hayes
        Administration, 1877–1881," Kent
        State U. Diss., 1973.
2132.   Isaacs, H. "United States–Mexican Rela-
        tions during the González Administra-
        tion, 1880–1884," U. of Ala. Diss.,
        1968.

2133.   Meier, M. S. "History of the Tehuan-
        tepec Railroad," U. of Calif. Diss.,
        1954.
2133a. Munch, F. J. "The Anglo-Dutch-
        American Petroleum Industry in Mexico:
        Formative Years during the Porfiriato,
        1900–1910," *RHA* 84 (July–Dec.,
        1977) 135–188.
2134.   Niblo, S. R. "The Political Economy of
        the Early Porfiriato: Politics and
        Economics in Mexico 1876–1880,"
        Northern Ill. U. Diss., 1972.
2135.   Raat, W. D. "The Diplomacy of Sup-
        pression: Los *Revoltosos* Mexico and the
        United States, 1906–1911," *HAHR* 56
        (Nov., 1976) 529–550.
           Concerns U.S. activities against the
        Flores Magón brothers and other radicals.
2136.   Roberts, D. F. "Mining and Moderniza-
        tion: The Mexican Border States during
        the Porfiriato, 1876–1911," U. of
        Pittsburgh Diss., 1974.
2137.   Romney, J. B. "American Interests in
        Mexico: Development and Impact during
        the Rule of Porfirio Díaz," U. of Utah
        Diss., 1969.
2138.   Roux López, F. B. "El Surgimiento del
        Imperialismo Económico de los Estados
        Unidos: La Penetración Económica en
        México (1896–1910)," UNAM Diss.,
        1965.
2139.   Ryan, H. J. "Selected Aspects of Ameri-
        can Activities in Mexico, 1876–1910,"
        U. of Chicago Diss., 1964.
2140.   Trenner, R. A. "The Southern Pacific
        Railroad of Mexico," *PHR* 35 (Aug.,
        1966) 265–284.
2141.   Wasserman, M. "Oligarquía e Intereses
        Extranjeros en Chihuahua durante el Por-
        firiato," *HM* 22 (Jan.–Mar., 1973)
        279–319.

XIII-G   cross references:
   a)   See item 2403.
   b)   In the Trask, Meyer, and Trask *Bibliography*
         see items 2085, 2508, 5867, 5871, 5880,
         5931–6008, 6070, 6751.

H. THE UNITED STATES AND THE MEXICAN REVOLUTION, 1910–1940

1. GENERAL ACCOUNTS AND SPECIAL STUDIES

2142.   Anderson, W. W. "The Nature of th▪

Mexican Revolution as Viewed from the United States, 1910–1917," U. of Tex. Diss., 1976.

2143. Bodayla, S. D. "Financial Diplomacy: The United States and Mexico, 1919–1933," NYU Diss., 1975.

2144. Córdova, A. *La Ideología de la Revolución Mexicana*. Mexico, 1973.

2145. Engel, J. F. "The Revolution and Mexican Foreign Policy," *JIAS* 11 (Oct., 1969) 518–532.

Surveys the period 1910 to 1960.

2146. Gerome, F. A. "United States–Mexican Relations during the Initial Years of the Mexican Revolution," Kent State U. Diss., 1968.

2147. Gilly, A. *La Revolución Interrumpida*. Mexico, 1972.

2148. Gómez Quiñones, J. *Las Ideas Políticas de Ricardo Flores Magón*. Mexico, 1977.

2149. Grieb, K. J. "Standard Oil and the Financing of the Mexican Revolution," *CHSQ* 50 (Mar., 1971) 59–71.

As the author admits, the case presented is inconclusive.

2150. Gunn, D. W. "The American and British Authorities in Mexico, 1911–1941," U. of N.C. Diss., 1968.

2151. Haley, P. E. *Revolution and Intervention: The Diplomacy of Taft and Wilson with Mexico, 1910–1917*, Cambridge, Mass., 1970.

2152. Landau, M. "American Enterprise in Mexico: A Case Study of the Discrimination in an Underdeveloped Country during a Revolutionary Period," NYU Diss., 1959.

2153. Levenstein, H. A. "The United States Labor Movement and Mexico, 1910–1951," U. of Wis. Diss., 1966.

2154. Lieuwen, E. *Mexican Militarism: The Political Rise and Fall of the Revolutionary Army, 1910–1940*. Albuquerque, N.M., 1968.

Describes the process of curbing militarism during the first 30 years of the revolution.

2155. Meyer, J. *La Revolution Mexicaine, 1910–1940*. Paris, 1972.

2156. Meyer, L. *Los Grupos de Presión Extranjeros en el México Revolucionario: 1910–1940*. Mexico, 1973.

Concentrates on the pressures of foreign-owned petroleum and mining companies.

2156a. Prisco, S. "John V. Barrett's Plan to Mediate the Mexican Revolution," *TA* 28 (Apr., 1971) 413–426.

2157. Pyron, D. A. "Mexico as an Issue in American Politics, 1911–1916," U. of Va. Diss., 1975.

2158. Robertson, O. Z. "Mexico and Non-Intervention, 1910–1919: The Policy, the Practice, and the Law," UCLA Diss., 1969.

2159. Santibáñez, E. *México y sus Relaciones Internacionales*. Paris, 1917.

2160. Smith, R. F. *The United States and Revolutionary Nationalism in Mexico, 1916–1932*. Chicago, 1972.

Sp. ed., Mexico, 1973.

2161. Trow, C. W. "Senator Albert B. Fall and Mexican Affairs: 1912–1921," U. of Colo. Diss., 1966.

XIII-H-1 cross references:

a) See item 2128.

b) In the Trask, Meyer, and Trask *Bibliography* see items 3408, 4638, 5950, 5974, 6009–6084, 6479.

2. UNITED STATES–MEXICAN RELATIONS, 1910–1913

2162. Beezley, W. H. *Insurgent Governor: Abraham González and the Mexican Revolution in Chihuahua*. Lincoln, Nebr., 1973.

Contains a section on González's activities in the United States, including arms procurement.

2163. Calvert, P. *The Mexican Revolution 1910–1914: The Diplomacy of the Anglo-American Conflict*. Cambridge, Eng., 1968.

A heavily documented study.

2164. Greenleaf, F. L. "Diplomacy of the Mexican Revolution: Mexican Policy and the American Response, 1910–1913," U. of Tenn. Diss., 1976.

2165. Grieb, K. J. *The United States and Huerta*. Lincoln, Nebr., 1969.

Based heavily on U.S. archives.

2165a. Henderson, P. V. N. "Mexican Rebels in the Borderlands: 1910–1912," *RRVHR* 2 (Summer, 1975) 207–219.

2166. Holcombe, H. E. "United States Arms

Control and the Mexican Revolution, 1910–1914," U. of Ala. Diss., 1968.

2167. Martínez, P. (ed.). *El Magonismo en Baja California*. Mexico, 1958.

Treats the Dick Ferris episode of 1911.

2168. Meyer, M. C. *Huerta: A Political Portrait*. Lincoln, Nebr., 1972.

Contains a chapter on Huerta and Wilson.

2168a. Rangel, R. S. "Henry Lane Wilson and the Fall of Francisco I. Madero," American U. Diss., 1975.

2169. Rausch, G. J. "Poison Pen Diplomacy: Mexico, 1913," *TA* 24 (Jan., 1968) 272–280.

2170. Taracena, A. *Madero, Víctima del Imperialismo Yanqui*. 2d ed., Mexico, 1973.

2171. Turner, F. C. "Anti-Americanism in Mexico, 1910–1913," *HAHR* 47 (Nov., 1967) 502–518.

2172. Ulloa, B. "Carranza y el Armamento Norteamericano," *HM* 17 (Oct.–Dec., 1967) 253–262.

Treats the period of the Constitutionalist fight against Huerta.

2173. ———. *La Revolución Intervenida: Relaciones Diplomáticas entre México y Estados Unidos, 1910–1944*. Mexico, 1971.

An impressively documented study covering a wide variety of diplomatic relations during the first four years of the Mexican Revolution.

XIII-H-2   cross references: In the Trask, Meyer, and Trask Bibliography see items 5959, 5969, 5971, 6085–6145, 6195a.

3. UNITED STATES–MEXICAN RELATIONS, 1914–1920

2174. Baecker, T. "The Arms of the *Ypiranga*: The German Side," *TA* 30 (July, 1973) 1–17.

Treats German activities during the controversial arms shipment to Huerta.

2175. Balmaseda-Napoles, F. A. "Mexico and the U.S., 1912–1917—A Study of Selected Writings of Isidro Fabela," Case Western Reserve U. Diss., 1974.

2176. Blaisdell, L. L. "Henry Chandler and Mexican Border Intrigue, 1914–1917," *PHR* 35 (Nov., 1966) 385–393.

Chandler was an editor of the *Los Angeles Times*.

2177. Burdick, C. B. "A House on Navidad Street: The Celebrated Zimmermann Note on the Texas Border," *AAW* 8 (1966) 19–34.

2177a. Clements, K. A. "Emissary from a Revolution," *TA* 35 (Jan., 1979) 353–372.

2178. Coker, W. S. "Mediación Británica en el Conflicto Wilson-Huerta," *HM* 18 (Oct.–Dec., 1968) 244–257.

2179. Gerlach, A. "Conditions along the Border, 1915: The Plan de San Diego," *NMHR* 43 (July, 1968) 195–212.

Traces German influence and reproduces the plan.

2180. Gilderhus, M. T. *Diplomacy and Revolution: U.S.-Mexican Relations under Wilson and Carranza*. Tucson, Ariz., 1977.

2181. ———. "Senator Albert B. Fall and the 'Plot against Mexico,'" *NMHR* 48 (Oct., 1973) 299–311.

Fall protected American interests without the need for intervention.

2182. ———. "The United States and Carranza, 1917: The Question of De Jure Recognition," *TA* 29 (Oct., 1972) 214–231.

Treats the impact of World War I on U.S. recognition policy toward Carranza.

2183. ———. "The United States and the Mexican Revolution, 1915–1920," U. of Nebr. Diss., 1968.

Based on both U.S. and Mexican foreign archives.

2184. Glaser, D. P. "Pacific Northwest Reaction to Wilson's Mexican Diplomacy, 1913–1916," U. of Idaho Diss., 1965.

2185. Grieb, K. J. "El Caso Benton y la Diplomacia de la Revolución," *HM* 18 (Oct.–Dec., 1969) 282–301.

Benton was executed by the Villistas.

2186. ———. "The Lind Mission to Mexico," *CS* 7 (Jan., 1968) 25–43.

2187. Hall, L. B. "The Mexican Revolution and the Crisis in Naco," *JW* 16 (Oct., 1977) 27–35.

2188. Harper, J. W. "Hugh Lenox Scott: Soldier and Diplomat, 1876–1917," U. of Va. Diss., 1968.

Scott played an active role during the revolution.

2188a. ————. "Hugh Lenox Scott y la Diplomacia de los Estados Unidos Hacia la Revolución Mexicana," *HM* 27 (Jan.–Mar., 1978) 427–445.

2189. Hill, L. D. *Emissaries to a Revolution: Woodrow Wilson's Executive Agents in Mexico*. Baton Rouge, La., 1973.
Examines the activities of William Bayard Hale, John Lind, John Silliman, Paul Fuller, and others.

2190. ————. "The Progressive Politician as a Diplomat: The Case of John Lind in Mexico," *TA* 27 (Apr., 1971) 355–372.
Lind was President Wilson's special agent in Veracruz.

2191. Machado, M. A., and J. T. Judge, "Tempest in a Teapot? The Mexican–United States Intervention Crisis of 1919," *SHQ* 74 (July, 1970) 1–23.

2192. Mancisidor, J. *Carranza y su Política Internacional*. Mexico, 1929.

2193. Meyer, M. C. "The Arms of the Ypiranga," *HAHR* 50 (Aug., 1970) 543–556.
Traces the shipment from original purchase in the United States to ultimate delivery in Mexico.

2193a. O'Brien, D. J. "Petróleo e Intervención: Relaciones entre los Estados Unidos y México, 1917–1918," *HM* 27 (Jul.–Sept., 1977) 103–140.

2194. Richmond, D. W. "The First Chief and Revolutionary Politics: The Presidency of Venustiano Carranza, 1915–1920," U. of Wash. Diss., 1976.

2194a. Stein, H. H. "Lincoln Steffens and the Mexican Revolution," *AJES* 34 (Apr., 1975) 197–212.

2195. Webster, A. *Woodrow Wilson y México*. Mexico, 1964.

XIII-H-3   cross references:
a) For more general accounts of President Wilson's Latin American policy, see items 833–844.
b) See also item 857.
c) In the Trask, Meyer, and Trask *Bibliography* see items 3036–3083, 3153, 3159, 3160, 5999, 6108, 6113, 6117, 6118, 6124, 6130, 6134, 6141, 6146–6204, 6439a.

4. TAMPICO, VERACRUZ, AND THE ABC MEDIATION

2196. Guerrero Yoacham, C. *Las Conferencias del Niagara Falls: La Mediación de Argentina, Brasil y Chile en el Conflicto entre Estados Unidos y México en 1914*. Santiago, 1966.

2197. Knopp, A. K. "'The Will of the People': The International Public Opinion and the American Intervention in Mexico, 1914," Tex. Technical U. Diss., 1973.

2198. Melo de Remer, M. L. *Veracruz Mártir: La Infamia de Woodrow Wilson*. Mexico, 1966.

2199. Sweetmen, J. *The Landing at Veracruz: 1914*. Annapolis, Md., 1968.

2200. Woodbury, R. G. "Wilson y la Intervención de Veracruz," *HM* 17 (Oct.–Dec., 1967) 263–292.

XIII-H-4   cross references:
a) Many of the general works on United States–Mexican relations for this period also treat these topics. See items 2142–2162.
b) For works on the Wilson administration, see items 833–834.
c) In the Trask, Meyer, and Trask *Bibliography* see items 3036–3083, 6146–6225, 9495.

5. THE COLUMBUS RAID AND PERSHING'S PUNITIVE EXPEDITION

2201. Beltrán, E. "Fantasía y Realidad de Pancho Villa," *HM* 16 (July–Sept., 1966) 71–84.
Discusses Villa's relationship with the United States.

2202. Calzadíaz Barrera, A. *Porqué Villa Atacó Colombus: Intriga Internacional*. Mexico, 1972.
Blames the attack on a German-Jewish conspiracy.

2203. Clendenen, C. C. "The Punitive Expedition of 1916: A Re-evaluation," *AAW* 3 (1961) 311–320.

2204. Cramer, S. "The Punitive Expedition from Boquillas," *CJ* 27 (Nov., 1916) 200–227.

2205. Farrell, C. H. *Incidents in the Life of General John J. Pershing*. N.Y., 1918.

2205a. Harris, C. H., and L. R. Sadler. "Pancho Villa and the Columbus Raid: The Missing Documents," *NMHR* 50 (Oct., 1975) 335–346.

2206. Mason, H. M. *The Great Pursuit*. N.Y., 1970.

2207. Munch, F. J. "Villa's Columbus Raid: Practical Politics or German Design?" *NMHR* 44 (July, 1969) 189–214.

2208. Rodney, G. B. *As a Cavalryman Remembers*. Caldwell, Idaho, 1944.
Author was a member of the punitive expedition.

2209. Thomas, R. S., and I. V. Allen. *The Mexican Punitive Expedition under Brigadier General John J. Pershing, United States Army, 1916–1917*. Wash., 1954.

2210. Vandiver, F. E. *Black Jack: The Life and Times of John J. Pershing*. 2 vols., College Station, Tex., 1977.

2211. White, E. B. "The Muddied Waters of Columbus, New Mexico," *TA* 32 (July, 1975) 92–116.

XIII-H-5   cross references:
a) Many of the general works on United States–Mexican relations for this period treat these topics. See items 2142–2162.
b) In the Trask, Meyer, and Trask *Bibliography* see items 6146–6204, 6226–6257.

I. UNITED STATES–MEXICAN RELATIONS, 1920–1940

2212. Alvarez Sepúlveda, E. *Las Relaciones de México y los Estados Unidos durante el Período en que Fué Presidente el General Calles, 1924–1928*. Mexico, 1966.

2213. Beelen, G. D. "Harding and Mexico: Diplomacy by Economic Persuasion," Kent State U. Diss., 1971.

2214. Carmona, I. "Anatomy of a Diplomatic Failure: A Study of the Tenure of Ambassador James Rockwell Sheffield in Mexico, 1923–1927," U.S.C. Diss., 1969.

2215. Di Piazza, D. D. "The Bucareli Conference and United States–Mexican Relations," U. of Mo. Diss., 1966.

2216. Fabela, I. (ed.). *La Política Internacional del Presidente Cárdenas*. Mexico, 1953.

Documents treating Cárdenas's foreign policy.

2217. ———. "La Política Internacional del Presidente Cárdenas," *CA* 30 (Jan.–Feb., 1971) 73–90.

2218. Hindman, E. J. "¿Confusión o Conspiración? Estados Unidos Frente a Obregón," *HM* 25 (Oct.–Dec., 1975) 271–301.

2219. ———. "The U.S. and Alvaro Obregón: Diplomacy by Proxy," Tex. Technical U. Diss., 1972.

2220. Horn, J. J. "Did the United States Plan an Invasion of Mexico in 1927?" *JIAS* 15 (Nov., 1973) 454–471.
Suggests that no serious plans were undertaken.

2221. ———. "Diplomacy by Ultimatum: Ambassador Sheffield and Mexican-American Relations, 1924–1927," State U. of N.Y. Buffalo Diss., 1969.

2222. ———. "El Embajador Sheffield contra el Presidente Calles," *HM* 20 (Oct.–Dec., 1970) 265–284.
Concentrates on the controversy over the implementation of Article 27 of the Constitution of 1917.

2223. ———. "U.S. Diplomacy and the Specter of Bolshevism in Mexico, 1924–1927," *TA* 32 (July, 1975) 31–45.

2224. Ignasias, C. D. "Reluctant Recognition: The United States and the Recognition of Alvaro Obregón of Mexico, 1920–1924," Mich. State U. Diss., 1967.

2225. ———. "Propaganda and Public Opinion in Harding's Foreign Affairs: The Case for Mexican Recognition," *JQ* 48 (Spring, 1971) 41–52.

2226. ———. "Charles Evans Hughes and Mexican–American Relations, 1921–1924," U. of Colo. Diss., 1970.

2226a. Kane, N. S. "American Businessmen and Foreign Policy: The Recognition of Mexico, 1920–1923," *PSQ* 90 (Summer, 1975) 293–313.

2226b. ———. "Corporate Power and Foreign Policy: Efforts of American Oil Companies to Influence United States Relations with Mexico, 1921–1928," *DH* 1 (Spring, 1977) 170–198.

2227. Lane, J. A. "United States–Mexican Diplomatic Relations, 1917–1942," Georgetown U. Diss., 1972.

2228. Levenstein, H. A. "The AFL and Mexican Immigration in the 1920's: An Experiment in Labor Diplomacy," *HAHR* 48 (May, 1968) 206–219.

2229. Medin, T. *Ideología y Praxis Política de Lázaro Cárdenas*. Mexico, 1972.

2230. Sawatzy, L. *They Sought a Country: Mennonite Colonization in Mexico*. Berkeley, Calif., 1971.

    The colonization occurred in the 1920s.

2231. Scholes, W. V., and M. V. Scholes, "Gran Bretaña, los Estados Unidos y el no Reconocimiento de Obregón," *HM* 19 (Jan.–Mar., 1970) 388–396.

2232. Tyler, T. C. "The Cárdenas Doctrine and Twentieth-Century Mexican Foreign Policy," La. State U. Diss., 1974.

2233. White, D. A. "Mexico in World Affairs, 1928–1968," UCLA Diss., 1968.

XIII-I cross references:

  a) For United States–Mexican relations during World War II, see items 952–957.

  b) In the Trask, Meyer, and Trask *Bibliography* see items 3343, 3345, 3350, 3364, 3627a–3646, 3814, 6258–6323.

J. UNITED STATES–MEXICAN RELATIONS SINCE 1940

2234. Arreola Resendiz, S. *Inversiones Norteamericanas en México y sus Consecuencias Económicas*. Mexico, 1953.

    A nationalistic treatment.

2234a. Bohrisch, A., and W. König. *La Política Mexicana sobre Inversiones Extranjeras*. Mexico, 1968.

2235. Bustamante, J. A. *Espaldas Mojadas: Materia Prima para la Expansión del Capital Norteamericano*. Mexico, 1975.

2236. Cecena, J. L. *México en la Orbita Imperial: Las Empresas Transnacionales*. Mexico, 1974.

2237. Clash, T. W. "United States–Mexican Relations, 1940–1946: A Study of U.S. Interests and Policies," State U. of N.Y. Buffalo Diss., 1972.

2238. Cranston, A. "Policies of the U.S. and Mexican Governments: Opportunities for Cooperation," *FRON* 8 (Nov., 1976) 17–22.

2238a. Fagen, R. R. "The Realities of U.S.-Mexican Relations," *FA* 55 (July, 1977) 685–700.

2239. Green, R. *El Endeudamiento Público Externo de México, 1940–1973*. Mexico, 1976.

2239a. Hamilton, W. H. "Mexico's 'New' Foreign Policy: A Reexamination," *IEA* 29 (Winter, 1975) 51–58.

2240. Jeannero, M. J. "The Question of Mexico's Dependence on the United States Relative to the Rest of the World, 1945–1962," Tufts U. Diss., 1969.

2240a. Kaye, H. J. "How 'New' Is Mexico's Foreign Policy?" *IEA* 28 (Spring, 1975) 87–92.

    Argues that the policy of Echeverría is similar to that of López Mateos.

2241. López Mateos, A. *La Voz de México en los Estados Unidos y Canadá*. Mexico, 1959.

    Speeches delivered in the two countries during a presidential visit.

2242. Machado, M. A. "An Industry in Crisis: Mexican–United States Cooperation in the Control of Foot-and-Mouth Disease," U. of Calif. Santa Barbara Diss., 1964.

2242a. Mexico. Secretaría de Industria y Comercio. *La Proyección Económica de México en el Exterior (1971–1973)*. Mexico, 1974.

2243. Meyer, M. C. "United States–Mexican Relations in the 1970's: The Persistent Problems of the Border," *FRON* 8 (Nov., 1976) 23–27.

2243a. Ojeda, M. *Alcances y Límites de la Política Exterior de México*. Mexico, 1976.

2244. ———. *México y América Latina: La Nueva Política Exterior*. Mexico, 1974.

    Treats Mexican relations with Cuba, Chile, Central America, LAFTA, and the Pacto Andino.

2245. Paredes, A. "The Role of Folklore in Border Relations and How It Expresses Intercultural Conflict and Cooperation," *FRON* 8 (Nov., 1976) 17–22.

2246. Pellicer de Brody, O. "Cambios Recientes en la Política Exterior Mexicana," *FI* 12 (Oct.–Dec., 1972) 139–154.

    Treats Mexican foreign policy under President Echeverría.

2247. ———. *México y la Revolución Cubana*. Mexico, 1972.

    Mexican-Cuban relations prior to and during the Castro revolution.

2248. Rondero, J. *Nacionalismo Mexicano y*

Política Mundial. Mexico, 1969.

2249. Sánchez Navarro, J. *Ensayo sobre una Política de Inversiones Extranjeras en México*. Mexico, 1955.

2250. Scott, D. H. "The Cultural Institute in Mexico City as an Example of United States Policy in Cultural Relations," U.S.C. Diss., 1959.

2250a. Sepúlveda, B., and A. Chumacero. *La Inversión Extranjera en México*. Mexico, 1973.

2251. ———. *et al*. *Las Empresas Transnacionales en México*. Mexico, 1974.

2252. Serra Rojas, A. "La Política Internacional del Señor Presidente Gustavo Díaz Ordaz," *JUS* 26 (Mar., 1966) 29–46.

2252a. Tello, M. *México: Una Posición Internacional*. Mexico, 1972.

2253. ——— (ed.). *La Política Exterior de México, 1970–1974*. Mexico, 1975.
    Primarily collected speeches of Luis Echeverría.

2254. "United States and Mexico Reaffirm Friendship and Goodwill," *USDSB* 57 (Nov., 1967) 673–684.
    Treats the visit of Díaz Ordaz to Washington and to the border with Lyndon Johnson to celebrate the Chamizal settlement.

2255. USC. Joint Economic Committee. *Recent Developments in Mexico and Their Economic Implications for the United States*. Wash., 1977.
    Includes testimony by James Wilkie, Clark Reynolds, Al R. Wichtrich, Calvin Blair, Jimmye Hillman, Raul Castro, and others.

2256. USCH. Committee on Foreign Affairs. Subcommittee on Inter-American Affairs. *United States–Mexican Trade Relations: Hearings . . . .* (92d Cong., 2d Sess.) Wash., 1972.

2257. USCS. *Mexico–United States Interparliamentary Group Report of the Senate Delegation on the Sixth Meeting, Held at Washington, February, 1966 by Senator John Sparkman*. Wash., 1966.

2258. Valero, R. "La Política Exterior en Coyuntura Actual de México," *FI* 12 (Oct.–Dec., 1972) 292–310.

2259. Wilkie, J. W., M. C. Meyer, and E. Monzón de Wilkie. *Contemporary Mexico: Papers of the IV International Congress of Mexican History*. Berkeley, Calif., 1976.
    Full text of over 45 papers read at the Santa Monica Conference.

2259a. Williams, E. J. "Oil in Mexican-U.S. Relations: Analysis and Bargaining Scenario," *OR* 22 (Spring, 1978) 201–216.

2260. Wright, H. K. *Foreign Enterprise in Mexico: Laws and Policies*. Chapel Hill, N.C., 1970.

XIII-J   cross references:
  a) For United States–Mexican relations during World War II, see items 952–957.
  b) See also items 1303, 1316, 1320, 1333, 1336, 1350, 1363, 1796, 2233.
  c) In the Trask, Meyer, and Trask *Bibliography* see items 3627a–3646, 4037, 4160, 4172, 4184, 4348, 4611, 4831a, 4831b, 4832, 4834, 5069c, 5403, 6028, 6050, 6324–6388, 6443, 6597, 7735.

K. SPECIAL ASPECTS OF UNITED STATES–MEXICAN RELATIONS

1. OIL CONTROVERSIES

2261. Acosta Saignés, M. *Petróleo en México y Venezuela*. Mexico, 1941.

2262. Archer, W. J. (ed.). *Mexican Petroleum: Description of Properties of the Pan American Petroleum and Transport Company and Principal Subsidiaries*. N.Y., 1922.

2263. Association of Producers of Petroleum in Mexico. *Documents Relating to the Attempt of the Government of Mexico to Confiscate Foreign-Owned Oil Properties*. Mexico, 1919.

2264. Baldridge, D. C. "Mexican Petroleum and United States–Mexican Relations, 1919–1923," U. of Ariz. Diss., 1971.

2265. Bermúdez, A. J. *La Política Petrolera Mexicana*. Mexico, 1976.

2266. Compañía Petrolera Comercial. *La Sombra Internacional de El Aguila*. Mexico, 1935.

2267. Corona, G. *Lázaro Cárdenas y la Expropiación de la Industria Petrolera en México*. Mexico, 1975.

2268. De la Peña, M. *El Dominio Directo del Soberano en las Minas de México y Génesis de la Legislación Petrolera Mexicana*. 2 vols., Mexico, 1928–1932.

2269. ———. *El Petróleo y la Legislación Frente a*

las Compañías Petroleras. Mexico, 1920.

2270. Fresco, M. Synthèse du Conflit de Pétrole au Mexique. Paris, 1938.

2270a. Hermida Ruiz, A. J. Bermúdez y la Batalla por el Petróleo. Mexico, 1974.
Bermúdez served as director of PEMEX from 1946 to 1958.

2271. López Portillo y Weber, J. "A los Veinticinco Años de la Expropiación Petrolera," MAMH 25 (Oct.–Dec., 1964) 329–415.

2272. Manterola, M. La Industria del Petróleo en México. Mexico, 1938.

2273. Mendoza, S. La Controversia del Petróleo. Mexico, 1921.

2274. Mexico. Secretaría de Relaciones Exteriores. Correspondencia Oficial Cambiada entre el Gobierno de México y los Estados Unidos con Motivo de las dos Leyes Reglamentarias de la Fracción Primera del Artículo 27 de la Constitución Mexicana. Mexico, 1926.

2275. Meyer, L. México y los Estados Unidos en el Conflicto Petrolero, 1917–1942. Mexico, 1968.
Rev. ed., Mexico, 1972. Actually covers the period between 1900 and 1942.

2276. Reyes Heroles, J. "El Petróleo en México," CA 158 (May–June, 1968) 7–25.

2277. Ring, J. "American Diplomacy and the Mexican Oil Controversy, 1938–1943," U. of N.M. Diss., 1974.

2278. Rippy, M. Oil and the Mexican Revolution. Leiden, 1972.
Eng. ed. of work published in Sp. in 1954.

2279. Rodríguez, A. El Rescate del Petróleo: Epopeya de un Pueblo. Mexico, 1975.

2280. Santaella, J. El Petróleo en México: Factor Económico. Mexico, 1937.

2281. Turchen, L. Van Der Wert. "The Oil Controversy, 1917–1942, in United States–Mexican Relations," Purdue U. Diss., 1972.

2282. Universidad Obrera de México. El Conflicto del Petróleo en México, 1937–1938. Mexico, 1938.

XIII-K-1 cross references:
a) See items 2133a, 2193a, 2259a.
b) In the Trask, Meyer, and Trask Bibliography see items 3343, 6023, 6042, 6389–6486.

2. CLAIMS SETTLEMENTS

2282a. Niblo, S. R. "The United States–Mexican Claims Commission of 1868," NMHR 50 (Apr., 1975) 101–121.

2283. Sepúlveda, C. (ed.). Dos Reclamaciones Internacionales Fraudulentes contra México. Mexico, 1965.
Treats the Weil and La Abra claims.

2284. ———. "Sobre Reclamaciones de Norteamericanos a México," HM 11 (Oct.–Dec., 1961) 180–206.
Covers the period 1825 to 1942.

2285. United States and Mexico Claims Commission. Opinions of Commissioners under the Convention Concluded September 8, 1923 as Extended by the Convention Signed August 6, 1927 between the United States and Mexico. Wash., 1929.

2286. USCS. Report of the Select Committee of the Senate, in Relation to the Proceedings of the Board of Commissioners on the Claims against Mexico. Wash., 1854.

2287. ———. Committee on Foreign Relations. Claims of American Nationals against Mexico. Wash., 1942.

XIII-K-2 cross references: In the Trask, Meyer, and Trask Bibliography see items 5856, 6487–6519.

3. PIOUS FUND

2288. Johnson, K. M. The Pious Fund. Los Angeles, 1963.
Surveys the case from the colonial period through the Mexican Revolution.

2289. Moreno, D. "El Fondo Piadoso de las Californias," RFDM 15 (Jan.–Mar., 1965) 209–214.

2290. Vallarta, I. L. "Dictámen sobre el Fondo Piadoso de las Californias," RFDM 15 (Jan.–Mar., 1965) 215–252.

2291. Weber, F. J. The United States versus Mexico: The Final Settlement of the Pious Fund. Los Angeles, 1969.

XIII-K-3 cross references: In the Trask, Meyer, and Trask Bibliography see items 6504, 6520–6528.

4. BOUNDARY AND WATER CONTROVERSIES

2292. "Agreement to Conclude Treaty to Resolve Boundary Problems," USDSB 63 (Sept., 1970) 298–300.

Treats agreement reached by Presidents Nixon and Díaz Ordaz at their Puerto Vallarta meeting in Aug., 1970.

2292a. Baerresen, D. W. *The Border Industrialization Program of Mexico*. Lexington, Mass., 1971.

2293. Carbajal Rodríguez, C. "La Solución del Caso del Chamizal," UNAM Diss., 1964.

2294. Coyro Enríquez, E. *El Tratado entre México y Estados Unidos sobre Rios Internacionales: Una Lucha Mexicana de 90 Años*. 2 vols., Mexico, 1976.

2295. Demaris, O. *Poso del Mundo: Inside the Mexican-American Border from Tijuana to Matamoros*. Boston, 1970.

2296. Graue, D. "Estudio Geohistórico de la Frontera Internacional entre México y los Estados Unidos de Norteamérica," *MANHG* 16 (1959) 11–47.

2297. Herrera, H. "Estudio sobre el Límite Internacional Terrestre de los Estados Unidos de Norte América con la República Mexicana," *BSMGE* 65 (1948) 169–194.
Covers the period 1846 to 1889.

2298. Hill, J. E., Jr. "El Chamizal: A Century-Old Boundary Dispute," *GR* 50 (Oct., 1965) 510–522.

2299. Hine, R. V. *Bartlett's West: Drawing the Mexican Boundary*. New Haven, Conn., 1968.
Treats the boundary survey of 1850–1853.

2300. Hundley, N. "The Politics of Water and Geography: California and the Mexican Treaty of 1944," *PHR* 36 (1967) 209–226.

2301. ———. *Water and the West: The Colorado River Compact and the Politics of Water in the American West*. Berkeley, Calif., 1975.

2302. Jessup, P. C. "El Chamizal," *AJIL* 67 (July, 1973) 423–445.

2303. Jordan, D. H. "The United States–Mexican International Boundary and Water Commission," *ASILP* 68 (1974) 226–229.

2304. Jury Germany, S. H. "Un Siglo de Negociación de los Límites entre México y los Estados Unidos (1819–1900)," UNAM Diss., 1965.

2305. Langston, E. L. "The Impact of Prohibition on the Mexican U.S. Border: The El Paso–Ciudad Juárez Case," Tex. Technical U. Diss., 1974.

2306. Leonard, G. M. "Western Boundary-Making: Texas and the Mexican Cession, 1844–50," U. of Utah Diss., 1970.

2307. Moberly, A. L. "Fences and Neighbors: El Chamizal and the Colorado River Salinity Disputes in U.S. Mexican Relations," U. of Calif. Santa Barbara Diss., 1974.

2308. Mori, T. "Mekishiko no Hoppô Kokkyô Chitai to Hoaresu Shi," *WS* 185 (Dec., 1965) 99–121.
Translated title: "The Northern Border Area of Mexico and Ciudad Juárez."

2309. Rabasa, O. *El Problema de las Aguas Entregadas a México en el Rio Colorado*. Mexico, 1968.

2310. Rojas Garcidueñas, J. "El Caso Internacional de la Salinidad de las Aguas Entregadas a México en el Rio Colorado," *RFDM* 14 (Apr.–June, 1964) 443–464.

2311. USCS. Committee on Foreign Relations. *Hearings . . . on Treaty with Mexico Relating to the Utilization of the Waters of Certain Rivers, January 22, 23, 24, 25 and 26, 1945*. Wash., 1945.

2312. Werner, J. R. "Guadalupe Hidalgo and the Mesilla Controversy," Kent State U. Diss., 1972.
Treats the international boundary survey.

2313. Yeilding, K. D. "The Chamizal Dispute: An Exercise in Arbitration, 1845–1945," Tex. Christian U. Diss., 1973.

XIII-K-4   cross references:
a) See items 1677, 2254.
b) In the Trask, Meyer, and Trask *Bibliography* see items 5872, 5885, 5903, 5905, 5915, 5968, 6006, 6152, 6529–6569.

5. CONTROVERSIES OVER THE RELIGIOUS ISSUE

2314. Bailey, D. C. *Viva Cristo Rey: The Cristero Rebellion and the Church-State Conflict in Mexico*. Austin, Tex., 1974.

2315. Berbusse, E. J. "The Unofficial Intervention of the United States in Mexico's Religious Crisis, 1926–1930," *TA* 23 (July, 1966) 28–62.

2316. Bravo Ugarte, J. "Como se Llegó al 'Modus Vivendi' de 1929," *HU* 6 (1965) 395–405.

Treats the settlement of the church-state controversy.

2317. Davis, M. C. "American Religious and Religiose Reaction to Mexico's Church-State Conflict: Background to the Morrow Mission," *JCS* 13 (Winter, 1971) 79–96.

2318. Dooley, F. P. "The Cristeros, Calles and Mexican Catholicism," U. of Md. Diss., 1972.

2319. Gotshall, E. R., Jr. "Catholicism and Catholic Action in Mexico, 1929–1941: A Church's Response to a Revolutionary Society and the Politics of the Modern Age," U. of Pittsburgh Diss., 1970.

2320. Kelly, B. J. "The Cristero Rebellion, 1926–1929: Its Diplomacy and Solution," U. of N.M. Diss., 1973.

2321. López Ortega, A. J. *Las Naciones Extranjeras y la Persecución Religiosa*. Mexico, 1944.

2322. Meyer, J. A. *The Cristero Rebellion*. Cambridge, Eng., 1976.

2323. Olivera Sedano, A. *Aspectos del Conflicto Religioso de 1926 a 1929: Sus Antecedentes y Consecuencias*. Mexico, 1966.
Treats the Cristero Rebellion.

2324. Quigley, R. E. "American Catholic Opinions of Mexican Anti-Clericalism, 1910–1936," U. of Pa. Diss., 1965.

2325. Quijano León, L. "El Conflicto Religioso en México durante el Gobierno de Calles: 1924–1928," *CS* 14 (Dec., 1970) 519–532.

2326. Quirk, R. E. *The Mexican Revolution and the Catholic Church 1910–1929*. Bloomington, Ind., 1973.

2327. Uroz, A. *La Cuestión Religiosa en México*. Mexico, 1926.

XIII-K-5 cross references: In the Trask, Meyer, and Trask Bibliography see items 3350, 5813, 6291, 6298, 6306, 6312, 6313, 6570–6591.

6. MEXICAN IMMIGRATION TO THE UNITED STATES AND THE BRACERO QUESTION

2328. Acuña, R. *Occupied America: The Chicano's Struggle toward Liberation*. San Francisco, 1972.

2329. Alvarez, J. H. "A Demographic Profile of the Mexican Immigration to the United States, 1910–1950," *JIAS* 8 (July, 1966) 471–496.

2330. Anderson, H. P. *The Bracero Program in California with Particular Reference to Health Status, Attitudes and Practices*. Berkeley, Calif., 1961.

2331. Bogardus, E. S. "The Mexican Immigrant and Segregation," *AJS* 36 (July, 1930) 74–80.

2332. Browning, H. L., and S. D. McLemore. *A Statistical Profile of the Spanish Surname Population of Texas*. Austin, Tex., 1964.

2333. Burma, J. H. *Spanish-Speaking Groups in the United States*. Durham, N.C., 1954.

2334. Bustamante, J. A. "Impact of Undocumented Immigration from Mexico on the U.S.-Mexican Economies," *FRON* 3 (Nov., 1976) 28–50.

2335. ———. "Mexican Immigration and the Social Relations of Capitalism," U. of Notre Dame Diss., 1975.

2336. California Department of Employment. *Mexican Nationals in California Agriculture 1942–1959*. Sacramento, Calif., 1959.

2337. California State Relief Administration. *Migratory Labor in California*. San Francisco, 1936.

2338. Cardoso, L. A. "Mexican Emigration to the U.S., 1900 to 1930: An Analysis of Socio-Economic Causes," U. of Conn. Diss., 1974.

2338a. ———. "La Repatriación de Braceros en Epoca de Obregón," *HM* 26 (Apr.–June, 1977) 576–595.

2339. Carreras de Velasco, M. *Los Mexicanos que Devolvió la Crisis, 1929–1932*. Mexico, 1974.
Concerns the repatriation of hundreds of thousands of Mexicans from the United States.

2340. Colorado Commission on Spanish Surnamed Citizens. *The Status of Spanish Surnamed Citizens in Colorado: Report to the Colorado General Assembly*. Greeley, Colo., 1967.

2341. Corwin, A. F. "Historia de la Emigración Mexicana, 1900–1970," *HM* 22 (Oct.–Dec., 1972) 188–220.

2342. Criag, R. B. *The Bracero Program: Interest Groups and Foreign Policy*. Austin, Tex., 1971.
Covers the period 1942 to 1965.

2343.   Davila, J. M. *The Mexican Migration Prob-lem*. Los Angeles, 1929.

2344.   De León, A. "White Racial Attitudes toward Mexicanos in Texas, 1821–1900," Tex. Christian U. Diss., 1974.

2345.   Dinwoodie, D. H. "Deportation: The Immigration Service and the Chicano Labor Movement in the 1930's," *NMHR* 52 (July, 1977) 193–206.

2346.   Galarza, E *Merchants of Labor: The Mexican Bracero Story*. San Jose, Calif., 1964.

2347.   ———. *Strangers in Our Fields*. Wash., 1956.
        A publication of the Joint United States–Mexico Trade Committee.

2348.   Gamio, M. *The Mexican Immigrant: His Life Story*. Chicago, 1930.

2349.   ———. *Quantitative Estimate of Sources and Distribution of Mexican Immigration into the United States*. Mexico, 1930.

2350.   García, J. R. "Operation Wetback: 1954," U. of Notre Dame Diss., 1977.
        Treats the mass repatriation of un-documented workers in 1954.

2351.   Gilmore, N. R., and G. W. Gilmore. "Bracero in California," *PHR* 32 (Aug., 1963) 265–282.

2352.   Gómez, D. F. *Somos Chicanos: Strangers in Our Own Land*. Boston, 1973.

2353.   Grebler, L. *Mexican Immigration to the United States: The Record and Its Implica-tions*. Los Angeles, 1966.
        Advance Report no. 2 of the Mexican-American Study Project.

2354.   ———, J. W. Moore, and R. C. Guz-mán. *The Mexican-American People: The Nation's Second Largest Minority*. New York, 1970.
        An interdisciplinary study with an ex-cellent bibliography.

2355.   Guzmán, R. *The Socio-Economic Position of the Mexican-American Migrant Farm Worker*. Wash., 1967.

2356.   Handman, M. S. "Economic Reasons for the Coming of the Mexican Immigrant," *AJS* 35 (Jan., 1930) 601–611.

2357.   ———. "The Mexican Immigrant in Texas," *SPSSQ* 7 (June, 1926) 33–40.

2358.   Hoffman, A. *Unwanted Mexican Ameri-cans in the Great Depression: Repatriation Pressures, 1929–1939*. Tucson, Ariz., 1974.
        Critical of the deportation policies of the U.S. government.

2359.   Hoover, G. E. "Our Mexican Immi-grants," *FA* 8 (Oct., 1929) 99–107.

2360.   Jones, R. C. *Mexican War Workers in the United States: The Mexico–United States Manpower Recruiting Program, 1942–1944*. Wash., 1945.

2361.   Kivstein, P. N. "Anglo over Bracero: A History of the Mexican Worker in the U.S. from Roosevelt to Nixon," St. Louis U. Diss., 1973.

2362.   Lamb, R. S. *Mexican Americans: Sons of the Southwest*. Claremont, Calif., 1970.

2362a. Maciel, D. (comp.). *La Otra Cara de México: El Pueblo Chicano*. Mexico, 1977.

2363.   Manuel, H. T. "The Mexican Population of Texas," *SSSQ* 15 (June, 1934) 29–51.

2364.   McCain, J. M. "Contract Labor as a Fac-tor in United States–Mexican Relations, 1942–1947," U. of Tex. Austin Diss., 1970.

2365.   McWilliams, C. *North from Mexico: The Spanish Speaking People of the United States*. Philadelphia, Pa., 1948.

2366.   Meier, M. S., and F. Rivera. *The Chicanos: A History of the Mexican Ameri-cans*. N.Y., 1972.

2367.   Menefee, S. C. *Mexican Migratory Workers of South Texas*. Wash., 1941.

2368.   Peón Máximo (pseud.). *Como Viven los Mexicanos en los Estados Unidos*. Mexico, 1966.

2369.   Pitt, L. M. "Submersion of the Mexican in California, 1846–1890," UCLA Diss., 1958.

2370.   Prago, A. *Strangers in Their Own Land: A History of Mexican-Americans*. N.Y., 1973.

2371.   Redfield, R. "Antecedents of Mexican Immigration to the United States," *AJS* 35 (Nov., 1929) 433–438.

2372.   Reisler, M. *By the Sweat of Their Brow: Mexican Immigrant Labor in the United States, 1900–1940*. Westport, Conn., 1976.

2373.   ———. "Passing through Our Egypt: Mexican Labor in the U.S., 1900–1940," Cornell U. Diss., 1973.

2373a. Revel Mouroz, J. "Les Migrations vers la Frontière Mexique–Etats Unis," *CAL* 12 (1975) 315–350.

2374. Rubel, A. J. *Across the Tracks: Mexican Americans in a Texas City*. Austin, Tex., 1966.

2375. Salinas, J. L. *La Emigración de Braceros*. Mexico, 1955.

2376. Sánchez, G. I. *Forgotten People*. Albuquerque, N.M., 1940.

2377. Santibáñez, E. *Ensayo Acerca de la Inmigración Mexicana en los Estados Unidos*. San Antonio, Tex., 1930.

2378. Saunders, L. *The Spanish-Speaking Population of Texas*. Austin, Tex., 1949.

2379. Scotford, J. R. *Within These Borders: Spanish Speaking Peoples in the U.S.A.* N.Y., 1953.

2380. Servin, M. P. "The Pre—World War II Mexican American: An Interpretation," *HSQ* 45 (1966) 325–338.

2381. Stowell, J. S. "The Danger of Unrestricted Mexican Immigration," *CH* 28 (Aug., 1928) 763–768.

2382. Topete, J. *Aventuras de un Bracero*. Mexico, 1949.

Traces the author's experiences as a bracero in California in 1944.

2383. U.S. Bureau of Employment Security. Farm Placement Service. *Information Concerning Entry of Mexican Agricultural Workers into the United States*. Wash., 1952.

2384. USCH. Committee on the Judiciary. *Illegal Aliens: A Review of Hearings Conducted during the 92nd Congress*. Wash., 1973.

2385. ———. Committee on Immigration and Naturalization. *Seasonal Agricultural Laborers from Mexico, Hearing*. (69th Cong., 1st Sess.) Wash., 1926.

2386. U.S. Department of Labor. *Fact Sheet on the Labor Department Hearings Concerning the Importation of Foreign Farm Workers*. Wash., 1964.

2387. Waters, L. L. "Transient Mexican Agricultural Labor," *SSSQ* 22 (June, 1941) 49–66.

2388. Weaver, T., and T. Downing (eds.). *Mexican Migration*. Tucson, Ariz., 1976.

2389. Weber, D. J. *Foreigners in Their Native Land: Historical Roots of the Mexican Americans*. Albuquerque, N.M., 1973.

XIII-K-6   cross references: In the Trask, Meyer, and Trask Bibliography see items 6592–6610a.

7. COMMUNISM

2390. Andrieu, R. *Los Comunistas y la Revolución*. Mexico, 1969.

2391. Barrera, M. *Infiltración Comunista en la Prensa*. Mexico, 1967.

2391a. Bassols Batalla, A. "Cincuenta Años de Amistad del Pueblo de México con el de la Unión Soviética," *CA* 198 (Jan.–Fcb., 1975) 177–207.

2392. Herman, D. L. *The Comintern in Mexico*. Wash., 1974.

A history of the Mexican Communist Party.

2393. Martínez Náteras, A. *El Partido Comunista en la Sociedad Mexicana Actual*. Mexico, 1975.

2394. Prieto Laurens, J. *La Subversión Comunista en México*. Mexico, 1961.

2395. Schmitt, K. M. "Communism in Mexico Today," *WPQ* 15 (Mar., 1962) 111–124.

XIII-K-7   cross references:
 a)   See item 2223.
 b)   In the Trask, Meyer, and Trask *Bibliography* see items 6611–6629.

Chapter XIV The United States and the Central American–Caribbean Region

A. GENERAL WORKS

2396. Huck, E., and E. Moseley (eds.). *Militarists, Merchants and Missionaries: United States Expansion in Middle America*. University, Ala., 1970.

2397. Langley, L. D. *Struggle for the American Mediterranean: United States–European Rivalry in the Gulf-Caribbean, 1776–1904*. Athens, Ga., 1976.

2398. Molineau, J. H. "The Concept of the Caribbean in the Latin American Policy of the United States," American U. Diss., 1968.

2399. Williams, E. *From Columbus to Castro: The History of the Caribbean, 1492–1969*. N.Y., 1971.

    The author is prime minister of Trinidad and Tobago.

2400. Woodward, R. L. *Central America: A Nation Divided*. N.Y., 1976.

XIV-A   cross references:
  a) For works dealing with canal diplomacy in Central America, see items 711–730.
  b) For works on the Central American–Caribbean region and the Inter-American system, see items 1797–1798.
  c) See also items 555, 1524a.
  d) In the Trask, Meyer, and Trask *Bibliography* see items 1758, 2349–2458, 4837–4847, 6630–6669.

B. THE UNITED STATES AND THE CENTRAL AMERICAN–CARIBBEAN REGION DURING THE NINETEENTH CENTURY

2401. Connick, G. P. "The United States and

Central America 1823–1850," U. of Colo. Diss., 1969.

2402. May, R. E. *The Southern Dream of a Caribbean Empire, 1854–1861*. Baton Rouge, La., 1973.

    Treats desires of the southern states to acquire Cuba, Nicaragua, and Mexico prior to the Civil War.

2403. O'Horo, T. K. "American Foreign Investments and Foreign Policy: The Railroad Experience, 1865–1898," Rutgers U. Diss., 1976.

    Treats U.S. railroad policy in Central America and Mexico.

2404. Shoemaker, R. L. "Diplomacy from the Quarterdeck: The United States Navy in the Caribbean, 1815–1830," Ind. U. Diss., 1976.

2405. Turk, R. W. "United States Naval Policy in the Caribbean, 1865–1915," Tufts U. Diss., 1968.

XIV-B   cross references:
  a) For general accounts of filibustering during the nineteenth century, see items 731–737.
  b) For general works on canal diplomacy in Central America, see items 711–730.
  c) For British incursions on the Mosquito Coast, see items 719–723.
  d) In the Trask, Meyer, and Trask *Bibliography* see items 1877, 2183–2189, 2349–2493, 6670–6705.

C. THE UNITED STATES AND THE CENTRAL AMERICAN–CARIBBEAN REGION, 1900–1940

2406. Butler, S. D. *Old Gimlet Eye: The Adven-*

tures of Smedley Butler as Told to Lowell Thomas. N.Y., 1933.

Treats U.S. policy in Central America from 1903 to 1917.

2407. Gerome, F. "Secretary of State Philander C. Knox and His Good Will Tour of Central America, 1912," *SECOLAS* 8 (Mar., 1977) 72–83.

2408. Grieb, K. "The United States and the Central American Federation," *TA* 24 (Oct., 1967) 107–121.

Focuses on the period 1921 to 1922.

2409. Kneer, W. G. "Great Britain and the Caribbean, 1901–1913: A Study in Anglo-American Relations," Mich. State U. Diss., 1967.

2410. Lommel, A. W., "United States Efforts to Foster Peace and Stability in Central America, 1923–1954," U. of Minn. Diss., 1967.

2411. Munro, D. G. *The United States and the Caribbean Republics, 1921–1933*. Princeton, N.J., 1974.

A sequel to the author's 1964 volume, which covered the period 1900 to 1921.

2412. Olch, I. "A Résumé of National Interests in the Caribbean Area," *USNIP* 66 (Feb., 1940) 165–176.

XIV-C   cross references:

a) For works on the Central American Peace Conference held in Washington (1907), see item 1849.

b) See also items 816, 835, 1351, 1977.

c) In the Trask, Meyer, and Trask *Bibliography* see items 2896, 2897, 2899, 2901, 2904–2906, 2910, 2915, 2921, 2932, 2934, 2938, 2960, 2967, 2970, 3000, 3005, 3036, 3039, 3091, 3228, 3268, 3605, 5128–5143, 6682, 6706–6758.

D. THE UNITED STATES AND THE CENTRAL AMERICAN–CARIBBEAN REGION SINCE 1940

2413. Ameringer, C. D. *The Democratic Left in Exile: The Anti-Dictatorial Struggle in the Caribbean, 1945–1959*. Coral Gables, Fla., 1974.

Details the activities and interrelationships of various exile groups.

2414. Castillo, C. M. *Growth and Integration in Central America*. N.Y., 1966.

2415. Cochrane, J. D. "U.S. Attitudes toward Central American Economic Integration," *IEA* 18 (Autumn, 1964) 73–91.

2415a. Corkran, H. *Patterns of International Cooperation in the Caribbean, 1942–1969*. Dallas, Tex., 1970.

2416. Crassweller, R. D. *The Caribbean Community: Changing Societies and U.S. Policy*. N.Y., 1972.

2417. Etchison, D. L. *The United States and Militarism in Central America*. N.Y., 1975.

Treats the period 1960 to 1974.

2418. Inoue, T. "Raten Amerika Niokeru Beikoku Banana Kigyo no Keiken," *KKKN* 16 (1966) 75–107.

Translated title: "Experiences of U.S. Banana Companies in Latin America."

2419. Kadt, E. de (ed.). *Patterns of Foreign Influence in the Caribbean*. London, 1972.

Papers from a series of symposia held at the Royal Institute of International Affairs in 1967 and 1968.

2419a. Martin, J. B. *U.S. Policy in the Caribbean*. Boulder, Colo., 1978.

Heavy emphasis on the Nixon and Ford administrations.

2420. Martínez-Sotomayor, C. *El Nuevo Caribe: La Independencia de las Colonias Británicas*. Santiago, 1974.

2421. Molineu, H. "The Concept of the Caribbean in the Latin American Policy of the U.S.," *JIAS* 15 (Aug., 1973) 285–307.

2422. "President Johnson Meets with Central American Presidents," *USDSB* 59 (July, 1968) 109–120.

2423. Rys, J. F. "Tensions and Conflicts in Cuba, Haiti, and the Dominican Republic between 1945 and 1959," American U. Diss., 1966.

2424. Szulc, T. (ed.). *The United States and the Caribbean*. Englewood Cliffs, N.J., 1971.

Eight essays by participants at the Thirty-Eighth American Assembly, which met in New York in 1970.

2425. Toledo, M. M. "La Violencia en Centro-América," *CA* 30 (May–June, 1971) 7–41.

2426. USCS. *Study Mission in the Caribbean and Northern South America, November, 1959*. Wash., 1960.

Report of Senator Homer E. Capehart

presented to the 86th Cong., 2d Sess.

2427. ———. *Study Mission in the Caribbean Area, December, 1957.* Wash., 1958.
Report of Senator George D. Aiken presented to the 85th Cong., 2d Sess.

2428. USDS. *The Woven Strand: Cooperation in Central America.* Wash., 1968.
A pamphlet treating Lyndon Johnson's Central American visit in July, 1968.

XIV-D   cross references:
a) For works on this area relating to World War II, see items 958–960.
b) See also items 1423, 1435, 1445, 1467, 2410.
c) In the Trask, Meyer, and Trask *Bibliography* see items 3647–3667, 3707, 3964a, 4364, 6739, 6759–6818.

E. THE UNITED STATES AND GUATEMALA

1. UNITED STATES–GUATEMALAN RELATIONS: GENERAL WORKS AND SPECIAL STUDIES

2429. Díaz, V. M. *Guatemala Independiente: Recopilación de Documentos Históricos.* Guatemala, 1932.

2430. Guerrero, C. J. N. *Geografía e Historia de Guatemala.* Guatemala, 1961.

XIV-E-1   cross references: In the Trask, Meyer, and Trask Bibliography *see items 6819–6834.*

2. UNITED STATES–GUATEMALAN RELATIONS: NINETEENTH CENTURY

2431. Barrientos, A. E. *Justo Rufino Barrios, el Reformador de Guatemala.* Guatemala, 1971.

2432. Carranza, J. E. *Algunos Datos e Referencias para la Biografía del Benemérito Gral. J. Rufino Barrios.* Totonicapan, Guatemala, 1901.

2433. Díaz, V. M. *Barrios ante la Posteridad.* Guatemala, 1935.

2434. Griffith, W. J. *Empires in the Wilderness: Foreign Colonization and Development in Guatemala, 1834–1844.* Chapel Hill, N.C., 1965.

2435. Herrick, T. R. *Economic and Political Development in Guatemala during the Barrios Period, 1871–1885.* Chicago, 1967.

2436. Ross, D. G. "The Construction of the

Interoceanic Railroad of Guatemala," *TA* 33 (1977) 430–456.
The line was built between 1878 and 1908.

XIV-E-2   cross references:
a) See item 2525.
b) In the Trask, Meyer, and Trask *Bibliography* see items 5993, 5995, 6835–6847a.

3. UNITED STATES–GUATEMALAN RELATIONS: TWENTIETH CENTURY

2437. Arévalo, J. J. *Informe del Ciudadano Presidente de la República, Doctor Juan José Arévalo, al Congreso Nacional en la Inauguración de su Primer Período de Sesiones Ordinarias del Año de 1947.* Guatemala, 1947.

2437a. Aybar, J. M. *Dependency and Intervention: The Case of Guatemala in 1954.* Boulder, Colo., 1978.

2438. ———. "Dictatorial Repression and U.S. Imperialism in Guatemala in Miguel Angel Asturias' *La Triología Bananera,*" *SECOLAS* 6 (Mar., 1975) 42–47.

2439. Chardkoff, R. B. "Communist Toehold in the Americas: A History of Official United States Involvement in the Guatemalan Crisis, 1954," Fla. State U. Diss., 1967.

2440. Crain, D. A. "Guatemalan Revolutionaries and Havana's Ideological Offensive of 1966–1968," *JIAS* 17 (May, 1975) 175–205.

2441. Dinwoodie, D. H. "Dollar Diplomacy in the Light of the Guatemalan Loan Project, 1909–1913," *TA* 26 (Jan., 1970) 237–253.

2442. ———. "Expedient Diplomacy: The United States and Guatemala, 1898–1920," U. of Colo. Diss., 1966.

2443. Galeano, E. H. *Guatemala: Occupied Country.* N.Y., 1969.

2443a. García Laguardia, J. M. *La Democracia Liberal de Guatemala.* San José, C.R., 1977.

2444. Gilly, A. "The Guerrilla Movement in Guatemala," *MR* 17 (May, 1965) 9–40 and 17 (June, 1965) 7–44.

2445. Grieb, K. J. "The United States and General Jorge Ubico's Retention of

Power," *RHA* 71 (Jan.–June, 1971) 119–135.

Ubico used the Good Neighbor Policy to his own advantage.

2446. Jonas, S., and D. Tobis (eds.). *Guatemala*. Berkeley, Calif., 1974.

Papers read at the North America Congress on Latin America. Emphasizes U.S. imperialism in Guatemala since 1954.

2447. Maddox, R. C. "A Comparison of Wages in United States–Owned and Guatemalan–Owned Manufacturing Firms in Guatemala," U. of Tex. Diss., 1967.

2447a. Rodríguez, M. "Guatemala in Perspective," *CH* 51 (Dec., 1966) 338–343, 367.

2448. Vaughn, H. G. "The American School of Guatemala and Its Relation to Guatemalan Education: A Descriptive Case Study," Mich. State U. Diss., 1968.

2449. Wilson, H. *The Education of a Diplomat*. London, 1938.

Author was U.S. chargé d'affaires in Guatemala from 1912 to 1914.

XIV-E-3   cross references:

a) For the arbitration of the Guatemalan boundary dispute with Honduras, see items 2479–2483.

b) See also 2478.

c) In the Trask, Meyer, and Trask *Bibliography* see items 6847b–6925, 7016–7027, 7218, 10037.

4. THE ANGLO-GUATEMALAN (BELICE) DISPUTE

2450. Aguilar, A. *Belice es de Guatemala*. Guatemala, 1950.

2451. Anderson, A. H. *Brief Sketch of British Honduras*. Belice, 1958.

2451a. Ashcraft, N. *Colonialism and Underdevelopment: Processes of Political Change in British Honduras*. N.Y., 1973.

2452. Camejo Farfan, H. *Belice: Una Cuestión Continental*. Guatemala, 1941.

2453. Carrillo y Ancona, C. *El Orígen de Belice*. Mexico, 1879.

Presents the Mexican claims to Belice.

2454. Castillo Arriola, E. *Estatuto Jurídico de los Guatemaltecos Beliceños*. Guatemala, 1949.

2455. *Defensa del Tratado de Límites entre Yucatán y Belice*. Guatemala, 1966.

2456. Dobson, N. *A History of Belize*. Port-of-Spain, Trinidad, 1973.

A balanced appraisal.

2457. García Bauer, C. *La Controversia sobre el Territorio de Belice y el Procedimiento Ex-Acquo Et Bono*. Guatemala, 1966.

2458. González Davison, F. *Belice: Realidad y Posibilidades*. Guatemala, 1970.

2459. Grant, C. H. *The Making of Modern Belize*. Cambridge, Eng., 1976.

The slow move to independence is explained in terms of fear of Guatemalan aggression.

2459a. Grieb, K. J. "Jorge Ubico and the Belice Boundary Dispute," *TA* 30 (Apr., 1974) 448–474.

Treats the U.S. mediation.

2460. Grunewald, D. "The Anglo-Guatemalan Dispute over British Honduras," *CS* 5 (July, 1965) 17–44.

2461. Leyton Rodríguez, R. *Belice Es Tierra de Guatemala*. Mexico, 1953.

2462. Marin, R. *A Brief Resume of Guatemala's Dispute with Britain over the Belize Territory*. Guatemala, 1963.

2463. Martínez Alomía, S. *Belice Histórico, Político, y Legal sobre el Proyecto de Tratado de Límites Concertado Entre el Lic. Ignacio Mariscal, Secretario de Relaciones Exteriores y Sir Spencer St. John Ministro Plenipotenciario de Inglaterra*. Mexico, 1945.

2464. Recinos, M. A. *Les Droits de Guatemala sur Belice*. Paris, 1948.

2465. Rodríguez Beteta, V. *Solidarity and Responsibilities of the United States in the Belize Case*. Guatemala, 1965.

XIV-E-4   cross references:

a) For the nineteenth-century background of the Belice controversy, see items 676–677.

b) In the Trask, Meyer, and Trask *Bibliography* see items 2183–2189, 6926–6977.

F. THE UNITED STATES AND HONDURAS

1. GENERAL WORKS AND SPECIAL STUDIES

2466. Aguirre, J. *Honduras: The Reply of Colonel José M. Aguirre to Some Unjust Strictures Published against That Republic by the New York Times*. N.Y., 1884.

2467. Alvarado O., M. A. "Compilación de

Documentos y Textos Referentes a la Soberanía que Sostiene el Gobierno de Honduras sobre las Islas de El Cisne, ante los Estados Unidos de América," *RAHGH* 55 (July–Dec., 1971) 265–283; 56 (July–Sept., 1972) 39–66; 57 (Oct.–Dec., 1973) 74–83.

The Honduran case against the United States in the Swan Islands controversy.

2468.   Barahona, R. *Breve Historia de Honduras*. Mexico, 1955.

2469.   Cáceres Lara, V. "La Aventura Postrera de William Walker en Honduras," *EX* 1 (Sept., 1965) 27–44.

2470.   Cruz, R. E. *Historia Constitucional e Institucional de Honduras y Derecho Interno y Derecho Internacional*. Tegucigalpa, 1976.

2471.   Díaz Chávez, F. *La Revolución Morazanista: Génesis, Desarrollo y Aniquilamiento; Su Importancia Histórica*. Tegucigalpa, 1965.

2472.   Ferro, C. A. *El Caso de las Islas Santanilla*. 2d ed., Tegucigalpa, 1972.

Treats the U.S. transfer of the Swan Islands to Honduras.

2473.   Herrera Cáceres, H. R. *Estatuto Jurídico de la Bahia de Fonseca y Régimen de sus Zonas Adyacentes*. Tegucigalpa, 1974.

2474.   ———. *Honduras y la Problemática del Derecho Internacional Público del Mar*. Tegucigalpa, 1974.

2475.   Leiva Vivas, R. *Tratados Internacionales de Honduras*. Tegucigalpa, 1968.

Lists and discusses over 500 treaties covering the period 1839 to 1869.

2476.   Lombard, T. R. *The New Honduras: Its Situation, Resources, Opportunities and Prospects*. N.Y., 1887.

2477.   Ponce de Avalos, R. *La United Fruit Company y la Segunda República*. Comayaguela, Honduras, 1960.

Treats the relationship between President Villeda Morales and the United Fruit Company.

2478.   Ulloa, J. *La Frutera en Honduras, El Extraño Caso de su Defensor en Guatemala, Clemente Marroquín Rojas*. Guatemala, 1949.

Attack on United Fruit Company.

2478a.   Yeager, G. S. "The Honduran Foreign Debt, 1825–1953," Tulane U. Diss., 1975.

XIV-F-1   cross references: In the Trask, Meyer, and Trask Bibliography *see items 2476, 4193, 6696, 6978–7015, 7148.*

2. THE HONDURAN-GUATEMALAN BOUNDARY DISPUTE

2479.   Cruz, R. E. *Problemas Territoriales Centroamericanos*. Tegucigalpa, 1966.

2480.   Guatemala. *Anexos la République de Guatemala Presentada ante el Tribunal de Arbiraje Integrado*. Wash., 1932.

2481.   ———. *Guatemala Presentada ante el Tribunal de Arbitraje Integrado*. Wash., 1932.

2482.   *Opinions Given by Seven American Jurists Regarding the Litigation between Guatemala and Honduras Pending before the Court of Justice of Central America*. Guatemala, 1908.

2483.   USDS. Office of the Geographer. *British Honduras Guatemala Boundary*. Wash., 1961.

International Boundary Study Series, No. 8.

XIV-F-2   cross references: In the Trask, Meyer, and Trask Bibliography *see items 6666, 7016–7027.*

G. THE UNITED STATES AND NICARAGUA

1. UNITED STATES–NICARAGUAN RELATIONS: GENERAL WORKS AND SPECIAL STUDIES

2484.   Durón, R. E. *Límites de Nicaragua*. Tegucigalpa, 1938.

2484a.   Quintana Orozco, O. *Apuntes de Historia de Nicaragua*. Managua, 1968.

XIV-G-1   cross references:
a)   See item 715.
b)   In the Trask, Meyer, and Trask *Bibliography* see items 6653, 7028–7036.

2. UNITED STATES–NICARAGUAN RELATIONS: NINETEENTH CENTURY

2485.   Johnson, E. R. "The Nicaraguan Canal and the Economic Development of the United States," *AAAPSS* 7 (Jan., 1896) 1–31.

2486.   Rodríguez Serrano, F. *El Canal por*

Nicaragua: Estudio de la Negociación Canalera a su Proyección en la Historia de Nicaragua. Managua, 1968.

2487. Ross, G. M. "Anglo-American Diplomatic Relations with Regard to Nicaragua and Venezuela: February 1894–January 1896," Wash. State U. Diss., 1966.

2488. Sheldon, H. A. *Notes on the Nicaragua Canal*. Chicago, 1902.

2489. Simmons, W. E. *The Nicaraguan Canal*. N.Y., 1900.

2490. USCS. *Reports of Explorations and Surveys for the Location of a Ship Canal between the Atlantic and Pacific Oceans through Nicaragua, 1872–'73*. (43d Cong., 1st Sess., Sen. Exec. Doc. 57.) Wash., 1874.

2491. Wall, J. T. "American Intervention in Nicaragua, 1848–1861," U. of Tenn. Diss., 1974.

XIV-G-2 cross references:

a) For accounts of filibustering, and especially of William Walker, see items 731–737.

b) For questions of trans-isthmian diplomacy, most of which treat the Nicaraguan canal, see items 711–730.

c) See also item 2402.

d) In the Trask, Meyer, and Trask *Bibliography* see items 2350, 2354, 2356, 2359, 2360, 2363, 2365, 2373, 2376, 2380a, 2387a, 2390, 2398, 2403, 2404, 2406, 2425, 2433, 2434, 2436, 2440, 2443, 2445, 2448, 2449, 2451, 2453–2455, 2459–2493, 7037–7065, 7252, 7495a.

3. UNITED STATES–NICARAGUAN RELATIONS: TWENTIETH CENTURY

2492. Aquino, E. *La Intervención en Nicaragua*. Managua, 1928.

A 34-page pamphlet comprising articles originally published in *El Comercio*.

2493. "El Archivo del Doctor Adán Cárdenas del Castillo, Presidente de Nicaragua: 1883–188," *RAGHN* 36 (Dec., 1969) 3–38.

Contains correspondence on the U.S. intervention in the 1920s.

2494. Binder, C. "On the Nicaraguan Front," *NR* 50 (Mar., 1927) 87–90.

2495. Carter, C. B. "The Kentucky Feud in Nicaragua," *WW* 54 (July, 1927) 312–321.

Author was U.S. commander of the Nicaraguan Guard from 1925 to 1927.

2496. Cole Chamorro, A. *Desde Sandino Hasta los Somoza*. Granada, Nicaragua, 1971.

2497. Crad, J. *I Had Nine Lives Fighting for Cash in Mexico and Nicaragua*. London, 1938.

Pseud. for Clarence Trelawney Ansell, who fought with Sandino in Nicaragua.

2498. Dodd, T. J. "Los Estados Unidos en la Política Nicaraguense: Elecciones Supervisadas, 1928–1932," *RPC* 30 (1975) 5–102.

2499. ———. "The United States in Nicaraguan Politics: Supervised Election 1927–1932," George Washington U. Diss., 1966.

2500. Edson, M. "The Coco Patrol," *MCG* 20 (Aug., 1936) 18–23.

2501. Findling, J. E. "The U.S. and Zelaya: A Study in the Diplomacy of Expediency," U. of Tex. Diss., 1971.

2501a. Fonseca, C. "Crónica Secreta: Augusto César Sandino ante sus Verdugos," *CDLA* 15 (Sept.–Oct., 1974) 4–15.

2502. Hackett, C. W. "Nicaraguan Civil Strife Ended by United States Ultimatum," *CH* 26 (July, 1927) 634–637.

2503. ———. "United States Intervention in Nicaragua," *CH* 26 (Apr., 1927) 104–107.

2504. Ibarra Grijalva, D. *The Last Night of General Augusto C. Sandino*. N.Y., 1973.

Most of the book does not treat the last night.

2505. Johnson, D. D. "The North American in Sandinista Novels," *SECOLAS* 8 (Mar., 1977) 30–37.

2506. Kamman, W. *A Search for Stability: United States Diplomacy toward Nicaragua, 1925–1933*. Notre Dame, Ind., 1968.

2507. McNeill, V. A. "Nicaraguan Elections of 1928," *MCG* 50 (Sept., 1966) 32–33, 36–39.

The United States supervised these elections.

2508. Millett, R. *Guardians of the Dynasty: A History of the U.S. Created Guardia Nacional de Nicaragua and the Somoza Family*. Maryknoll, N.Y., 1977.

2509.   ———. "The History of the Guardia Nacional de Nicaragua, 1925–1965," U. of N.M. Diss., 1966.

2510.   Petrov, V. *A Study in Diplomacy: The Story of Arthur Bliss Lane.* Chicago, 1971.
Lane was minister to Nicaragua.

2511.   Recinos, L. F., and R. Hernández. *Sandino: Hazañas del Héroe.* San José, C.R., 1934.
Sandino led guerrilla forces against the U.S. Marines.

2512.   Rodríguez Serrano, F. *Estudios sobre la Convención Chamorro-Bryan.* Managua, 1965.

2513.   Strachan, H. W. "The Role of Business Groups in Economic Development: The Case of Nicaragua," Harvard U. Diss., 1973.

2514.   Sylvester, J. A. "Arthur Bliss Lane: American Career Diplomat," U. of Wis. Diss., 1967.
Lane served in Nicaragua from 1933 to 1936.

2515.   Tierney, J. J., Jr. "The Nicaraguan Experience and the United States Caribbean Policy," *WA* 132 (Dec., 1969) 195–208.
Treats U.S. interventions in 1912 and 1927.

2516.   ———. "The United States and Nicaragua, 1927–1932: Decisions for Deescalation and Withdrawal," U. of Pa. Diss., 1969.

2517.   ———. "U.S. Intervention in Nicaragua, 1927–1933: Lessons for Today," *OR* 14 (Winter, 1971) 1012–1028.

2518.   Vichas, R. P. "External Financing of the Nicaraguan Development Experiment," U. of Fla. Diss., 1967.

XIV-G-3   cross references:
  a)   See item 2522.
  b)   In the Trask, Meyer, and Trask *Bibliography* see items 3305, 3320, 6978, 6996, 7003, 7066–7198, 7200, 7203, 7220, 7230, 7233a, 7531.

H. THE UNITED STATES AND EL SALVADOR

2519.   Anderson, T. P. *Matanza: El Salvador's Communist Revolt of 1932.* Lincoln, Nebr., 1971.

2520.   Astilla, C. F. E. "The Martínez Era: Salvadorian-American Relations, 1931–1944," La. State U. Diss., 1976.

2521.   Barón Ferrufino, J. R. *Penetración Comunista en El Salvador y Veinte Años de Traición.* San Salvador, 1970.

2522.   Brooks, J. J. "The Impact of U.S. Cotton Policy on Economic Development: The Cases of El Salvador and Nicaragua," *PIA* 5 (1967) 191–214.

2523.   Browning, D. *El Salvador: Landscape and Society.* Oxford, Eng., 1971.

2524.   Elam, R. V. "Appeal to Arms, the Army and Politics in El Salvador, 1931–1964," U. of N.M. Diss., 1968.

2525.   García Bauer, C. *Antonio José de Isiarri, Diplomático de América: Su Actuación en los Estados Unidos.* Guatemala, 1970.
Isiarri served both El Salvador and Guatemala in the United States in mid-nineteenth century.

2526.   Grieb, K. J. "The United States and the Rise of General Maximiliano Hernández Martínez," *JLAS* 3 (Nov., 1971) 151–172.

2527.   Luna, D. A. *Manual de Historia Económica de El Salvador.* San Salvador, 1971.

2528.   Ramírez Peña, A. *Cartilla Consular.* San Salvador, 1916.
Guide for the Salvadorian consular service.

2529.   Royer, K. "Economic Development of El Salvador, 1945–1965," U. of Fla. Diss., 1966.

2530.   Salazar, P. C. "El Salvador en 1967," *CA* 155 (Nov.–Dec., 1967) 20–30.

2531.   White, A. *El Salvador.* N.Y., 1973.
A broadly based survey.

XIV-H   cross references:
  a)   See item 1879.
  b)   In the Trask, Meyer, and Trask *Bibliography* see items 4151d, 6696, 7005, 7199–7223b.

I. THE UNITED STATES AND COSTA RICA

1. UNITED STATES–COSTA RICAN RELATIONS: GENERAL WORKS AND SPECIAL STUDIES

2532.   Barahona J., L. *Historia de la Política en Costa Rica.* San José, C.R., 1971.

2533.   Bell, J. P. *Crisis in Costa Rica: The 1948*

Revolution. Austin, Tex., 1971.

2534. Brien, R. H. "Petroleum Refining in Costa Rica: A Study in Industrial Development," U. of Tex. Diss., 1966.

Treats a refinery owned jointly by U.S. Chemical Company and the Costa Rican government.

2535. Cordero, J. A. *El Ser de la Nacionalidad Costaricense*. Madrid, 1964.

Contains a section on Costa Rica's war against William Walker.

2536. Costa Rica. Congreso Legislativo. *Guía de Instituciones del Instituciones del Estado y Particulares: Principales Funcionarios y Cargos que Desempeñan*. San José, C.R., 1967.

2537. Denton, C. F. *Patterns of Costa Rican Politics*. Boston, 1971.

2538. Fernández Guardia, R. (ed.). *Costa Rica en el Siglo XIX*. San José, C.R., 1972.

2539. Marín, J. *La Crisis de Nuestra Independencia*. San José, C.R., 1962.

Treats foreign intervention in Costa Rica.

2540. O'Connor, S. M. "Costa Rica in the World Community of Nations, 1919–1935: A Case Study in Latin American Internationalism," Loyola U. of Chicago Diss., 1976.

2541. Peralta, H. *La Diplomacia en Costa Rica*. San José, C.R., 1969.

2542. Ramos, L. (ed.). *Júblio y Pena del Recuerdo*. San José, C.R., 1965.

Treats some of Minor Keith's activities in Costa Rica.

2543. Salisbury, R. V. "Domestic Politics and Foreign Policy: Costa Rica's Stand on Recognition, 1923–1934," *HAHR* 54 (Aug., 1974) 453–478.

XIV-I-1   cross references:
a) See item 723.
b) In the Trask, Meyer, and Trask *Bibliography* see items 2356, 2357, 2445, 3369, 4151d, 7189, 7196, 7224–7270.

2. THE COSTA RICAN BOUNDARY DISPUTE WITH COLOMBIA AND PANAMA

2544. Anderson, L. *El Laudo Loubet: Contribución al Estudio de Límites entre Costa Rica y Panamá*. San José, C.R., 1911.

2545. Bustamante, A. S. de. *Panama–Costa*

Rica Boundary Dispute. Panama, 1921.

2546. Conte Porras, J. "Reflexiones en Torno a la Guerra de Coto y de las Primeras Demandas Panameñas para Reformar el Tratado del Canal," *L* 192 (Nov., 1971) 19–34.

Holds the United States responsible for the outbreak of war between Panama and Costa Rica.

2547. Costa Rica. *Panama Arbitration: Maps Annexed to the Answer of Costa Rica to the Argument of Panama*. Wash., 1914.

2548. ———. Secretaría de Relaciones Exteriores. *Documentos Relativos al Conflicto de Jurisdicción Territorial con la República de Panamá y sus Antecedentes*. San José, C.R., 1921.

2549. Guevara Solano de Pérez, R. *Estudio sobre Lic. Pedro Pérez Zeledón*. San José, C.R., 1968.

Served as Costa Rican negotiator in the boundary dispute with Panama.

2550. Leiva Quirós, E. *Por Nuestras Fronteras Naturales*. San José, C.R., 1935.

In this pamphlet the author opposed the pending border treaty with Panama.

2550a. Méndez Pereira, O. "Causas y Efectos del Conflicto de Límites entre Panamá y Costa Rica," *L* 18 (Oct.–Nov., 1973) 15–22.

2551. Pereira Jiménez, B. "Historia de la Controversia de Límites entre Panamá y Costa Rica," *L* 7 (Sept., 1962) 7–141.

XIV-I-2   cross references:
a) For a discussion of the boundary arbitration between Panama and Costa Rica, see items 2544–2551.
b) In the Trask, Meyer, and Trask *Bibliography* see items 7271–7285.

J. THE UNITED STATES AND PANAMA

1. UNITED STATES–PANAMANIAN RELATIONS: GENERAL WORKS AND SPECIAL STUDIES

2552. Aguilera, F. *50 Millas de Heroicidad; Relato sobre el Canal*. Panama, 1954.

2553. Alfaro, R. J. *Los Acuerdos entre Panamá y los Estados Unidos*. Panama, 1960.

2554. ———. *Medio Siglo de Relaciones entre*

Panamá y los Estados Unidos. Panama, 1959.

By the president of Panama.

2555. Anguizola, G. *The Panama Canal: Isthmian Political Instability from 1821 to 1977*. Wash., 1977.

2556. Benedetti, E. *Tres Ensayos sobre el Canal de Panamá*. Panama, 1965.

2557. Borda Roldán, L. "Problemas Históricos del Canal de Panamá," *L* 10 (Sept., 1965) 55–66.

Treats the period from 1903 to 1964.

2558. Castillero Calvo, A. "Transitismo y Dependencia: El Caso del Istmo de Panamá," *L* 210 (July, 1973) 17–40.

2559. Castillero R., E. J. *El Canal de Panamá*. Panama, 1964.

Treats the idea of the canal from the colonial period.

2560. Chidsey, D. B. *The Panama Canal: An Informal History*. N.Y., 1970.

2561. Ealy, L. *Yanqui Politics and the Isthmian Canal*. University Park, Pa., 1971.

Surveys the history of relations between the countries.

2562. Kitchel, D. *The Truth about the Panama Canal*. New Rochelle, N.Y., 1978.

2563. Krotoski, L. *Kanal Panamski W Dyplomacji Stanów Zjednoczonych i Wielkiej Brytanii*. Warsaw, Poland, 1934.

Translated title: "The Panama Canal and the Diplomacy of the United States and Great Britain."

2564. LaFeber, W. *The Panama Canal: The Crisis in Historical Perspective*. N.Y., 1978.

2565. Leonard, T. M. "The Commissary Issue in United States–Panamanian Relations," American U. Diss., 1969.

2566. Liss, S. B. *The Canal: Aspects of United States–Panamanian Relations*. Notre Dame, Ind., 1967.

2567. Martínez Delgado, L. *Panamá, su Independencia su Incorporación a la Gran Colombia, su Separación de Colombia, el Canal Interoceánico*. Bogotá, 1972.

2568. Miro, R. *Documentos Fundamentales para la Historia de la Nación Panameña*. Panama, 1953.

2569. Moreno, M. B. *Status Jurídico de los Tratados del Canal de Pamamá, (1903–1963)*. Panama, 1964.

2570. Mount, G. S. "American Imperialism in Panama," U. of Toronto Diss., 1969.

2571. Niemeier, J. G. *The Panama Story*. Portland, Ore., 1968.

A survey history with emphasis on United States–Panamanian relations.

2572. Panamá. Ministero de Relaciones Exteriores. *Guía Consular*. Panama, 1944.

2573. Patterson, G. *Panama U.S. Relations*. Panama, 1962.

2574. Richard, A. C. "The Panama Canal in American National Consciousness, 1870–1922," Boston U. Diss., 1969.

2575. Ricord, H. E. "El Nuevo Canal Según Ellos y Nosotros," *L* 185 (Apr., 1971) 5–14.

2576. Ruiz-Eldredge, A. *La Cuestión de Panamá*. Lima, 1973.

A legalistic analysis of the Panama Canal issue.

XIV-J-1   cross references:

a) For canal projects and canal diplomacy during the nineteenth century, see items 711–730.

b) For studies pertaining to the role of the United States in Panama's separation from Colombia, see items 2898–2927.

c) In the Trask, Meyer, and Trask *Bibliography* see items 2349–2458, 7286–7307a, 8290–8382.

2. UNITED STATES–PANAMANIAN RELATIONS, 1903–1940

2577. Adams, W. R. "Strategy, Diplomacy and Isthmian Canal Security, 1880–1917," Fla. State U. Diss., 1974.

2578. Arosemena, J. D. *Historia del Canal de Panamá*. Panama, 1915.

2579. Burns, E. B. "The Recognition of Panama by the Major Latin American States," *TA* 26 (July, 1969) 3–14.

2580. Callejas, B. *Resumen Político de la Administración del Doctor Manuel Amador Guerrero*. Panama, 1933.

2581. Cameron, I. *The Impossible Dream: The Building of the Panama Canal*. N.Y., 1972.

Concerns itself with the engineering process rather than the diplomacy of the venture.

2582. Carles, R. D. *Reminiscencias de los Primeros*

Años de la República de Panamá. Panama, 1968.

Covers the period 1903 to 1912.

2583. Cornish, V. *The Panama Canal and Its Makers*. London, 1909.

2584. Edwards, A. *Panama, the Canal, the Country and the People*. London, 1912.

2585. Escobar, F. J. *Las Relaciones entre Panamá y los Estados Unidos*. Panama, 1933.

2586. Forbes, L. C. *Panama and the Canal Today*. Boston, 1912.

2587. ———. *Panama: The Isthmus and the Canal*. Philadelphia, Pa., 1906.

2588. Franck, H. A. *Zone Policeman 88*. N.Y., 1913.

2589. Fraser, J. F. *Panama, and What It Means*. London, 1913.

2590. Garay, N. *¿Es el Nuevo Tratado entre Panamá y los Estados Unidos una Alianza Militar?* Panama, 1937.

2591. ———. *Panamá y las Guerras de los Estados Unidos*. Panama, 1930.

2592. Guardia, S. de la. *La Intervención Fiscal Americana en Panamá*. Panama, 1917.

2593. Gause, F. A., and C. C. Carr. *The Story of Panama*. Boston, 1912.

Gause was superintendent of the Canal Zone schools.

2594. Hammond, R., and C. J. Lewin. *The Panama Canal*. London, 1966.

A survey of canal history with emphasis on the period 1903 to 1914.

2595. Haskins, W. C. *Canal Zone Pilot*. Panama, 1908.

2596. Langley, L. D. "Negotiating New Treaties with Panama: 1936," *HAHR* 48 (May, 1968) 220–233.

2597. ———. "The World Crisis and the Good Neighbor Policy in Panama, 1936–1941," *TA* 24 (Oct., 1967) 137–152.

2598. Mellander, G. A. *The United States in Panamanian Politics: The Intriguing Formative Years*. Danville, Ill., 1971.

Emphasizes the period 1903 to 1908.

2599. Morales, E. *Cuestiones del Canal*. Panama, 1914.

2600. Panamá. Secretaría de Relaciones Exteriores. *Relación de los Tratados, Convenciones y Convenios Vigentes Suscritos por la República de Panamá de Noviembre 1903 a Febrero 1929*. Panama, 1929.

2601. Pierre, C. G. "Panama's Demand for Independence," *CH* 19 (1923) 128–130.

2602. Porras, B. *Memorandum de las Reclamaciones Fiscales Formuladas por Panamá contra los Estados Unidos Presentado al Presidente Electo Harding durante su Visita a Panamá en Noviembre de 1920*. Panama, 1921.

2603. Rivera Reyes, J. *La Revisión de los Tratados*. Paris, 1929.

2604. ———, and M. A. Díaz. *Historia Auténtica de la Escandalosa Negociación del Tratado del Canal de Panamá, Escrita por el Propio Autor de esa Convención, Sr. Phillipe Bunau-Varilla*. Panama, 1930.

2605. U.S. Isthmian Canal Commission. *Digest of the Executive Orders, Resolutions of the Isthmian Canal Commission, Circulars of the Chairman and Chief Engineer, March 22, 1904 to April 1, 1907*. Wash., 1906.

2606. USCS. *A Convention between the United States and the Republic of Panama for the Construction of a Ship Canal to Connect the Waters of the Atlantic and Pacific Oceans, Signed November 18, 1903*. Wash., 1903.

The text of the Hay-Bunau-Varilla Treaty.

2607. ———. Committee on Interoceanic Canals. *Investigation of Panama Canal Matters*. 3 vols., Wash., 1906.

2608. Zapata, J. *La Cuestión de Panamá*. Panama, 1921.

XIV-J-2   cross references:

a) See items 888, 2910, 2911, 2914, 2921, 2925.

b) In the Trask, Meyer, and Trask *Bibliography* see items 3177, 3667, 7271–7285, 7308–7388, 7521, 7609, 8303, 8308, 8323, 8346, 8371, 8374.

3. UNITED STATES–PANAMANIAN RELATIONS SINCE 1940

2609. Arroyo C., D. "El Projecto de Tratado con los Estados Unidos de América Concerniente a la Construcción de un Canal a Nivel por Territorio Panameño," *L* 182 (Jan., 1971) 45–57.

2610. Bolívar Pedreschi, C. *Canal Propio vs. Canal Ajeno: Elementos para una Nueva Política Canalera*. Panama, 1973.

2611. ———. "La Estrategia del Tratado

Eminente," *TARE* 38 (Mar.–June, 1977) 16–28.

Analyzes Panamanian strategies in the negotiations with the Carter administration.

2612. Busey, J. L. *Political Aspects of the Panama Canal: The Problem of Location.* Tucson, Ariz., 1974.

A pamphlet published in Comparative Government Studies.

2613. Carles, R. D. *La Cuestión Económica en la Relaciones de Panamá con los Estados Unidos.* Panama, 1962.

2614. Center for Statistical Studies. *Panama: Canal Issues and Treaty Talks.* Wash., 1967.

Study conducted by Georgetown U.

2615. Galindo, J. de Arco. *Planteamiento para un Nuevo Tratado con los Estados Unidos.* Panama, 1964.

2616. Gorostiaga, X. "Diez Tesis sobre el Canal de Panamá," *RPC* 30 (1975) 19–27.

2617. Goytia, V. F. *Como Negocia Panamá su Canal.* San José, C.R., 1973.

2618. International Commission of Jurists. *Report on Events in Panama, January 9–12, 1964.* Geneva, 1965.

Report on the flag incidents in the Canal Zone.

2619. León, C. A. de. *Significado Histórico de la Actual Crisis entre Panamá y los Estados Unidos.* Panama, 1964.

Pamphlet interpreting the controversy of Jan., 1964.

2620. Martínez Hauradou, R. L. *Sangre en Panamá.* Panama, 1967.

Treats the 1964 flag incidents.

2621. Minor, K. J. "United States–Panamanian Relations: 1958–1973," Case Western Reserve U. Diss., 1974.

2622. Rivera Reyes, J. *El Problema de las Bases Militares de Defensa del Canal en Territorio Panameño y en Tiempos de Paz.* Panama, 1946.

2623. Rosenfeld, S. S. "The Panama Negotiations—A Close Run Thing," *FA* 54 (Oct., 1975) 1–13.

2624. Russo Berguido, A. *Panamá, Ave Fénix de América.* Panama, 1964.

Emphasizes the 1964 controversy.

2625. Speller, J. P. *The Panama Canal: Heart of America's Security.* N.Y., 1972.

Argues for continued U.S. control.

XIV-J-3 cross references:
a) See items 958, 1358.
b) In the Trask, Meyer, and Trask *Bibliography* see items 4186, 7290, 7389–7411.

K. THE UNITED STATES AND CUBA

1. UNITED STATES–CUBAN RELATIONS: GENERAL WORKS AND SPECIAL STUDIES

2626. Benjamin, J. B. *The United States and Cuba: Hegemony and Development, 1880–1934.* Pittsburgh, Pa., 1977.

2627. Cortina, J. M. *Estudios Realizados para un Proyecto de Ley: Organizando el Servicio Diplomático y Consular de la República de Cuba.* Havana, 1938.

2627a. García Montes, J., and A. A. Avila. *Historia del Partido Comunista de Cuba.* Miami, Fla., 1970.

2628. Langley, L. D. *The Cuban Policy of the United States: A Brief History.* N.Y., 1968.

2628a. Le Riverend, J. *Historia Económica de Cuba.* Barcelona, 1972.

A skillful Marxist analysis emphasizing the role of foreign interests.

2629. López Segrera, F. *Cuba: Capitalismo Dependiente y Subdesarrollo (1510–1959).* Havana, 1972.

2630. Ruiz, R. *Cuba: The Making of a Revolution.* Amherst, Mass., 1968.

2631. Thomas, H. *Cuba: The Pursuit of Freedom, 1762–1969.* N.Y., 1971.

An extensive survey history. Sp. ed., B.A., 1974.

XIV-K-1 cross references:
a) For references on the Spanish-American War, see items 774–815.
b) In the Trask, Meyer, and Trask *Bibliography* see items 2623–2891, 7412–7437.

2. THE UNITED STATES AND SPANISH CUBA TO 1898

2632. Aguirre, S. *Seis Actitudes de la Burguesía Cubana en el Siglo XIX.* Havana, 1944.

2633. Isern, J. *Pioneros Cubanos en U.S.A., 1575–1898.* Miami Springs, Fla., 1971.

2634. Katz, I. "August Belmont's Cuban Acquisition Scheme," *MA* 50 (1968) 52–63.

Treats the Ostend Manifesto.

2635. Langley, L. D. "The Whigs and the López Expeditions to Cuba, 1849–1851: A Chapter in Frustrating Diplomacy," *RHA* 71 (Jan.–June, 1971) 9–22.

2636. MacMaster, R. K. "The United States, Great Britain, and the Suppression of the Cuban Slave Trade, 1835–1860," Georgetown U. Diss., 1968.

XIV-K-2 cross references:

a) For the background of the Spanish-American War, see items 788–801.

b) See also items 790, 2402.

c) In the Trask, Meyer, and Trask *Bibliography* see items 1966, 2005, 2103, 2107b, 2137a, 2191, 7419, 7428, 7438–7499, 7541a, 7581.

3. UNITED STATES–CUBAN RELATIONS, 1898–1934

2637. Adams, J. M. *Pioneering in Cuba.* Concord, N.H., 1901.
Treats the American colony at La Gloria following the Spanish-American War.

2638. Aguilar, L. *Cuba 1933: Prologue to Revolution.* Ithaca, N.Y., 1972.

2639. Benjamin, J. R. "The U.S. and the Cuban Revolution of 1933: The Role of the U.S. Hegemony in the Cuban Political Economy, 1880–1934," U. of Pa. Diss., 1974.

2639a. Carlson, W. H. *Report of William H. Carlson, Special Commissioner of Railroads, to Major General Wood.* Baltimore, Md., 1901.

2640. Cirules, E. *Conversación con el Ultimo Norteamericano.* Havana, 1973.
Treats activities of the Cuban Land and Steamship Company.

2641. Clagett, J. H. "Skipper of the *Eagle*: Rehearsal for Greatness," *USNIP* 102 (1976) 56–58.
Treats H. Kent Hewitt's landing in Cuba in 1917 to protect American life and property.

2642. García Kohly, M. *Política Internacional Cubana.* Madrid, 1928.
Concentrates on Cuban-Spanish relations at the time of publication.

2643. Gaylor, S. K. "The Abrogation of the Platt Amendment: A Case Study in United States–Cuban Relations, with Special Emphasis on Public Opinion," NYU Diss., 1971.

2644. Hitchman, J. H. "The American Touch in Imperial Administration: General Leonard Wood in Cuba, 1898–1902," *TA* 24 (Apr., 1968) 394–403.

2645. ———. *Leonard Wood and Cuban Independence, 1898–1902.* The Hague, 1971.

2646. Holme, J. G. *The Life of Leonard Wood.* Garden City, N.Y., 1920.

2646a. Hunter, J. M. "Investment as a Factor in the Economic Development of Cuba, 1899–1935," *IEA* 5 (Winter, 1951) 82–96.

2647. Krogh, P. F. "Sumner Wells and United States Relations with Cuba: 1933," Tufts U. Diss., 1966.

2648. Lamar Schweyer, A. *Cómo Cayó el Presidente Machado: Una Página Oscura de la Diplomacia Norteamericana.* Madrid, 1934.

2649. Lippmann, W. "Second Thoughts on Havana," *FA* 6 (July, 1928) 541–554.

2650. Millett, A. R. *The Politics of Intervention: The Military Occupation of Cuba, 1906–1909.* Columbus, O., 1968.

2651. Milton, J. J. "William Howard Taft: Diplomatic Trouble Shooter," Tex. A. and M. U. Diss., 1977.
Contains section on Taft's mission to Cuba in 1906.

2652. Mondejar, J. P. "Neo-Colonialism as an Economic System: Cuba, 1898–1934," Ind. U. Diss., 1976.

2652a. Pérez, L. A. "Capital, Bureaucrats, and Policy: The Economic Contours of United States–Cuban Relations, 1916–1921," *IEA* 29 (Summer, 1975) 59–78.

2653. ———. "Supervision of a Protectorate: United States and the Cuban Army, 1898–1902," *HAHR* 52 (May, 1972) 250–271.

2654. Smith, R. F. "Cuba: Laboratory for Dollar Diplomacy, 1898–1917," *HIS* 28 (1966) 586–609.

2654a. U.S. Bureau of Insular Affairs. *Translation of the Proposed Constitution for Cuba, the Official Acceptance of the Platt Amendment, and the Electoral Law.* Wash., 1901.

2655. Woolsey, L. H. "The New Cuban Treaty," *AJIL* 28 (July, 1934) 530–534.

XIV-K-3   cross references:
a) For works on the Spanish-American War, see Chapter V.
b) In the Trask, Meyer, and Trask *Bibliography* see items 2651, 2675, 2681, 2785, 2886, 2956, 3158, 3161, 3174, 3222, 3342, 7437, 7500–7653.

4. ISLE OF PINES CONTROVERSY, 1898–1925

XIV-K-4   cross references:
a) See items 946, 960.
b) In the Trask, Meyer, and Trask *Bibliography* see items 7589, 7654–7669a.

5. UNITED STATES–CUBAN RELATIONS, 1934–1958

2656. Alienes Urosa, J. *Características Fundamentales de la Economía Cubana*. Havana, 1950.

2657. Asociación Nacional de Hacendados de Cuba. *El Tratado de Reciprocidad de 1934*. Havana, 1939.

2658. Beals, C. "American Diplomacy in Cuba," *N* 138 (Jan., 1934) 68–70.

2659. Bonachea, R. E. "United States Policy toward Cuba: 1954–1961," Georgetown U. Diss., 1976.

2660. Club Rotario de la Havana. *The Present Status of Cuban-American Trade Relations*. Havana, 1955.

2661. "Commission of the Social-Economic Union of Cuba Visits Washington," *BPAU* 69 (Sept., 1935) 667–671.

2662. Cuba. Cámara de Comercio de la República de Cuba. *Directorio Oficial de Exportación e Importacion, Producción y Turismo*. Havana, 1941.

2663. Farber, S. "Revolution and Social Structure in Cuba, 1933–1959," U. of Calif. Diss., 1969.

2664. Fitzgibbon, R., and H. M. Healey. "Cuban Elections of 1936," *APSR* 30 (Aug., 1936) 724–735.

2665. Gellman, I. F. "Good Neighbor Diplomacy and the Rise of Batista, 1933–1945," Ind. U. Diss., 1970.

2666. Gutiérrez y Sánchez, G. *El Desarrollo Económico de Cuba*. Havana, 1952.

2667. ———. *Presente y Futuro de la Economía Cubana*. Havana, 1950.

2668. International Bank for Reconstruction and Development. *Report on Cuba*. Wash., 1951.

2669. Lupien, A. L. "Presenting Cuba, Our Good Neighbor," *BPAU* 76 (Feb., 1942) 91–94.

2670. Magill, R., and C. Shoup. *The Cuban Fiscal System, 1939*. N.Y., 1939.

2670a. Ott, T. O. "The Corbitts, the H.A.H.R., and United States–Cuban Intellectual Relations," *HAHR* 59 (Feb., 1979) 108–119.

2671. Portell Vilá, H. *The Non-Intervention Pact of Montevideo and American Intervention in Cuba*. Havana, 1935.

2672. Sadler, L. R. "The Racambole Conspiracy: A Planned Invasion of Cuba from the United States in 1947," U. of South Carolina Diss., 1970.

2673. Shaw, P. V. "'Good Neighbor'—and Cuba," *NAR* 240 (Sept., 1935) 315–341.

2674. Stuart, G. H. "Cuba and the Platt Amendment," *WAI* 5 (Spring, 1934) 49–54.

2675. Unión Social Económica de Cuba. *Commercial Relations between Cuba and the United States of America*. Havana, 1936.

2675a. USDS. *Analysis of Cuban-American Trade during the First Two Years under Reciprocal Trade Agreement*. Wash., 1937.

XIV-K-5   cross references: In the Trask, Meyer, and Trask Bibliography *see items 4055, 7670–7696, 7827.*

6. UNITED STATES–CUBAN RELATIONS SINCE 1958

2676. Allison, G. T. *Essence of Decision: Explaining the Cuban Missile Crisis*. Boston, 1971.
Focuses on the theory of decision-making and how it was applied in the Cuban case.

2677. ———. "Policy, Process, and Politics: Conceptual Models and the Cuban Missile Crisis," Harvard U. Diss., 1968.

2678. Alvarez García, J. *Che Guevara*. Medellín, Colombia, 1968.
Contains biographical data, speeches, and conflicting interpretations of his death.

2679. Ayers, B. E. *The War That Never Was*. N.Y., 1976.
Author was hired by the CIA to train Cuban exiles for invasion.

2680. Bender, L. D. "Guantánamo: Its Political, Military and Legal Status," *CQ* 19 (Mar., 1973) 80–86.

2681. Benítez Cabrera, J. A. *David-Goliat: Siglo XX*. Havana, 1967.
Treats U.S. policy toward Castro.

2682. Bethel, P. D. *Cuba y los Estados Unidos*. Barcelona, 1962.

2683. Bonachea, R. E., and N. P. Valdés. *Che: Selected Works of Ernesto Guevara*. Cambridge, Mass., 1969.

2684. Bonsal, P. S. *Cuba, Castro, and the United States*. Pittsburgh, Pa., 1970.
Author was U.S. ambassador to Cuba, 1959–1960.

2685. Boorstein, E. *The Economic Transformation of Cuba*. N.Y., 1968.
Optimistic appraisals by an economic advisor to Castro.

2686. Boughton, G. J. "Soviet-Cuban Relations: 1956–1962," Mich. State U. Diss., 1972.

2687. ———. "Soviet Cuban Relations, 1956–1960," *JIAS* 16 (Nov., 1974) 436–453.

2688. Castro, F. *Major Speeches*. London, 1968.

2689. ———. *10 Años de Revolución Cubana*. Montevideo, 1969.
Castro speech.

2690. ———. *El Viaje de Fidel Castro a la Unión Soviética*. Montevideo, 1963.

2691. Castro, R. *Trascendencia de la Revolución Cubana y Denuncia del Diversionismo Ideológico Imperialista*. Lima, 1974.

2692. Collazo, E. *Los Americanos en Cuba*. Havana, 1972.

2693. Córdova-Claure, T. *Los Años 60: Cuba vs. U.S.A.* B.A., 1974.

2694. Cuba. Ministerio de Relaciones Exteriores. *Hyjacking of Aircraft: A Boomerang Hurled at Cuba by the Imperialist Government of the United States of America*. Havana, 1970.
A 26-page pamphlet.

2695. Dasziewicz, W. "Miedzynarodowa Sytuacja Kuby," *SM* 15 (1960) 3–38.
Translated title: "The International Situation of Cuba."

2696. Dinnerstein, H. S. *The Making of a Missile Crisis: October, 1962*. Baltimore, Md., 1976.

2697. Divine, R. A. (ed.). *The Cuban Missile Crisis*. Chicago, 1971.
Concerns the debate in the United States over Kennedy's actions.

2697a. Domínguez, J. I. *Cuba: Order and Progress*. Cambridge, Mass., 1978.

2698. Duncan, W. R. "Castro's New Approach toward Latin America," *WA* 133 (Mar., 1971) 275–282.

2699. Ebon, M. *Che: The Making of a Legend*. N.Y., 1969.

2700. Edelstein, J. C. "The Evolution of Goals and Priorities in the Thought of Fidel Castro Ruz," U. of Calif. Riverside Diss., 1975.

2701. *El Insólito Caso de Espía de la CIA bajo el Manto de Funcionario Diplomático de la Embajada de México en Cuba*. Havana, 1969.

2702. Franco, C. *Bloqueio de Cuba e Guerra Nuclear*. São Paulo, 1963.

2703. Friedberg, S. "The Measures of Damages in Claims against Cuba," *IEA* 23 (Summer, 1969) 67–86.
Discusses claims of U.S. citizens against the Cuban government.

2704. Garelli Farías, M. J. *La Crisis Internacional de 1962 y el Bloque de Cuba*. Mexico, 1967.

2705. Gelberg, L. *Kryzys Karaibski 1962, Problemy Prawa Miedzy-Norodowego*. Warsaw, Poland, 1964.
Translated title: "Caribbean Crisis of 1962, Problems of International Law."

2706. González, E. *Cuba under Castro: The Limits of Charisma*. Boston, 1974.

2707. Gordon, M. W. *The Cuban Nationalizations: The Demise of Foreign Private Property*. Buffalo, N.Y., 1976.
Nationalization is viewed in the context of U.S. relations with Cuba.

2708. Guevara, E. *Escritos y Discursos*. 3 vols., Havana, 1972.

2709. Halajczuk, B. T. "Autodefensa Preventativa a la Luz de la Cuarentena de Cuba en 1962," *REP* 186 (Nov.–Dec., 1972) 277–295.
A legal analysis of the quarantine.

2710. Halperin, E. "The Castro Regime in Cuba," *CH* 51 (Dec., 1966) 354–359.

2711. Halperin, M. *The Rise and Decline of Fidel*

Castro. Berkeley, Calif., 1972.

2712. Holler, J. S. *Fidelem Castrem Napřic Kubou*. Prague, Czechoslovakia, 1961.
Translated title: "Fidel Castro Redresses Cuba."

2713. Horowitz, I. L. (ed.). *Cuban Communism*. Chicago, 1970.

2713a. Hunt, H. *Give Us This Day: The Inside Story of the CIA and the Bay of Pigs Invasion . . . by One of Its Key Organizers*. New Rochelle, N.Y., 1973.

2714. Jackson, D. B. *Castro, the Kremlin and Communism in Latin America*. Baltimore, Md., 1969.

2715. Johnson, L. L. "U.S. Business Interests in Cuba and the Rise of Castro," *WP* 17 (Apr., 1965) 440–459.

2716. Kahan, J. H., and A. K. Long. "The Cuban Missile Crisis: A Study of Its Strategic Context," *PSQ* 87 (Dec., 1972) 564–590.

2717. Kennedy, R. F. *Thirteen Days: A Memoir of the Cuban Missile Crisis*. N.Y., 1969.
Contains some of the Kennedy-Khrushchev correspondence and various speeches.

2718. Layson, W. W. "The Political and Strategic Aspects of the 1962 Cuban Crisis," U. of Va. Diss., 1969.

2719. Lazo, M. *Dagger in the Heart: American Foreign Policy Failures in Cuba*. N.Y., 1968.
A disillusioned account of the U.S. position.

2720. Lévesque, J. *L'URSS et la Révolution Cubaine*. Montreal, 1976.

2721. Levinson, S., and C. Brightman. *Venceremos Brigade: Young Americans Sharing the Life and Work of Revolutionary Cuba*. N.Y., 1971.

2722. Lidert, M. *Kuba a Stany Zdednoczone*. Warsaw, Poland, 1961.
Translated title: "Cuba and the United States."

2723. Mesa Lago, C. *Cuba in the 1970's: Pragmatism and Institutionalization*. Albuquerque, N.M., 1974.
An objective analysis of how Cuban society changed from the late 1960s to the early 1970s.

2724. ——— (ed.). *Revolutionary Change in Cuba*. Pittsburgh, Pa., 1971.
Eighteen essays covering a wide variety of topics.

2725. Petras, J. "The U.S.-Cuban Policy Debate," *MR* 26 (Feb., 1975) 22–23.
Treats the Nixon administration's reluctance to normalize relations with Cuba.

2726. Pino-Santos, O. *El Asalto a Cuba por la Olarquía Yanqui*. Havana, 1973.

2727. ———. *El Imperialismo Norteamericana en la Economía de Cuba*. Havana, 1960.

2728. Plank, J. (ed.). *Cuba and the United States: Long Range Perspectives*. Wash., 1967.
Includes essays by Bayless Manning, Kalman H. Silvert, Robert F. Smith, Tad Szulc, and Raymond Aron.

2729. Quester, G. H. "Missiles in Cuba," *FA* 49 (Apr., 1971) 493–506.

2729a. Raymond, W. J. "The Feasibility of Rapprochement between the Republic of Cuba and the United States: The Case of Guantánamo Naval Base," *CQ* 5 (Mar.–June, 1975) 35–59.

2730. Sabri, M. *Thawrat Kāstrū*. Cairo, 1961.
Translated title: "Castro's Revolution."

2731. Semidel, M. *Les Etats-Unis et la Révolution Cubaine*. Paris, 1968.

2732. Sobel, L. A., *et al. Cuba, the U.S. and Russia, 1960–1963*. N.Y., 1973.

2733. Sonntag, H. R. *Che Guevara und die Revolution*. Frankfurt, 1968.

2734. Stagni, P. *¿Qué es la Cuba Comunista de Hoy?* B.A., 1963.
Anti-Castro account by a Paraguayan.

2735. Suchliki, J. (ed.). *Cuba, Castro, and Revolution*. Coral Gables, Fla., 1972.

2736. Tannenbaum, F. "Castro and Social Change," *PSQ* 77 (June, 1962) 178–204.

2737. Telalov, K. *Kuba-Da! Janki-Ne!* Varna, Bulgaria, 1961.
Translated title: "Cuba-Yes, Yankee-no."

2738. Turnell, A. *Cuba Hoy: Una Revolución en Marcha*. Barcelona, 1977.

2739. USCS. Committee on the Judiciary. Subcommittee to Investigate the Administration of the Internal Security Act and Other Internal Security Laws. *Castro's*

Network in the United States (Fair Play for Cuba Committee): Hearings. (88th Cong., 1st Sess.). Wash., 1963.

2740. Zeitlin, M. *Revolutionary Politics and the Cuban Working Class.* Princeton, N.J., 1967.

Sociological study based largely on interviews.

XIV-K-6   cross references:
a) For the expulsion of Cuba from the OAS, see items 1882–1887.
b) See also items 1125, 1385, 1698, 1785.
c) In the Trask, Meyer, and Trask *Bibliography* see items 4250, 4611, 4785, 4791a, 4840, 4841, 5287–5311, 6335, 6337, 7696a– 7852, 10135.

L. THE UNITED STATES AND THE DOMINICAN REPUBLIC (SANTO DOMINGO)

1. United States–Dominican Relations: General Works and Special Studies

2741. Llaverías, F. *Manual de Derecho Consular Dominicano.* Santo Domingo, 1925.
2742. PAU. *Dominican Constitution of 1955.* Wash., 1958.
2743. Pérez y Pérez, C. F. *Historia Diplomática de Santo Domingo.* Santo Domingo, 1973.
2744. Wiarda, H. J. *The Dominican Republic: A Nation in Transition.* N.Y., 1969.

XIV-L-1   cross references:
a) See item 2827.
b) In the Trask, Meyer, and Trask *Bibliography* see items 7853–7864.

2. United States–Dominican Relations: Independence to 1905

2745. Duin, C. E. "Dominican-American Relations, 1897–1907," Georgetown U. Diss., 1955.

XIV-L-2   cross references:
a) For works treating the short-lived Spanish reconquest (1861–1865), see items 678– 682.
b) In the Trask, Meyer, and Trask *Bibliography* see items 2192–2202, 7865–7882.

3. Attempted United States Annexation (1871)

2746. Donald, D. *Charles Sumner and the Rights of Man.* N.Y., 1970.

Sumner opposed the annexation.

2747. "Mensaje a la Comisión de Investigación de los E.U.A. en Santo Domingo," *BAGNDR* 23 (Jan.–Dec., 1960) 101– 108.
2748. Rodríguez Demorizi, E. (comp.) *Papeles de Buenaventura Baez.* Santo Domingo, 1969.

Baez was president during the projected annexation to the United States.

2749. ———. "Proyecto de Incorporación de Santo Domingo a Norte América," *BAGNDR* 35 (1960) 3–7.
2750. USCS. *Report of Davis Hatch. With Documents.* (41st Cong., 2d Sess.) Wash., 1870.

Treats possible annexation of Dominican Republic.

XIV-L-3   cross references: In the Trask, Meyer, and Trask Bibliography *see items 2094, 2112a, 7870, 7871, 7879, 7883–7899.*

4. United States–Dominican Relations, 1905–1924

2751. Baughman, C. C. "United States Occupation of the Dominican Republic," *USNIP* (Dec., 1925) 2306–2327.
2752. Burke, A. J. *Land of Checkerboard Families.* N.Y., 1932.

Treats U.S. intervention under President Ramón Cáceres, 1908–1911.

2752a. Calder, B. J. "Caudillos and Gavilleros versus the United States Marines." *HAHR* 58 (Nov., 1978) 649–675.
2752b. ———. "Some Aspects of the United States Occupation of the Dominican Republic, 1916–1924," U. of Tex. Diss., 1974.
2753. Fuller, S., and G. A. Cosmas. *Marines in the Dominican Republic, 1916–1924.* Wash., 1974.
2754. Grieb, K. J. "Warren G. Harding and the Dominican Republic: U.S. Withdrawal, 1921–1923," *JIAS* 11 (July, 1969) 425–440.

2755. Hoepelman, A., and J. A. Senior. *Documentos Históricos que se Refieren a la Intervención Armada de los Estados Unidos de Norte-América y la Implantación de un Gobierno Militar Americano en la República Dominicana*. Santo Domingo, 1973.

2756. León, C. V. *Casos y Cosas de Ayer*. Santo Domingo, 1972.

    Stresses the positive accomplishments of the intervention of 1916–1924.

2757. Rosa, A. de la. *Las Finanzas de Santo Domingo y el Control Americano*. Santo Domingo, 1969.

XIV-L-4   cross references:
  a) See item 2839.
  b) In the Trask, Meyer, and Trask *Bibliography* see items 7118, 7638, 7900–7933, 8085, 8092.

5. UNITED STATES–DOMINICAN RELATIONS SINCE 1924

2758. Acre Medina, J. *An Open Letter to the Editors of Life: Re the Galíndez-Murphey Case*. N.Y., 1957.

2759. Addison, T. G. *Reorganization of the Financial Administration of the Dominican Republic*. Wash., 1931.

2760. Almoina, J. *Yo Fuí Secretario de Trujillo*. B.A., 1950.

2761. Atkins, G. P., and L. C. Wilson. *The United States and the Trujillo Regime*. New Brunswick, N.J., 1972.

    Based on the doctoral dissertations of both authors.

2762. Balaguer, J. (ed.). *El Tratado Trujillo-Hull y la Liberación Financiera de la República Dominicana*. Bogotá, 1941.

2763. Bosch, J. "Trujillo: Problema de América," *COMB* 1 (Mar.–Apr., 1959) 9–13.

2764. Cestero Burgos, T. *Filosofía de un Régimen*. Cd. Trujillo, D.R., 1951.

2765. Crassweller, R. D. *Trujillo: The Life and Times of a Caribbean Dictator*. N.Y., 1966.

2766. Cruz y Berges, F. *Trujillo, Gobierno y Pueblo Dominicano Frente al Comunismo Internacional*. Cd. Trujillo, D.R., 1957.

2767. Curry, E. R. "The United States and the Dominican Republic, 1924–1933," U. of Minn. Diss., 1966.

2768. Ellender, A. J. *La Ley Azucarera de EU y el Azúcar Dominicano*. Cd. Trujillo, D.R., 1960.

2769. Ernst, M. L. *Report and Opinion in the Matter of Galindez*. N.Y., 1958.

2770. Felkel, G. *Menschen im Hurrikan: Trujillo und die Dominikanische Republik*. Berlin, 1962.

2771. Gil, F. *Trujillo y su Obra, 1930–1952*. La Romanan, D.R., 1954.

2772. Girona, F. *Las Fechorías del Bandolero Trujillo: Estudio Crítico de la Vida y Milagros del Tirano de Santo Domingo*. San Juan, P.R., 1937.

2773. Gruening, E. "Dictatorship in Santo Domingo: A Joint Concern," *N* 138 (May, 1934) 583–585.

2774. Herrera, C. A. *Las Finanzas de la República Dominicana*. Cd. Trujillo, D.R., 1955.

2775. Herring, H. "Scandal of the Caribbean: The Dominican Republic," *CH* 38 (Mar., 1960) 140–143, 164.

2776. Long, G. S. *El Caso de Gerry Murphy y la República Dominicana*. Cd. Trujillo, D.R., 1957.

2777. Medina Benet, V. M. *Fracaso de la Tercera República: Narraciones de Historia Dominicana (1924–1930)*. Santo Domingo, 1974.

    Treats the period from the U.S. withdrawal to the rise of Trujillo.

2778. Millington, T. "U.S. Diplomacy and the Dominican Crisis," *SAISR* 7 (Summer, 1963) 25–30.

2779. Monclus, M. A. *El Caudillismo en la República Dominicana*. 3d ed., Cd. Trujillo, D.R., 1962.

2780. Ornes Coiscu, G. E. *Trujillo, Brownell, and Braden*. Cd. Trujillo, D.R., 1953.

2781. Osori Lizarazo, J. A. *Birth and Growth of Anti-Trujillism in America*. Madrid, 1958.

2782. PAU. Comisión Interamericana de Derechos Humanos. *Informaciones sobre el Respecto de los Derechos Humanos en la República Dominicana*. Wash., 1961.

2783. ———. ———. *Informe sobre la Situación de los Derechos Humanos en la República Dominicana*. Wash., 1962.

2784. Penzini, J. *Las Acusaciones contra Trujillo: Assault by Slander*. Cd. Trujillo, D.R., 1956.

2785. Pulley, R. H. "The United States and the

Trujillo Dictatorship, 1933–1940: The High Price of Caribbean Stability," *CS* 5 (Oct., 1965) 22–31.

2786. Rodríguez Demorizi, E. *De Política Dominicana-Americana: Discurso ante la Estatua de Cordell Hull*. Cd. Trujillo, D.R., 1957.

2787. ———. *Trujillo y Cordell Hull: Un Ejemplo de Política Panamericanista*. Cd. Trujillo, D.R., 1956.

2788. Rubin, S. F. "The Overthrow of the Trujillo Regime: Implications for the United States," U. of Miami Diss., 1972.

2789. Thomson, C. A. "Dictatorship in the Dominican Republic," *FPAR* 12 (Apr., 1936) 30–40.

2790. Troncoso, J. M. *La Política Económica de Trujillo*. Cd. Trujillo, D.R., 1953.

2791. Trujillo, H. B. *Strengthening Relations between the Dominican Republic and the United States*. Wash., 1958.

2792. U.S. Tariff Commission. *Economic Controls and Commercial Policy in the Dominican Republic*. Wash., 1946.

2793. ———. ———. *Mining and Manufacturing Industries in the Dominican Republic*. Wash., 1948.

2794. USCH. *Legislation Relating to Amounts of Sugar Which May Be Purchased in Dominican Republic*. Wash., 1960.

2795. Varney, H. L. "What Is behind the Galindez Case?" *AME* 84 (June, 1957) 34–42.

XIV-L-5   cross references:
   a) See items 734, 3108.
   b) In the Trask, Meyer, and Trask *Bibliography* see items 7906, 7914, 7934–7994.

6. THE UNITED STATES INTERVENTION OF 1965

2796. Acosta Garrido, M., and C. M. Vilas, "Santo Domingo y Checoslovakia en la Política de Bloques," *RCS* 16 (June, 1972) 249–261.
   Compares the U.S. intervention in the Dominican Republic and the Soviet intervention in Czechoslovakia.

2797. Almuli, J. "Intervencÿa u Dominikanskoj Republici," *SOCI* 8 (1965) 656–666.
   Translated title: "Intervention in the Dominican Republic."

2798. Brown-John, C. L. *Multinational Sanctions in International Law: A Comparative Analysis*. N.Y., 1975.
   Chapter 4 treats sanctions against the Dominican Republic.

2799. Carey, J. *The Dominican Republic Crisis, 1965*. Dobbs Ferry, N.Y., 1967.

2800. Clark, J. A. *The Church and the Crisis in the Dominican Republic*. Westminster, Md., 1967.
   The author was a Roman Catholic clergyman in the Dominican Republic at the time of the U.S. intervention.

2801. Draper, T. "The Dominican Intervention Reconsidered," *PSQ* 86 (Mar., 1971) 1–36.

2802. ———. *The Dominican Revolt: A Case Study in American Policy*. N.Y., 1968.

2803. ———. "As Raízes da Crise Dominicana," *CB* 7 (Sept.–Oct., 1965) 21–46.

2804. Georgetown U. Center for Strategic Studies. *Dominican Action, 1965: Intervention or Cooperation?* Wash., 1966.
   Concludes that the intervention was necessary to prevent a Communist takeover.

2805. Gleijeses, P. *La Crise Dominicaine, 1965*. Milan, Italy, 1973.

2805a. ———. *The Dominican Crisis: The 1965 Constitutionalist Revolt and American Intervention*. Baltimore, 1978.

2806. Goff, F., and M. Locker. "La Violencia de la Dominación: El Poder de los Estados Unidos en la República Dominicana," *RCEDR* 1 (Mar.–June, 1972) 3–43.

2807. Gutiérrez, C. M. *The Dominican Republic: Rebellion and Repression*. N.Y., 1972.
   Argues that the United States has continued to control the Dominican Republic since the intervention of 1965.

2808. Harmel, C. "Contribución a la Historia de la Crisis Dominicana," *EYO* 5 (July, 1966) 1–12.

2809. Lowenthal, A. F. *The Dominican Intervention*. Cambridge, Mass., 1972.
   The criticism of the United States is restrained.

2810. Mann, T. C. "The Dominican Crisis: Correcting Some Misconceptions," *USDSB* 53 (Nov., 1965) 730–738.

2811. Mansbach, R. W. *Dominican Crisis, 1965*. N.Y., 1971.

A quick reference to the major facts of the U.S. intervention.

2812. Meeker, L. C. "The Dominican Situation in the Perspective of Internal Law," *USDSB* 53 (July, 1965) 60–65.

2813. Millington, T. M. "U.S. Diplomacy and the Dominican Crisis," *SAISR* 7 (Summer, 1965) 25–30.

2814. Moreno, J. *Barrio in Arms: Revolution in Santo Domingo*. Pittsburgh, Pa., 1970.

The author, a sociologist in Santo Domingo during the revolution, argues that the role of Communists and Fidelistas was exaggerated by the Johnson administration.

2814a. Morris, M. A. "The Problem of Control of American Military Interventions: Vietnam and the Dominican Republic," Johns Hopkins U. Diss., 1971.

2815. Odena, I. J. *La Intervención Illegal en Santo Domingo*. B.A., 1965.

2816. Ortega, G. *Santo Domingo, 1965*. Havana, 1965.

2817. Ovalles, A. *Caamaño, el Gobierno y las Guerrillas*. Santo Domingo, 1973.

2818. PAU. Inter-American Commission on Human Rights. *Report on the Situation Regarding Human Rights in the Dominican Republic*. Wash., 1962.

2819. Schreiber, A. P., and P. S. Schreiber, "The Inter-American Commission on Human Rights in the Dominican Crisis," *IO* 22 (Spring, 1968) 508–528.

2820. Slater, J. *Intervention and Negotiation: The United States and the Dominican Revolution*. N.Y., 1970.

Argues that the United States intervened to stop the bloodshed and to assure free elections.

2821. ———. "The Limits of Legitimization in International Organizations: The OAS and the Dominican Crisis," *IO* 33 (Winter, 1969) 48–72.

2822. Wilson, L. C. "The Dominican Policy of the United States: The Illusions of Economic Development and Elections," *WA* 128 (July–Aug., 1965) 93–101.

2823. ———. "Estados Unidos y la Guerra Civil Dominicana: El Reto de las Relaciones Interamericanas," *FI* (Oct.–Dec., 1967) 155–178.

2824. ———. "La Intervención de los Estados Unidos de América en el Caribe: La Crisis de 1965 en la República Dominicana," *RPI* 122 (July–Aug., 1972) 37–82.

XIV-L-6   cross references:
a) See items 137, 1385, 2423.
b) In the Trask, Meyer, and Trask *Bibliography* see items 7994a–8004a.

M. THE UNITED STATES AND HAITI

1. UNITED STATES–HAITIAN RELATIONS: GENERAL WORKS

2825. Alexis, S. *La Nègre Masqué*. Port-au-Prince, 1933.

2825a. Heinl, R. D. *Written in Blood: The Story of the Haitian People, 1492–1971*. Boston, 1978.

2826. Laurent, M. *Erreurs et Verités dans L'Histoire D'Haiti*. Port-au-Prince, 1945.

2827. Logan, R. D. *Haiti and the Dominican Republic*. N.Y., 1968.

A comparative history.

XIV-M-1   cross references: In the Trask, Meyer, and Trask Bibliography *see items 8005–8020.*

2. UNITED STATES–HAITIAN RELATIONS: NINETEENTH CENTURY

2828. Cole, H. *Christophe: King of Haiti*. N.Y., 1967.

2828a. De Vidas, A. "The Foreign Relations of Haiti in Hemispheric Affairs from Independence to Occupation, 1804–1915," NYU Diss., 1971.

Hunt, A. N. "The Influence of Haiti on the Antebellum South, 1791–1865," U. of Texas Diss., 1975.

2829. Lubin, M. A. "Les Premiers Rapports de la Nation Haïtienne avec L'Etranger," *JIAS* 10 (Apr., 1968) 277–305.

Contains a section on early relations with the United States.

2830. Mathewson, T. M. "Slavery and Diplomacy: The United States and Saint Domingue, 1791–1893," U. of Calif. Santa Barbara Diss., 1976.

2831. Ott, T. O. *The Haitian Revolution, 1789–1804*. Knoxville, Tenn., 1973.

2831a. Seraille, W. "Afro-American Emigration to Haiti during the American Civil War," *TA* 35 (Oct., 1978) 185–200.

2832. Tyson, G. F. (ed.). *Toussaint L'Overture*. Englewood Cliffs, N.J., 1973.

2833. USCH. *Claims on Hayti. Message from the President of the United States*. (27th Cong., 2d Sess., Exec. Doc. 36.) Wash., 1842.

Treats claims of U.S. citizens from the Christophe and Boyer administrations.

XIV-M-2   cross references: In the Trask, Meyer, and Trask Bibliography *see items 8021–8064.*

3. UNITED STATES–HAITIAN RELATIONS, 1900–1941

2834. Allen, J. H. "An Inside View of Revolutions in Haiti," *CH* 32 (May, 1930) 325–329.

2835. Bausman, F., *et al. The Seizure of Haiti by the United States*. N.Y., 1922.

2836. Blanchet, J. *Politique Étrangère et Représentation Extérieure*. Port-au-Prince, 1936.

2837. Blassingame, J. W. "The Press and American Intervention in Haiti and the Dominican Republic, 1904–1920," *CS* 4 (July, 1969) 27–43.

2838. Borno, L. "Problems of Interest to Haiti and the United States," *BPAU* 40 (Sept., 1926) 845–851.

2839. Brown, P. M. "International Responsibility in Haiti and Santo Domingo," *AJIL* 16 (1922) 433–437.

2840. Castor, S. *La Ocupación Norteamericana de Haití y sus Consecuencias: 1915–1934*. Mexico, 1971.

Explains the intervention almost entirely in economic terms.

2841. Cauvin, E. *Un Désastre: L'Accord du 7 Août 1933*. Port-au-Prince, 1933.

A 20-page pamphlet.

2842. Craige, J. H. *Cannibal Cousins*. N.Y., 1934.

Account by a marine colonel of the occupation of Haiti.

2843. ———. "The Haitian Situation," *MCG* 15 (Mar., 1930) 16–20.

2844. Cumberland, W. W. "Haiti's Foreign Commerce," *BPAU* 59 (Nov., 1925) 1133–1136.

2845. ———. "Notable Commercial and Financial Progress in Haiti," *BPAU* 61 (Apr., 1927) 316–319.

2846. Dehoux, L. *L'Accord Américano-Hatien du 7 Août 1933 le Pouvoir Législatif d'Haiti*. Port-au-Prince, 1933.

2847. Gould, J. W. DuB. *General Report on Haiti*. Chicago, 1916.

2848. Gruening, E. "Haiti under American Occupation," *CE* 103 (Apr., 1922) 836–845.

2849. Haiti. Département des Affaires Étrangères. *Six Mois de Ministère en Face des Estats Unis par H. Pauléus Sannon*. Port-au-Prince, 1936.

2850. Healy, D. *Gunboat Diplomacy in the Wilson Era: The U.S. Navy in Haiti, 1915–1916*. Madison, Wis., 1976.

Emphasis on Haiti rather than Washington.

2851. Hinshaw, A. "The American Occupation of Haiti," *WT* 57 (Apr., 1931) 457–465.

2852. Hudicourt, P. L. *Pour Notre Libération Économique et Financière*. Port-au-Prince, 1946.

A 25-page pamphlet.

2853. Kernisan, C. E. *La République d'Haiti et la Gouvernement Democratique de M. Woodrow Wilson*. Port-au-Prince, 1919.

2854. Kuser, J. D. *Haiti, Its Dawn of Progress after Years in a Night of Revolution*. Boston, 1921.

2855. Manigat, L. F. "La Substitution de la Prépondérance Américaine a la Prépondérance Française en Haïti au Début du XX siècle: La Conjoncture de 1910–1911," *RHMC* 14 (Oct.–Dec., 1967) 321–355.

2856. Morpeau, M. *L'Inconstitutionalité de la Convention Americáno-Haitienne*. Port-au-Prince, 1929.

A speech read before the Haitian Senate.

2857. Munro, D. G. "The American Withdrawal from Haiti," *HAHR* 49 (Feb., 1969) 1–26.

Author was U.S. minister to Haiti, 1930–1932.

2858. Padmore, G. *Haiti, an American Slave Colony*. Moscow, 1931.

2859. Pierre-Paul, A. *La Première Protestation Armée contre L'Intervention Américaine de 1915 et 260 Jours dans le Maquis*. Port-au-Prince, 1968.

2860. *Reciprocal Trade Agreement between the United States of America and Haiti*. Wash., 1935.

No. 78 of the Executive Agreement Series.

2861. Russell, J. H. *Annual Reports of the American High Commissioner, 1923–1929*. 4 vols., Wash., 1925–1929.

2862. Schmidt, H. *The United States Occupation of Haiti, 1915–1934*. New Brunswick, N.J., 1971.
    The Haitian intervention is viewed in the context of U.S. imperialism of the epoch.

2863. Slyvain, G. *Dix Années de Lutte pour la Liberté: 1915–25*. 2 vols., Port-au-Prince, 1950.

2864. Spector, R. M. "W. Cameron Forbes in Haiti: Additional Light on the Genesis of the 'Good Neighbor' Policy," *CS* 6 (July, 1966) 28–45.

2865. Streit, C. K. "Haiti: Intervention in Operation," *FA* 6 (July, 1966) 28–45.

2866. U.S. American High Commissioner to Haiti. *Data on the Physical Features and Political, Financial, and Economic Conditions of the Republic of Haiti*. Port-au-Prince, 1924.

2867. USDS. *Report on the United States Commission on Education in Haiti, Oct. 1, 1930*. Wash., 1931.

2868. ———. *Report of the President's Commission for the Study and Review of Conditions in the Republic of Haiti*. Wash., 1930.

2869. Vincent, S. *Sur la Route de la Seconde Indépendence*. Port-au-Prince, 1934.

XIV-M-3   cross references: In the Trask, Meyer, and Trask Bibliography see items 7513, 7920, 8065–8106.

4. UNITED STATES–HAITIAN RELATIONS SINCE 1941

2870. Diederich, B. *Papa Doc: The Truth about Haiti Today*. N.Y., 1969.

2871. Manigat, L. F. *Haiti of the Sixties, Object of International Concern*. Wash., 1964.

2872. PAU. Inter-American Commission on Human Rights. *Report on the Situation Regarding Human Rights in Haiti*. Wash., 1963.

2873. Rotberg, R. I. *Haiti: The Politics of Squalor*. Boston, 1971.

2874. Sherman, G. "Nonintervention: A Shield for 'Papa Doc,'" *REPORT* 38 (June, 1963) 27–29.

XIV-M-4   cross references: In the Trask, Meyer, and Trask Bibliography see items 4185, 8093, 8107–8119.

Chapter XV The United States and Colombia

A. UNITED STATES–COLOMBIAN RELATIONS: GENERAL WORKS AND SPECIAL STUDIES

2875. Academia Colombiana de Historia. *Historia Extensa de Colombia*. 24 vols., Bogotá, 1965–1974.

Vol. 17 by José Joaquín Caicedo Castilla treats Colombia's diplomatic history.

2876. Calvo, J. A. *Prontuario Consular Colombiano: Leyes, Decretos, Circulares, Convenciones, Reglamentos y Modelos de Documentos y Cuadros*. Bogotá, 1938.

2877. Cavelier, G. *Lista Cronológica de los Tratados y Convenios de Colombia, 1811–1974*. Bogotá, 1975.

2878. Ortega Torres, J. (comp.). *Constitución Política de Colombia*. Bogotá, 1969.

2879. Pérez Sarmiento, J. M. *Manual Diplomático y Consular Colombiano*. 5th ed., Bogotá, 1927.

XV-A cross references:
- a) For the role of the United States in attempting to mediate the boundary dispute with Costa Rica, see items 2544–2551.
- b) In the Trask, Meyer, and Trask *Bibliography* see items 1289, 1473, 7271–7285, 8120–8148.

B. THE UNITED STATES AND THE INDEPENDENCE OF GRAN COLOMBIA

2880. Bowman, C. H. "The Activities of Manuel Torres as a Purchasing Agent, 1820–1821," *HAHR* 48 (May, 1968) 234–246.

Torres, from Gran Colombia, was the first Latin American diplomat to be officially received in the United States.

2881. ———. "Manuel Torres in Philadelphia and the Recognition of Colombian Independence, 1821–1822," *RACHS* 80 (Mar., 1969) 17–38.

2882. Carrera Damas, G. *El Culto a Bolívar: Esbozo para un Estudio de la Historia de las Ideas en Venezuela*. Caracas, 1973.

2883. Gómez Hoyas, R. "Un Granadino Traductor de Thomas Paine en 1819," *BHA* 57 (Apr.–June, 1970) 181–194.

2884. Mijares, A., (ed.). *Simón Bolívar: Doctrina del Libertador*. Caracas, 1976.

2885. Olson, W. C. "Early North Americans in Venezuelan Commerce, 1810–1830," U. of N.C. Diss., 1974.

2886. Paez-Pumar, M. *Las Proclamas de Filadelfia de 1774 y 1775 en la Caracas de 1777*. Caracas, 1973.

2887. Salcedo-Bastardo, J. L. *Bolívar: Un Continente y un Destino*. Caracas, 1972.

2888. Sherman, J. H. *A General Account of Miranda's Expedition, Including the Trial and Execution of Ten of His Officers. . . .* N.Y., 1808.

Author was a participant in the *Leander* expedition.

2889. Vivian, J. F. "The Orinoco River and Angostura Venezuela in the Summer of 1819: The Narrative of a Maryland Naval Chaplain," *TA* 24 (Oct., 1967) 160–183.

The chaplain, John Needles Hambleton, was on the naval mission of Captain Oliver Perry.

XV-B cross references:
- a) For more general works on the role of the United States during the period of Latin

American independence, see items 582–636.

b) See also items 123, 3255.

c) In the Trask, Meyer, and Trask *Bibliography* see items 1805–1896, 8149–8241.

C. THE UNITED STATES AND GRAN COLOMBIA, 1819–1830

2890. Bushnell, D. "The Religion Question in the Congress of Gran Colombia," *TA* 31 (July, 1974) 1–17.

2891. Galvis Madero, L. *La Gran Colombia: 1819–1830*. Bogotá, 1970.

2892. Seckinger, R. L. "La Gran Colombia ante el Imperio Brasileño," *BHA* 60 (Jan.–Mar., 1973) 45–54.

2893. Winn, W. B. "The Issue of Religious Liberty in the United States Commercial Treaty with Colombia of 1824," *TA* 26 (Jan., 1970) 291–301.

Suggests that the Colombian treaty became a pattern for U.S. treaties with other Latin American countries.

XV-C cross references: In the Trask, Meyer, and Trask Bibliography *see items 2341, 2582, 8149, 8175, 8191, 8192, 8220, 8241–8260.*

D. UNITED STATES–COLOMBIAN RELATIONS, 1830–1903

2894. Biddle, C. J. *Comunicaciones entre el Señor Carlos Biddle, Coronel de los Estados Unidos del Norte i la Sociedad Amigos del País*. Panama, 1836.

2895. Safford, F. "Empresarios Nacionales y Extranjeros en Colombia durante el Siglo XIX," *ACHSC* 4 (1969) 87–111.

2896. ———. "Foreign and National Enterprise in Nineteenth Century Colombia," *BHR* 39 (Winter, 1965) 503–526.

2897. Scheips, P. J. "Buchanan and the Chiriquí Naval Station Sites," *MAF* 18 (Summer, 1954) 64–80.

2897a. Wolff, W. G. "The Diplomatic Career of William L. Scruggs: United States Minister to Colombia and Venezuela and Legal Advisor to Venezuela, 1872–1912," Southern Ill. U. Diss., 1975.

XV-D cross references:

a) See item 2919.

b) In the Trask, Meyer, and Trask *Bibliography* see items 2346, 2388, 8220, 8246, 8247, 8253, 8261–8289.

E. THE PANAMA DISPUTE

2898. Aguilera, R. *Documentos Históricos sobre la Fundación de la República de Panamá*. Panama, 1904.

2899. Araúz, M. *Relatos sobre la "Guerra de los Mil Dias" y Otros Artículos*. Panama, 1951.

Argues that Colombia neglected Panama.

2900. Arbena, J. L. "Colombian Reactions to the Independence of Panama, 1903–1904," *TA* 33 (July, 1976) 130–148.

Colombia did not act decisively because of internal dissention.

2901. ———. "The Loss of Panama and Colombian Poetry of the Early Twentieth Century," *SECOLAS* 6 (Mar., 1975) 94–104.

2902. ———. "The Panama Problem in Colombian History," U. of Va. Diss., 1970.

2903. Arosemena, C. C., and N. A. de Obarrio. *Datos Históricos Acerca de los Movimientos Iniciales de la Independencia Relatados por los Próceres*. Panama, 1937.

2904. Arosemena, M. *Independencia del Istmo*. Panama, 1959.

2905. Arrocha Graell, C. *Historia de la Independencia de Panamá: Sus Antecedentes y sus Causas*. Panama, 1933.

2906. Becerra, R. *Opiniones de un Patriota*. Barranquilla, Colombia, 1904.

2907. Blanco, A. R. *Canal: Artículos Referentes al Tratado Hay-Herrán*. Cartagena, Colombia, 1903.

2908. Boyd, F. *Exposición Histórica Acerca de los Motivos que Causaron la Emancipación*. Panama, 1911.

2909. ———. *Exposición Histórica Acerca de los Motivos que Causaron la Separación de Panamá de la República de Colombia*. Panama, 1911.

2910. Burns, E. B. "The Recognition of Panama by the Major Latin American States," *TA* 26 (July, 1969) 3–14.

2911. Castillero Reyes, E. *El Doctor Manuel Amador Guerrero, Prócer de la Independencia* y *Primer Presidente de la República*. Panama, 1933.

2912. ———. *Documentos Históricos sobre la Independencia del Istmo*. Panama, 1930.

2913. ———. *Panamá y Colombia: Historia de su Reconciliación*. Panama, 1974.

2914. ———. "El Profeta de Panamá y su Gran Tración: El Tratado del Canal y la Intervención de Bunau-Varilla en su Confección," *BAPH* 10 (Jan.–Apr., 1936) 3–60.

2915. Chamberlain, L. T. *A Chapter of National Dishonor*. Bogotá, 1915.

Extremely critical of Roosevelt's actions.

2916. Lemaitre, E. *Panamá y su Separación de Colombia*. Bogotá, 1971.

2916a. Lowrie, W. E. "France, the United States and the Lesseps Panama Canal: Renewed Rivalry in the Western Hemisphere, 1879–1889," Syracuse U. Diss., 1975.

2917. Ortega B., I. *La Independencia de Panamá en 1903*. Panama, 1930.

2918. ———. *La Jornada del Dia 3 de Noviembre de 1903 y sus Antecedentes*. Panama, 1931.

2919. Ortiz, D., and R. Galvis. *Los Estados Unidos y su Robo de Panamá. Tratado de 1846: Antecedentes y Consecuencias*. Bogotá, 1920.

2920. Panamá. Instituto Nacional de Panamá. *Documentos Históricos sobre la Independencia del Istmo de Panamá*. Panama, 1930.

Contains many Panamanian government documents.

2921. Susto, J. A. (comp.). *Homenaje al Doctor Manuel Amador Guerrero en el Centenario de su Nacimiento*. Panama, 1933.

First-hand accounts.

2922. USCH. Committee on Foreign Affairs. *Message from the President of the United States Transmitting in Response to Resolution of the House of Representatives of November 9, 1903, All Correspondence and Other Official Documents Relating to the Recent Revolution on the Isthmus of Panama*. Wash., 1903.

2923. USCS. Committee on Foreign Relations. *Correspondence Concerning the Convention between the United States and Colombia for the Construction of an Interoceanic Canal across the Isthmus of Panama*. Wash., 1903.

2924. ———. ———. *Message of the President of the United States Transmitting a Statement of Action in Executing the Act Entitled, "An Act to Provide for the Construction of a Canal Connecting the Waters of the Atlantic and Pacific Oceans."* Wash., 1904.

2925. USDS. *Relations between the United States with Colombia and the Republic of Panama*. Wash., 1904.

2926. ———. Office of the Geographer. *Colombia-Panama Boundary*. Wash., 1966.

International Boundary Series, No. 62.

2927. USDW. General Staff. *Notes on Panama: November, 1903*. Wash., 1903.

XV-E   cross references:

a) For specialized works on the background of the Panama dispute, see items 713, 719, 721, 722, 726–730.

b) For general accounts of the Theodore Roosevelt administration, see items 821–832.

c) See also items 167, 2598, 2606.

d) In the Trask, Meyer, and Trask *Bibliography* see items 2350, 2351, 2353, 2358, 2361, 2365, 2368–2370, 2377–2379, 2380, 2381, 2387, 2388, 2395, 2397, 2401, 2403, 2408–2411, 2414, 2432, 2435, 2437–2439, 2447, 2450, 2454, 2457, 2458, 2506, 2984–3035, 8283, 8290–8382, 8426.

F. UNITED STATES–COLOMBIAN RELATIONS, 1903–1948

2928. Bushnell, D. *Eduardo Santos and the Good Neighbor Policy, 1938–1942*. Gainesville, Fla., 1967.

2929. Calvert, P. "The Murray Contract: An Episode in International Finance and Diplomacy," *PHR* 35 (1966) 203–224.

Treats oil concessions in 1913.

2930. Coletta, P. "William Jennings Bryan and the United States–Colombia Impasse, 1903–1921," *HAHR* 47 (Nov., 1967) 486–501.

2931. Gillman, I. F. "Prelude to Reciprocity: The Abortive United States–Colombian Treaty of 1933," *HIS* 32 (Nov., 1969) 52–68.

The treaty negotiations preceded the Montevideo Conference.

2932. Lael, R. L. "Dilemma over Panama:

United States–Colombian Relations, 1903–1922," U. of N.C. Diss., 1976.

2932a. ———. "Struggle for Ratification: Wilson, Lodge and the Thomson-Urrutia Treaty," *DH* 2 (Winter, 1978) 81–106.

2933. Randall, S. J. "The Barco Concession in Colombian-American Relations, 1926–1932," *TA* 33 (July, 1976) 95–108.
Treats oil concessions to the United States.

2934. ———. "Colombia, the United States and Inter-American Aviation Rivalry, 1927–1940," *JIAS* 14 (Aug., 1972) 297–324.

2935. ———. *The Diplomacy of Modernization: Colombian-American Relations, 1929–1940*. Toronto, 1977.

2936. ———. "Good Neighbours in Depression: The United States and Colombia, 1928–1938," U. of Toronto Diss., 1972.

2937. Zúñiga G., C. I. "Consideraciones Histórico-Políticas sobre el Tratado Urrutia-Thompson," *L* 210 (July, 1973) 1–16.
Treats the 1914 treaty between the United States and Colombia.

XV-F   cross references:
a) For a discussion of the Costa Rica–Panama boundary arbitration, see items 2544–2551.
b) In the Trask, Meyer, and Trask *Bibliography* see items 2903, 3408, 4854, 7085, 7271–7285, 7311, 7375, 8351, 8354, 8368, 8383–8439.

G. THE LETICIA DISPUTE

2938. Pavia y Suñol, J. *El Incidente de Leticia a la luz del Derecho Internacional*. Mexico, 1933.

2939. Perú. *Correspondencia Diplomática con Colombia sobre el Incidente de Leticia*. Lima, 1933.

2940. Santos Chocano, J. *El Escándalo de Leticia ante las Conferencias de Rio de Janeiro*. Santiago, 1933.

XV-G   cross references:
a) See items 994, 1305, 1353.
b) In the Trask, Meyer, and Trask *Bibliography* see items 8440–8461, 8760, 8779, 9120.

H. UNITED STATES–COLOMBIAN RELATIONS SINCE 1948

2940a. Dailey, S. M. C. "United States Reactions to the Persecutions of Protestants in Colombia during the 1950's," St. Louis Diss., 1971.

2941. Díaz-Alejandro, C. F. *Foreign Trade Regimes and Economic Development*. Vol. IX: *Colombia*. N.Y., 1976.

2942. Dix, R. H. *Colombia: The Political Dimensions of Change*. New Haven, Conn., 1967.
A volume in the Yale Studies in Political Science.

2943. Echavarría Oloazaga, H. *Las Relaciones Comerciales con Estados Unidos*. Bogotá, 1969.

2943a. Espinosa, J. M. *Las Inversiones Extranjeras en Colombia*. Bogotá, 1976.

2944. López Michelsen, A. *Memoria de Relaciones Exteriores*. 2 vols., Bogotá, 1970.
Covers the period 1968 to 1970.

2945. Nieto Rojas, J. M. *La Batalla contra el Comunismo en Colombia*. Bogotá, 1956.

2946. Ramsey, R. W. "The Colombian Battalion in Korea and Suez," *JIAS* 9 (Oct., 1967) 541–560.

2947. Varela, T. *Colombia: Los Monopolios y la Penetración Imperialista*. 2d ed., Medellín, Colombia, 1974.

2948. Villegas, J. *Petróleo Colombiano: Ganancia Gringa*. Medellín, Colombia, 1973.

2949. Zea Hernández, G. *Memoria de Relaciones Exteriores*. Bogotá, 1969.
Covers the period 1966 to 1967.

XV-H   cross references:
a) See items 1305, 1687.
b) In the Trask, Meyer, and Trask *Bibliography* see items 4152b, 4152e–4152g, 7221, 8413, 8462–8490.

Chapter XVI   The United States and Venezuela

A. UNITED STATES–VENEZUELAN RELATIONS: GENERAL WORKS AND SPECIAL STUDIES

2950. Arcaya, P. M. *Historia de las Reclamaciones contra Venezuela*. Caracas, 1964.

2951. Arellano Moreno, A. *Breve Historia de Venezuela*. Caracas, 1973.
   Covers from the colonial period to the date of publication.

2952. Brito, F. *Venezuela, Siglo XX*. Havana, 1967.
   Marxist interpretation of Venezuela's twentieth-century experience. Was given the Cuban Casa de las Américas Award.

2952a. Liss, S. B. *Diplomacy and Dependency: Venezuela, the United States and the Americas*. Salisbury, N.C., 1978.

XVI-A   cross references: In the Trask, Meyer, and Trask Bibliography see items 1473, 8133, 8491–8515.

B. UNITED STATES–VENEZUELAN RELATIONS, 1830–1908

2953. Carl, G. E. "British Commercial Interest in Venezuela during the Nineteenth Century," Tulane U. Diss., 1968.

2954. Hood, M. *Gunboat Diplomacy, 1895–1905: Great Power Diplomacy in Venezuela*. London, 1975.

2955. Johnson, J. W. *Along the Way: The Autobiography of James W. Johnson*.
   Author was U.S. consul in Venezuela from 1906 to 1909.

2956. Lioni, T. V. *La Política Exterior del General Cipriano Castro Juzgada por un Tratadista de Derecho Internacional Hispanoamericano*. Santiago, 1908.

2957. Pino Iturrieta, E. (comp.). *Castro: Epistolario Presidencial (1899–1908)*. Caracas, 1974.
   Contains 460 documents.

2958. Rojas, A. *Las Misiones Diplomáticas de Guzmán Blanco*. Caracas, 1972.
   Critical view of Guzmán Blanco's foreign policy.

2959. Sullivan, W. M. "The Rise of Despotism in Venezuela. Cipriano Castro, 1899–1908," U. of N.M. Diss., 1974.

XVI-B   cross references:
a) For works on the Olney Corollary (1895), see items 738–739.
b) The role of the United States in the independence of Gran Colombia is treated in items 2080–2889.
c) In the Trask, Meyer, and Trask *Bibliography* see items 2494–2515, 8149–8241, 8516–8561, 8606, 8607, 8614.

C. THE VENEZUELAN–BRITISH GUIANA BOUNDARY CONTROVERSY

2960. Cárdenas C., A. L., and R. Chalbaud. *Usurpación de la Guayana Esequiba: Enfoque Geográfico, Estudio Histórico Jurídico*. Mérida, Venezuela, 1965.
   The boundary dispute from the Venezuelan viewpoint.

2961. Grow, M. M. "Boundaries and United States Diplomacy: Two Case Studies," Tufts U. Diss., 1969.

2962. Guayana. Ministry of External Affairs. *Guayana-Surinam Boundary*. Georgetown, Guayana, 1968.

2963. ———. ———. *Guayana-Venezuela Re-*

lations. Georgetown, Guayana, 1968.

2964. Humphreys, R. H. "Anglo-American Rivalries and the Venezuela Crisis of 1895," *TRHS* 17 (1967) 131–164.

2965. Kissler, B. J. "Venezuela-Guayana Boundary Dispute: 1899–1966," U. of Tex. Austin Diss., 1971.

2966. Reyner, A. S., and W. B. Hope. "Guyana's Disputed Borders: A Factual Background," *WA* 130 (July–Sept., 1967) 107–113.

2967. Rout, L. B. *Which Way Out? A Study of the Guayana-Venezuela Boundary Dispute*. East Lansing, Mich., 1971.

2968. USDS. Office of the Geographer. *British Guiana–Venezuela Boundary*. Wash., 1963.
    International Boundary Study Series, No. 21.

2969. Venezuela. Ministerio de Relaciones Exteriores. *Informes que los Expertos Venezolanos para la Cuestión de Límites con Guayana Británica Presenta al Gobierno Nacional*. Caracas, 1967.

2970. ———. ———. *Reclamación de la Guayana Esequibo: Documentos, 1962–1966*. Caracas, 1967.

XVI-C   cross references:
  a) For works on the Olney Corollary (1895), see items 738–739.
  b) See also items 2487, 2954.
  c) In the Trask, Meyer, and Trask *Bibliography* see items 2112, 2112b, 2494–2515, 2638, 8562–8605a.

D. THE VENEZUELAN DEBTS CONTROVERSY

2971. Barral de Monteferrat, H. D. *Le Président Castro et le Conflit Franco-Vénezuélien*. Paris, 1906.

2972. Bowman, H. W. *Correspondence and Cablegrams Relating to the Venezuelan Protocols*. Wash., 1903.

2973. Calhoun, W. J. *Report of the Hon. William J. Calhoun, Special Commissioner between the New York and Bermúdez Company and the Government of Venezuela*. Wash., 1906.

2974. Chacón, R. (comp.). *Documentos Relativos al Asunto Internacional*. San Cristóbal, Venezuela, 1903.
    A 46-page pamphlet documenting the blockade.

2975. Holbo, P. "Perilous Obscurity: Public Diplomacy and the Press in the Venezuelan Crisis, 1902–1903," *HIS* 32 (May, 1970) 428–448.

2976. Planas Suárez, S. *El Conflicto Venezolano con Alemania, Gran Bretaña e Italia y la Famosa Doctrina Drago: Historia y Diplomacia*. B.A., 1963.

2977. Ralston, J. H., and W. T. S. Doyle. *Venezuelan Arbitrations of 1903. Including Protocols, Personnel and Rules of Commissions. . . .* Wash., 1904.

2977a. Rodríguez Campos, M. *Venezuela 1902: La Crisis Fiscal y el Bloqueo*. Caracas, 1977.

2978. United States and Venezuelan Claims Commission, 1889–1890. *Opinions Delivered by the Commissioners in the Principal Cases to Which Is Prefixed a Copy of the Conventions between the Two Governments and of the Rules of the Commission*. Wash., 1890.

2979. USCS. *Correspondence Relating to Wrongs Done to American Citizens by the Government of Venezuela*. (60th Cong., 1st Sess., Sen. Exec. Doc. 413.) Wash., 1909.

2980. ———. *Report of Robert C. Morris, Agent of the United States, before the United States and Venezuelan Claims Commission, Organized under the Protocol of February 16, 1903 between the United States of America and the Republic of Venezuela*. Wash., 1904.

2981. Vibert, P. *Questions Américaines: Castro e le Vénezuéla*. Paris, 1909.

XVI-D   cross references: In the Trask, Meyer, and Trask Bibliography *see items 8605b–8627.*

E. UNITED STATES–VENEZUELAN RELATIONS, 1908–1948

2982. Blendon, E. M. J. "Venezuela and the United States, 1928–1948: The Impact of Venezuelan Nationalism," U. of Md. Diss., 1971.

2983. Carreras, C. E. "United States Economic Penetration of Venezuela and Its Effects on Diplomacy: 1895–1906," U. of N.C. Diss., 1971.

2984. Duffy, E. G. "Politics of Expediency: Diplomatic Relations between the U.S.

and Venezuela during the Vicente Gómez Era," Pa. State U. Diss., 1970.

2985. Hendrickson, E. J. "The New Venezuela Controversy: The Relations of the United States and Venezuela, 1904 to 1914," U. of Minn. Diss., 1964.

2985a. Knudson, D. L. T. "Petroleum, Venezuela and the United States: 1920–1941," Michigan State U. Diss., 1975.

2986. McBeth, B. S. "Juan Vicente Gómez and the Oil Companies: The Political-Economic Effects of the Oil Companies on Venezuela during the Gómez Dictatorship, 1908–1935," Oxford U. Diss., 1977.

2986a. Mohr, C. J. B., "Revolution, Reform and Counter-revolution: The United States and Economic Nationalism in Venezuela, 1945–1948," U. of Denver Diss., 1975.

2987. Venezuela. Ministerio Relaciones Exteriores. *El Libro Amarillo de los Estados Unidos de Venezuela Presentado al Congreso Nacional en sus Sesiones de 1929*. Caracas, 1929.

XVI-E cross references:
a) See item 2261.
b) In the Trask, Meyer, and Trask *Bibliography* see items 8531, 8628–8645.

F. UNITED STATES–VENEZUELAN RELATIONS SINCE 1948

2987a. Acosta H., E. *Este Petróleo es Venezolano*. Caracas, 1970.

2988. Alexander, R. J. *The Communist Party of Venezuela*. Stanford, Calif., 1970.

2988a. Anzala, E. *Función del Capital Extranjero en el Desarrollo de Venezuela*. Caracas, 1965.

2989. Baptista, F. G. *Historia de la Industria Petrolera en Venezuela*. Caracas, 1966.

2990. Betancourt, R. *Venezuela: Dueña de su Petróleo*. Caracas, 1975.
Argues for the nationalization of the industry.

2991. Blanchard, W. *U.S. Army Handbook for Venezuela*. Wash., 1964.

2992. Bond, R. D. (ed.). *Contemporary Venezuela and Its Role in International Affairs*. N.Y., 1977.
Contains chapters by the ed. and by Pedro Pablo Kuczynski, Daniel H. Levine, Frank Tugwell, Kim Fuad, and John D. Martz.

2993. Bravo, D. *Avec Douglas Bravo dans les Maquis Venezuéliens*. Paris, 1968.

2994. Brito Figueroa, F. *Venezuela Contemporánea, ¿País Colonial?* Caracas, 1972.
Argues that U.S. monopolists, especially the oil companies, have controlled Venezuela during the entire post–World War II period.

2994a. Burggraaff, W. *The Venezuelan Armed Forces in Politics, 1935–1959*. Columbia, Mo., 1972.

2995. Caldera, R. *La Nacionalización del Petróleo*. Caracas, 1975.

2996. Calvani, A. *Las Bases de la Nueva Política Exterior de Venezuela*. Caracas, 1972.
Consists of speeches made by Venezuelan delegates to the UN General Assembly.

2996a. Carrillo Batalla, T. E. *La Economía del Comercio Internacional de Venezuela*. Caracas, 1962.

2997. Cooke, T. M. "The Dynamics of Foreign Policy Decision-Making in Venezuela," American U. Diss., 1968.

2997a. Córdoba, A. *Inversiones Extranjeras y Subdesarrollo*. Caracas, 1973.

2998. Crazut, R. J. *Consideraciones Acerca de las Inversiones Privadas Extranjeras en Venezuela*. Caracas, 1967.

2998a. Ewell, J. "The Extradition and Trial of Marcos Pérez Jiménez, 1959–1968," U. of N.M. Diss., 1972.

2999. Faraco, F. J. (ed.). *Reversión Petrolera en Venzuela*. Caracas, 1975.

3000. Feinstein, O. "Foreign Investment and the Development of Venezuela," U. of Chicago Diss., 1965.

3001. Friedmann, J. *Regional Development Policy: A Case Study of Venezuela*. Cambridge, Mass., 1966.

3002. Kolb, G. L. *Democracy and Dictatorship in Venezuela, 1945–1958*. Hamden, Conn., 1974.
Holds the United States partially responsible for the return of dictatorship in the person of Marcos Pérez Jiménez.

3002a. Levine, D. H. *Conflict and Political Change in Venezuela*. Princeton, N.J., 1973.

3002b. Martínez, A. R. *Cronología del Petróleo Venezolano*. Caracas, 1970.

3003.   Mayobre, J. A. *Las Inversiones Extranjeras en Venezuela*. Caracas, 1970.

3004.   ————. *La Verdad sobre el Petróleo*. Caracas, 1968.
        By the Venezuelan minister of mines and hydrocarbons.

3005.   Maza Zavala, D. F. *Venezuela: Una Economía Dependiente*. Caracas, 1964.

3005a. Mejía Alarcón, P. E. *La Industria del Petróleo en Venezuela*. Caracas, 1972.
        Treats the nationalization debate.

3006.   Peñaloza, H. *El Cuadro Político del Petróleo Venezolano*. Caracas, 1970.

3007.   Pérez, C. A. *La Nacionalización Petrolera: Hacia la Gran Venezuela*. Caracas, 1975.
        By the president of Venezuela.

3008.   Pérez Alfonzo, J. P. *El Pentágono Petróleo: La Política Nacionalista de Defensa y Conservación del Petróleo*. Caracas, 1967.
        Extremely critical of U.S. petroleum interests.

3009.   Quintero, R. *¿Interviene la CIA en Investigaciones Sociológicas que se Realizan en Venezuela?* Caracas, 1968.

3010.   Robledo, L. R. "El Partido Comunista de Venezuela: Sus Tácticas Políticas de 1964 a 1969," *FI* 11 (Apr.–June, 1971) 531–551.

3011.   Sáder Pérez, R. *Petróleo Nacional y Opinión Pública*. Caracas, 1966.

3012.   Salazar-Carrillo, J. *Oil in the Economic Development of Venezuela*. N.Y., 1976.

3013.   Tinoco, P. R. (ed.). *Análisis de la Política Petrolera Venezolana*. Caracas, 1966.

3013a. Torrealba Alvarez, R. *El Petróleo en la Economía Venezolana*. Caracas, 1974.

3014.   Tugwell, F. *The Politics of Oil in Venezuela*. Stanford, Calif., 1975.
        Covers the period 1959 to 1974.

3015.   Vallenilla, L. *Oil: The Making of a New Economic Order*. N.Y., 1975.

XVI-F   cross references:
   a)   See items 1527a, 3108.
   b)   In the Trask, Meyer, and Trask *Bibliography* see items 3844, 3873, 3888, 3896, 3897, 4119a, 4192, 4289, 8632, 8646–8670.

Chapter XVII   The United States and Ecuador

A. UNITED STATES–ECUADORIAN RELATIONS: GENERAL WORKS AND SPECIAL STUDIES

3016.   Guzmán Polanco, M. de. *Doctrinas Ecuatorianas en el Derecho Internacional*. Quito, 1975.

3017.   Martz, J. D. *Ecuador: Conflicting Political Culture and the Quest for Progress*. Boston, 1972.

3018.   Montero Toro, J. *Práctica del Derecho Consular y Comercial Ecuatoriana*. Quito, 1956.

3019.   Monteverde Paz, O. *Recopilación de los Instrumentos Internacionales Celebrados por el Ecuador en Materia Económica y Comercial*. Quito, 1962.
  Contains texts of treaties.

3020.   Puig Vilazar, C. *Derecho Consular Ecuatoriano*. Guayaquil, Ecuador, 1951.

3021.   Villacrés Moscoso, J. W. *Derecho Internacional Ecuatoriano*. Guayaquil, Ecuador, 1972.

3022.   ———. *Historia Diplomática de la República de Ecuador*. Guayaquil, Ecuador, 1967.

XVII-A   cross references:
  a)   See item 3049.
  b)   In the Trask, Meyer, and Trask *Bibliography* see items 1473, 8671–8694.

B. UNITED STATES–ECUADORIAN RELATIONS: NINETEENTH CENTURY

3023.   Gold, R. L. "Negro Colonization Schemes in Ecuador, 1801–1864," *PHY* 30 (Fall, 1969) 306–316.
  Treats efforts of the Ecuadorians to acquire black labor from the United States.

3024.   Price, J. "Ecuadorian Opinions of the United States in the Nineteenth Century: An Attitudinal Study," U. of N.C. Diss., 1968.

XVII-B   cross references:
  a)   For the role of the United States in the independence of Gran Colombia, see items 2880–2889.
  b)   In the Trask, Meyer, and Trask *Bibliography* see items 2339–2343, 2347, 2348, 8149–8241, 8695–8709.

C. UNITED STATES–ECUADORIAN RELATIONS: TWENTIETH CENTURY

3025.   Cabezas, R. *Problemas Petroleros Ecuatorianos*. Quito, 1968.

3026.   Cueva, A. *El Proceso de Dominación Política en Ecuador*. Quito, 1973.

3027.   Erickson, E. E. *Area Handbook for Ecuador*. Wash., 1966.

3028.   Gibson, C. R. "The Role of Foreign Trade in Ecuadorian Economic Development," U. of Pa. Diss., 1968.

3029.   Paredes, R. A. *El Imperialismo en el Ecuador: Oro y Sangre en Portovelo*. 2d ed., Guayaquil, Ecuador, 1970.
  Treats labor struggles against U.S. companies in Ecuador. Originally published in 1938.

3030.   Rosenberg, E. S. "Dollar Diplomacy under Wilson: An Ecuadorian Case," *IAEA* 25 (Autumn, 1972) 47–53.
  An excellent treatment of a relatively unknown subject.

XVII-C   cross references:
  a)   See items 1301, 1307, 1803.
  b)   In the Trask, Meyer, and Trask *Bibliography*

see items 3224, 4109, 4150, 4673, 4850, 4855, 4988, 5259, 6212, 8702, 8710–8719.

D. ECUADORIAN–PERUVIAN BOUNDARY DISPUTE

3031. Barra, F. de la. *El Conflicto Peruano-Ecuatoriano y la Vigorosa Campaña de 1941 en las Fronteras de Zarumilla*. Lima, 1969.

3032. Larrea Alba, L. *La Campaña de 1941. La Agresión Peruana al Ecuador: Sus Antecedentes Históricos, Políticos y Militares*. Quito, 1964.

3033. Maier, G. "Ecuadorian-Peruvian Boundary Dispute," *AJIL* 63 (Jan., 1969) 28–46.

3034. Montero Ríos, E., *et al. Los Límites Territoriales de las Repúblicas del Perú y el Ecuador*. Madrid, 1908.
        Contains documentary appendices.

3035. Monteza Tafur, M. *El Conflicto Militar del Perú con el Ecuador*. Lima, 1976.

3036. Pardo y Barreda, D. J. *Alegato del Perú en la Arbitraje sobre sus Límites con el Ecuador*. Madrid, 1905.

3037. Perú. Ministerio de Relaciones Exteriores. *Documentos Relativos a la Conferencia Peru-Ecuatoriana de Washington*. Lima, 1938.

3038. Puente, R. A. *La Mala Fe Peruana y los Responsables del Desastre de Zarumilla*. Quito, 1961.

3039. Vázquez, H. "Memoria Histórico-Jurídica sobre los Límites Ecuatoriano-Peruanos," *AUC* 23 (July–Sept., 1967) 1–321.

3040. Villamil, H. *Invasiones Peruanas al Ecuador*. Quito, 1965.

3040a. Wood, B. *Aggression and History: The Case of Ecuador and Peru*. Ann Arbor, Mich., 1978.

3041. Zambria Zamudio, R. *Luchas y Victorias por la Definición de una Frontera: La Lucha en el Dominio Político*. Lima, 1969.

XVII-D   cross references:
  a) See item 1301.
  b) In the Trask, Meyer, and Trask *Bibliography* see items 8690, 8720–8800, 8813, 8954, 9120.

Chapter XVIII   The United States and Peru

A. UNITED STATES–PERUVIAN RELATIONS: GENERAL WORKS AND SPECIAL STUDIES

3041a. Alba, V. *Peru*. Boulder, Colo., 1977.

3042. García Salazar, A. *Historia Diplomática del Perú*. Lima, 1928.

3043. González Dittoni, E. *Textos Internacionales del Perú*. Lima, 1962.

3044. Mora, J. J. de *Del Perú en la Historia y en el Consorcio de los Pueblos de Ibero-América*. Lima, 1928.

   A 34-page pamphlet.

3045. Nieves Ayala, A. *Los Extranjeros ante la Ley Peruana*. 2 vols., Lima, 1976.

3046. Ortega, E. H. *Manual de Historia General del Perú*. Lima, 1968.

3047. Pérez de Cuéllar, J. *Manual de Derecho Diplomático*. Lima, 1964.

3048. Pike, F. B. *The Modern History of Peru*. N.Y., 1967.

3049. ———. *The United States and the Andean Republics: Peru, Bolivia and Ecuador*. Cambridge, Mass., 1977.

3050. Rivera Serna, R. *Historia del Perú República 1822–1968*. Lima, 1974.

3051. Romero, E. *Historia del Perú*. 2 vols., Lima, 1968.

3052. Sharp, D. A. (ed.). *U.S. Foreign Policy and Peru*. Austin, Tex., 1972.

   Consists of twelve essays and two official policy statements.

3052a. Werlich, D. P. *Peru: A Short History*. Carbondale, Ill., 1978.

   Heavy emphasis on the twentieth century.

XVIII-A   cross references:

a) For works on the Peruvian boundary controversy with Ecuador, see items 3031–3041.

b) In the Trask, Meyer, and Trask *Bibliography* see items 1473, 8800a–8817.

B. UNITED STATES–PERUVIAN RELATIONS: NINETEENTH CENTURY

3053. *Antología de la Independencia del Perú*. Lima, 1972.

   Contains documentary extracts.

3054. Zegarra, F. C. C. *La Condición Jurídica de los Extranjeros en el Perú*. Santiago, 1872.

XVIII-B   cross references:

a) For accounts of the attempted Spanish reconquest of 1863–1866, see items 683–686.

b) See also item 3282.

c) In the Trask, Meyer, and Trask *Bibliography* see items 1863–1866, 2203–2232, 8818–8849, 9330, 9360.

C. THE WAR OF THE PACIFIC, 1879–1884

3055. Benavides Santos, A. *Historia Compendiada de la Guerra del Pacífico 1879–1884*. B.A., 1972.

3056. García Calderón, F. *Mediación de los Estados Unidos de Norte América en la Guerra del Pacífico*. B.A., 1884.

3057. Guerrero, J. C. *1879–1883: La Guerra de las Ocasiones Perdidas*. Lima, 1975.

   Contains the treaties of Ancón and Arica as documentary appendices.

3058. Mantilla, V. *Nuestros Héroes: Episodios de la Guerra del Pacífico 1879–1883*. Lima, 1902.

3059. Molina, M. *Hojas del Proceso: Datos para la Historia de la Guerra del Pacífico*. Lima, 1922.

3060. Páez, A. *La Guerra del Pacífico y los Deberes de América*. Bogotá, 1881.

3061. Peterson, D. W. "The Diplomatic and Commercial Relations between the United States and Peru from 1883 to 1918," U. of Minn. Diss., 1969.

3062. Phillips, R. S., Jr. "Bolivia in the War of the Pacific, 1879–1884," U. of Va. Diss., 1973.

3063. Sater, W. F. "Chile during the First Months of the War of the Pacific," *JLAS* 5 (May, 1973) 133–158.

3064. ———. "La Intervención Norteamericana durante la Guerra del Pacífico: Refutaciones a Vladimir Smolenski," *BACH* 83–84 (1970) 185–206.

3065. Smolenski, V. "Los Estados Unidos y Guerra del Pacífico: Historia de una Intervención que no Llegó a Efectuarse," *BACH* 78 (1968) 96–120.

Argues that the United States was responsible for the war.

3066. Valdez Franck, A. *Fase Oculta en la Historia de la Guerra con Chile*. Lima, 1971.

3067. Varigny, C. de. *La Guerra del Pacífico*. B.A., 1971.

XVIII-C   cross references: In the Trask, Meyer, and Trask Bibliography see items 2607, 2608, 8850–8879, 8880.

D. THE TACNA–ARICA DISPUTE

3068. Campo, M. del. *Conflicto del Pacífico*. Santiago, 1920.

3069. Guerra, M. L. *El Tratado de Ancón y el Laudo Arbitral de los Estados Unidos de Norte América, 1883–1925*. Lima, 1925.

3070. Malaga Grenet, F. E. *Una Carta a Wilson*. Lima, 1919.

Treats U.S. arbitration of the Tacna-Arica dispute.

3071. Palacios y Rodríguez, R. *La Chilenización de Tacna y Arica, 1883–1929*. Lima, 1975.

Treats Peruvian desire to regain the lost territory.

3072. Pérez Canto, J. *El Conflicto Después de la Victoria: Recuerdos e Impresiones de un Ex-Diplomático Chileno en el Perú*. Santiago, 1918.

3073. Perú. Ministerio de Relaciones Exteriores. *Documentos Relativos al Plebiscito de Tacna y Arica*. 4 vols., Lima, 1926.

3074. Rumbold, H. *Further Recollections of a Diplomatist*. London, 1903.

Contains information on the Tacna-Arica dispute by the British minister to Chile.

3075. Soder, J. P. "The Impact of the Tacna-Arica Dispute on the Pan American Movement," Georgetown U. Diss., 1970.

3076. USDS. Office of the Geographer. *Chile-Peru Boundary*. Wash., 1966.

International Boundary Studies Series, No. 65.

3077. Wilson, J. F. "An Evaluation of the Failure of the Tacna-Arica Plebiscitory Commission, 1925–1926," U. of Ga. Diss., 1965.

XVIII-D   cross references: In the Trask, Meyer, and Trask Bibliography see items 3214, 8760, 8804, 8862, 8880–8932, 8966, 8972, 9425.

E. UNITED STATES–PERUVIAN RELATIONS: TWENTIETH CENTURY

3078. Allen, H. W. "Miles Poindexter: A Political Biography," U. of Wash. Diss., 1959.

U.S. ambassador, 1922–1928.

3079. Alvarado G., L. "Posición del Perú en la VIII Reunión de Consulta de Ministros de Relaciones Exteriores Americanos," *RPDI* 22 (Jan.–Dec., 1962) 180–190.

3080. Anaya, F. E. *Imperialismo, Industrialización y Transferencia de Tecnología en el Perú*. Lima, 1974.

3081. Boesen, R. M. *Rights and Duties of Foreign Business under Peruvian Law. . . .* Lima, 1952.

3082. Brundenius, C. "The Anatomy of Imperialism: The Case of the Multinational Mining Corporations in Peru," *JPR* 3 (1972) 189–207.

3083. Bunker, R. "Linkages and the Foreign Policy of Peru: 1958–1966," *WPQ* 22 (June, 1969) 280–297.

3084. Catacora Pino, J. A. *La Enmienda Hickenlooper contra la Alianza para el Progreso*. Lima, 1969.

3085. Chaplin, D. (ed.). *Peruvian Nationalism:*

A Corporatist Revolution. New Brunswick, N.J., 1976.
A series of essays.

3086. Deal, J. M. *El Estado e Inversión Extranjera en el Proceso de Industrialización Peruana*. Lima, 1976.

3087. Echecopar García, L. *Informe Jurídico sobre el Caso de la Brea y Pariñas*. Lima, 1960.

3088. Einaudi, L. *Peruvian Military Relations with the United States*. Santa Monica, Calif., 1970.

3089. Goodsell, C. T. *American Corporations and Peruvian Politics*. Cambridge, Mass., 1974.
Treats most of the major U.S. corporations in Peru.

3089a. ———. "The Multinational Corporation as a Political Actor in a Changing Environment: Peru," *IEA* 29 (Winter, 1975) 3–21.

3090. González Aguayo, L. "Perú: Historia de un Conflicto," *RMS* 15 (Jan.–Mar., 1969) 49–64.
Treats Peruvian expropriations of the International Petroleum Company in 1968.

3091. Kuo, D. W. "Peru's Foreign Policy: Ends and Means, 1945–1968," Tulane U. Diss., 1969.

3092. Laurie Solis, L. *La Diplomacia del Petróleo y el Caso de "La Brea y Pariñas."* Lima, 1967.

3093. Loring, D. C. "The United States–Peruvian Fisheries Dispute," *SLR* 23 (Feb., 1971) 391–453.

3094. McIrvin, R. R. "Buying Time: The International Petroleum Company's Public Relations Campaign in Peru, 1946–1966," *SECOLAS* 8 (Mar., 1977) 94–105.

3095. Molina, A. (ed.). *Ensayos Revolucionarios del Perú: Antología*. Lima, 1969.

3096. Noriega Calmet, F. *La Brea y Pariñas y la Integración del Perú*. Lima, 1968.

3097. Peeler, J. A. "The Politics of the Alliance for Progress in Peru," U. of N.C. Diss., 1968.

3098. Perú. Ministerio de Relaciones Exteriores. *El Perú y su Política Exterior: Recopilación de los Principales Discursos Pronunciados por el Ministro de Relaciones Exteriores General de División E. P. Edgardo Mercado Jarrín*. Lima, 1971.

3099. Phillip, G. D. E. "Policy Making in the Peruvian Oil Industry: With Special Reference to the Period October 1968 to September 1973," Oxford U. Diss., 1976.

3100. Pinelo, J. *The Multinational Corporation as a Force in Latin American Politics: A Case Study of the International Petroleum Company in Peru*. N.Y., 1973.
Emphasizes that Peruvian politicians used the IPC rather than the reverse.

3101. Prado, J. del. *Una Tercera Posición*. Lima, 1960.
Calls for Peruvian neutrality in world power struggles.

3102. Pratt, B. S. "Diplomatic and Business Relations between Peru and the United States Since 1959," Cambridge U. Diss., 1977.

3103. Ramírez Novoa, E. *Recuperación de la Brea y Pariñas: Soberanía Nacional y Desarrollo Económico*. Lima, 1964.

3104. Rocca Torres, L. *Imperialismo en el Perú: Viejas Ataduras con Nuevos Nudos*. Lima, 1976.

3105. Sharp, D. A. (ed.). *Estados Unidos y la Revolución Peruana*. B.A., 1972.

3106. ——— (ed.). *U.S. Foreign Policy and Peru*. Austin, Tex., 1972.

3107. Stackman, R. R. "Laurence Steinhardt: New Deal Diplomat, 1933–1945," Mich. State U. Diss., 1967.
Steinhardt served in Peru prior to World War II.

3108. Sugrue, M. M. "Reform and Stability: U.S. Foreign Policy Goals and Actions in Peru, the Dominican Republic, and Venezuela—1958–1964," U. of Chicago Diss., 1969.

3109. U.S. Embassy, Lima, Peru. *Fojas Expositivas sobre el Punto Cuatro en el Perú*. Lima, 1958.

3110. Zink, D. W. *The Political Risks of Multinational Enterprises in Developing Countries: With a Case Study of Peru*. N.Y., 1974.

XVIII-E cross references:

a) For works on the Leticia controversy, see items 2938–2940.

b) For works on Aprismo, see items 1994–2019.

c) See also items 870, 1306, 1379, 1475, 1664, 1672, 1678, 3061.

d) *In the Trask, Meyer, and Trask Bibliography*   3888, 3896, 3897, 4151c, 4673, 5446–
    see items 3147, 3166, 3286, 3844, 3873,   5515a, 8440–8461, 8933–8959a.

Chapter XIX   The United States and Bolivia

A. UNITED STATES–BOLIVIAN RELATIONS: GENERAL WORKS AND SPECIAL STUDIES

3111. Bolivia. Ministerio de Información. Dirección General de Informaciones. *Una Política Internacional Digna y Independiente*. La Paz, 1971.

3112. Carter, W. *Bolivia: A Profile*. N.Y., 1971.

An introduction for the nonspecialist.

3113. Escobari Cusicanqui, J. *Historia Diplomática de Bolivia*. Cochabamba, Bolivia, 1975.

3114. Fifer, J. V. *Bolivia: Land Location and Politics Since 1825*. Cambridge, Eng., 1972.

3115. Helper, H. R. *Oddments of Andean Diplomacy and Other Oddments*. St. Louis, Mo., 1879.

3116. Shipe, S. H., Jr. "The American Legation in Bolivia: 1848–1879," St. Louis U. Diss., 1967.

XIX-A   cross references:

a) For works on the War of the Pacific, see items 3055–3067.

b) See also item 3049.

c) In the Trask, Meyer, and Trask *Bibliography* see items 1473, 8850–8879, 8960–8989.

B. UNITED STATES–BOLIVIAN RELATIONS: TWENTIETH CENTURY

3117. Alemán Ugarte, H. *Frente a la Conjura de la Gulf, Vigoricemos: Yacimientos Petrolíferos Fiscales Bolivianos*. Potosí, Bolivia, 1969.

Treats the Bolivian government's relations with Gulf Oil.

3118. Alliance for Progress. Comité Interamericano de la Alianza para el Progreso. *El Esfuerzo Interno y la Necesidades de Financiamiento Externo para el Desarrollo de Bolivia*. Wash., 1966.

3119. Arnade, C. W. "Communism in Bolivia," *SAQ* 53 (Oct., 1954) 454–463.

3120. ———. "The U.S. and the Ultimate Roots of the Bolivian Revolution," *IIISPR* 1 (Jun., 1962) 35–49.

3121. Barrientos Ortuño, R. *El Che Guevara, el Intervencionismo un Pueblo Libre y Heróico*. La Paz, 1967.

Text of presidential speeches given before the Bolivian Congress.

3122. Blasier, C. "The United States, Germany, and the Bolivian Revolutionaries (1914–1946)," *HAHR* 52 (Feb., 1972) 52–73.

3123. Bolivia. Dirección Nacional de Informaciones. *El Gobierno Revolucionario de Bolivia y la Política Hemisférica de Nixon*. La Paz, 1969.

A 20-page pamphlet.

3124. ———. Ministerio de Industria y Comercio. *Bolivia Exporta: Directorio de Exportadores*. La Paz, 1972.

3125. Burke, M. "Does Food for Peace Assistance Damage the Bolivian Economy?" *IEA* 25 (Summer, 1971) 3–19.

3126. Camacho Omiste, E. (comp.). *Bolivia: Convenios y Declaraciones Internacionales, Bilaterales, 1948–1966, Multilaterales, 1950–1966*. La Paz, 1966.

3127. Gonzalez, L. J. *The Great Rebel: Che Guevara in Bolivia*. N.Y., 1969.

3128. Goodrich, C. "Bolivia: Test of Technical Assistance," *FA* 32 (1954) 473–481.

3129. Greene, G. "Revolution and the

Rationalization of Reform in Bolivia," *IAEA* 19 (1965) 3–25.

3130. Gutiérrez, A. *Notas e Impresiones de los Estados Unidos*. Santiago, 1904.

Author was Secretary of the Bolivian legation in Washington.

3131. Hanson, G. "Fraud in Foreign Aid: The Bolivia Program," *IAEA* 11 (1957) 65–89.

3132. Harris, R. *Death of a Revolutionary: Che Guevara's Last Mission*. N.Y., 1970.

3133. Holland, E. J. "A Study of Bolivian Foreign Relations, 1935–1946," American U. Diss., 1967.

3134. James, D. (comp.). *The Complete Bolivian Diaries of Ché Guevara*. N.Y., 1968.

3135. Klein, H. S. "American Oil Companies in Latin America: The Bolivian Experience,"*IAEA* 18 (Autumn, 1964) 47–72.

3136. Llosa M., J. A. *René Barrientos Ortuño: Paladín de la Bolivianidad*. La Paz, 1966.

3137. Malloy, J. M. *Bolivia: The Uncompleted Revolution*. Pittsburgh, Pa., 1970.

3138. ———, and R. S. Thorn (eds.). *Beyond the Revolution: Bolivia Since 1952*. Pittsburgh, Pa., 1971.

Carter Goodrich and Cole Blasier authored the chapters treating United States–Bolivian relations.

3139. Mariaca, E. *Mito y Realidad del Petróleo Boliviano*. La Paz, 1966.

3140. Molina Céspedes, T. *Las Guerrillas en Bolivia: La Ultima Trinchera del "Che."* Cochabamba, Bolivia, 1969.

3141. Pérez Patón, R. "La Penetración Comunista en Bolivia," *ESC* 11 (Oct.–Dec., 1963) 48–66.

3142. Quiroga Santa Cruz, M. *Acta de Transacción con Gulf: Análisis del Decreto de Indemnificación*. La Paz, 1970.

Treats the expropriation of Gulf Oil Company holdings.

3143. Sanders, G. E. "The Quiet Experiment in Diplomacy: An Interpretive Essay on United States Aid to the Bolivian Revolution," *TA* 33 (July, 1976) 25–49.

3144. Sauvage, L. *Che Guevara: The Failure of a Revolutionary*. Englewood Cliffs, N.J., 1973.

3145. Scott, R. "Economic Aid and Imperialism in Bolivia," *MR* 24 (May, 1972) 48–60.

3146. Selser, G. *La CIA en Bolivia*. B.A., 1970.

3147. Sinclair, A. *Che Guevara*. N.Y., 1970.

3148. Standard Oil Company of Bolivia. *Confiscation: A History of the Oil Industry in Bolivia*. N.Y., 1939.

3149. U.S. Agency for International Development. *An Agreement Transferring the Responsibility and Functions of the Servicio Cooperativo Boliviano Americano de Caminos to the Government of Bolivia*. La Paz, 1961.

3150. USCS. *Administration of United States Foreign Aid Programs in Bolivia*. (86th Cong., 2d Sess., Sen. Rept. 1030.) Wash., 1960.

3151. Valdivieso, J., and C. F. Salamanca. *La Standard Oil en Bolivia: Caducidad de Concesiones Petrolíferas*. La Paz, 1942.

3152. Wilkie, J. W. *The Bolivian Revolution and U.S. Aid Since 1952*. Los Angeles, 1969.

Detailed statistical analysis of U.S. aid programs.

3153. Zondag, H. *The Bolivian Economy, 1952–1965: The Revolution and Its Aftermath*. N.Y., 1966.

XIX-B cross references:

a) See items 879, 1306, 1342, 1379, 2678.

b) In the Trask, Meyer, and Trask *Bibliography* see items 3213, 4857, 8990–9048.

C. THE CHACO WAR, 1932–1936

3154. Arce Quiroga, E. (ed.). *Documentos para una Historia de la Guerra del Chaco: Seleccionados del Archivo de Daniel Salamanca*. 3 vols., La Paz, 1951–1960.

3155. Argentina. Ministerio de Relaciones Exteriores y Culto. *La Política Argentina en la Guerra del Chaco*. 2 vols., B.A., 1937.

3156. ———. ———. *La Conferencia de Paz del Chaco 1935–1939*. B.A., 1939.

3157. Ayala, J. B. *Planes de Operaciones en la Guerra del Chaco*. Asunción, 1969.

3158. Baldiviesco, E. *El Proceso Diplomático en el Chaco: Exposición Sinóptica del Derecho de Bolivia sobre Todo el Chaco Boreal*. Santiago, 1934.

3159. Campos, A. *Misión de Paz en el Chaco Boreal*. 2 vols., Montevideo, 1954.

3160. Centurión, C. R. *El Conflicto del Chaco Boreal: Gestiones Diplomáticas*. 2 vols., Asunción, 1937.

3161. Chartrain, F. "Causes de la Guerre du

Chaco: Eléments de Jugement," *CAR* 14 (1970) 97–123.

Holds Standard Oil partially responsible for the outbreak of hostilities and the U.S. government partially responsible for not preventing them.

3162. Christman, C. L. *The Chaco Dispute and United States Diplomatic Involvement, 1928–1935*. Nashville, Tenn., 1966.

3163. Ciancio, P. N. *La Guerra del Chaco: Bolivia y el Paraguay ante la Historia: América y el Conflicto*. B.A., 1933.

Holds Bolivia totally accountable.

3164. Eguino, J. R. *La Guerra del Chaco: Interpretación de Política Internacional Americana*. B.A., 1938.

3165. Garner, W. R. *The Chaco Dispute: A Study of Prestige Diplomacy*. Wash., 1966.

3166. González, A. E. *La Guerra del Chaco: Contribución a la Historia*. São Paulo, 1941.

Emphasis on the military history.

3167. Grez Pérez, C. E. *La Delimitación Artificiosa del Chaco a Espaldas del Arbitraje Jurídico, Consitituiría un Depojo que Violaría la Justicia, el Derecho, el Uti Possidetis y la Doctrina Continental del 3 de Agosto*. Santiago, 1933.

3168. Hyde, C. C. "Looking towards the Arbitration of the Dispute over the Chaco Boreal," *AJIL* 28 (Oct., 1934) 718–723.

3169. Kain, R. S. "Behind the Chaco War," *CH* 42 (Aug., 1935) 468–474.

3170. Laconich, M. A. *La Paz del Chaco*. Montevideo, 1939.

3171. Laguna, A. *La Diplomacia Paraguaya en la Cuestión del Chaco Boreal*. B.A., 1932.

3172. Loureiro, P. *La Conferencia de Paz del Chaco*. Rio, 1936.

3173. Mercado Moreira, M. *Historia Diplomática de la Guerra del Chaco*. La Paz, 1966.

3174. Orrego Vicuña, F. *La Labor Internacional de don Andrés Bello*. Santiago, 1966.

3175. Paraguay. *Libro Blanco: Documentos Relativos a los Acuerdos de Mendoza y la Declaración del Estado de Guerra con Bolivia*. Asunción, 1933.

3176. Pérez, C. E. *La Agresión de Bolivia en el Chaco y el Uti Possidetis*. Santiago, 1932.

3177. Querejazu Calvo, R. *Masmaclay: Historia Política, Diplomática y Militar de la Guerra del Chaco*. La Paz, 1965.

3178. Ramirez, J. I. *La Paz del Chaco*. B.A., 1942.

3179. Rout, L. B., Jr. "The Chaco War: A Study in Inter-American Diplomacy," U. of Minn. Diss., 1966.

3180. ———. *Politics of the Chaco Peace Conference, 1935–1939*. Austin, Tex., 1970.

Discusses Inter-American efforts to prevent hostilities and subsequently to reach a peaceful settlement.

3181. U.S. Commission of Inquiry and Conciliation, Bolivia and Paraguay. *Proceedings of the Commission of Inquiry and Conciliation. Bolivia and Paraguay, March 18, 1929–September 13, 1929*. Baltimore, Md., 1929.

3182. USCS. *Munitions Industry: Chaco Arms Embargo*. Wash., 1936.

3183. Vergara Vicuña, A. *La Guerra del Chaco*. 7 vols., La Paz, 1940–1944.

XIX-C cross references:

a) For works on Latin America and the League of Nations, see items 878–895.

b) See also items 96, 994.

c) In the Trask, Meyer, and Trask *Bibliography* see items 3210–3242, 8444, 8446, 9009, 9049–9123, 9203.

Chapter XX   The United States and Uruguay

A. UNITED STATES–URUGUAYAN RELATIONS: GENERAL WORKS AND SPECIAL STUDIES

3184. Acevedo, E. *Historia Económica y Financiera del Uruguay*. 2 vols., Montevideo, 1903.

3185. Araujo, O. *Historia Compendiada de la Civilización Uruguaya*. Montevideo, 1906.

3186. Benvenuto, L. C. *Breve Historia del Uruguay*. Montevideo, 1967.

3187. Trais, V. *Uruguay y sus Claves Geopolíticas*. Montevideo, 1972.

3188. Zum Felde, A. *Proceso Histórico del Uruguay*. 5th ed., Montevideo, 1967. Originally published in 1920.

XX-A   cross references:
a) See item 3365.
b) In the Trask, Meyer, and Trask *Bibliography* see items 9124–9138.

B. UNITED STATES–URUGUAYAN RELATIONS: NINETEENTH CENTURY

3189. Bacon, J. E., and P. L. Bridgers. *United States Consular Reports: The Republic of Uruguay*. Wash., 1887.

3190. Duomarco, C. A. *Interpretación del Artiguismo: Influencia de los Estados Unidos de Norte en la Formación del Pensamiento Político de José Artigas*. Montevideo, 1946.

3191. Narancio, E. M. (ed.). *Artigas, Estudios Publicados . . . en el Centenario de su Muerte, 1850–1950*. Montevideo, 1951.

3192. Pivel Devoto, J. E. *Historia de los Partidos y de las Ideas Políticas en el Uruguay: La Definición de los Bandos, 1829–1838*. 2 vols., Montevideo, 1956.

XX-B   cross references:
a) For works on the Paraguayan War, see items 3228–3236.
b) In the Trask, Meyer, and Trask *Bibliography* see items 2157, 9139–9159. 9232–9247, 9692.

C. UNITED STATES–URUGUAYAN RELATIONS: TWENTIETH CENTURY

3193. Abadie-Aicardi, O. *El Uruguay, los Estados Unidos y la Unión Panamericana (1916–1918)*. Montevideo, 1969.

3194. Alisky, M. *Uruguay: A Contemporary Survey*. N.Y., 1969.

3195. Cassinelli Muñoz, H. (ed.). *A Statement of Laws of Uruguay in Matters Affecting Business*. 4th ed., Wash., 1963.

3196. Costa, O. *Los Tupamaros*. Mexico, 1971.

3197. Directorio del Partido Nacional. *El Partido Nacional y la Política Exterior del Uruguay*. Montevideo, 1947.

3198. Gilio, M. E. *La Guerrilla Tupamara*. B.A., 1970.

3199. ————. *The Tupamaro Guerrillas: The Structure and Strategy of the Urban Guerrilla Movement*. N.Y., 1972.

3200. Giudice, R. B., and E. González Conzi. *Batlle y el Batllismo*. 2d ed., Montevideo, 1959.

3201. Giudice, R. B. *Los Fundamentos del Batllismo*. Montevideo, 1946.

3202. Haedo, Eduardo V. *En Defensa de la Soberanía: Discursos*. Montevideo, 1961.

3203. Herrera, L. A. de. *El Uruguay Internacional*. Paris, 1912.

3204. Labrousse, A. *Los Tupamaros: Guerrilla en el Uruguay*. B.A., 1971.

3205. Martínez Ces, R. *El Uruguay Batllista*. Montevideo, 1962.

3206. Michelini, Z. *Batllismo y Antimperialismo*. Montevideo, 1971.

3207. Movimiento de Liberación Nacional. *Actas Tupamaras*. B.A., 1971.

3208. Núñez, C. *The Tupamaros*. N.Y., 1970.

3209. Ramírez, G. *La Fuerzas Armadas Uruguayas en la Crisis Continental*. Montevideo, 1971.

3210. Ramírez, J. A., *et al. Uruguay and the United Nations*. N.Y., 1958.

3211. Real de Azua, C. *El Impulso y su Freno; Tres Décadas de Batllismo y las Raíces de la Crisis Uruguaya*. Montevideo, 1964.

3212. Soleri, A., *et al. Uruguay en Cifras*. Montevideo, 1966.

3213. Trías, V. *El Plan Kennedy y la Revolución Latino Americana*. Montevideo, 1961.

3214. Weinstein, M. *Uruguay: The Politics of Failure*. Westport, Conn., 1975.
Covers the twentieth century.

XX-C *cross references:*
a) See items 1365, 1680.
b) In the Trask, Meyer, and Trask *Bibliography* see items 3676, 4154, 4849, 4867, 9084, 9160–9191.

Chapter XXI The United States and Paraguay

A. UNITED STATES–PARAGUAYAN RELATIONS: GENERAL WORKS AND SPECIAL STUDIES

3215. Benítez, L. G. *Historia Cultural: Reseña de su Evolución en el Paraguay*. Asunción, 1966.

3216. ———. *Historia Diplomática del Paraguay*. Asunción, 1972.

3217. Salum-Flecha, A. *Historia Diplomática del Paraguay: De 1869 a 1938*. Asunción, 1972.

XXI-A cross references: In the Trask, Meyer, and Trask Bibliography see items 9192–9202.

B. UNITED STATES–PARAGUAYAN RELATIONS: NINETEENTH CENTURY

3218. Appleton, J., and C. S. Bradley. *Argument for Claimants in the Case of the U.S. and Paraguay Navigation Co. vs. the Republic of Paraguay.* Wash., 1860.

3219. Bermejo, I. A. *La Vida Paraguaya en Tiempos del Viejo López*. B.A., 1973.

3220. Chaves, J. D. *El Presidente López: Vida y Gobierno de Don Carlos*. B.A., 1955.

3221. Cooney, J. W. "Paraguayan Independence and Doctor Francia," *TA* 28 (Apr., 1972) 407–428.

3222. Elliott, M. H. *Uncle Sam Ward and His Circle*. N.Y., 1938.

3223. Flickema, T. O. "Sam Ward's Bargain: A Tentative Reconsideration," *HAHR* 50 (Aug., 1970) 538–542.
   Concerns the U.S. naval expedition, 1858–1859.

3224. ———. "The Settlement of the Paraguayan-American Controversy of 1859: A Reappraisal," *TA* 25 (July, 1968) 49–69.
   Stresses the roles played by U.S. Commissioner James B. Bowlin and Paraguayan President Carlos Antonio López.

3225. ———. "The United States and Paraguay, 1845–1860: Misunderstanding, Miscalculation and Misconduct," Wayne State U. Diss., 1966.

3226. Paraguay. Ministerio de Relaciones Exteriores. *Documentos Relativos a la Reclamación Norteamericana*. Asunción, 1887.

3227. Washburn, C. A. *The History of Paraguay with Notes of Personal Observations and Reminiscences of Diplomacy under Difficulties*. 2 vols., N.Y., 1973.
   By U.S. minister to Paraguay, 1861–1868. Original ed., 1871.

3227a. White, R. A. *Paraguay's Autonomous Revolution, 1810–1840*. Albuquerque, N.M., 1978.

3227b. Williams, J. H. "Foreign Técnicos and the Modernization of Paraguay, 1840–1870," *JIAS* 19 (May, 1977) 233–258.

XXI-B cross references: In the Trask, Meyer, and Trask Bibliography see items 9144a, 9203–9231, 9692.

C. THE PARAGUAYAN WAR, 1864–1870

3228. Amarilla Fretes, E. *El Paraguay en el Primer Cincuentenario del Fallo Arbitral del Presidente Hayes*. Asunción, 1932.

3229. Bonifazi, W. *Rugidos de Leones*. Asunción, 1968.
3230. Cardozo, E. *Hace 100 Años: Crónicas de la Guerra de 1864–1870*. 6 vols., Asunción, 1971–1972.
3231. Dallegri, S. *El Paraguay y la Guerra de la Triple Alianza*. B.A., 1964.
3232. Franco, V. *La Sanidad en la Guerra contra la Triple Alianza*. Asunción, 1976.
3233. González, J. N. *La Guerra del Paraguay*. B.A., 1968.
3234. Hersch, R. C. "American Interest in the War of the Triple Alliance, 1865–1870," NYU Diss., 1974.
3234a. Patterson, L. S. "The War of the Triple Alliance: Paraguayan Offensive Phase —A Military History," Georgetown U. Diss., 1975.
3235. Peña, D. *Alberdi, los Mitristas y la Guerra de la Triple Alianza*. B.A., 1965.
3236. Saunders, J. H. "Diplomacy under Difficulties: United States Relations with Paraguay during the War of the Triple Alliance," U. of Ga. Diss., 1966.

XXI-C   cross references: In the Trask, Meyer, and Trask Bibliography see items 9232–9247.

D. UNITED STATES–PARAGUAYAN RELATIONS: TWENTIETH CENTURY

3237. Arens, R. *Genocide in Paraguay*. Philadelphia, Pa., 1976.
3238. Grow, M. R. "The Good Neighbor Policy: United States Economic Expansion and Great-Power Rivalry in Paraguay," George Washington U. Diss., 1977.
3239. Méndez, E. *Psicología del Colonialismo: Imperialismo Yanqui-Brasilero en el Paraguay*. B.A., 1971.

XXI-D   cross references:
  a)   For works on the Chaco War (1932–1936), see items 3154–3183.
  b)   In the Trask, Meyer, and Trask *Bibliography* see items 3401, 9049–9123, 9248–9258.

Chapter XXII   The United States and Chile

A. UNITED STATES–CHILEAN RELATIONS: GENERAL WORKS AND SPECIAL STUDIES

3240. Barros, M. *Historia Diplomática de Chile, 1541–1938*. Barcelona, 1970.

3241. Bustons L., E. *Legislación Diplomática y Consular de Chile*. Santiago, 1914.

3242. Carrasco, G., and F. López. *Recopilación de Tratados Convenciones y Acuerdos Internacionales Bilaterales Celebrados por la República de Chile*. Santiago, 1960.

3243. Eyzaguirre, J. *Breve Historia de las Fronteras de Chile*. Santiago, 1967.

3244. Frank, A. G. *Capitalism and Underdevelopment in Latin America: Historical Studies of Chile and Brazil*. N.Y., 1969.

3245. Frías Valenzuela, F. *Manual de Historia de Chile*. Santiago, 1967.

3246. Girvan, N. *Copper in Chile: A Study in Conflict between Corporate and National Economy*. Kingston, Jamaica, 1972.

Contains histories of Anaconda and Kennecott in Chile in the twentieth century.

3247. Guerra Araya, J. *Prontuario de Derecho Consular Chileno*. Santiago, 1948.

3248. Kinsbruner, J. *Chile: An Historical Interpretation*. N.Y., 1973.

A brief survey.

3249. Lagos, G. *Las Fronteras de Chile*. Santiago, 1966.

3250. Millar, V. *Historia de Chile*. 11th ed., Santiago, 1960.

3251. Montaner Bello, R. *Historia Diplomática de Chile*. Santiago, 1961.

3252. Talbott, R. D. *A History of Chilean Boundaries*. Ames, Ia., 1974.

3253. Vera, R. *Manual para Diplomático y Cónsules*. Santiago, 1909.

Outlines procedures for Chilean foreign service.

XXII-A   cross references:
a) See item 3365.
b) In the Trask, Meyer, and Trask *Bibliography* see items 1474, 4275, 9259–9306.

B. THE UNITED STATES AND CHILEAN INDEPENDENCE

3254. Aldridge, A. O. "Camilo Henríquez and the Fame of Thomas Paine and Benjamin Franklin in Chile," *IBR* 37 (Jan.–Mar., 1967) 51–67.

Henríquez publicized the ideas of Paine and Franklin in Chile.

3255. Billingsley, E. B. *In Defense of Neutral Rights: The United States Navy and the Wars of Independence in Chile and Peru*. Chapel Hill, N.C., 1967.

3256. Bland, T. *The Present State of Chile from the Report Laid before Congress by Judge Bland, the Commissioner Sent to That Country by the Government of the United States in 1818*. London, 1820.

3257. Carrasco, A. *Pensamiento de O'Higgins*. Santiago, 1974.

3258. Clissold, S. *Bernardo O'Higgins and the Independence of Chile*. London, 1968.

3259. Coffin, J. E. *Diario de un Joven Norteamericano Detenido en Chile durante el Período Revolucionario de 1817–1819*. B.A., 1968.

Originally published in 1823.

3260. Collier, S. *Ideas and Politics of Chilean Independence, 1808–1833*. London, 1967.

3261. Fernández Larraín, S. *O'Higgins*. Santiago, 1974.

3262. Johnson, S. B. *Cartas de un Tipógrafo*

Yanqui en Chile y Perú durante la Guerra de Independencia. B.A., 1967.

Originally published in 1823.

3263. Pereira Salas, E. *La Influencia Norteamericana en las Primeras Constituciones de Chile*. Santiago, 1945.

3264. ———. *Los Primeros Contactos entre Chile y los Estados Unidos, 1778–1809*. Santiago, 1971.

Details relations on the eve of independence.

3265. Reyno Gutiérrez, M. *Carrera: Su Vida, Sus Vicisitudes, Su Epoca*. Santiago, 1973.

Treats Carrera's trip to the United States in search of aid for the Chilean independence movement.

3266. Rodríguez, J. A. *La Vida Militar de O'Higgins: Síntesis de la Historia de la Independencia*. Santiago, 1975.

Eulogistic biography.

XXII-B cross references:

a) For more general works on the role of the United States in the Latin American independence movements, see items 582–636.

b) In the Trask, Meyer, and Trask *Bibliography* see items 1805–1896, 1972–1988, 5604, 5616, 5619–5621, 5626, 9307–9354, 9545, 9566, 9569, 9576, 9577.

C. UNITED STATES–CHILEAN RELATIONS, 1823–1891

3267. Alberdi, J. B. *The Life and Industrial Labors of William Wheelwright in South America*. Boston, 1877.

3268. Bader, T. M. "A Willingness to War: A Portrait of the Republic of Chile during the Years preceding the War of the Pacific," UCLA Diss., 1967.

3269. Beilharz, E. A., and C. U. López. *We Were 49ers: Chilean Accounts of the California Gold Rush*. Pasadena, Calif., 1976.

Experiences of some of the 7,000 Chileans who went to California.

3270. Brown, C. H. *Insurrection at Magellan*. Boston, 1854.

Concerns the treatment of U.S. citizens by the Chilean government.

3271. Carcovic, L. *Portales y la Política Internacional Hispanoamericana*. Santiago, 1937.

3272. Cruchaga Ossa, A. *Los Primeros Años del Ministerio de Relaciones Exteriores*. Santiago, 1919.

3273. Duncan, R. E. "William Wheelwright and Early Steam Navigation in the Pacific, 1820–1840," *TA* 32 (Oct., 1975) 257–281.

3274. Dupuys, J. *La Relaciones Internacionales Bajo el Gobierno de Jorge Montt*. Santiago, 1967.

3275. Edwards, A. *Cuatro Presidentes de Chile, 1841–1876*. Valparaíso, 1932.

Contains biographical sketches of Presidents Bulnes, Montt, Pérez, and Errázuriz.

3276. Faugsted, G. E., Jr. *The Chilenos in the California Gold Rush*. Saratoga, Calif., 1973.

3277. Giacobbi, S. *Chile and Her Argonauts in the Gold Rush, 1848–1856*. Saratoga, Calif., 1974.

3278. Herrmann, A. *Comercio Exterior de Chile: Observaciones a la Estadística del Comercio Exterior de Chile, 1889–1890*. Santiago, 1892.

3279. Kinsbruner, J. "Water for Valparaíso: A Case of Entrepreneurial Frustration," *JIAS* 10 (Oct., 1968) 653–661.

Traces the activities of William Wheelwright in mid-nineteenth century.

3280. López Loyola, A. *Las Relaciones Diplomáticas entre Chile y los Estados Unidos*. Santiago, 1961.

Covers the years 1822 to 1829.

3281. López Urrutia, C. *Episodios Chilenos en California, 1849–60*. Valparaíso, 1975.

3282. Mery Squella, C. *Las Relaciones Diplomáticas entre Chile y los Estados Unidos*. Santiago, 1965.

Covers the years 1829 to 1841.

3283. Monaghan, J. *Chile, Peru and the California Gold Rush of 1849*. Berkeley, Calif., 1973.

Discusses the anti-Chilean demonstrations in California.

3284. Richards, C. A. H. "Chilean Attitudes toward the United States, 1860–1867," Stanford U. Diss., 1970.

3285. Ross, C. A., Jr. "Chile and Its Relations with the United States during the Ministry of Thomas Henry Nelson 1861–1866," U. of Ga. Diss., 1966.

3286. Shurbutt, T. R. "United States Charges

d'Affaires to Chile, 1835–1848," U. of Ga. Diss., 1971.

XXII-C   cross references:

a) For accounts of the attempted Spanish reconquest (1836–1866), see items 683–686.

b) For works on the War of the Pacific, see items 3068–3077.

c) In the Trask, Meyer, and Trask *Bibliography* see items 1879–1884, 2203–2232, 2524, 2616, 8850–8879, 9310, 9322, 9324, 9336–9338, 9348, 9355–9405, 9495, 9611, 9637, 9694.

D. THE *BALTIMORE* AFFAIR, 1891

3287. Bravo Kendrick, A. *La Revolución de 1891: Relación Histórica en Vista de los Partes Oficiales, Documentos de la Epoca y Datos Recogidos Personalmente*. Santiago, 1946.

3288. Estellé, P. "La Controversia Chileno-Americana de 1891 a 1892," *EHIPS* 1 (1967) 149–277.

3289. *Final Report of George H. Shields, Agent and Counsel of the United States before the United States and Chilean Claims Commission, Held under Treaty Signed at Santiago, Chile, August 7, 1892*. Wash., 1894.

3290. Pizarro, C. *La Revolución de 1891*. Valparaíso, 1971.

3291. *United States and Chilean Claims Commission Organized under the Convention of August 7, 1892. Minutes of Proceedings and Decisions*. Wash., 1894.

3292. Valdés Vergara, I. *La Revolución de 1891*. 2d ed., B.A., 1970.

XXII-D   cross references:

a) For additional works pertaining to the *Baltimore* affair, consult the histories of the revolution of 1891 and the biographies of José Balmaceda cited in the previous section.

b) In the Trask, Meyer, and Trask *Bibliography* see items 2803, 9379, 9406–9417.

E. UNITED STATES–CHILEAN RELATIONS, 1891–1925

3293. Varley, M. G. "Aftermath of the War of the Pacific: A Study in the Foreign Policy

of Chile, 1891–1896," Cambridge U. Diss., 1969.

XXII-E   cross references:

a) For works relating to the Tacna-Arica dispute and settlement, see items 3068–3077.

b) In the Trask, Meyer, and Trask *Bibliography* see items 2909, 3144, 3152, 3155, 3157, 3164, 3165, 3167–3169, 3171, 3176, 4161, 5440, 6112, 6145, 8880–8932, 9417a–9434, 9645a.

F. UNITED STATES–CHILEAN RELATIONS SINCE 1925

3294. Allende, S. *La Conspiración contra Chile*. B.A., 1973.

3295. Ambacher, J. R. "International Communism and the Chilean Left: Case Study in the Evolution of Soviet Foreign Policy Objectives and Leftist Political Fragmentation in Chile, 1964–1969," Fletcher School Diss., 1970.

3296. Baklanoff, E. N. "The Expropriation of Anaconda in Chile: A Perspective on an Export Enclave," *SECOLAS* 4 (Mar., 1973) 16–38.

3297. Barnard, A. G. "The Chilean Communist Party 1929–1947, with Particular Reference to the Popular Front," U. of London Diss., 1977.

3298. Behrman, J. R. *Foreign Trade Regimes and Economic Development*. Vol. VIII: *Chile*. N.Y., 1976.

3299. Birns, L. (ed.). *The End of Chilean Democracy: An IDOC Dossier on the Coup and Its Aftermath*. N.Y., 1974.
        U.S. intervention was indirect but effective.

3300. Blanco, H. *La Tragedia Chilena*. B.A., 1974.

3301. Bohan, M. L., and M. Pomeranz. *Investment in Chile: Basic Information for U.S. Businessmen*. Wash., 1960.

3301a. Bruna, S. *Chile: La Legalidad Vencida*. Mexico, 1976.

3302. Burbach, R. J. "The Chilean Industrial Bourgeoisie and Foreign Capital, 1920–1970," Ind. U. Diss., 1975.

3303. Cannabrava Filho, P. *Chile: Anatomía de un Golpe*. Lima, 1975.

Treats U.S. role in overthrow of Allende.

3304. Chile. Senate. Oficina de Informaciones. *El Presidente Eisenhower en el Congreso de Chile*. Santiago, 1960.

3305. Ehrman, L. *Opportunities for Investment in Chile: A Program for Encouragement of Private Industry*. N.Y., 1966.
A study undertaken by the Surveys and Research Corporation at the request of the Chilean government.

3306. Farnsworth, E., *et al. Chile: El Bloqueo Invisible*. B.A., 1973.

3306a. Feinberg, R. *The Triumph of Allende: Chile's Legal Revolution*. N.Y., 1972.
A sympathetic analysis.

3307. French-Davis, R. *El Cobre en el Desarrollo Nacional*. Santiago, 1974.
Treats the nationalization of the copper industry.

3308. García Márquez, G. *Chile, el Golpe y los Gringos*. Bogotá, 1974.
Colombia's most famous novelist turns journalist for this attack on U.S. policy.

3309. Gil, F. G. "Socialist Chile and the United States," *IEA* 27 (Autumn, 1973) 29–47.

3310. ———, R. Lagos E., and H. A. Landsberger (eds.). *Chile, 1970–1973: Lecciones de una Experiencia*. Madrid, 1977.
Papers from a special seminar at the U. of N.C.

3311. Gross, L. *Last Best Hope, Eduardo Frei and Chilean Democracy*. N.Y., 1967.

3312. Hanson, S. G. "Kissinger on the Chilean Coup," *IEA* 27 (Winter, 1973) 61–85.

3313. Horowitz, I. L. (ed.). *The Rise and Fall of Project Camelot: Studies in the Relationship between Social Science and Practical Politics*. Rev. ed., Cambridge, Mass., 1974.

3314. Jordan, D. C. "Marxism in Chile: An Interim View of Its Implications for U.S. Latin American Policy," *OR* 15 (Spring, 1971) 315–337.

3315. Labarca Goddard, E. *Chile Invadido: Reportaje a la Intromisión Extranjera*. Santiago, 1968.

3316. Lau, S. F. *The Chilean Response to Foreign Investment*. N.Y., 1972.
Based on 57 interviews.

3317. Littwin, L. "An Integrated View of Chilean Foreign Policy," NYU Diss., 1967.

3318. Maira, L. "Algunas Antecedentes de la Victoria de la Unidad Popular en Chile y su Posterior Conflicto con Estados Unidos," *FI* 15 (1971) 252–278.

3319. Marín, G. *Una Historia Fantástica y Calculada: La CIA en el País de los Chilenos*. Mexico, 1976.

3320. Moran, T. H. *Multinational Corporations and the Politics of Dependence: Copper in Chile*. Princeton, N.J., 1974.
Treats the role of the copper companies from 1945 to 1973.

3321. Moss, R. *Chile's Marxist Experiment*. London, 1973.
By a reporter for the *London Economist*.

3322. Novoa Monreal, E. *La Nacionalización Chilena del Cobre: Comentarios y Documentos*. Santiago, 1972.

3323. Orrego Vicuña, F. (ed.). *Chile: The Balanced View*. Santiago, 1975.
Collection prepared by the International Studies Department of the U. of Chile.

3324. ———. *Chile y el Derecho del Mar*. Santiago, 1972.

3325. ——— *La Participación de Chile en el Sistema Internacional*. Santiago, 1974.

3326. Petras, J., and M. Morley. *The United States and Chile: Imperialism and the Overthrow of the Allende Government*. N.Y., 1975.
Holds the multinational corporations largely responsible.

3327. Puga Vega, M. *El Cobre Chileno*. Santiago, 1965.
Analyzes contracts with Cerro, Kennecott, and Anaconda.

3328. ———. *El Petróleo Chileno*. Santiago, 1964.

3329. Ramiréz Necochea, H. *História de Imperialismo en Chile*. 2d ed., Santiago, 1970.
Revised version of the study published in 1960.

3330. Rojas, R. *El Imperialismo Yanqui en Chile*. Santiago, 1971.

3331. ———. *The Murder of Allende and the End of the Chilean Way to Socialism*. N.Y., 1975.
Journalist argues that the Chilean military received approval from the Pentagon.

3332.   Sibeck, G. P. "The 'Invisible Blockade' and the Overthrow of Allende," *FA* 52 (Jan., 1974) 322–348.
        Treats economic warfare against Allende.

3333.   Snyder, J. R. "William S. Culbertson in Chile: Opening the Door to a Good Neighbor, 1928–1933," *IAEA* 26 (Summer, 1972) 81–98.

3334.   Tapia Sokom, J. G. "The Effects of the World Depression of 1929 on the Chilean Political System," U. of Essex Diss., 1977.

3335.   Teitelboim V., S. *Chile y la Soberanía en el Mar.* Santiago, 1966.

3336.   Touraine, A. *Vie et Mort du Chili Populaire.* Paris, 1973.
        A diary covering the summer and fall of 1973.

3337.   Uribe, A. *The Black Book of American Intervention in Chile.* Boston, 1974.
        Highly critical of U.S. policy.

3338.   ———. *El Libro de la Intervención Norteamericana en Chile.* Mexico, 1974.
        Treats U.S. role in the overthrow of Allende.

3339.   USCH. Committee on Foreign Affairs. Subcommittee on Inter-American Affairs. *Human Rights in Chile. Hearings. . . .* Wash., 1974.

3339a. ———. *United States and Chile during the Allende Years, 1970–1973. Hearing before the Subcommittee on Inter-American Relations of the Committee on Foreign Affairs, House of Representatives.* Wash., 1975.
        Includes testimony given by leading academic specialists.

3340.   USCS. Committee on Appropriations. *Hearings, Inter-American Social and Economic Cooperation Program and the Chilean Reconstruction Program.* (87th Cong., 1st Sess.) Wash., 1961.

3341.   ———. Committee on Foreign Relations. *Hearings on the International Telephone and Telegraph Company and Chile, 1970–1971, March 20–April 2, 1973.* Wash., 1973.

3342.   ———. Select Committee on Intelligence Activities. *Covert Action in Chile, 1963–1973.* Wash., 1975.

3343.   Valencia Goelkel, H. (trans.). *La Cía: 10 Años contra Chile. Documentos del Senado de los Estados Unidos.* Bogotá, 1976.
        Documents translated from the Senate hearings.

3344.   Varas, F., and J. M. Vergara. *Operación Chile: La Caída de Allende Relatado Minuto a Minuto.* Barcelona, 1973.

3345.   Vera Valenzuela, M. *La Política Económica del Cobre en Chile.* Santiago, 1961.

3346.   Watson, L. "The Communist Movement in Chile," *SAISR* 12 (Autumn, 1967) 23–32.

3347.   White, J. (ed.). *Chile's Days of Terror: Eyewitness Accounts of the Military Coup.* N.Y., 1974.
        Fifteen accounts of the overthrow of Allende.

3348.   Wolpin, M. D. "The Influence of the Cuban Revolution upon Chilean Politics and Foreign Policy: 1959–1965," Columbia U. Diss., 1968.

XXII-F   cross references:
   a) See items 949, 963, 1379, 1671, 1679, 1953.
   b) In the Trask, Meyer, and Trask *Bibliography* see items 3408, 3409e, 4055, 4146a, 4673, 5235, 7674, 9420, 9422, 9426, 9427, 9435–9482.

Chapter XXIII The United States and Argentina

A. UNITED STATES–ARGENTINE RELATIONS: GENERAL WORKS AND SPECIAL STUDIES

3349. Alexander, R. J. *An Introduction to Argentina*. N.Y., 1969.

3350. Antokoletz, D. *Tratado Teórico y Práctico de Derecho Diplomático y Consular, con Referencias Especiales a la República Argentina y las Demás Repúblicas Americanas*. 2 vols., B.A., 1948.

3351. Centeno, F. *Digesto de Relaciones Exteriores, 1810–1913*. B.A., 1913.

3352. Conil Paz, A. A., and G. Ferrari. *Política Exterior Argentina*. B.A., 1972.
Covers the period 1929 to 1962.

3353. Ferns, H. S. *The Argentine Republic, 1516-1971*. N.Y., 1973.
An economic history.

3354. García Lupo, R. *Historia de unas Malas Relaciones*. B.A., 1964.
Surveys United States–Argentine relations.

3355. Goldschmidt, W., and J. R. Nova. *American-Argentine Private International Law*. Dobbs Ferry, N.Y., 1966.

3356. López, V. F. *Historia de la República Argentina*. 8th ed., 8 vols., B.A., 1970.
Treats Argentine history to 1966.

3357. McGann, T. F. *Argentina: The Divided Land*. Princeton, N.J., 1966.

3358. Ortega, E. C. *Cómo fue la Argentina, 1516–1972*. 2 vols., B.A., 1973.

3359. ———. *Historia de la República Argentina: Política, Social, y Económica*. B.A., 1970.
From conquest to 1966.

3360. Rodríguez Araya, R. *La Diplomacia: Evolución, Profesionalidad, Reglamentación*. Rosario, Arg., 1932.

3361. Ruiz Moreno, I. J. *Estudios sobre Historia Diplomática*. B.A., 1973.

3362. Sampay, A. E. (ed.). *Las Constituciones de la Argentina, 1810–1972*. B.A., 1975.

3363. Scenna, M. A. *Cómo Fueron las Relaciones Argentino-Norteamericanas*. B.A., 1970.
Covers from independence to date of publication.

3363a. Solberg, C. E. *Oil and Nationalism in Argentina: A History*. Stanford, Calif., 1979.

3364. Suárez, J. L. *Las Embajadas en la Diplomacia Argentina: Consideraciones Históricas, Constitucionales y Diplomáticas*. B.A., 1918.

3365. Whitaker, A. P. *The United States and the Southern Cone: Argentina, Chile and Uruguay*. Cambridge, Mass., 1976.

XXIII-A *cross references: In the Trask, Meyer, and Trask* Bibliography *see items 1474, 9483–9535.*

B. THE UNITED STATES AND ARGENTINE INDEPENDENCE

3366. Carril, B. del. *La Declaración de Independencia*. B.A., 1966.
Comparative analysis of the U.S. and Argentine declarations of independence.

3367. Fitte, E. J. "Los Primeros Buques Mercantes Norteamericanos en el Río de la Plata," *BANHA* 43 (1970) 231–324.
U.S. commercial interests had a difficult time with English competition.

3368. García, F. A. (ed.). *Espigas de la Patria Vieja*. Montevideo, 1949.
Contains correspondence between Thomas Halsey, U.S. consul in Buenos Aires, and Secretary of State John Q. Adams, 1817–1818.

3369. Gianello, L. *Historia del Congreso de Tucu-*
mán. B.A., 1968..

3370. Goldberg de Flichman, M. B. "Los Intereses Económicos que Influyeron en la
Orientación Diplomática Norteamericana en el Río de la Plata: 1810–1823,"
BIHA 12 (1969) 190–204 and 13 (1970)
192–228.

Treats United States–British economic
rivalry at the time of independence.

3371. Tesler, M. D. "El Apresamiento de la
Galeta 'Rampart' y sus Implicaciones
Diplomáticas," *HRTH* 11 (Apr.–June,
1960) 78–98.

The *Rampart* was a U.S. ship.

3372. ———. "John Murray Forbes y David
Jewett: Presencia de un Agente Diplomático y un Corsario en un Caso con
Implicaciones Diplomáticas," *UNI* 81
(1970) 269–300.

Treats the capture of the U.S. ship
Rampart.

3373. ———. "Martin Jacobo Thompson: Un
Capitán de Puerto en Misión Diplomático," *GU* 23 (1970) 65–74.

Treats the mission of 1816.

XXIII-B   cross references:

a) For more general works on the role of the
United States in Latin American independence, see items 582–636.

b) In the Trask, Meyer, and Trask *Bibliography*
see items 1805–1896, 1972–1988, 9536–
9581.

C. UNITED STATES–ARGENTINE
   RELATIONS, 1820–1852

3374. Barba, E. M. *Quiroga y Rosas*. B.A.,
1974.

Brings together articles originally
published in periodicals.

3375. Cárcano, M. A. *La Política Internacional
en la Historia Argentina*. B.A., 1972.

Covers the period 1810 to 1880.

3376. Carretero, A. M. *El Pensamiento Político de
Juan M. de Rosas*. B.A., 1970.

3377. Clementi, H. *Rosas en la Historia Nacional*. B.A., 1970.

3378. Fodor, J., and A. O'Connell. "La Argentina y la Economía Atlántica en la Primera Mitad del Siglo XIX," *DE* 13 (Apr.–

Discusses the triangular trade among
Argentina, Great Britain, and the United
States.

3379. Irozusta, J. *Via Política de Juan Manuel de
Rosas a Través de su Correspondencia*. 8
vols., B.A., 1970.

XXIII-C   cross references:

a) For the French and British interventions in
the Rio de la Plata (1838–1850), see items
667–674.

b) In the Trask, Meyer, and Trask *Bibliography*
see items 2150–2177, 2344, 9542, 9579,
9582–9610, 9841, 9844, 9852.

D. UNITED STATES–ARGENTINE
   RELATIONS, 1853–1930

3380. Buchanan, J. E. "Politics and Petroleum
Development in Argentina, 1916–
1930," U. of Mass. Diss., 1973.

3381. Caillet-Bois, R. R. *Cuestiones Internacionales 1852–1966*. B.A., 1970.

3382. Campobassi, J. S. *Sarmiento y su Epoca*. 2
vols., B.A., 1975.

Contains sections on Sarmiento's visits
to the United States.

3383. Castro, D. S. "The Development of
Argentine Immigration Policy, 1852–
1914," UCLA Diss., 1970.

3384. Cortés Conde, R., and E. Gallo. *La Formación de la Argentina Moderna*. B.A.,
1967.

Emphasis is on the period 1860 to
1914.

3385. Etchepareborda, R. "Los Armamentos
Navales de 1908: Enfrentamiento de
Empresas y Diplomacias," *IYE* 13
(July–Dec., 1972) 179–209.

Many of the ships were built by U.S.
shipbuilders.

3386. Ferrer, J., Jr. "United States–Argentine
Economic Relations, 1900–1930," U. of
Calif. Diss., 1965.

3387. Hodge, J. E. "Benjamin Aphrorp Gould
and the Founding of the Argentine National Observatory," *TA* 28 (Oct., 1971)
151–175.

U.S. astronomer who established the
observatory in Córdoba in 1870–1871.

3388. ———. "Juan M. Thorne, Argentine

Astronomer from the Quaker State," *JIAS* 13 (Apr., 1971) 215–229.

3389. Hollander, F. A. "Oligarchy and the Politics of Petroleum in Argentina: The Case of the Salta Oligarchy and Standard Oil, 1918–1933," UCLA Diss., 1976.

3390. Johnson, H. L. "Sarmiento's Participation in Educator's Meetings in Indianapolis in 1866," *IRB* 23 (Oct.–Dec., 1973) 438–446.

3391. Letts de Espil, C. *La Segunda Presidencia Roca Vista por los Diplomáticos Norteamericanos*. B.A., 1972.

The second presidency of Roca coincided with those of McKinley and Roosevelt in the United States.

3392. Rock, D. *Politics in Argentina, 1890–1930: The Rise and Fall of Radicalism*. Cambridge, Eng., 1975.

Deals primarily with the evolution of the Radical Party.

3393. Rockland, M. A. "Domingo Faustino Sarmiento and the United States," U. of Minn. Diss., 1968.

3394. ———. *Sarmiento's Travels in the United States in 1847*. Princeton, N.J., 1970.

3395. Roig, A. A. "Algunos Aspectos de las Influencias Francesa y Norteamericana en el Pensamiento Argentino de la Segunda Mitad del Siglo," *RJEHM* 1 (1972) 415–431.

3396. Ruiz Moreno, I. *El Pensamiento Internacional de Alberdi*. B.A., 1969.

3397. Sweet, D. R. "A History of United States–Argentine Commercial Relations, 1918–1933: A Study of Competitive Farm Economics," Syracuse U. Diss., 1972.

3398. Vivian, J. F. "Splendid Isolation: Argentina, the United States, and the San Martín Monument in Washington, 1921–1925," *NDQ* 45 (Spring, 1977) 24–35.

XXIII-D   cross references:

a) For works treating the Paraguayan War, see items 3228–3236.

b) See also items 866, 867, 869, 871, 1689, 3375.

c) In the Trask, Meyer, and Trask *Bibliography* see items 2119, 2245, 2621, 2909, 3151, 3162, 3170, 3173a, 3176, 3211, 3236, 3286, 4531, 8610, 9232–9247, 9594, 9601, 9610a–9698, 9803.

E. UNITED STATES–ARGENTINE RELATIONS SINCE 1930

3399. Argentina. Ministerio del Interior. *La Política Internacional de la Nación Argentina*. B.A., 1946.

3400. Barager, J. R. *Why Perón Came to Power: The Background to Peronism in Argentina*. N.Y., 1968.

3401. Bunge, C. A. *El Mundialismo: Una Doctrina para la Argentina del Futuro*. B.A., 1972.

3402. Campo Wilson, E. *Confusión en la Argentina*. B.A., 1964.

Treats Argentine political history from 1958 to 1962.

3403. Ciria, A. *Estados Unidos nos Mira*. B.A., 1973.

An Argentine's impressions of how specialists in the United States view Argentina.

3403a. ———. *Perón y el Justicialismo*. Mexico, 1971.

3404. Cooper, W. G. "New Light on the Good Neighbor Policy: The United States and Argentina, 1933–1939," U. of Pa. Diss., 1972.

3404a. Dagnino Pastore, J. M. *Política Económica Argentina, 1969–1970*. B.A., 1971.

3405. Ely, R. T. "Hoover y Uriburu ante la Gran Depresión," *TC* 21 (1972) 83–114.

3405a. Escipion (pseud.). *La Política Exterior Peronista*. B.A., 1974.

3406. Falcoff, M., and R. H. Dolkhart (eds.). *Prologue to Perón: Argentina in Depression and War, 1930–1943*. Berkeley, Calif., 1975.

Seven essays. Joseph Tulchin treats foreign policy.

3407. Fayt, C. S. *La Naturaleza del Peronismo*. B.A., 1967.

Contains useful documentary appendices.

3408. Feldman, E. V. "Foreign Capital in the Banking Sector and Financial Practice of Multinational Firms: The Argentine Experience during the Period 1958–1970," Oxford U. Diss., 1977.

3409. Ferre, P. *El Comunismo en la Universidad*. B.A., 1962.

3410. Franworth, C. H., and A. G. Kervorkian. *Argentina: Competitor of U.S. Agriculture in World Markets*. Wash., 1957.

3411. García Lupo, R. *La Argentina en la Selva Mundial*. B.A., 1973.
Treats Argentine relations with the rest of the world.

3412. ———. *Contra la Ocupación Extranjera*. 3d ed., B.A., 1971.
Criticizes U.S. intervention in the Argentine economy.

3413. Giacalone, R. A. "From Bad Neighbors to Reluctant Partners: Argentina and the United States, 1946–1950," Ind. U. Diss., 1977.

3414. Grupp, R. J. "La Argentina y la Alianza para el Progreso," *RDN* 1 (May–Aug., 1962) 29–33.

3415. Lafer, C., and F. Peña. *Argentina e Brasil no Sistema das Relações Internacionais*. São Paulo, 1973.
Argentina's and Brazil's relations with the rest of the world are conditioned in large part by the influence of the United States. Sp. ed., B.A., 1973.

3415a. Luna, F. *De Perón a Lanusse, 1943–1973*. B.A., 1972.

3416. Lux-Wurm, P. *Le Peronisme*. Paris, 1965.
Anti-Perón biography.

3417. Martínez Paz, E. "The Influence of the United States on Argentine Institutions," *BPAU* 75 (June, 1941) 337–343.

3418. Martorell, G. *Las Inversiones Extranjeras en la Argentina*. B.A., 1969.

3418a. Milenky, E. S. *Argentina's Foreign Policies*. Boulder, Colo., 1978.
Chapter 4 treats Argentine relations with the United States.

3419. Morales, E. *Uturunco y las Guerrillas en la Argentina*. Montevideo, 1964.

3419a. Niosi, J. *Los Empresarios y el Estado Argentino, 1955–1969*. B.A., 1974.

3420. Perón J. *Habla Juan Perón: Conceptos Políticos*. B.A., 1973.

3421. Puiggrós, R. *El Peronismo: Las Causas*. B.A., 1969.

3422. Ramos, J. A. *El Partido Comunista en la Política Argentina: Su Historia y su Crítica*. B.A., 1962.

3423. Reeder, R. R. "The United States and Argentina, 1943–1948: An Ethical Case Study," American U. Diss., 1969.

3424. Richmond, L. T. *La Tercera Posición Argentina y Otros Sistemas Comparados*. B.A., 1950.

3425. Rommi, L. V. *Los Capitales Yanquis en la Argentina*. B.A., 1949.

3426. Sabato, E. *Economía y Política del Petróleo Argentina (1939–1956)*. B.A., 1957.

3427. Snow, P. *Political Forces in Argentina*. Boston, 1971.

3428. Sweeney, E. S. *Foreign Missionaries in Argentina, 1938–1962*. Cuernavaca, Mexico, 1970.

XXIII-E   cross references:
a) See items 963, 964, 966–970, 994, 1248, 1315, 1337, 1364, 1367, 3381.
b) In the Trask, Meyer, and Trask *Bibliography* see items 2331, 3401, 3409c, 3681, 3683, 3684, 3688, 3694–3696, 3698, 4086, 4113, 4848, 4852, 4856, 4861, 5233, 5234, 9037, 9056, 9667, 9676, 9677, 9699–9830.

F. THE MALVINAS (FALKLAND) ISLANDS DISPUTE

3429. Almeida, J. L. *¿Qué Hizo el Gaucho Rivero en las Malvinas?* B.A., 1971.
Concerns the removal of the English flag in 1833.

3430. Asociación Integridad Argentina. *¿Son Argentinas las Islas Malvinas?* B.A., 1918.

3431. Burzio, H. F. "El Acto de Soberanía del Coronel de Marina David Jewett," *BANHA* 43 (1970) 283–287.
Treats the raising of the flag in the islands in 1820.

3432. Caillet-Bois, R. R. "Los Títulos Argentinos sobre las Islas Malvinas," *ESTR* 6 (1970) 88–103.

3433. Carril, B. *El Dominio de las Islas Malvinas*. B.A., 1964.
Defends the Argentine position.

3434. Fitte, E. J. *La Agresión Norteamericana a las Islas Malvinas*. B.A., 1966.
Treats the *U.S.S. Lexington* incident of 1831 and attempts to resolve the controversy throughout the nineteenth century.

3435. ———. *Las Malvinas Bajo la Ocupación Británica*. B.A., 1970.

3436. ———. "Sangre en Malvinas: El Asesinato del Comandante Meslivier," *IYE* 12 (Jan.–June, 1972) 121–166.

3437. Groussac, P. *Las Islas Malvinas*. B.A., 1936.

3438. Hadfield, W. *Brazil, the River Plate, and the Falkland Islands*. London, 1854.

3439. Luder, I. A. *Argentina en Latinamérica y en el Mundo*. B.A., 1976.

3440. MacKinnon, L. B. *Some Account of the Falkland Islands*. London, 1840.

3441. Martínez Moreno, R. S. *La Cuestión Malvinas*. Tucumán, Arg., 1965.

3442. Metford, J. C. J. "Falklands or Malvinas? The Background to the Dispute," *IAF* 44 (July, 1968) 463–481.

　　　Disputes Argentine claims to the islands.

3443. Moneta, J. M. *¿Nos Devolverán las Malvinas?* B.A., 1970.

3444. Moreno, J. C. *La Recuperación de las Malvinas*. B.A., 1973.

3445. Pereyra, E. F. *Las Islas Malvinas: Soberanía Argentina*. B.A., 1968.

3446. Torre Revello, J. "Historia del Archipiélago Malvinero," *HU* 3 (1962) 513–530.

3447. Zorraquín Becú, R. *Inglaterra Prometió Abandonar las Malvinas*. B.A., 1975.

XXIII-F　　*cross references:*
　a)　See item 3372.
　b)　In the Trask, Meyer, and Trask *Bibliography* see items 2168, 4698, 6957, 9831–9862.

Chapter XXIV The United States and Brazil

A. UNITED STATES–BRAZILIAN RELATIONS: GENERAL WORKS AND SPECIAL STUDIES

3448. Accioli, R. B., and A. d'E Accioli Taunay. *História Geral da Civilização Brasileira: Das Origens à Atualidade*. Rio, 1973.

More emphasis on twentieth century than most surveys.

3449. Bandeira, M. *Presença dos Estados Unidos no Brasil: Dois Séculos de História*. Rio, 1973.

3450. Brasil. Ministério das Relações Exteriores. *Coleção das Portarias (Normativas) do Ministro de Estado, 1893 a 1960*. Rio, 1960.

3451. Burns, E. B. *A History of Brazil*. N.Y., 1970.

3452. Campanhole, A., and H. L. Campanhole. *Tôdas as Constituições do Brasil*. São Paulo, 1971.

3453. Graham, R. (ed.). *A Century of Brazilian History Since 1865*. N.Y., 1969.

3454. Mello, R. de. *Tratado de Direito Diplomático*. 2d ed., 2 vols., Rio, 1949.

3455. Poppino, R. E. *Brazil: The Land and People*. N.Y., 1968.

An interpretive survey from the colonial period to date of publication.

3456. Silva, G. E. do Nascimento. *Manual de Derecho Consular*. Rio, 1952.

3457. Worcester, D. E. *Brazil: From Colony to World Power*. N.Y., 1973.

A survey text from discovery to the 1970s.

XXIV-A   cross references:
a) See item 3244.
b) In the Trask, Meyer, and Trask *Bibliography*

see items 1235, 1474, 4869–4876, 9863–9943.

B. THE UNITED STATES AND BRAZILIAN INDEPENDENCE

3458. Barretto, V. *A Ideologia Liberal no Processo da Independência do Brasil, 1789–1824*. Brasília, 1973.

3459. Bonnabeau, R. F. "The Pursuit of Legitimacy: The Stuart Mission and the Recognition of Brazilian Independence, 1824–1826," Ind. U. Diss., 1974.

3460. Kahler, M. E. "Relations between Brazil and the United States, 1815–1825, with Special Reference to the Revolutions of 1817 and 1824," American U. Diss., 1968.

3461. Ministerio das Relações Exteriores. *Archivo Diplomático da Independência*. 5 vols., Rio, 1923.

3462. Montello, J. *Historia da Independência do Brazil*. Rio, 1972.

3463. Pereira, H. da Costa. *Diario de Minha Viagem para Filadélfia—1798–1799*. Rio, 1955.

3464. Russell-Wood, A. J. R. (ed.). *From Colony to Nation: Essays on the Independence of Brazil*. Baltimore, Md., 1975.

3465. Tjarks, A. V. "As Primeiras Relações dos Estados Unidos com o Brasil," *RBEP* 36 (June, 1973) 115–159.

Covers the period 1808 to 1824.

XXIV-B   cross references:
a) For more general works on the role of the United States in Latin American independence, see items 582–636.
b) In the Trask, Meyer, and Trask *Bibliography*

see items 1805–1896, 1972–1988, 9944–9960.

C. UNITED STATES–BRAZILIAN RELATIONS, 1824–1889

3466. Andrew, C. C. *Brazil: Its Conditions and Prospects.* N.Y., 1887.
Author was U.S. consul general in Rio from 1882 to 1885.

3467. Baker, J. M. *A View of the Commerce between the United States and Rio de Janeiro.* Wash., 1838.

3467a. Bernstein, H. *Dom Pedro II.* N.Y., 1973.

3467b. Brasil. Ministério da Fazenda. *Informações sobre a Posição Comercial do Brasil nas Praças Estrangeiras.* Rio, 1875.

3468. Browne, G. P. "Government Immigration Policy in Imperial Brazil, 1822–1870," Catholic U. of America Diss., 1972.

3469. Brunetti, A. de Campos. "D. Pedro II em Nova Orleans, *RHIS* 32 (Oct.–Dec., 1975) 869–874.

3470. Carneiro de Mendoça, F. M. (ed.). *Consular Regulations of the Empire of Brazil and Other Legal Dispositions and Orders Connected Therewith: Collected and Published in English for the Use of the Respective Consular Agents in the Countries of the Same Language.* London, 1872.

3471. Corbin, D. F. *A Life of Matthew Fontaine Maury.* London, 1888.
Maury favored the settlement of U.S. slave owners in the Amazon valley.

3472. Da Costa, J. F. *Joaquím Nabuco e a Política Exterior do Brasil.* Rio, 1968.

3473. Froehlich, R. C. "The United States Navy and Diplomatic Relations with Brazil, 1822–1871," Kent State U. Diss., 1971.

3474. Goldman, F. P. *Os Pioneiros Americanos no Brasil: Educadores, Sacerdotes, Covos e Reis.* São Paulo, 1972.
Treats the southern emigration after the Civil War.

3475. Grier, D. A. "Confederate Emigration to Brazil, 1865–1870," U. of Mich. Diss., 1968.

3476. Iiams, T. M., Jr. "Prolegoma to the Study of Brazilian Foreign Relations from the Court in Rio to the U.S. Trade Agreement of 1891," *STU* 35 (Dec., 1972) 207–233.

3477. Jones, J. M. *Soldado Descansa: Uma Epopéia sob os Céus do Brasil.* São Paulo, 1967.
Treats the migration of ex-Confederates to Brazil.

3478. Kalso, H. H. "Christopher C. Andrews," U. of Minn. Diss., 1954.
Andrews was U.S. consul general in Brazil from 1882 to 1885.

3479. Luz, N. V. *A Amazônia para os Negros Americanos (As Origens de uma Controversia Internacional).* Rio, 1969.

3480. Magalhães Mota, D. "Relações entre Estados Unidos e a América Latina durante a Guerra de Secessão: Mudança Operada em 1861," *RHIS* 54 (Oct.–Dec., 1976) 555–561.

3481. Saboia de Medeiros, F. *A Libertade de Navegação do Amazonas: Relações entre o Império e os Estados Unidos.* São Paulo, 1938.

3482. Strauss, N. T. "Brazil in the 1870's as Seen by American Diplomats," NYU Diss., 1971.

3483. ———. "Rise of American Growth in Brazil: Decade of the 1870's," *TA* 32 (Jan., 1976) 437–444.

3484. Therry, J. R. "The Life of General Robert Cumming Schenck," Georgetown U. Diss., 1968.
Schenck was U.S. minister to Brazil from 1851 to 1853.

3485. Trester, D. J. "The Political Career of David Todd," O. U. Diss., 1950.
Todd was U.S. minister to Brazil from 1847 to 1851.

3486. Williams, F. L. *Matthew Fontaine Maury, Scientist of the Sea.* New Brunswick, N.J., 1963.

3487. Wright, A., and A. F. Pacca de. *Desafio Americano à Preponderância Britânica no Brasil, 1808–1850.* Rio, 1972.
Discusses Anglo-American rivalry in Brazil in the first half of the nineteenth century.

XXIV-C cross references:
a) For works treating the Paraguayan War, see items 3228–3236.
b) See also item 1804.

c) In the Trask, Meyer, and Trask *Bibliography* see items 9232–9247, 9692–9947, 9961–10010a.

D. UNITED STATES–BRAZILIAN RELATIONS, 1890–1930

3487a. Barros Pimentel, J. F. de. *Nossa Expansão Econômica: O Brasil, sua Situação Econômica, Comercial e Financeira na Política Internacional*. Rio, 1928.

3488. Basbaum, L. *História Sincera da República (de 1889 a 1930)*. Rio, 1958.

3489. Dulles, J. W. F. *Anarchists and Communists in Brazil, 1900–1935*. Austin, Tex., 1973.

3490. Hahner, J. E. *Civil-Military Relations in Brazil, 1889–1898*. Columbia, S.C., 1969.

3491. House, L. "Edwin V. Morris and Brazilian-American Diplomatic Relations, 1912–1933," NYU Diss., 1969.

3492. McCamant, J. F. *Development Assistance in Central America*. N.Y., 1968.

3493. Nabuco, J. *A Intervenção Estrangeira durante a Revolta*. Rio, 1896.

3494. Valla, V. "Os Estados Unidos e a Influência Estrangeira na Economia Brasileira: Um Período de Transição, 1904–1928," *RHIS* 44 (Jan.–Mar., 1972) 173–195.

XXIV-D cross references: In the Trask, Meyer, and Trask Bibliography *see items 2909, 3143, 3146, 3149, 3150, 3163, 3229, 4672, 4675, 4871, 9697, 9698, 10011–10088.*

E. UNITED STATES–BRAZILIAN RELATIONS SINCE 1930

3495. Abreu, M. "Brazilian Foreign Economic Policy under Vargas, 1930–1945," Cambridge U. Diss., 1977.

3496. Adams, D. "What Can Underdeveloped Countries Expect from Foreign Aid to Agriculture? Case Study: Brazil, 1950–1970," *IEA* 25 (1971) 47–63.

3497. Archer, R. *Política Nacional de Energia Atômica*. Rio, 1956.
Speech read in the Câmara dos Deputados.

3497a. Arruda, M., H. de Soreza, and C. Afonso. *Multinationals and Brazil*. Toronto, 1975.

3498. Baer, W. *The Development of the Brazilian Steel Industry*. Nashville, Tenn., 1969.

3499. ————. *Industrialization and Economic Development in Brazil*. Homewood, Ill., 1965.

3500. ————, and M. H. Simonsen. "American Capital and Brazilian Nationalism," *YR* 53 (Dec., 1963) 192–198.

3501. Bailey, N. A., and R. M. Schneider. "Brazil's Foreign Policy: A Case Study in Upward Mobility," *IEA* 27 (1974) 3–25.

3502. Bandeira, M. *Presença dos Estados Unidos no Brasil*. Rio, 1973.

3503. Bates, L. W. "The Petroleum Industry in Brazil," U. of Tex. Diss., 1975.

3504. Black, J. D. *United States Penetration of Brazil*. University Park, Pa., 1977.
Treats U.S. influences in the 1960s and 1970s.

3505. Brasil. Congresso. Câmara dos Deputados. *Deputados Brasileiros: Repertório Biográfico dos Membros da Câmara dos Deputados. Sexta Legislatura (1967–1971)*. Brasília, 1968.

3506. ————. Inspetoria Geral das Polícias Militares. *Guerrilha e Contra-Guerrilha Urbanas*. Brasília, 1968.

3507. Burns, B. E. "Brazil's Foreign Policy: Traditionalism vs. Nationalism," *OR* 13 (1969) 643–644.

3508. ————. "Tradition and Variation in Brazilian Foreign Policy," *JIAS* 9 (Apr., 1967) 195–212.
Emphasis on the period since the military takeover in 1964.

3509. Callero, M. F. "International Business Promotion by State Governments: A Case Study of the Potential for Bi-National Cooperation, the United States and Brazil," American U. Diss., 1977.

3510. Carneiro Leão, A. *Visão Panorámica dos Estados Unidos*. Rio, 1950.

3511. Carvalho, A. de. *O Brasil Não é dos Brasileiros*. São Paulo, 1937.

3512. Castro, J. A. de Araújo. "O Congelamento do Poder Mundial," *RBEP* 33 (Jan., 1972) 7–30.
Considers United States–Brazilian relations in the light of changing world relationships.

3513. Chilcote, R. H. *The Brazilian Communist Party: Conflict and Integration, 1922–1972*. N.Y., 1974.

3514. Cohn, G. *Petróleo e Nacionalismo*. São Paulo, 1968.

Deaton, R. H. "The Impact of United States Private Investment, Aid, and Trade Policies toward Brazil during the Alliance for Progress," U. of Kan. Diss., 1973.

3515. De Holanda, N. *Diálogo Brasil-URSS*. Rio-Bahia, 1960.

3516. Duarte Pereira, O. *Multinacionais no Brasil: Aspectos Sociais e Políticos*. Rio, 1974.

3516a. Edfelt, R. B. "Direct Foreign Investment in a Developing Economy: Toward Evaluation of the Human Resource Development Impact in Brazil," UCLA Diss., 1975.

3517. Federação das Indústrias do Estado de São Paulo. *Resultados dos Acordos Comerciais entre o Brasil e Outros Países*. São Paulo, 1972.

3518. Ferreira, P. *Capitais, Estrangeiros e Dívida Externa*. São Paulo, 1965.

3519. Fontaine, R. W. *Brazil and the United States: Toward a Maturing Relationship*. Stanford, Calif., 1974.

3520. Garvey, E. "Meddling in Brazil: The CIA Bungles On," *COM* 37 (1968) 553–554.

3521. Geiger, T., and L. Goode. *The General Electric Company in Brazil*. N.Y., 1961.

3522. Gordon, L. "Brazil's Future World Role," *OR* 16 (1972) 621–631.

Author was U.S. ambassador to Brazil and later Secretary of State for Inter-American Affairs.

3523. Governo do Estado do Rio Grande do Sul. *Encampação da Companhia Telefónica Nacional*. Porto Alegre, 1962.

Treats the expropriation of International Telephone and Telegraph Company.

3524. Guilherme, O. *O Brasil e a Era Atômica*. Rio, 1959.

3525. Hilton, S. E. "Brazil and Great Power Trade Rivalry in South America, 1934–1939," U. of Tex. Diss., 1969.

3526. Hopp, J. C. "A Study of Investment Policy and Performance of Subsidiaries of United States Manufacturing Corporations in Brazil," Mich. State U. Diss., 1969.

3527. Instituto Argentino del Petróleo. *El Petróleo en la República Argentina*. B.A., 1967.

3528. Kaplan, S. S., and N. C. Bonsor, "Did United States Aid Really Help Brazilian Development? A Perspective of a Quarter-Century," *IEA* 14 (1973) 25–46.

3529. Lafer, C. "Una Interpretación del Sistema de las Relaciones Internacionales del Brasil," *FI* 9 (Jan.–Mar., 1969) 298–318.

Except for the Quadros and Goulart administration Brazil has always been under U.S. control in foreign policy.

3530. Levine, R. M. *The Vargas Regime: The Critical Years, 1934–1938*. N.Y., 1970.

3531. Maia, J. *O Brasil no Terceiro Mundo*. Rio, 1968.

3532. Marinho Júnior, I. P. *Petróleo, Soberania e Desenvolvimento*. Rio, 1969.

3533. Marzo, A. "Il Partito Comunista Nella Lotta Politica Argentina," *RSPI* 32 (Apr.–June, 1965) 215–234.

3534. McCann, F. D. *The Brazilian-American Alliance, 1937–1945*. Princeton, N.J., 1973.

3535. McMillan, C. *International Enterprise in a Developing Economy: A Study of U.S. Business in Brazil*. Ann Arbor, Mich., 1964.

3536. Novaes, R. de F. *Investimentos Estrangeiros no Brasil, Uma Análise Econômica*. Rio, 1975.

3537. Odalia, N. "As Relações Externas do Brasil: 1945–1964," *EHI* 5 (1966) 233–250.

Views the years under consideration as the only period in which Brazil tried to free itself of U.S. influence. The military coup of 1964 returned the old policy.

3538. Onody, O. "Relações Comerciais do Brasil com o Bloco Soviético," *RBPI* 3 (1960) 38–74.

3539. Parker, P. R. *1964: O Papel dos Estados Unidos no Golpe de Estado de 31 de Março*. Rio, 1977.

Based on a U. of Tex. Diss.

3540. Perry, W. *Comtemporary Brazilian Foreign Policy: The International Strategy of an Emergency Power*. Beverly Hills, Calif., 1976.

Concentrates on United States–Brazilian relations.

3541.   Pinsky, J. "O Brasil nas Relações Inter-
        nacionais, 1930–1945," *EHIS* 5 (Dec.,
        1966) 199–212.
3542.   Rabelo, G. *O Capital Estrangeiro na Im-
        prensa Brasileira*. Rio, 1966.
3543.   Rodrigues, J. H. *Interêsse Nacional e
        Política Externa*. Rio, 1966.
3544.   Roett, R. "Brazil Ascendant: Interna-
        tional Relations and Geopolitics in the
        Late 20th Century," *JIAS* 29 (1975)
        139–154.
3545.   ———. *Brazil: Politics of a Patrimonial
        Society*. Boston, 1972.
3546.   ———. *The Politics of Foreign Aid in the
        Brazilian Northeast*. Nashville, Tenn.,
        1972.
        A highly critical view of USAID.
3547.   Rosenbaum, H. J. "Brazil's Foreign Pol-
        icy and Cuba, 1959–1966," Tufts U.
        Diss., 1967.
3548.   ———. "Brazil's Foreign Policy: De-
        velopmentalism and Beyond," *OR* 16
        (1972) 58–84.
3549.   Sakurai, T. *Burajiru Niokeru Gaikoku
        Shihon no Hôseido*. Tokyo, 1965.
        Translated title: "Legal Institutions
        Relating to Foreign Investment in
        Brazil."
3550.   Salles, D. *Energia Atómica—Um Inquérito
        que Abalou o País*. São Paulo, 1958.
3551.   Santos, R. G. "Brazilian Foreign Policy
        and the Dominican Republic," *TA* 29
        (July, 1972) 62–77.
        Brazil's support of the U.S. position
        marks the abandonment of the indepen-
        dent foreign policy.
3552.   Schilling, P. R. *Una Historia Sucia: El
        Capital Extranjero en el Brasil*. Mon-
        tevideo, 1968.
3553.   Schneider, R. M. *Brazil: Foreign Relations
        of a Future World Power*. Boulder, Colo.,
        1977.
3554.   Sibeck, G. P. "Brazil's Independent
        Foreign Policy," U.S.C. Diss., 1971.
3555.   Skidmore, T. E. *Politics in Brazil,
        1930–1964*. N.Y., 1968.
3556.   Smith, P. S. *Oil and Politics in Modern
        Brazil*. Toronto, 1976.
3557.   Stepan, A. (ed.). *Authoritarian Brazil:
        Origins, Policies, and Future*. New Haven,

        Conn., 1973.
        Papers from an interdisciplinary work-
        shop held at Yale U. in 1971.
3558.   Storrs, K. L. "Brazil's Independent
        Foreign Policy, 1961–1964," Cornell U.
        Diss., 1973.
3559.   Távora, J. *Átomos para o Brasil*. Rio,
        1958.
3560.   Tuthill, J. W. "Economic and Political
        Aspects of Development in Brazil and
        U.S. Aid," *JIAS* 11 (Apr., 1969) 186–
        208.
3561.   "U.S. and Brazil: Partners in Progress,"
        USDSB 54 (Apr., 1966) 620–624.
3562.   USCS. Committee on Foreign Relations.
        *Hearings on United States Policies and Pro-
        grams in Brazil, May 4–11, 1971*.
        Wash., 1971.
3563.   USDS. *Report of the Joint Brazilian–United
        States Technical Commission, Rio de Janeiro,
        February 7, 1949*. Wash., 1949.
3564.   ———. "United States and Brazil Sign
        Extradition Treaty," *USDSB* 44 (Jan.,
        1961) 164–168.
3565.   Victor, M. *A Batalha do Petróleo
        Brasileiro*. Rio, 1970.
3566.   Vieira, J. M. G. *O Capital Estrangeiro no
        Desenvolvimento do Brasil*. São Paulo,
        1975.
3567.   Wiley, R. J. "An Analysis of Financing
        by a Multinational Group of Companies
        in Brazil, 1964–1965," Columbia U.
        Diss., 1969.
3568.   Wirth, J. *The Politics of Brazilian De-
        velopment, 1930–1954*. Palo Alto, Calif.,
        1970.

XXIV-E   *cross references:*
a)   For the role of Brazil during World War II,
       see items 971–980.
b)   See also items 1662, 1731, 1805, 3415.
c)   In the Trask, Meyer, and Trask *Bibliography*
       see items 3408, 3409c, 3709–3724, 4106,
       4107, 4136, 4152c, 4152d, 4158, 4171,
       4180, 4289, 4348, 4870, 4871, 5423,
       7701, 9072, 9810, 10086, 10089–
       10205a.

Index

Only items with identifiable authors are listed in this index. Each entry includes the author's name, followed by the serial number(s) assigned to his work(s) in the text. There are no entries for organizations like "Pan American Union" or "United States" or "United Nations," because in the editor's judgment they would be of little value. In such instances the detailed Table of Contents will be helpful in locating information on specific topics.

A